COLORADO CACHE

A goldmine of recipes from the Junior League of Denver

Cover design and illustrations by Ann W. Douden

Proceeds from the sale of this cookbook
support the Junior League of Denver

Junior League
of Denver

The Junior League of Denver, Inc.
Denver, Colorado

THE JUNIOR LEAGUE OF DENVER, INCORPORATED (founded in 1918), is an organization of women committed to promoting voluntarism and to improving the community through the effective action and leadership of trained volunteers. Its purpose is exclusively educational and charitable.

The revenue received from our fundraising efforts support the Junior League of Denver's purpose and community program.

Additional copies may be obtained by addressing:
C & C PUBLICATIONS
The Junior League of Denver, Inc.
6300 E. Yale Avenue
Denver, Colorado 80222
(303) 782-9244

Colorado Cache Cookbook and **Creme de Colorado Cookbook** may be obtained for fundraising projects or by retail outlets at special rates. Write above address for further information. Prices subject to change without notice.

For your convenience, order blanks are included in the back of the book.

Copyright © 1978
The Junior League of Denver, Inc.
Denver, Colorado

First Edition
First printing: 10,000 copies September 1978

Second Edition
First printing: 20,000 copies December 1978
Second printing: 20,000 copies June 1979
Third printing: 20,000 copies December 1979
Fourth printing: 20,000 copies July 1980
Fifth printing: 30,000 copies September 1980
Sixth printing: 30,000 copies January 1981
Seventh printing: 50,000 copies May 1981
Eighth printing: 50,000 copies December 1981
Ninth printing: 50,000 copies August 1982
Tenth printing: 60,000 copies April 1983
Eleventh printing: 60,000 copies April 1984
Twelfth printing: 60,000 copies December 1984
Thirteenth printing: 60,000 copies December 1985
Fourteenth printing: 60,000 copies December 1986
Fifteenth printing: 30,000 copies March 1988
Sixteenth printing: 30,000 copies September 1989
Seventeenth printing: 30,000 copies November 1989
Eighteenth printing: 45,000 copies October 1990
Nineteenth printing: 45,000 copies October 1991
Twentieth printing: 45,000 copies October 1992
Twenty-First printing: 15,000 copies January 1994
Twenty-Second printing: 25,000 copies October 1994

Third Edition
First printing: 35,000 copies September 1988

The Library of Congress Catalog Number: TX546-485
ISBN: 0-9603946-1-3

Printed by Eastwood Printing, Denver, Colorado

TABLE OF CONTENTS

METRIC CONVERSION CHART

MEASURE	EQUIVALENT	METRIC(ML)
1 tsp.		5 milliliters
1 Tbsp.	3 tsp.	14.8 milliliters
1 jigger	1½ oz.	44.4 milliliters
1 cup	16 Tbsp.	236.8 milliliters
1 pint	2 cups	473.6 milliliters
1 quart	4 cups	947.2 milliliters
1 liter	4 cups + 3½ Tbsp.	1000.0 milliliters
1 oz. (dry)	2 Tbsp.	28.35 grams
1 pound	16 oz.	453.59 grams
2.21 pounds	35.3 oz.	1.00 kilogram

APPROXIMATE CONVERSION FACTORS FOR UNITS OF VOLUME

to convert from	to	multiply by
teaspoons	milliliters	5
Tablespoons	milliliters	15
fluid ounces	milliliters	30
cups	liters	0.24
pints	liters	0.47
quarts	liters	0.95
gallons	liters	3.8

250 degrees Farenheit = 106 degrees Centigrade
350 degrees Farenheit = 162 degrees Centigrade
450 degrees Farenheit = 218 degrees Centigrade

A NOTE FROM THE COOKBOOK COMMITTEE

Colorado Cache is a collection of over 700 recipes selected from approximately 2800 submitted. Wherever possible, there is an emphasis on the use of fresh ingredients, and each recipe has been tested and enthusiastically approved by one of twelve separate testing teams. We are most grateful to all the League members and friends who shared their ideas and recipes, and gave unselfishly of their time. A special thank you to our families who have been so patient and supportive during the past two years.

COOKBOOK COMMITTEE

Chairman	Jaydee Boat
Editor	Louise Steinhauer
Cover design and illustrations	Ann Douden
Testing Coordinator	Karen Kruse
Hors d'oeuvres and Appetizers	Diane Seccombe
Soups	Karen Albin
Brunch	Karen Albin
Salads and Salad Dressings	Rebecca Sexson
Fish and Game	Desse Anthony
Entrees	Ellin Schroeder
Vegetables	Betty Winslow
Pasta, Rice and Potatoes	Jaydee Boat, Karen Kruse
Breads	Molly Waters
Mexican Food	Marilyn McWilliams
Microwave Cooking	Chartan Martin
Picnics and Camping	Desse Anthony
Desserts	Betty Clark, Anne Curran
Potpourri	Mary Grow
Restaurants	Louise Steinhauer
Index	Rebecca Sexson
Secretary	Anne Curran
Treasurer	Chartan Martin
Production	Suzy Witzler
Marketing Chairman	Christie Truitt
Consultant	Barbara Conwell

The cookbook committee would like to thank Katie Stapleton for her advice and support, Nancy Byrd, Bev Howell, Betty Lynn Jackson, Kathy Kugeler, Juliana Olin, and Kathy Thomason for their initial research and Pat Harwood for her invaluable assistance in getting us started.

MESA VERDE

8

Hors d'oeuvres and Appetizers

RADO CACHE COLORADO CACHE COLORADO CACHE COLORADO CACHE COLORADO CACHE COLORADO CACHE COLORADO CACHE COLORADO CACHE COLORADO CACHE COLORADO CACHE COLORADO CACH

Hints from the **Royal Gorge**

Unexpected guests?

Cover an 8 ounce block of cream cheese with one the the following (see index for recipes) and serve with crackers:

> Tabasco jelly
> Pear chutney
> Tomato-apple chutney
> Steak sauce
> Chutney, Piquante sauce and sprinkling of
>   crumbled bacon
> Jezebel sauce
>   or

> Mixture of 8 ounces of crabmeat, 1 cup cat-
>   sup, 2 tablespoons horseradish and 1 ta-
>   blespoon honey.

Spread crackers with peanut butter and top with a dollop of chutney.

Peel fresh kiwi fruit, slice it and serve with thin, rolled slices of prosciutto.
                or
Wrap cubes of fresh pears in prosciutto.

Spread thin slices of pumpernickel with Camembert or Brie and pop in the oven until hot. Top with a thin slice of apple or pear.

Mix 4 ounces of cream cheese, 2 tablespoons mayonnaise, and ¼ teaspoon curry powder. Spread on toast rounds and top with a dollop of chutney. Broil to heat.

Wrap ¼ of a marinated artichoke heart with a 1 by 4½ inch strip of boiled ham, secure with a toothpick and broil to heat.

Serve cherry tomatoes with small bowls of vodka and curry powder. Dip each tomato in vodka then in curry powder, pop them in your mouth and enjoy a new taste.

Bake pieces of Italian sausage, drain well and serve in a chafing dish filled with about 2 inches of warmed dry white wine. Have plenty of toothpicks.

Crudites may be served with the following:
> Creme Fraiche seasoned to taste with
>   grated onion, curry powder and Worces-
>   tershire sauce.
> A small bowl of Beau Monde seasoning for
>   dipping is great for calorie counters.
> Try including quickly blanched asparagus,
>   fresh green beans and strips of raw tur-
>   nip along with the usual carrots, celery
>   etc.

The **Royal Gorge,** once a favorite Ute campground, lies at the mouth of the Grand Canyon of the Arkansas, the most accessible and best known of the great river canyons in Colorado. At one time the main line of the Denver and Rio Grande railroad ran through the bottom of the canyon, which was an engineering marvel. The world's highest suspension bridge now crosses the canyon of red granite walls, rising 1,000 feet above the foaming river. The bridge has enough wire to reach from Colorado Springs to New York and continue halfway to London.

9

Hors d'oeuvres and Appetizers

COLORADO CACHE COLORADO CACHE COLORADO CACHE COLORADO CACHE COLORADO CACHE COLORADO CACHE COLORADO CACHE COLORADO CACHE COLORADO

Anchoyade

8-10 servings

2 2-ounce cans flat anchovy
   fillets
2 medium cloves garlic, finely
   chopped
1 teaspoon tomato paste
1 - 1½ tablespoons olive oil
2 teaspoons lemon juice (or red
   wine vinegar)
   freshly ground black pepper
8 to 10 slices French bread, ½ inch
   thick, cut into strips
1 teaspoon finely chopped,
   fresh parsley

Soak anchovies 10 minutes in cold water and pat dry with paper towels. Place in a large mortar or heavy bowl with the garlic and tomato paste. Pound with a pestle, wooden masher or spoon into a very smooth puree, or use food processor with steel blade. Dribble the oil in, a few drops at a time, stirring constantly until thick and smooth, like mayonnaise. Stir in lemon juice and a few grounds of black pepper. Preheat oven to 500 degrees. Brown bread lightly on one side. While bread is warm, spread untoasted side with anchovy mixture, pressing it into bread with back of fork or spoon. Bake for 10 minutes. Sprinkle with parsley and serve at once.

Note: For a first course, use whole slices of French bread spread with anchovy mixture.

Daube Glace

8-10 servings

2 10½-ounce cans consomme
½ can water
½ lemon, cut in half
1 tablespoon vinegar
½ teaspoon cayenne pepper
¾ teaspoon Worcestershire
   sauce
2 stalks celery, cut in eighths
1 onion, cut in quarters
½ green pepper, cut in half
1½ teaspoons salt
½ teaspoon Tabasco sauce
1 clove garlic
2 packages unflavored gelatin
½ cup water
1 pound left-over pot roast
   mayonnaise for garnish

In a large covered pot, simmer consomme, ½ can water, lemon, vinegar, cayenne, Worcestershire sauce, celery, onion, green pepper, salt, Tabasco sauce and garlic for 1½ hours. Melt the gelatin in ½ cup water in a saucepan. Shred pot roast and add to gelatin. Strain the stock through a collander, add the meat-gelatin mixture and pour into an 8 × 8 inch pan. Chill. Before gelatin has completely set, mix meat through so it is evenly distributed. Chill thoroughly. Cut into squares and serve on a lettuce leaf with a dollop of mayonnaise.

Note: This may also be served for luncheon or as a hot weather dinner with fresh fruit and rolls or French bread.

COLORADO CACHE COLORADO CACHE COLORADO CACHE COLORADO CACHE COLORADO CACHE COLORADO CACHE COLORADO CACHE COLORADO CACHE COLORADO CACHE COLORADO CACHE COLORADO CACHE COLORADO CACHE COLORADO CACHE COLORADO CACH

Caviar Helen

8 servings

6 **eggs, hard cooked and chopped**
mayonnaise to moisten
salt and pepper to taste
dry mustard to taste
8 **slices of firm white sandwich bread cut into 3 inch rounds**
caviar

Mix chopped eggs with mayonnaise, salt and pepper. Mound egg mixture on each bread round so that it is completely covered on top. Top with a generous tablespoon of caviar. Serve as a first course.

Mushroom Roulade

8 servings

6 **egg yolks**
1½ **pounds fresh mushrooms**
½ **cup butter, melted and cooled**
2 **tablespoons fresh lemon juice**
salt and pepper to taste
6 **egg whites**
pinch of salt
⅓ **cup minced green onions**
2 **tablespoons butter**
6 **ounces boiled ham, cut in julienne strips**
½ **cup Mornay sauce (see index)**
minced parsley
whole mushrooms for garnish
lemon juice
salt and pepper to taste
¾ **cup light cream**

Beat egg yolks until they are thick and fold in the mushrooms which have been trimmed, finely chopped, and the moisture squeezed out. Add ½ cup butter, 2 tablespoons lemon juice, salt and pepper. In a large bowl, beat egg whites with a pinch of salt until they hold soft peaks. Stir ¼ of the whites into the mushroom mixture, and fold the mixture into the remaining whites. Spread mixture on a buttered 15 × 10½ inch jelly roll pan lined with a buttered sheet of waxed paper and bake at 350 degrees for 30 minutes, or until the edges have pulled away from the sides of the pan. Let the mushroom sheet cool, invert it onto another sheet of waxed paper, and carefully peel off the top sheet of paper.

In a skillet, saute green onions in 2 tablespoons butter until they are softened. Add ham and saute the mixture for 3 minutes. Stir in Mornay sauce and spread ⅔ of the filling on the mushroom sheet, 1 inch from the long edge, reserving the remaining third. Carefully fold up the mushroom sheet to enclose the filling, lifting the waxed paper as the sheet is rolled and transfer the roll, seam side down, to a platter. Sprinkle the roll with parsley and garnish the platter with fluted and sauteed whole mushrooms seasoned with lemon juice, salt and pepper. Thin the remaining filling with cream and serve it separately as a sauce.

COLORADO CACHE COLORADO CACHE COLORADO CACHE COLORADO CACHE COLORADO CACHE COLORADO CACHE COLORADO CACHE COLORADO CACHE COLORADO CACHE COLORADO C

Mushrooms Silver Plume

1 pound mushrooms, cleaned
   and sliced
6 tablespoons butter
1 cup dry sherry
¼ cup brandy
½ cup heavy cream
   dash of salt

4 servings

Simmer mushrooms in butter and sherry until liquid is almost evaporated. Add brandy, heat and ignite. Heat ½ cup heavy cream, add salt and pour over mushrooms. Serve on toast triangles as a first course.

Escargots in Wine

1 cup dry white wine
1 shallot, finely chopped
4 dozen snails and shells
1 cup butter, softened
1 tablespoon fresh lemon juice
2 tablespoons parsley, finely
   chopped
3 cloves garlic, minced
1 teaspoon salt
¼ teaspoon freshly ground
   pepper

4 dozen

Simmer wine and shallot for about 5 minutes. Place about 1 teaspoon of this mixture in each of the shells. Tuck a snail into each shell. Combine remaining ingredients. Fill each shell with mixture. Place on snail plates and bake in a preheated 400 degree oven for about 10 minutes.

Note: As snails cook, some of the sauce oozes out. Soak it up with French bread and eat along with the snails.

Queen City Consomme

2 10½-ounce cans consomme
   Madrilene, chilled
½ cup sour cream
   chopped chives for garnish
   red caviar for garnish

4 servings

Spoon well chilled consomme into consomme cups or sherbet glasses. Top with a generous dollop of sour cream and a sprinkling of chopped chives. Top all with a teaspoon of red caviar.

Note: This is a very refreshing first course.

12

Hors d'oeuvres and Appetizers

ORADO CACHE COLORADO CACHE COLORADO CACHE COLORADO CACHE COLORADO CACHE COLORADO CACHE COLORADO CACHE COLORADO CACHE COLORADO CACHE COLORADO CAC

Oysters Hempel

4 tablespoons butter
7 green onions, chopped
4 tablespoons flour
1¾ cups milk
3 ounces Cheddar cheese
3 tablespoons freshly grated
   Parmesan cheese
4 tablespoons mayonnaise
1 teaspoon Worcestershire
   sauce
¼ pound fresh crabmeat
½ pound fresh mushrooms
   lightly sauteed
   white pepper to taste
1 quart oysters
¼ cup sweet vermouth
¼ cup Cognac

2 quarts

In the top of a double boiler over direct heat, melt butter and saute the green onions. Place over hot water and make a thick white sauce by adding the flour and milk. Add Cheddar, Parmesan, mayonnaise, Worcestershire sauce, crab, mushrooms and pepper. Heat chafing dish pan until hot and add 1 quart oysters. Start to heat over stove and finish over open flame in chafing dish. When all are curled, drain liquor. Heat vermouth and Cognac and flame. Pour over oysters. Flame again. When flame dies, add crab mixture and mix gently. Serve over crisp bread triangles.

Steak Tartare

2 pounds ground filet of beef
   (or trimmed sirloin)
4 egg yolks
8 anchovy filets, chopped
   capers to taste
½ cup finely chopped onion
4 tablespoons finely chopped
   parsley
   salt and freshly ground
   pepper to taste
   rose paprika
   cayenne pepper
   catsup
   Worcestershire sauce
   prepared mustard
   Cognac or Port to taste
1 lemon, quartered
   buttered toast

12-16 servings

In a large bowl gently mix all ingredients except toast and lemon. Ingredients without proportions should be added to taste. Serve in a well-chilled bowl surrounded by pieces of buttered toast. Sprinkle with lemon juice.

COLORADO CACHE COLORADO CACHE COLORADO CACHE COLORADO CACHE COLORADO CACHE COLORADO CACHE COLORADO CACHE COLORADO CACHE COLORADO CA

Colorado Pate

¼ pound butter
1 pound chicken livers
1 medium onion, chopped
3 shallots, chopped
½ teaspoon thyme
½ teaspoon rosemary
1 bay leaf
12 large fresh mushrooms, chopped
¼ cup brandy
½ teaspoon salt
⅛ teaspoon pepper

1 pint

In a large skillet, melt the butter. Add chicken livers, onion and shallots. Stir over medium heat about 10 minutes. Add spices and mushrooms. Stir frequently while cooking for 5 minutes. Discard bay leaf and pour mixture into blender. Pour in brandy, salt and pepper. Blend 2 minutes, then pour into a 2 cup souffle dish. Chill. Garnish with parsley. Serve with melba toast rounds.

Note: Dish may be covered with plastic wrap and kept in the refrigerator for a week.

Hawaiian Pate

1½ cups butter
1 onion, chopped
1½ pounds chicken livers, cut up
¾ cup chicken broth
2 tablespoons dry sherry
½ teaspoon paprika
½ teaspoon curry powder
½ teaspoon salt
⅛ teaspoon pepper
2 cloves garlic, crushed
⅓ cup brandy
1 cup chopped walnuts, toasted
2 tablespoons unflavored gelatin
sliced stuffed olives for garnish
fresh pineapple top

1½ quarts

In a large skillet heat 1 cup butter and saute onion until golden. Add chicken livers and cook 10 minutes, stiring occasionally. Add sherry, seasonings, garlic and ½ cup broth. Cook 5 minutes. Puree mixture in blender. Add ¼ cup broth and gelatin to mixture and puree. Melt remaining butter and blend into puree with brandy. Stir in walnuts with a fork. Chill overnight in refrigerator. Shape mixture with hands into pineapple shape. Decorate "pineapple" with sliced stuffed olives and cap with a fresh pineapple top. Serve with crackers.

14
Hors d'oeuvres and Appetizers

Shrimp Pate

2½ cups

4 **7½-ounce cans shrimp**
½ **cup butter, melted**
⅓ **cup mayonnaise**
1 **small onion, minced**
2 **tablespoons fresh lemon juice**
   dash of Tabasco sauce

Mash shrimp well and add onion. Pour butter over shrimp and onion. Add mayonnaise, lemon juice and Tabasco sauce. Mix and pack into a mold. Refrigerate for 3 hours. Unmold and pour sauce over pate. Serve with crackers.

Sauce:

1 **cup catsup**
2 **tablespoons horseradish**
2 **teaspoons fresh lemon juice**

Blend all ingredients. Refrigerate.

Lobster Pate

2½ cups

1 **8-ounce package cream cheese, softened**
¼ **cup dry white wine**
½ **teaspoon onion salt**
½ **teaspoon seasoned salt**
⅛ **teaspoon dill weed**
1½ **cups lobster meat, finely chopped**

Beat cheese and wine until smooth and creamy. Blend in salts and dill; add lobster. Cover and refrigerate several hours or overnight to mellow. Serve with crackers.

Bourbon Pate

3 cups

1 **10½-ounce can beef broth**
1 **4-ounce can Sell's or other good quality pate**
1 **3-ounce package cream cheese**
2 **teaspoons unflavored gelatin**
½ **cup cold water**
¼ **cup bourbon**

Mix cream cheese and pate and spread in bottom of 3 cup mold. Chill. Dissolve gelatin in cold water. Heat beef broth and combine with gelatin. When pate mixture is firm, pour gelatin on top. Chill. Unmold and serve with club crackers.

COLORADO CACHE COLORADO CACHE COLORADO CACHE COLORADO CACHE COLORADO CACHE COLORADO CACHE COLORADO CACHE COLORADO CACHE COLORADO CACHE COLORADO C

Royal Camembert Mousse

2½ cups

¼	cup cold water
1	tablespoon unflavored gelatin
2½	ounces Camembert cheese
3¾	ounces Roquefort cheese
1	teaspoon Worcestershire sauce
1	egg, separated
½	cup whipping cream, whipped
	parsley for garnish

Soften gelatin in water. Set cup in hot water until dissolved. Blend cheeses together until smooth. Beat in Worcestershire sauce, egg yolk and then gelatin. Beat egg white until stiff. Fold with cream into cheese mixture. Pour into 2 or 3 cup mold. Refrigerate overnight. Unmold and garnish with parsley.

Crabmeat Mousse

4 cups

1	tablespoon unflavored gelatin
¼	cup cold water
1	cup undiluted mushroom soup
1	8-ounce package cream cheese, softened
1	cup mayonnaise
¾	cup finely chopped celery
1	6½-ounce can Alaskan king crab meat, drained
1	tablespoon grated onion
1½	teaspoons Worcestershire sauce

Soak gelatin in cold water to soften. Heat soup. Stir gelatin into hot soup, making sure it is dissolved. Add cream cheese and mayonnaise. Beat until smooth. Add celery, crabmeat, onion and Worcestershire sauce. Pour into mold and chill. Serve with club crackers.

Roquefort Mousse

3⅓ cups

½ **pound Roquefort cheese**
4 **tablespoons butter**
4 **ounces cream cheese**
1 **egg, separated**
1 **tablespoon unflavored gelatin**
½ **teaspoon Dijon mustard**
½ **cup whipping cream**

Have cheese and butter at room temperature. Whip cream and set aside. Beat egg white until stiff and set aside. In a large bowl beat egg yolk. Add Roquefort and beat until smooth. Add cream cheese and butter and beat until smooth. Dissolve gelatin in cold water, then place dish of gelatin in hot water and stir until gelatin is dissolved. Add gelatin and mustard to cheese mixture. Fold in egg white, then fold in whipped cream. Pour into greased mold. Chill. Serve with crackers or fruit.

Note: Good with pears for dessert.

Domestic Boursin Cheese

1 cup

1 **3-ounce package cream cheese**
4 **tablespoons butter**
¼ **teaspoon garlic powder**
2 **tablespoons freshly grated Parmesan cheese**
1 **tablespoon dry white wine**
1 **tablespoon minced parsley**
dash of thyme
dash of marjoram

Cream all ingredients thoroughly or use food processor with steel blade. Chill for at least four hours. Serve with crackers.

Liptauer Cheese

3 cups

½ **pound butter**
1 **pound cream cheese**
1½ **teaspoons caraway seeds**
1 **tablespoon grated onion**
2 **teaspoons chopped parsley**
2 **teaspoons chopped capers**
1½ **teaspoons prepared mustard**

Soften butter and cream cheese. Combine all ingredients. Pack in a crock and sprinkle with parsley. This can be made into a ball and rolled in parsley. Serve with crackers.

COLORADO CACHE COLORADO CACHE COLORADO CACHE COLORADO CACHE COLORADO CACHE COLORADO CACHE COLORADO CACHE COLORADO CACHE COLORADO

Green Oaks Cheese Spread

4 cups

- 2 8-ounce packages cream cheese
- 1 1-pound jar sharp Cheddar cheese (Kaukauna Klub)
- ¼ pound soft butter
- ¼ cup dry sherry
- 2 tablespoons dry vermouth
- ½ teaspoon dry mustard
- ½ teaspoon Worcestershire sauce
- 2 - 3 drops Tabasco sauce
- ½ teaspoon seasoned salt
- ½ teaspoon celery salt
- ¼ teaspoon oregano

Mix cheese with butter until thoroughly blended. Add remaining ingredients and stir until well mixed. Pack in a crock, cover and refrigerate. Bring to room temperature to serve with crackers.

Note: This keeps for weeks. It is also good as a stuffing for celery.

The Bee Cheese

2 cups

- 10 ounces sharp cheese, grated
- 10 ounces butter, softened
- 2 tablespoons sherry
- 1 tablespoon horseradish
- ½ teaspoon garlic salt

Blend all ingredients well and pack in a crock. Serve with crackers. This is better if it is made several days before serving.

Curried Chutney Spread

3 cups

- 2 8-ounce packages cream cheese
- ½ cup Major Grey's chutney
- ½ cup chopped almonds, toasted
- 1 teaspoon curry powder
- ½ teaspoon dry mustard

Bring cream cheese to room temperature. Mix all ingredients together well. Pack in a crock. Chill. Serve with crackers or use spread to stuff dates or celery.

RADO CACHE COLORADO CACHE COLORADO CACHE COLORADO CACHE COLORADO CACHE COLORADO CACHE COLORADO CACHE COLORADO CACHE COLORADO CACHE COLORADO CACH

Pineapple Cheese Spread

5 cups

2 **8-ounce packages cream cheese**
1 **8½-ounce can crushed pineapple drained**
1 **cup chopped pecans**
½ **cup chopped green pepper**
2 **tablespoons chopped green onions**
1 **teaspoon Lawry's seasoned salt**

Soften cheese and mix with pineapple, pecans, green pepper, onion and salt. Pack in a crock and refrigerate or you may roll the mixture in a ball and cover with more pecans. Serve with crackers.

Crab and Water Chestnut Spread

2¼ cups

1 **pound cooked crabmeat**
½ **cup finely chopped water chestnuts**
2 **tablespoons soy sauce**
½ **cup mayonnaise**
2 **tablespoons minced green onions**

Chop crabmeat and combine with water chestnuts, soy sauce, mayonnaise and onions. Refrigerate. Serve with crisp crackers.

Crab-Swiss Bites

36 hors d'oeuvres

1 **7½-ounce can crabmeat, drained and flaked**
1 **tablespoon sliced green onion**
1 **cup grated Swiss cheese**
½ **cup mayonnaise**
1 **teaspoon fresh lemon juice**
¼ **teaspoon curry powder**
1 **package flakey refrigerator rolls (12 rolls)**
1 **5-ounce can water chestnuts, drained and sliced**

Combine crabmeat, green onion, Swiss cheese, mayonnaise, lemon juice and curry powder. Mix well. Separate each roll into 3 layers. Place on ungreased baking sheet and spoon on crabmeat mixture. Top each with a few slices of water chestnuts. Bake at 400 degrees for 10 to 12 minutes.

Sauerkraut Loaf

1   29-ounce can sauerkraut
2   cups grated, sharp Cheddar
      cheese
2   tablespoons chopped onion
2   tablespoons chopped pimento
3   tablespoons chopped green
      pepper
1   hard cooked egg, chopped
¼   cup mayonnaise
½   teaspoon salt
½   cup corn flake crumbs
      (or bread crumbs)
1   tablespoon sugar
1   8-ounce package cream
      cheese at room temperature
    sliced, stuffed green olives
      and pimento for garnish

1 loaf

Drain sauerkraut and squeeze as dry as possible. Mix all ingredients except cream cheese and shape into a loaf. Chill overnight. Ice loaf with cream cheese. Garnish with olives and pimento.

Hot Ryes

1   cup finely grated Swiss
      cheese
¼   cup cooked and crumbled
      bacon
1   4½-ounce can chopped ripe
      olives
¼   cup minced green onions or
      chives
1   teaspoon Worcestershire
      sauce
¼   cup mayonnaise
    party rye bread

36 hors d'oeuvres

Mix together all ingredients except bread. Spread on party rye or pumpernickel and bake at 375 degrees for 10 to 15 minutes or until browned.

Note: These may be frozen after baking and reheated.

Hot Artichoke Canapes

5 dozen

1 cup mayonnaise
1 cup freshly grated Parmesan cheese
1 4-ounce can green chiles, chopped
1 cup artichoke hearts, chopped
melba toast rounds

Mix mayonnaise, Parmesan cheese, green chiles and artichoke hearts together. Put 1 teaspoon of the mixture on bite-sized toast round. Put under broiler until lightly browned on top.

Ham 'n Cheese Cocktail Bagels

40 pieces

¾ pound boiled ham
¾ pound American cheese
¼ cup olive oil
8 stuffed green olives
6 green onions
1 green pepper
2 celery stalks
½ cup tomato sauce
20 mini-bagels

Chop ham, cheese, olives, green onions, green pepper and celery. Combine with olive oil and tomato sauce. Let stand overnight in refrigerator. Put 2 teaspoons of mixture on a split mini-bagel and broil until bubbly.

Bacon Roll-ups

24 roll-ups

½ cup sour cream
½ teaspoon onion salt
½ pound bacon, cooked and crumbled
1 8-ounce package crescent rolls

Separate rolls. Mix the rest of the ingredients and spread on rolls. Cut each into thirds and roll up. Bake for 12 to 15 minutes at 375 degrees.

21

Hors d'oeuvres and Appetizers

COLORADO CACHE COLORADO CACHE COLORADO CACHE COLORADO CACHE COLORADO CACHE COLORADO CACHE COLORADO CACHE COLORADO CACHE COLORADO

Brie en Croute

3 small rounds Brie cheese
1 package frozen patty shells
1 egg yolk, beaten

3 rounds

Roll out 2 patty shells for each Brie. Place Brie on top of one round of pastry and fold up sides. Cut circle in second pastry round with empty Brie container. Place this round on top of Brie. Cut 2 strips of pastry 3 × ½ inches. Use this to wrap around top edges and crimp to join top crust and folded-up sides. Brush with egg yolk. This can be frozen at this point. Bake at 450 degrees for 10 minutes, then reduce heat to 350 degrees and bake for 20 minutes more or until crust is lightly browned. Cut into wedges and serve with crackers or fruit.

Note: A super make-ahead appetizer.

Curried Beef Pasties

¼ cup butter, softened
1 3-ounce package cream cheese
½ cup flour, sifted

Filling:

1 tablespoons butter
¼ pound ground beef
6 green onions, chopped (including tops)
½ garlic clove, minced
¼ teaspoon ground ginger
⅛ teaspoon ground cloves
⅛ teaspoon ground cinnamon
1 teaspoon fresh lemon juice
1 teaspoon curry powder
½ teaspoon salt

25 pieces

Cream together butter and cheese. Add flour. Chill the dough. Roll dough on floured board to 1/8 inch thickness, or as thin as possible. Cut into 2 inch squares or circles. Place 1 teaspoon filling on half of each piece. Wet edges and fold remaining half over. Press edges together. Bake at 350 degrees for 20 minutes.

Saute ground beef and onions in butter. Add garlic, ginger, cloves, cinnamon, lemon juice, curry powder and salt. Simmer covered for 5 minutes and use as filling.

RADO CACHE COLORADO CACHE COLORADO CACHE COLORADO CACHE COLORADO CACHE COLORADO CACHE COLORADO CACHE COLORADO CACHE COLORADO CACH

Hot Feta Cheese Pastries

8 dozen

2 **eggs**
½ **pound Feta cheese, crumbled**
1 **8-ounce package cream cheese**
¼ **cup coarsely chopped parsley**
¼ **cup coarsely chopped green onion**
½ **teaspoon dried mint leaves**
16 **filo leaves**
1 **cup butter, melted**

Combine eggs, feta and cream cheeses in a blender. Blend at medium speed until smooth. Add parsley, onion and mint. Blend until combined. Refrigerate for at least 1 hour. Remove filo dough from refrigerator and cut into six strips, each 16 by 1½ inches. Keep 1 stack of dough out to work with, wrap remaining leaves airtight to keep from drying out. Keep a damp cloth over strips you are working with, removing 1 at a time. Place 1 rounded teaspoon of filling on end of each strip. Fold corner to opposite side, forming a triangle. Continue folding, keeping triangle shape to other end. Place filled pastries on ungreased cookie sheets and keep covered with a damp cloth. Brush pastries liberally with melted butter. Bake in a 375 degree oven for 20 minutes, or until golden. Serve hot.

Mushroom Turnovers

36 pieces

Pastry:
3 **3-ounce packages cream cheese at room temperature**
½ **cup butter at room temperature**
1½ **cups flour**
½ **teaspoon salt**

Mix cream cheese and butter thoroughly. Add flour and salt and work until smooth. Chill well for at least 30 minutes. Preheat oven to 450 degrees. Roll dough into 1/8 inch thickness on lightly floured surface and cut into round with a 3 inch biscuit cutter.

Filling:
3 **tablespoons butter**
1 **large onion, finely chopped**
¼ **teaspoon thyme**
½ **teaspoon salt**
½ **teaspoon pepper**
2 **tablespoons flour**
¼ **cup sour cream**
½ **pound fresh mushrooms, chopped**
1 **egg**
1 **teaspoon milk**

In a skillet, heat butter, add onion and brown. Add mushrooms and cook, stirring often, about 3 minutes. Add seasonings and sprinkle with flour. Stir in sour cream and cook gently until thickened. Place 1 teaspoon filling on each round and fold dough over. Press edges together with a fork. Pinch top crust. Place on greased cookie sheet. Brush tops with 1 egg, lightly beaten, mixed with 1 teaspoon milk. Bake 10 to 15 minutes or until lightly browned.
Note: May be frozen before baking.

Hors d'oeuvres and Appetizers

Spinach and Cheese Squares

4 ounces butter
3 eggs
1 cup flour
1 cup milk
1 teaspoon salt
1 teaspoon baking powder
1 pound Monterey Jack cheese, grated
4 cups chopped, fresh spinach

40 squares

Melt butter in a 9 × 13 inch pan. Beat eggs. Add flour, milk, salt and baking powder. Add cheese and spinach, mixing well. Spread into pan and bake at 350 degrees for 35 minutes. Cool 30 minutes before serving. Cut into squares.
Note: These freeze well in plastic bags.

Artichoke Squares

2 6-ounce jars marinated artichoke hearts
1 small onion, finely chopped
¼ cup fine, dry bread crumbs
⅛ teaspoon pepper
⅛ teaspoon oregano
⅛ teaspoon Tabasco sauce
2 cups grated Cheddar cheese
2 tablespoons chopped parsley
¼ teaspoon salt
4 eggs

40 squares

Drain artichokes, saving marinade from one jar. In marinade, saute onion. Cut up artichokes. Beat eggs and add crumbs and seasoning. Stir in remaining ingredients. Turn into a greased 7 × 11 inch pan. Bake at 325 degrees for 30 minutes. Let cool a little before cutting into squares. Serve hot or cold.

Cheese Squares

½ pound processed Old English cheese
½ pound butter, softened
1 teaspoon grated onion
2 - 3 dashes Tabasco sauce
1 egg, beaten
1 loaf sandwich bread, unsliced
   salt to taste

4½ dozen

Cream together cheese and butter. Mixture will be lumpy. Add onion and Tabasco sauce. Add egg. Remove crusts from bread and cut into 1-inch cubes. Spread mixture on all sides of cubes except bottom and bake on greased cookie sheet at 450 degrees for 3 minutes, or until lightly browned.
Note: Cheese squares may be frozen and then baked.

Hors d'oeuvres and Appetizers

Parmesan Strips

130 strips

1	loaf sliced white bread
2	8-ounce packages cream cheese
¼	pound butter, melted
6	tablespoons mayonnaise
6	green onions with tops, chopped
6	drops of Tabasco sauce
	Parmesan cheese

Cut crusts from bread. Cut each slice into strips. Spread 1 side of bread strip with butter. Place under broiler and toast lightly on both sides. Mix other ingredients and spread on buttered side of bread. Pour Parmesan cheese in a shallow bowl and dip each piece of bread (spread-side down) in the cheese. Freeze. To serve, thaw slightly and broil until brown and bubbly. Watch carefully.

Cocktail Trout Burgers

trout
bacon

Cook trout. Skin, bone and filet. Place a piece of trout on a cocktail bun and top with tartar sauce and a partial slice of crisply cooked bacon.

1¼ cups sauce

Mix all of the ingredients well.

Tartar Sauce:

1	cup mayonnaise
1½	tablespoons finely chopped green onions, including tops
1	teaspoon fresh lemon juice
1	tablespoon minced parsley
1	tablespoon finely chopped, sweet pickle relish

Ham Balls

120 balls

1	pound ground ham
1	pound ground round steak
1	pound lean ground pork
2	cups soft bread crumbs
1	cup milk
2	eggs

Mix all ingredients together. Form into balls the size of a walnut. Drop meat balls into sauce and cook slowly for 1 hour.

COLORADO CACHE COLORADO CACHE COLORADO CACHE COLORADO CACHE COLORADO CACHE COLORADO CACHE COLORADO CACHE COLORADO CACHE COLORADO

Sauce (for Ham Balls):
- 2 cups brown sugar, packed
- 1 cup vinegar
- 2 teaspoons dry mustard
- 1 cup water

Cook until bubbly.
> Note: These freeze well.

French Pizza

- 1 package Pepperidge Farm patty shells
- 1 tablespoon butter
- ⅓ cup bottled spaghetti sauce
- 16 slices pepperoni
- 6 ounces ham
- ¼ cup chopped green onion
- ½ teaspoon oregano
- 6 ounces Mozzarella cheese

18 pieces

Thaw patty shells and roll into a 9 × 16 inch rectangle. Cut into two rectangles, one 4-inch and one 5-inch in width. Brush edges with egg yolk and 1 teaspoon water. Place larger rectangle on cookie sheet. Pour spaghetti sauce down center of dough to within one inch of edge. Place a layer of pepperoni, cheese, ham and onions on sauce. Place other crust on top. Crinkle edge with a fork. Brush top with egg yolk and water mixture. Make 3 slits across top. Bake at 425 degrees for 25 minutes. Cut into bite-size pieces.

Green Chile Won Tons

- ½ pound Monterey Jack cheese, grated
- 1 4-ounce can green chiles, chopped
- 1 package Won Ton skins

30 Won Tons

Mix cheese and green chiles. Place 1 teaspoon mixture on a Won Ton skin and fold like an envelope. Fry in 2 inches of hot oil until brown, turning so that both sides will be brown. Drain. Serve hot with guacamole dip.

Guacamole Dip:
- 2 large, ripe avocados
- 3 tablespoons fresh lime juice
- ½ teaspoon salt
- ½ teaspoon ground coriander
- 2 teaspoons minced green onion
- 3 tablespoons mayonnaise

Mash pulp of avocado and blend in lime juice. Add remaining ingredients and blend until smooth. Cover and refrigerate until used.

ADO CACHE COLORADO CACHE COLORADO CACHE COLORADO CACHE COLORADO CACHE COLORADO CACHE COLORADO CACHE COLORADO CACHE COLORADO CACHE COLORADO CACHE COLORADO CACHE

Crab Won Tons

3 dozen

1 8-ounce package cream cheese
1 6-ounce package frozen crabmeat
Won Ton skins

Mix cream cheese and crab. Place 1 teaspoon of mixture in middle of Won Ton skin and fold like an envelope. Fry in hot oil on both sides. Serve hot with sweet and sour sauce.

Sweet and Sour Sauce:

1 cup sugar
½ cup wine vinegar
½ cup water
1 scant teaspoon white pepper
1 tablespoon finely diced green pepper
1 tablespoon finely diced pimento
2 tablespoons corn starch

Combine all ingredients. Cook over low heat until thick, stirring constantly. Simmer 5 minutes.

Pork Won Tons

6 cups filling

1½ pounds pork, finely ground
1 tablespoon dry white wine
1 teaspoon salt
1 teaspoon minced garlic
1 10-ounce can Chinese vegetables, drained and chopped
1 4-ounce can mushrooms, drained and chopped
½ teaspoon sugar
1 tablespoon soy sauce
1 small onion, diced
Won Ton skins
oil for frying

Brown pork and drain well. Saute onions in a little of the pork grease. Combine all ingredients except Won Ton skins. Place a spoonful of filling in center of each skin. Fold like an envelope (may put a dab of water in each corner to secure). Fry in 2 inches hot oil until golden. Drain on paper towel. Arrange on plate with small cup of soy sauce for dipping.
Note: These may be frozen before frying.

Egg Rolls

60 egg rolls

2 tablespoons oil
3 stalks celery, cut into 1-inch julienned pieces
6 green onions, cut into 1-inch julienned pieces
¾ teaspoon salt
¾ teaspoon sugar
¾ pound cooked, leftover pork
1 can bamboo shoots, sliced
½ pound shrimp, cooked and slivered
1½ pounds fresh bean sprouts
2 tablespoons soy sauce
1 package egg roll wrappers (or Won Ton skins) cut in quarters
1 egg white, beaten
oil for frying
mustard sauce (see index)
sweet and sour sauce (see index)

Heat 1 tablespoon oil in wok. Add celery, onion, salt, sugar and stir-fry 2 minutes. Remove to large bowl. Add a bit more oil to wok, add pork and bamboo shoots and stir-fry 1 minute. Remove to bowl. Add more oil, shrimp and bean sprouts to wok and stir-fry 2 minutes. Add to ingredients in bowl with soy sauce. Combine well, place in strainer and drain thoroughly. Roll in egg roll wrappers and seal with egg white. Fry in oil at 350 degrees until golden brown. Serve with mustard sauce and sweet and sour sauce (see index).

Crab-Stuffed Mushrooms

25 mushrooms

25 fresh mushrooms
1 8-ounce package cream cheese
1 tablespoon milk
1 6½-ounce can crabmeat
2 tablespoons minced onions
½ teaspoon horseradish
dash of Worcestershire sauce
salt to taste

Blend all ingredients except mushrooms. Clean mushrooms and remove stems. Fill mushroom caps with mixture. Sprinkle top with bread crumbs. Bake at 350 degrees for 10 minutes in a shallow buttered dish until hot and bubbly.

Hors d'oeuvres and Appetizers

Marinated Mushrooms

1½ cups

25 fresh mushrooms
1 hard cooked egg yolk, mashed
⅓ cup malt vinegar
½ cup vegetable oil
   salt and pepper to taste
2 teaspoons chopped parsley
1 teaspoon prepared mustard
1 tablespoon brown sugar

Mix together all ingredients except mushrooms. Bring to a boil and add mushrooms. Cook 5 to 6 minutes. Refrigerate and marinate overnight. Serve with toothpicks.

Stuffed Mushroom Caps

20 mushrooms

20 large mushroom caps
6 - 8 tablespoons butter
3 tablespoons minced green onions or chives
1 tablespoon flour
¾ cup heavy cream
3 tablespoons minced parsley
¼ cup grated Swiss cheese
   salt and pepper to taste

Clean mushroom caps and stems. Remove stems and save. Brush caps with melted butter and arrange, hollow side up, in baking dish. Season with salt and pepper. Mince stems of mushrooms and saute with chives in 4 or 5 tablespoons butter for 4 or 5 minutes. Lower heat and stir in flour for 1 minute. Add cream and simmer until thickened. Stir in parsley and seasonings. Fill mushroom caps with mixture. Top each with 1 teaspoon cheese and drizzle with melted butter. 15 minutes before serving, bake at 375 degrees in upper ⅓ of oven for about 15 minutes.

Sausage Stuffed Mushrooms

About 50 mushrooms

1 pound Jimmy Dean's hot pork sausage
1 pound large fresh mushrooms

Clean mushrooms and remove stems. Fill mushrooms with raw sausage and pat until sausage is mounded and secure. Bake on ungreased cookie sheet at 350 degrees for 30 minutes or until sausage looks well browned. Serve hot.

Note: May sprinkle with Parmesan cheese before baking.

29

Hors d'oeuvres and Appetizers

E COLORADO CACHE COLORADO CACHE COLORADO CACHE COLORADO CACHE COLORADO CACHE COLORADO CACHE COLORADO CACHE COLORADO CACHE COLORADO CACHE COLORADO

Stuffed Cocktail Tomatoes

Cherry tomatoes

Fillings:
Seasoned cottage cheese
Smoked oysters
Guacamole (see index)
Roquefort softened with Cognac and butter
Yogurt generously flavored with dill and grated cucumber
Smoked salmon, cream cheese, Worcestershire sauce and chopped chives

Stuff hollowed-out, drained cherry tomatoes with one of the following fillings and serve chilled.

Fillings for Stuffed Eggs

Crisply fried, crumbled bacon and chopped chutney

Cooked, chopped lobster meat, Dijon mustard, capers (optional)

Black caviar, fresh lemon juice and grated onion

Chopped ham, mustard, parsley, fresh dill and freshly grated lemon rind

Minced, smoked salmon, grated onion, capers, lemon juice, mayonnaise, freshly ground pepper

Sour cream, dill weed, mashed anchovy, chopped chives, parsley, salt and pepper

Minced cooked ham, minced sweet pickle, mayonnaise, Dijon mustard, salt and pepper

Cheese Wrapped Grapes

1 **8-ounce package cream cheese, softened**
1 **8-ounce package sharp Cheddar cheese, grated**
½ **cup butter, softened**
1 **tablespoon prepared mustard**
½ **teaspoon Worcestershire sauce**
   fresh seedless grapes
   paprika
   walnuts or pecans, chopped

50 appetizers

Beat together cheeses, butter, mustard and Worcestershire sauce. With damp hands, form mixture around individual grapes. Roll each ball in paprika and then chopped nuts. Chill.

COLORADO CACHE COLORADO CACHE COLORADO CACHE COLORADO CACHE COLORADO CACHE COLORADO CACHE COLORADO CACHE COLORADO CACHE COLORADO CACHE COLORADO CACHE COLORADO

Artichoke Dip

1½ cups

1   **14-ounce can artichoke hearts, chopped**
4   **pieces bacon, crisply fried and crumbled**
1   **tablespoon minced onion**
1   **tablespoon fresh lemon juice**
½   **cup mayonnaise**
    dash of cayenne pepper
    salt and pepper to taste
    Worcestershire sauce to taste

Mix all ingredients and refrigerate overnight. Serve with crackers.

Avocado-Crab Dip

2 cups

1   **large avocado, mashed**
1   **tablespoon fresh lemon juice**
2   **tablespoons grated onion**
1   **teaspoon Worcestershire sauce**
1   **8-ounce package cream cheese, softened**
½   **cup sour cream**
½   **teaspoon salt**
1   **7½-ounce can crabmeat, drained and flaked**

Mix mashed avocado with lemon juice, onion and Worcestershire sauce. Stir in cream cheese, sour cream and salt. Add crabmeat and mix thoroughly. Serve with tortilla chips or crackers.

Avocado and Leek Dip

1½ cups

½   **package dry leek soup mix**
1   **cup sour cream**
1   **large ripe avocado, mashed**
1   **tablespoon fresh lemon juice**
    large red cabbage, hollowed

Mix soup and sour cream and avocado mixed with lemon juice. Serve in a hollowed-out red cabbage with crudites.

Crab Spinach Fondue

2 cups

- 2 **10-ounce packages frozen, chopped spinach, defrosted**
- 1 **bunch green onions, thinly sliced**
- ¼ **pound butter**
- 8 **ounces crabmeat**
- ¼ **cup grated Parmesan Cheese**
- ¼ **teaspoon garlic powder**
  dash of salt
  dash of pepper
  dash of Tabasco sauce

Squeeze all liquid from chopped spinach. Saute onions in butter and mix with rest of ingredients. Serve warm in a fondue pot. Dip with corn chips or crackers.

Pickadillo Almond Dip

6 cups

- ½ **pound ground beef**
- ½ **pound ground pork**
- 1 **teaspoon salt**
- ¼ **teaspoon pepper**
- 4 **medium tomatoes, peeled and diced**
- 2½ **cloves garlic, minced**
- 3 **green onions, minced**
- 1 **6-ounce can tomato paste**
- 2 **Jalapeno peppers, rinsed, seeded and diced**
  dash of oregano
- ¾ **cup chopped pimento**
- ¾ **cup seedless raisins**
- ¾ **cup whole, blanched almonds**

In a saucepan crumble beef and pork; brown. Add salt, pepper and enough water to cover meat. Bring to a boil, reduce heat and simmer for 30 minutes. Drain and add remaining ingredients. Bring to a boil and simmer for 45 minutes, or until mixture is very thick. Serve hot with tortilla chips.

33

Hors d'oeuvres and Appetizers
COLORADO CACHE COLORADO CACHE COLORADO CACHE COLORADO CACHE COLORADO CACHE COLORADO CACHE COLORADO CACHE COLORADO CACHE COLORADO

Sour Dough-Beef Dip

1 8-ounce package cream
     cheese
1 cup sour cream
1 4-ounce package chipped
     beef, chopped
¼ cup finely chopped green
     onion
     dash of Worcestershire sauce
2 tablespoons chopped green
     pepper
1 8-inch round loaf sour dough
     bread

12 servings

Mix well all ingredients except bread. Slice top off bread round and hollow out carefully, making sure there are no weak places in bread shell. Fill bread shell with chipped beef mixture and put top back on. Wrap in foil and bake at 300 degrees for 1½ hours. Use soft bread from the interior of the loaf to dip in hot mixture.

Count Arnaud's Shrimp Cocktail Sauce

3 tablespoons vegetable oil
3 tablespoons olive oil
2 tablespoons vinegar
1 tablespoon paprika
½ teaspoon white pepper
     chopped parsley to taste
½ teaspoon salt
4 tablespoons Creole mustard
½ heart celery, chopped
½ small white onion, finely
     chopped

1 cup

Mix ingredients in blender. Chill. Serve on shrimp.
     Note: This recipe reportedly comes from Count Arnaud's family, founders of the renowned Arnaud's Restaurant in New Orleans.

ASPEN TREES AND THE MAROON BELLS

Hints from the **Front Range**

Stock may be stored refrigerated, but must be refreshed. After 5 days, it should be reheated and boiled for 2 minutes and returned to the refrigerator.

Stock may be frozen, but because freezing causes ingredients to separate it should be brought to a boil before using.

If fresh stock is to be used immediately, skim off as much surface fat as possible, then float an ice cube to congeal the rest. A piece of chilled lettuce will collect the remaining fat.

To clarify stock: for each quart of stock add 1 egg white beaten slightly with 2 teaspoons of cold water and 1 crumbled egg shell. Stir and heat to boiling. Boil 2 minutes, remove from heat and let stand without stirring for 20 minutes. Pour stock through a strainer lined with cheesecloth.

Stocks may be conveniently frozen in ice cube trays. Store the frozen cubes in plastic bags and use as needed.

Use the bones from a left-over standing rib roast in your stock. They give it a rich flavor and a wonderful dark color.

If you do not have time to soak dried beans over night, cover and bring them to a boil, boil for 2 minutes, remove from heat and let them soak covered in the cooking water for one hour.

The **Front Range,** one of the principal mountain chains in the Rockies, extends a full 100 miles. From Pike's Peak, an isolated monarch at the southern end, to Mount Evans, and north to Longs' Peak, the visible magnitude of nature's creation is a constant backdrop to the cities and arid plains of Eastern Colorado.

COLORADO CACHE COLORADO CACHE COLORADO CACHE COLORADO CACHE COLORADO CACHE COLORADO CACHE COLORADO CACHE COLORADO CACHE COLORADO

Chilled Raspberry Soup

12 servings

1½	tablespoons unflavored gelatin
⅓	cup cold water
¾	cup hot water
3	10-ounce packages frozen raspberries, thawed
3½	cups sour cream (28 ounces)
1⅓	cups pineapple juice
1⅓	cups half and half
1⅓	cups dry sherry
⅓	cup grenadine
2	tablespoons lemon juice

Garnishes:
mint
whole raspberries

Soak gelatin in cold water for 5 minutes. Stir in hot water and dissolve over low heat. Push raspberries through a strainer to remove seeds, then puree. Combine all ingredients and place in a glass bowl. Cover and refrigerate overnight. Garnish with mint and/or whole raspberries.

Note: Great served as a first course for a luncheon. Leftover soup can be frozen for a yogurt-like snack.

Cream Consomme

10 servings

1	large onion, grated
1	tart apple, unpeeled and grated
3	10½-ounce cans beef consomme
1½	cups heavy cream
½	teaspoon paprika
½	teaspoon imported curry powder
1	red apple, unpeeled and chopped, for garnish
2	tablespoons fresh lemon juice

Add the grated onion and apple to the consomme and cook until tender, about 12 minutes. Puree in a blender, then put through a strainer. Stir in cream and season with paprika and curry powder. Refrigerate until ready to serve. Reheat slowly, just until heated through. Serve in small cups garnished with chopped unpeeled apple sprinkled with lemon juice.

Consomme de Mer

6 servings

1	**10½-ounce can consomme**
1	**can water**
1	**8-ounce bottle clam juice**
2	**teaspoons lemon juice**
½	**cup whipping cream**
½	**teaspoon salt**

Heat the consomme, water, clam juice and lemon juice to boiling. Whip the cream with the salt. Serve hot with a large dollop of cream on each portion.

Katie Stapleton's Colorado Cantaloupe Soup

6 servings

1	**ripe cantaloupe, peeled, seeded and cut into chunks**
½	**cup dry sherry**
2	**tablespoons honey**
1	**tablespoon fresh lime juice**

Put all ingredients into food processor or blender and mix well. Chill covered in refrigerator. Blend again before serving to mix altogether.

39
Soups

COLORADO CACHE COLORADO CACHE COLORADO CACHE COLORADO CACHE COLORADO CACHE COLORADO CACHE COLORADO CACHE COLORADO CACHE COLORADO CACHE COLORADO C

Cold Cucumber and Spinach Soup

8 servings

1   **bunch green onions, sliced**
2   **tablespoons butter**
4   **cups diced cucumbers**
3   **cups chicken broth**
1   **cup chopped, fresh spinach**
½   **cup sliced, peeled potatoes**
½   **teaspoon salt**
1   **tablespoon lemon juice**
    Pepper to taste
1   **cup light cream**

Garnishes:
    radishes
    green onions

In a saucepan, saute green onions in butter until they are softened. Add cucumbers, chicken broth, spinach, potatoes, salt, lemon juice and pepper. Simmer uncovered until the potatoes are tender. Transfer the mixture to a blender in batches and puree. Transfer the puree to a bowl and stir in the light cream. Let soup cool and chill for several hours, or overnight. Garnish each serving with thin slices of radishes and/or green onions.

Zucchini Soup

6-8 servings

4   **medium zucchini, quartered
    and sliced**
2   **15-ounce cans chicken broth
    bunch of green onions,
    chopped**
1   **teaspoon salt**
1   **teaspoon pepper
    dill weed to taste**
2   **8-ounce packages cream
    cheese**
1   **cup sour cream with chives
    (½ pint)
    chopped chives or paprika for
    garnish**

In a saucepan, add zucchini, chicken broth, green onions, salt, pepper and dill weed to taste. Cook mixture until soft, approximately 20 to 30 minutes. Blend the cream cheese and sour cream in a blender until smooth. Then blend in zucchini mixture, a portion at a time, until smooth. Chill overnight or until very cold. Garnish with chopped chives or paprika.

40
Soups

Tomato Bisque

2 pounds ripe tomatoes (or 2 15-ounce cans tomatoes) chopped
1 medium onion, thinly sliced
1 tablespoon butter
1 bay leaf
1 heaping tablespoon brown sugar
2 teaspoons finely chopped fresh basil (or 1 teaspoon dried basil)
2 whole cloves
1 teaspoon salt
½ teaspoon black pepper
1 pint light cream
1 cup milk
6 large croutons, buttered
2 tablespoons chopped chives

6 servings

Peel and seed tomatoes. Saute onion in butter and add the chopped tomatoes. Add bay leaf, sugar, cloves, salt, pepper and basil. Simmer, stirring occasionally, until tomatoes are thoroughly cooked, about 25 minutes. Remove bay leaf and cloves and transfer mixture to blender or food processor to puree. Strain. Add cream and milk and heat through. Serve topped with toasted buttered croutons. Sprinkle with chopped chives.

COLORADO CACHE COLORADO CACHE COLORADO CACHE COLORADO CACHE COLORADO CACHE COLORADO CACHE COLORADO CACHE COLORADO CACHE COLORADO C

Clear Tomato Consomme

6-8 servings

1   1 pound, 14-ounce can
       tomatoes
2   10½-ounce cans beef bouillon
2   cups water
3   tablespoons chopped onion
1   bay leaf
1   stalk celery
6   cloves
     Salt and pepper to taste

Combine all ingredients and simmer uncovered for 30 minutes. Strain. Taste and correct seasonings. Serve hot with puffed crackers.

Note: Prepare the day before so that the flavors have a chance to mingle.

Potage Crecy

6 servings

2   tablespoons butter
¾   cup finely chopped onions
3   cups finely chopped carrots
1   quart chicken stock (or 4 10½-
       ounce cans chicken broth)
2   teaspoons tomato paste
2   tablespoons raw white rice
     salt to taste
     white pepper to taste
½   cup heavy cream
1   tablespoon softened butter
8 - 12   carrot curls for garnish

In a heavy 3 to 4 quart saucepan over moderate heat, melt butter. Stir in onions and cook 5 minutes. Add carrots, stock, tomato paste and rice. Simmer 30 minutes. Puree in blender in small batches until smooth. Return to pan. Add salt and pepper and stir in cream. Simmer for 10 minutes; stir in softened butter. Garnish with carrot curls.

Swiss Broccoli Soup

8 servings

5½ cups whole milk
1 10-ounce package frozen chopped broccoli, or 1½ cups chopped fresh broccoli
3 tablespoons chopped onion
2 tablespoons butter
1 tablespoon flour
2 cups grated Swiss cheese (8 ounces)
¼ teaspoon salt

Heat milk in large saucepan until simmering. Cook broccoli and onions in milk until tender. Melt butter in small saucepan. Stir in flour. Add butter-flour mixture to milk. Cook and stir 3 minutes. Remove from heat and add grated cheese and salt. Stir until cheese is melted. Serve immediately.

Soupe a l'Oignon

6 servings

6 large yellow onions, thinly sliced
4 tablespoons butter
1 teaspoon sugar
1 tablespoon flour
1 cup chablis
1 quart beef stock or 2 10½-ounce cans consomme plus 2 cans water
6 large croutons, made from sliced French bread
2 cups grated Swiss cheese (8 ounces)
½ cup freshly grated Parmesan cheese (2 ounces)

In a heavy-bottomed pan, slowly brown the onions in butter and sugar until the onions are a dark brown, about 30 minutes. (With a wooden spoon, occasionally scrape the brown off the bottom of the pan.) Add flour and cook, stirring for 2 or 3 minutes. Add the chablis and cook for 2 or 3 minutes. Add stock and simmer partially covered for 1 hour. To serve, place a crouton on top of each bowl of soup. Cover generously with Swiss cheese and sprinkle with Parmesan cheese. Bake covered at 325 degrees for 15 minutes, then uncover and bake another 10 minutes.

COLORADO CACHE COLORADO CACHE COLORADO CACHE COLORADO CACHE COLORADO CACHE COLORADO CACHE COLORADO CACHE COLORADO CACHE COLORADO

Fresh Mushroom Soup

6 servings

- 6 tablespoons butter
- 2 cups finely minced yellow onions
- ½ teaspoon sugar
- 1 pound fresh mushrooms
- ¼ cup flour
- 1 cup water
- 1¾ cups chicken broth
- 1 cup dry vermouth
- 1 teaspoon salt
- ¼ teaspoon pepper

In a large saucepan melt butter and cook onions and sugar slowly until golden, about 30 to 45 minutes. Slice ⅓ of the mushrooms and finely chop the rest. Add all mushrooms and saute for 5 minutes. Stir in flour until smooth. Cook for 2 minutes, stirring constantly. Pour in water and stir until smooth. Add remaining ingredients and heat to boiling, stirring constantly. Reduce heat and simmer uncovered 10 minutes.

Note: May be prepared in advance, refrigerated, and reheated covered over low heat for 10 minutes.

Bay Scallop Chowder

4 servings

- 3 medium potatoes, diced
- 1 small carrot, chopped
- 1 stalk celery, chopped
- 1 medium onion, chopped
- 2 cups chicken stock
- ½ teaspoon salt
- ¼ teaspoon freshly ground pepper
- ½ bay leaf
- ½ teaspoon thyme, crumbled
- 1 pound fresh bay scallops
- ½ pound fresh mushrooms, sliced
- 1½ tablespoons butter
- ½ cup dry white wine
- 1 cup heavy cream
- 1 egg yolk, lightly beaten
- 2 tablespoons chopped parsley paprika

Place potatoes, carrot, celery and onion in a large pot, cover with chicken stock and bring to a boil. Add salt, pepper, bay leaf and thyme. Simmer covered until vegetables are tender. Remove bay leaf and transfer mixture to blender or food processor. Blend until smooth. Meanwhile, saute mushrooms in butter. Add scallops and wine and cook for 1 minute. Stir in cream mixed with egg yolk. Combine this mixture with the pureed vegetables and broth. Heat through and serve with a sprinkling of parsley and paprika.

Cream of Mushroom Soup

4 servings

¼ **cup butter**
¾ **cup chopped green onions, including tops**
2 **cups chopped, fresh mushrooms**
2 **tablespoons flour**
1 **cup half and half**
1 **cup chicken broth or stock**
¼ **teaspoon salt**
⅛ **teaspoon pepper**

In a large skillet cook green onions in butter over low heat for 5 minutes or until tender. Add the chopped mushrooms and cook mixture, stirring, for 2 minutes. Add flour and cook, stirring, for 3 minutes. Remove the pan from the heat and add chicken stock and half and half in a steady stream, whisking. Bring the soup to a boil over moderate heat. Simmer, stirring, for 5 minutes. Add salt and pepper.

Note: This is better if made ahead and reheated.

Corn Chowder

6 servings

½ **cup diced salt pork**
2 **slices onion**
1 **small bay leaf**
4 - 5 **sprigs of parsley**
pinch of dried sage
salt and pepper to taste
1 **cup raw, diced potatoes**
2 **cups hot water**
3 **tablespoons flour**
2½ **cups corn kernels**
2 **cups scalded milk**
2 **egg yolks, lightly beaten**
1 **tablespoon butter**
paprika for garnish

In a large saucepan lightly brown salt pork. Add onion slices and cook for 2 to 3 minutes, stirring frequently. Add bay leaf, parsley, sage, salt and pepper. Stir in raw potatoes and hot water and cook the mixture until potatoes are tender. Thicken mixture with the flour mixed with a little cold water or milk. Add corn kernels and scalded milk to the potato mixture. Bring chowder to a boil and remove saucepan from heat. Just before serving, mix a little of the chowder liquid with egg yolks and butter and stir this mixture into the chowder. Sprinkle the chowder with paprika and serve very hot.

COLORADO CACHE COLORADO CACHE COLORADO CACHE COLORADO CACHE COLORADO CACHE COLORADO CACHE COLORADO CACHE COLORADO CACHE COLORADO C.

Coach House Black Bean Soup

8 servings

1	pound black beans
2½	quarts water
5	strips bacon, cut in small pieces
2	stalks celery, chopped
2	medium-sized onions, chopped
2	tablespoons flour
	rind and bone from smoked ham or
2	smoked ham hocks, split
3	pounds beef bones
3	sprigs parsley
2	bay leaves
2	cloves garlic, halved
2	carrots, cut in pieces
2	parsnips, chopped
¼	teaspoon ground pepper
2	teaspoons salt
¾	cup Madeira
2	hard cooked eggs
	lemon slices, sprinkled with parsley

Wash beans, cover with cold water and soak overnight. Drain and wash again. Place them in a casserole and add 2½ quarts water. Cover and simmer 90 minutes. Cook bacon in heavy kettle for a few minutes. Add celery and onion and cook until tender; do not brown. Blend in flour and cook, stirring for 1 minute. Add ham and beef bones, parsley, bay leaves, garlic, carrots, parsnips, pepper, salt and beans with the cooking liquid. Cover and simmer over low heat, stirring occasionally, for 4 hours. Add more water if necessary. Remove bone and ham rind or hocks and blend half of the soup in blender. Remove any meat from ham bone or hocks, chop fine and return to soup. Add blended soup. Add wine and chopped eggs. Mix well. Garnish with lemon.

Split Pea Soup

6-8 servings

1	pound split peas
2	cups water
1	47-ounce can regular-strength chicken broth
3	slices thick bacon, chopped
½	teaspoon dry mustard
1	cup diced celery
¼	teaspoon coarsely ground pepper
1	teaspoon salt
⅛	teaspoon oregano
1	cup diced ham

Combine all ingredients except oregano and ham and simmer covered for 3 to 4 hours. Skim off grease. Add oregano and ham and simmer 1 hour. Serve hot.

Pistou

6 servings

1	**cup diced onion**
1	**leek, white part only, sliced**
2	**tablespoons butter**
1	**cup green beans, cut into ½ inch pieces**
1	**cup diced potatoes**
1	**cup canned tomatoes, chopped and drained**
6	**cups beef bouillon**
½	**cup spaghetti, broken into 1 inch pieces**
2	**teaspoons salt**
1	**teaspoon pepper**
2	**cloves garlic**
2	**teaspoons crushed basil**
½	**teaspoon crushed thyme**
¼	**teaspoon ground sage**
2	**egg yolks**
¼	**cup olive oil**
2	**tablespoons tomato paste**
2	**tablespoons freshly grated Parmesan cheese**

Saute the onions and leek in butter until soft. Transfer to a large pot with a cover. Add green beans, potatoes, tomatoes and beef bouillon. Cover and simmer gently for 30 minutes. Add salt, pepper and spaghetti and cook 15 minutes longer. In a bowl, mash the garlic with the basil, thyme and sage. Add egg yolks and gradually stir in the oil and tomato paste. Add a little soup to this mixture and stir back into the soup. Sprinkle with Parmesan cheese.

Minestrone

6 servings

5 - 6	ounces salt pork
1	yellow onion, thinly sliced
1	leek, thinly sliced
2	carrots
2	potatoes
¼	celery root
2	quarts chicken stock
1	cup tomatoes
2	tablespoons tomato paste
2	cloves garlic
1	cup broken spaghetti
1½	teaspoons basil
	freshly ground pepper to taste
	chopped parsley to taste
	freshly grated Parmesan cheese to taste

Pare carrots and potatoes. Cut all vegetables and salt pork into thin strips, about 2 inches long. Saute the pork without allowing it to brown. Add tomato paste and season with freshly ground pepper. Press juice from the garlic cloves into pork mixture. Add sliced onion, leek, carrots, potatoes, tomatoes and celery. Pour in the chicken stock and let the soup boil for 10 minutes uncovered. Add the spaghetti and season with basil and parsley. Add salt only if needed. Cook until spaghetti is al dente. Sprinkle with Parmesan cheese just before serving.

Garbanzo Soup

16 servings

1	large ham bone, about 2 pounds with meat on
3	quarts water
2	large onions, finely chopped
2	cloves garlic, minced
2	bay leaves
2	tablespoons salt
½	teaspoon pepper
	pinch saffron
4	peeled, medium potatoes, cut in eighths
2	16-ounce cans garbanzo beans
3	chorizos (or approximately ¼ pound any other well-seasoned Spanish or Italian sausage)

Cover ham bone with water and cook covered with the onions, garlic and bay leaves for 2 hours. Add salt, pepper and saffron. Add potatoes and cook covered for 30 minutes. Add garbanzos and sliced chorizos. Remove meat from ham bone, dice and add to soup. Cook covered for 30 minutes longer over low heat. Remove bay leaves and check seasoning.

Note: Keeps at least 2 weeks, refrigerated, and the flavor improves daily.

48
Soups

Tiffany's Bean Pot Soup

12 servings

2 cups dry pinto beans
1 pound ham, cubed
1 quart water
2 13½-ounce cans tomato juice
4 cups chicken stock
1 medium onion, chopped
2 medium cloves garlic, minced
3 tablespoons chopped parsley
¼ cup chopped green pepper
4 tablespoons brown sugar
1 teaspoon salt
1 teaspoon crushed bay leaves
½ teaspoon celery seed
4 whole cloves
1½ teaspoons Fines Herbes
¼ cup dry vermouth (optional)

Thoroughly wash beans and soak overnight covered in water. Drain and rinse again. Add all of the ingredients except the vermouth. Bring to a boil, reduce heat and simmer covered until the beans are tender, about 6 to 8 hours. At this point, cool and blend half of the soup in a blender. Return to pot, add vermouth and heat to serving temperature.

Note: This is good reheated and freezes well.

White Russian Vegetable Soup

8 servings

2 cups diced beets
4 cups shredded cabbage
3½ - 4 pounds chuck roast
2 large onions, chopped
3½ cups tomatoes
boullion cubes to taste
¾ cup fresh lemon juice
6 garlic cloves, minced
¼ cup chopped parsley
1 small bay leaf, crumbled
1 teaspoon paprika
2 tablespoons sugar
1 teaspoon salt
1 teaspoon pepper
sour cream

Cover roast with 1½ quarts water. Bring to a boil, cover and simmer 1 hour. Taste stock for flavor and add bouillon cubes as needed. Add vegetables, lemon juice, and seasonings and simmer covered 2 hours. Remove the roast, take out bones and cut meat into bite-size pieces. Return meat to soup. Serve with a generous spoonful of sour cream per serving.

Pot Luck Chili

14-16 servings

1	**pound pinto beans**
½	**cup butter**
2	**onions, chopped**
6	**shallots, chopped**
1	**7-ounce can green chiles, seeded, chopped and drained**
2	**cloves garlic, minced**
3	**pounds chopped sirloin or round steak**
1	**pound pork sausage**
½	**cup flour**
1	**pound can baked beans**
1	**4-ounce can pimentos**
3	**pounds fresh tomatoes, chopped**
¾	**cup chopped celery**
½	**pound fresh mushrooms, sliced**
1	**sweet red pepper, chopped (optional)**
1	**hot red pepper, chopped**
2	**cups pitted ripe olives, chopped**
½	**cup minced parsley**
1	**12-ounce bottle chili sauce**
	salt
1	**tablespoon garlic salt**
2	**tablespoons pepper**
2	**teaspoons ground coriander**
1	**tablespoon oregano**
4	**tablespoons chili powder**
2	**cups sour cream (1 pint)**

Wash pinto beans, soak overnight in water to cover. Bring to a boil in soaking water and lower heat. Simmer covered for 3 hours until tender. Drain. Melt butter in skillet, add onions, shallots, chiles and garlic. Saute until onion is soft. Add chopped sirloin and cook over moderate heat until meat is brown. In a separate pan, brown sausage, pour off grease and add to meat-onion mixture. Stir flour into meat mixture and blend. Put meat mixture into a pot. Add beans, pimento, tomatoes, celery, mushrooms, sweet and hot peppers, olives, parsley and chili sauce. Bring to a boil, lower heat and simmer uncovered for 30 minutes. Add salt to taste, garlic salt, pepper, coriander, oregano and chili powder. Simmer uncovered 1¼ hours, stirring occasionally. Skim off grease. Before serving, remove from heat, stir in sour cream and return to low heat to heat through.

Spanish Soup

6-8 servings

2	tablespoons butter
1	tablespoon olive oil
4	cups thinly sliced onions
3	tablespoons flour
1	16-ounce can tomato puree
4	14-ounce cans regular strength beef broth
1	clove garlic, minced
1	tablespoon red wine vinegar
1	tablespoon Worcestershire sauce
1	tablespoon sugar
1½	teaspoons salt
¼	teaspoon pepper
¼	teaspoon oregano
¼	teaspoon tarragon
¼	teaspoon Tabasco sauce
½	teaspoon ground cumin

Melt butter in a 4 to 5 quart pot over medium-low heat. Add olive oil and onions. Slowly cook the onions, stirring occasionally, until they are limp and slightly golden, about 45 minutes. Sprinkle flour over onions and blend. Gradually stir in tomato puree and beef broth. Add garlic, vinegar, Worcestershire sauce, sugar, salt, pepper, oregano, tarragon, Tabasco sauce and cumin. Stir until well blended. Bring to a boil over high heat, reduce heat to low and simmer uncovered for 30 to 40 minutes, stirring occasionally. This soup is fun because it is served with several condiments. Ask your guests to choose 2 or 3 from each of the condiment groups.

Condiments:
Group #1 Meat

2	large linguica, chorizo, or kielbasa sausages, sliced ¼ inch thick and browned
¼ - ½	pound tiny shrimp, cooked and shelled
¾	pound ham, cooked and cubed, sauteed until lightly browned

Group #2 Fresh Vegetables

1	cup diced red or green pepper
1	cup peeled and diced cucumber
1	cup diced fresh tomato
1	cup diced onion
½	pound fresh mushrooms, sliced and sauteed in butter
½	pound fresh carrots, sliced and cooked until tender, drained

Garnishes:

3	hard cooked eggs, chopped
1	cup sour cream
¼	pound Cheddar cheese, grated
2	limes, cut into wedges
1	8-ounce can garbanzos, drained
1	2¼-ounce can sliced ripe olives, drained
½	cup chopped parsley

51
Soups

COLORADO CACHE COLORADO CACHE COLORADO CACHE COLORADO CACHE COLORADO CACHE COLORADO CACHE COLORADO CACHE COLORADO CACHE COLORADO

Chasen's Chili

8 servings

½ **pound pinto beans**
5 **cups canned tomatoes**
1 **pound green peppers,**
   chopped
1½ **tablespoons vegetable oil**
1½ **pounds onions, chopped**
2 **cloves garlic, crushed**
½ **cup chopped parsley**
1 **pound ground lean pork**
2½ **pounds coarsely ground beef**
   chuck
2 **tablespoons chili powder**
2 **tablespoons salt**
1 **teaspoon pepper**
1½ **teaspoons ground cumin**

Wash the pinto beans and soak overnight. Simmer in the soaking water until tender. Add tomatoes and simmer for 5 minutes. Saute the peppers in oil for 5 minutes. Add onions and cook until tender, stirring often. Add garlic and parsley. Saute pork and beef in butter for 15 minutes. Add meat to onion, tomato and pepper mixture, stir in the chili powder and cook for 10 minutes. Add the beans and spices and simmer covered for 1 hour. Uncover the pot and simmer for another 30 minutes. Skim the grease from the top before serving.

OLD MINE SHAFT NEAR ESTES PARK/CHASM FALLS IN ROCKY MOUNTAIN NATIONAL PARK

Hints from the **Frying Pan**

Egg whites should be at room temperature before beating.

If you are beating egg whites in a non-copper bowl, add a pinch of cream of tartar when they have been beaten to the foamy stage. This adds acidity, which helps the whites increase in volume and keeps their stability after beating.

Beaten egg whites are stiff enough if they do not slide when the bowl is turned upside down.

Crepe batter should sit 2 to 3 hours before it is used.

To prevent a quiche crust from becoming soggy:
• Partially bake the pastry shell in a 425 degree oven for 14 to 16 minutes. Remove from oven, brush with lightly beaten egg yolk, white, whole egg or Dijon mustard and return it to the oven for 2 minutes.
• Do not pour the filling into the pastry shell until just before baking.
• When baking in a Pyrex pie plate, reduce oven temperature 25 degrees, as glass conducts heat quicker than metal.
• To test a quiche for doneness, shake the pan gently to see if the custard is set or slide a knife tip into the center. If it comes out clean, the quiche is done.

Add Grand Marnier, to taste, to French toast batter. Cook as usual then put in a moderate oven to "puff". Serve with warm maple syrup flavored with brandy and butter.

Add shredded ham or crumbled bacon to corn bread or corn stick batter. Serve with melted butter and honey.

Add broken pecans, crumbled bacon or shredded ham to your favorite waffle batter.

Hot maple syrup becomes extraordinary with the addition of a little freshly squeezed orange juice, including some of the crushed pulp, and melted butter.

The **Frying Pan River,** a fishing paradise surrounded by some of the most spectacular scenery in the state, was named for the story of a murdered miner whose last will and testament was found beside his body under his frying pan. Nearby Glenwood Springs, a popular resort, boasts the world's largest hot sulfur spring.

Oranges with Sour Cream

8-10 servings

6 large seedless oranges
1 tablespoon brown sugar
1 cup sour cream
½ teaspoon ground cinnamon
2 tablespoons freshly grated
    orange peel

Peel and slice oranges crosswise ¼ inch thick. Place on a shallow serving dish and sprinkle with brown sugar. Cover with sour cream and sprinkle with cinnamon and orange peel.

Brandy Fruit Compote

6 servings

1 6-ounce can frozen orange
    juice concentrate
2 pints fresh strawberries
8 fresh peaches
    sugar to taste
½ cup brandy or Cognac

Defrost unopened can of orange juice concentrate. Wash and hull berries, blot dry on paper towels. Peel peaches, cut into halves and remove pits. Place in a shallow crystal bowl. Sprinkle with sugar. Cover with strawberries and sprinkle lightly with sugar to taste. Stir brandy into undiluted orange juice concentrate. Pour over fruits and mix gently. Cover and refrigerate for 2 hours. Stir occasionally. Serve in individual small bowls.

Note: Do not prepare ahead as the fruit will become soft.

Fruit Salad Ice

30 servings

1 17-ounce can apricots
1 17-ounce can crushed
    pineapple
1 cup liquid
½ cup sugar
3 10-ounce packages frozen
    strawberries
1 6-ounce can frozen orange
    juice
2 tablespoons lemon juice
3 bananas, diced

Drain apricots and pineapple, reserving liquid and add water to make 1 cup, if necessary. Heat liquid and sugar until sugar dissolves. Add strawberries and their juice, orange juice and lemon juice. Cut up apricots and bananas and add to mixture along with the pineapple. Spoon into cupcake papers. Place in muffin tins and freeze until solid. Remove from tins and store in plastic bags. Remove from freezer 10 to 20 minutes before serving.

Candied Oranges

12 servings

1⅓	**cups sugar**
4	**cups water**
2	**teaspoons vanilla extract**
½	**teaspoon ground cinnamon**
6	**seedless oranges**
	juice of 1 lemon
1	**cup whipped cream**
1	**tablespoon brandy**

In a heavy pot that will hold the oranges snugly, make a syrup of the sugar, water, vanilla and cinnamon. Bring to a boil, reduce heat to medium, cover, and simmer for 15 minutes. Grate skin of the orange lightly to allow syrup to penetrate into the fruit. Add oranges to the syrup. The oranges should be ¾ covered by the syrup. Reduce heat to low, cover, and slowly cook oranges for 2 hours. Turn once or twice during cooking. Remove pot from heat, add lemon juice, re-cover and let oranges cool in the syrup. Chill overnight. To serve, slice oranges cross-wise and arrange on a shallow serving plate. Top with a dollop of brandy flavored whipped cream. Candied oranges will keep for at least 2 weeks in the refrigerator.

Note: Try using 2 pounds of kumquats instead of oranges. You will need to cook these for only 1 hour. To serve, place in small glass bowls and top with brandy flavored whipped cream.

Fruit Slush

6-8 servings

2	**oranges**
2	**lemons**
1	**cup sugar**
1	**16-ounce can crushed pineapple**
2	**cups ginger ale**
3	**bananas, mashed**

Grate the rinds of 1 orange and 1 lemon. Squeeze the juice from the oranges and lemons. Combine juice with sugar, pineapple, ginger ale and bananas. Pour into a 6 cup ring mold and freeze. Remove from mold and thaw 20 to 30 minutes before serving.

Peches Brulee

8 servings

8	fresh or canned peach halves
6	tablespoons butter, melted
6	tablespoons light brown sugar
	grated rind of 2 oranges
1½	teaspoons fresh lemon juice
2	ounces Cognac
1	cup whipped cream
1	teaspoon almond extract

Place peaches in a shallow casserole. Sprinkle with butter, brown sugar, orange rind and lemon juice. Place under broiler until hot and bubbling. Pour Cognac over and ignite. Serve warm, plain, or with almond-flavored whipped cream.

Note: A delicious way to use fresh peaches.

Honey Baked Apples

6 servings

6	tart red or green apples
	brown sugar
6	tablespoons butter
	honey
	ground cinnamon
24	whole cloves

Wash and core the apples, scooping out some of the fruit. Stuff each apple nearly to the top with brown sugar, pressing it down firmly with the back of a spoon. Dot butter on top of brown sugar, fill each apple to the top with honey and sprinkle generously with cinnamon. Stick 4 cloves in each apple and set in a shallow pan. Add ½ cup water to the pan and bake at 300 degrees for 30 minutes or until apples are tender.

Cheese Strata

6 servings

2	**cups (3 slices) bread cubes, crusts trimmed**
½	**pound sharp Cheddar cheese, cubed**
½	**pound bacon, cooked and crumbled (ham or shrimp may be substituted)**
¼	**cup butter, melted**
½	**pound whole fresh mushrooms**
3	**large eggs**
2	**cups milk**
1	**teaspoon prepared mustard**
¼	**teaspoon salt**

Place half the bread cubes in a 1½ quart casserole. Layer half the cheese, bacon and butter. Repeat layers and arrange mushrooms on top. Beat eggs, milk, mustard and salt and pour over the layered mixture. Set casserole in pan of hot water. Bake uncovered at 300 degrees for 1½ hours.

Note: This is better if prepared in advance and refrigerated overnight until baking time.

Cheese Souffle

4 servings

2	**rounded tablespoons freshly grated Parmesan cheese**
2	**rounded tablespoons finely grated Gruyere cheese (4 rounded tablespoons finely grated Cheddar cheese may be substituted for the Parmesan and Gruyere cheeses)**
3	**tablespoons butter**
1	**rounded tablespoon flour**
	salt
	cayenne pepper
¾	**cup milk**
1	**teaspoon prepared mustard**
4	**egg yolks**
5	**egg whites**
1	**tablespoon browned bread crumbs**

Lightly butter a 1 quart souffle dish and dust with browned bread crumbs. Tie a collar of doubled waxed paper around outside of dish so that it stands about 4 inches above top of dish. Lightly butter the waxed paper. In a medium-large saucepan melt butter. Remove from heat. Add flour, salt and cayenne pepper to taste. Gradually stir in the milk and return to heat, stirring until it boils. Remove from heat and add mustard and Gruyere cheese and 1 tablespoon Parmesan cheese (or 3 tablespoons Cheddar cheese). Add egg yolks, one at a time, mixing well after each addition. Whip egg whites to form stiff peaks. Stir 2 tablespoons of egg whites into sauce using metal spoon. Stir in remainder of egg whites in two parts. Fold in carefully. Turn lightly into souffle dish. Sprinkle with remaining cheese and browned crumbs. Bake at 375 degrees for 25 to 30 minutes or until firm to the touch. Serve immediately.

Easy Cheese Souffle

6 servings

6 large eggs
1 cup heavy cream
1 teaspoon salt
   freshly ground pepper
      to taste
¼ teaspoon ground nutmeg
1½ cups grated Cheddar or Swiss
      cheese (6 ounces)
½ cup grated Parmesan cheese

Beat eggs until thick and light. Mix in cream, salt, pepper and nutmeg, beating well. Fold in the cheeses. Pour into a well buttered 1½ quart baking dish or an ovenproof 10½ inch skillet. Bake 425 degrees for 35 to 40 minutes or until set.

Orange Souffle

6 servings

7 egg whites
7 tablespoons sugar
6 tablespoons orange
      marmalade

Sauce:
2 egg yolks
⅔ cup powdered sugar
1 cup whipping cream
1 tablespoon brandy

Beat egg whites until stiff, then beat in the sugar gradually. Add orange marmalade. Butter the top of a double boiler and the lid, pour in the souffle and put the lid on. Steam for 1 hour. If your guests are late, don't worry, just turn down the flame and keep the water under the souffle hot. It won't fall.

To make the sauce, beat egg yolks, gradually adding powdered sugar until the mixture is too stiff to beat. Whip the cream and just before serving carefully blend together. Flavor with brandy.

Note: You may serve fewer people by using 1 egg white for each person and 1 for the double boiler, and 1 tablespoon sugar for each egg white. Add 1 tablespoon less marmalade than the number of egg whites.

Artichoke Frittata

6 servings

½ **pound fresh mushrooms, sliced**
1 **cup chopped onions**
1 **tablespoon vegetable oil**
1 **10-ounce package frozen spinach**
5 **large eggs**
2 **6-ounce jars marinated artichoke hearts, drained**
1½ **cups grated sharp Cheddar cheese (6 ounces)**

Slice mushrooms and saute with onions in oil. Thaw spinach and drain well. (Allow 3 to 4 hours for spinach to thaw and drain.) Beat eggs lightly and combine with mushrooms, spinach, artichoke hearts and cheese. Bake covered in buttered 1½ quart casserole at 350 degrees for 45 minutes.

Windrift Farm Scrambled Eggs

6 servings

1 **7-ounce package frozen shrimp**
1 **7½-ounce can crab**
3½ **tablespoons dry sherry**
6 **tablespoons butter**
2 **tablespoons flour**
¾ **cup milk**
1 **tablespoon chopped chives**
12 **eggs**
  pinch of tarragon
1 **teaspoon salt**
  pepper
  Tabasco sauce
  chopped parsley
  paprika

Cook shrimp, drain and rinse and cut into pieces. Drain, rinse and flake crab. Mix shrimp, crab and sherry. Set aside. Melt 2 tablespoons of butter and 2 tablespoons flour. Add milk, stirring constantly and simmer 1 minute. Add chives and shrimp mixture. Set aside. Mix eggs and seasonings and a pinch of tarragon in blender. Melt remaining butter in skillet. Add eggs and stir until partially cooked (until wet looking and set up). Add seafood mixture. Cook until set and all ingredients are hot. Sprinkle with chopped parsley and paprika.

Note: The eggs may be cooked in a double boiler over hot water. This will keep them moist longer than the conventional frying pan method.

Katie Stapleton's Hawaiian Eggs

6 servings

½ cup butter
2 slices ham, 1-inch thick
1 pineapple, skinned and sliced
3 bananas, skinned and quartered
4 tablespoons honey or ⅓ cup brown sugar
6 eggs, beaten

Melt butter in large skillet. Add ham. Fry until brown on both sides. Remove ham from skillet. Keep warm on platter. Put sliced pineapple and quartered bananas in skillet with the honey or brown sugar. Fry until they are barely soft, not mushy. Remove fruit from skillet, keep warm on platter with ham. Scramble the 6 beaten eggs in skillet.

Note: Be sure that each guest gets a little of each: ham, pineapple, bananas and scrambled egg.

Baked Eggs Provencale

8 servings

8 ripe tomatoes, hollowed out salt and pepper
8 teaspoons chopped parsley Nature's Seasoning
8 eggs
1 teaspoon butter basil
Parmesan cheese, freshly grated

Preheat oven to 400 degrees. Place tomato shells in a buttered baking dish. Sprinkle each with salt, pepper, parsley and a pinch of Nature's Seasoning. Bake 5 minutes, uncovered. Remove from oven and break an egg into each tomato, dot with butter, sprinkle with basil and return to oven for 15 minutes. Sprinkle with Parmesan cheese and bake another 10 minutes.

Basic Omelet

1 omelet

2 large eggs
¼ teaspoon salt pinch of pepper
1 tablespoon water
1 tablespoon butter

Break the eggs into a bowl, add seasonings and water and beat lightly with a fork, just to blend the yolks and whites. Heat omelet pan over high heat. When the pan is hot, add butter and swirl it around until it melts and foams. Quickly pour in the eggs and stir lightly with a fork, but not breaking through to the pan. When the eggs have set to the degree you like, add filling and roll. Tip the pan forward so the omelet rolls onto itself. Serve immediately.

ADO CACHE COLORADO CACHE COLORADO CACHE COLORADO CACHE COLORADO CACHE COLORADO CACHE COLORADO CACHE COLORADO CACHE COLORADO CACHE COLORADO CACHE COLORADO CACHE

Ham and Potato Omelet

2 servings

1 **cooked potato, thinly sliced**
½ **onion, thinly sliced**
5 **tablespoons butter**
 salt and pepper
½ **cup diced, cooked ham**
4 **eggs, beaten**
 parsley

Saute potato and onion in 4 tablespoons hot butter in a skillet until well cooked. Add salt and pepper to taste. Stir in ham and quickly cook until crisp. In an omelet pan, melt 1 tablespoon butter and add well beaten eggs. As mixture begins to thicken add ham, onion and potato. Place omelet pan under broiler. Broil, watching closely until it is well done and brown on top. Serve hot on warm plates. Garnish with parsley.

How to Clarify Butter

Place butter in the top of a double boiler over hot water. Place over heat and let stand just until the butter melts. When the whey (milky sediment) has separated from the melted fat, pour off the clear fat, which is the clarified butter, and discard the whey.

Katie Stapleton's Own Basic Crepe Batter

2 **eggs**
2 **cups Wondra instant flour**
2 **cups water**

Blend in your food processor or blender very briefly, only 1 minute. If you want to create dessert crepes, add 2 table-spoons sugar and 1 tablespoon pure vanilla extract. If you're making Crepes Suzette, pour 2 tablespoons or more of Grand Marnier right into your batter. Because of using instant flour, you only have to rest this batter for 30 minutes at room temperature.

Savory Crepe Batter (for meat-filled crepes)

16-18 6-inch crepes

3 eggs
⅛ teaspoon salt
1¼ cups beer
1 cup less 2 tablespoons flour
4 tablespoons butter, melted

Put all ingredients in a blender or food processor at one time and blend until smooth and well mixed. For best results, let the batter rest at room temperature for 2 to 3 hours or up to 12 hours in the refrigerator. Heat a 6-inch skillet and brush it with clarified butter (see index). Pour in one tablespoon batter and tilt the pan immediately so that the batter will spread over the entire bottom of the pan. Cook the crepe quickly on both sides.

Curried Chicken Crepes

16 crepes

1½ tablespoons olive oil
½ onion, chopped
1 apple, chopped
2 tablespoons flour
1½ tablespoons curry powder
1½ cups chicken stock
2½ cups milk
   pinch of sugar
½ teaspoon salt
1 carrot, grated
2 tablespoons lemon juice
4 - 6 cups chicken, cooked and
      shredded
16 crepes

Heat olive oil in a large skillet. Add onion and apple and saute until onion is transparent. Add flour and curry and cook 1 minute. Add chicken stock and milk slowly, stirring constantly. Then add sugar and salt. Bring to a slow boil, add the carrot and lemon juice and simmer covered for 7 to 10 minutes. Sauce should be on the thin side as the chicken will absorb some moisture and some will bake off. Divide the chicken among the crepes, cover with two tablespoons of the sauce and roll up. Place crepes in a buttered baking dish and spoon over the rest of the sauce. Bake uncovered at 350 degrees for 20 minutes or until bubbling.

Crepes Clinton

Filling:

- 4 tablespoons butter
- 2 onions, chopped
- ½ pound fresh mushrooms, sliced
- ½ 10-ounce package frozen, chopped spinach, thawed and well drained
- 2 cups coarsely chopped cooked chicken or turkey
- 6 tablespoons sour cream
- 2 tablespoons sherry
  salt

Sauce:

- 6 tablespoons butter
- 6 tablespoons flour
- ½ cup sherry
- 2 cups chicken stock
- 1 cup milk
- ¾ cup freshly grated Parmesan cheese
- ½ cup grated Swiss or Gruyere cheese
  salt
- 8 - 12 crepes

4-6 servings

Melt butter in a large skillet. Add onions and saute until soft. Add mushrooms and saute for a few minutes. Remove from heat. Add spinach, chicken, sour cream, sherry and salt to taste. Stir until well blended. This mixture may be done ahead and refrigerated.

Melt butter and remove from heat. Add flour and stir until smooth. Stir in sherry, stock and milk. Return pan to the heat and cook, stirring constantly, until mixture is thick and at a full boil. Reduce heat and simmer. Add the cheese and salt to taste. Stir over low heat until cheese is melted. Remove pan from heat and cover it with a piece of waxed paper so that a skin does not form. The sauce may be frozen.

To assemble crepes, fill the crepes with the warmed filling, roll up and place side by side in a baking dish. Spoon some of the sauce over the crepes and bake at 350 degrees for 15 minutes. Reheat the rest of the sauce gently and serve it separately.

Note: These are delicious and guaranteed to get raves from your guests!

Ham and Zucchini Crepes

Filling:

- 8 ounces sharp Cheddar cheese, grated
- 12 thin slices boiled ham
- 2 fresh zucchini, about 6 inches long, cut in eighths

6 servings

Fill each crepe with a sprinkling of cheese and a slice of ham. Place a length of zucchini on each crepe and roll up. Place them crosswise in a buttered 13 × 9 × 2 inch baking pan. Bake uncovered at 350 degrees for about 20 to 25 minutes.

Sauce:

- 1 pound fresh mushrooms, sliced
- 2 green onions, finely chopped
- 8 tablespoons butter
- ½ teaspoon salt
- 1 cup heavy cream
- 12 crepes

In a large, heavy skillet, saute mushrooms and onions in butter until onions are cooked through and mushrooms are tender. Sprinkle with salt. Add the cream and simmer uncovered for about 30 minutes. Spoon sauce over crepes just before serving.

Crab Crepes Mornay

Filling:

- 7½ ounces canned crab, drained (can use frozen)
- 3 ounces cream cheese
- 2 tablespoons sour cream
- ⅛ teaspoon garlic salt
- 2 tablespoons sherry

6 servings

In a saucepan, soften cream cheese over low heat. Add crab, sour cream, garlic salt and sherry and stir until blended.

Mornay Sauce:

- 2 tablespoons flour
- 2 tablespoons butter
- 1 cup milk
- ½ teaspoon salt
  dash of pepper
- ¼ cup grated Swiss cheese
- 1 tablespoon freshly grated Parmesan cheese
- ¼ teaspoon dry mustard
- 12 crepes

Melt butter and stir in flour until well blended. Add milk, salt, pepper, swiss cheese, parmesan cheese, and mustard, stirring until mixture is smooth.

To assemble, fill crepes and roll. Place in an ungreased, shallow casserole and bake at 375 degrees for 12 minutes. Spoon heated Mornay sauce over each crepe and serve.

Baked German Pancake

4 servings

3 **eggs**
½ **cup flour**
½ **teaspoon salt**
½ **cup milk**
2 **tablespoons butter, melted**
2 **tablespoons butter, softened**

Using a wire whisk or fork, beat eggs until blended. Sift flour, measure, and sift again with salt. Add flour mixture to beaten eggs in 4 additions, beating after each addition just until mixture is smooth. Add milk in 2 additions, beating slightly after each. Lightly beat in butter. Using 2 tablespoons butter, butter bottom and sides of a 9 or 10 inch heavy skillet. Pour batter into skillet and bake at 450 degrees for 20 minutes. Slip onto a heated platter and serve immediately. It is traditionally served with melted butter, a squeeze of lemon and a dusting of powdered sugar, or serve with the following fillings.

Almond filling:
¼ - ½ **cup sliced almonds**
2 **tablespoons butter, melted**
¼ **cup sugar**

When pancake has baked 15 minutes, quickly sprinkle center with almonds, drizzle with melted butter and sprinkle generously with sugar. Return to oven and bake remaining 5 minutes.

Swiss Honey Butter:
½ **cup soft butter**
½ **cup honey**
½ **cup whipping cream**
1 **teaspoon vanilla**

Cream butter with honey. Slowly add whipping cream, beating constantly until mixture is fluffy. Add vanilla. Spoon over hot pancakes.

Pan-Glazed Cinnamon Apple Slices
2 **tablespoons butter**
2 **apples, peeled and sliced**
2 **tablespoons sugar**
½ **teaspoon ground cinnamon**

Filling for 1 pancake

Melt butter in small frying pan. Add apples. Sprinkle with sugar and cinnamon. Slowly cook over low heat, stirring occasionally until slices are glazed and tender. Spoon into center of baked pancake.

67
Brunch

COLORADO CACHE COLORADO CACHE COLORADO CACHE COLORADO CACHE COLORADO CACHE COLORADO CACHE COLORADO CACHE COLORADO CACHE COLORADO

Wheat Germ Pancakes

15-18 pancakes

- 1 cup flour, unsifted
- 1 tablespoon sugar
- 1 teaspoon baking powder
- ½ teaspoon baking soda
- ½ teaspoon salt
- ¼ cup wheat germ
- 2 large eggs, separated
- 2 cups buttermilk
- 3 tablespoons butter, melted

In a bowl thoroughly mix flour, sugar, baking powder, soda and salt. Stir in wheat germ. In a small mixing bowl beat egg yolks with ½ cup buttermilk. Add remaining 1½ cups buttermilk and melted butter. Beat to combine. Gradually stir into dry ingredients. With clean beater beat egg whites until they hold soft peaks. Fold into flour mixture. Cook on hot, lightly greased griddle until bubbly on top and dry around edges. Turn and cook until brown. Serve at once with melted butter and warm maple syrup.

Gougere with Mushrooms and Ham

6 servings

- 4 tablespoons butter
- 1 cup chopped onions
- ½ pound mushrooms, sliced
- 1½ tablespoons flour
- 1 teaspoon salt
- ¼ teaspoon pepper
- 1 teaspoon instant chicken broth (or 1 cube)
- 1 cup hot water
- 2 cups tomato strips, about 2 large tomatoes
- 2 - 3 cups cooked ham strips
- 1 cup sifted flour
  pinch of salt and pepper
- 1 cup water
- ½ cup butter, cut up
- 4 large eggs
- 1 cup grated Cheddar cheese (reserve 2 tablespoons for top)

Melt 4 tablespoons butter in a large skillet. Saute onion until soft, but not browned. Add mushrooms and continue cooking for 2 minutes. Sprinkle with flour, salt and pepper. Mix and cook for 2 minutes longer. Add chicken broth and water; mix well. Bring to boil, stirring constantly. Simmer for 4 minutes. Remove sauce from heat. Add tomato strips and ham strips. Set aside. To make the pate a choux, heat water and butter in a large saucepan until the butter melts. Bring water to a boil, add flour, salt and pepper all at once and stir vigorously until mixture forms a ball in center of pan, about 1 minute. Allow mixture to cool for 5 minutes. Add eggs, one at a time, beating well with a wooden spoon after each addition. This beating is important or gougere will not puff. Stir in grated cheese. Butter an 11- or 12-inch ovenproof skillet or shallow baking dish. Spoon the pate a choux in a ring around the edge, leaving the center open. Pour the ham, tomato and mushroom filling into the center and sprinkle with remaining 2 tablespoons Cheddar cheese. Bake at 400 degrees for 20 minutes. Reduce oven temperature to 350 degrees and bake for 20 to 25 minutes, or until the gougere is puffed and brown and the filling is bubbling. Serve at once.

Note: Great with fresh fruit and pecan rolls.

Swedish Pancakes Lucken

4 servings

3 eggs
1¾ cups milk
1 cup flour
1 teaspoon salt
2 tablespoons sugar
1 tablespoon oil

In a blender mix eggs and milk. Add flour, salt, sugar and oil and blend until smooth, much like a crepe batter. Cook on a lightly greased griddle or skillet.

Note: They should be very thin and delicate.

Chicken Quiche in Lemon Pastry Shell

Lemon pastry shell

Filling:
2 whole chicken breasts, skinned, boned and cut into 1 inch cubes
1½ teaspoons salt
⅛ teaspoon white pepper
¼ cup corn oil
1 large onion, thinly sliced and separated into rings
1 large, firm tomato, peeled, seeded, cut into cubes and drained
3 large eggs
¾ cup milk
¾ cup light cream
4½ - 5 ounces Gruyere cheese, cut into small cubes
¼ cup freshly grated Parmesan cheese
pinch of ground nutmeg
1 teaspoon butter, cut into small pieces

Add ½ teaspoon salt and pepper to chicken. Heat corn oil, saute chicken slowly, 5 to 6 minutes. Remove chicken, add onion rings and cook until nearly tender. Add tomato, cover and cook 7 minutes or until moisture evaporates. Beat eggs, add milk, cream, cheeses, nutmeg and remaining teaspoon salt. Arrange onion, tomato and chicken on bottom of pastry shell. Pour over egg mixture and dot with butter. Bake in a pre-heated 375 degree oven for 35 to 40 minutes. Check by inserting knife 3 inches from edge. If the knife comes out clean it is done.

Sauce:

10	small mushrooms, chopped
3	tablespoons butter
	salt and pepper to taste
2	tablespoons flour
½	cup light cream
2	tablespoons chutney, chopped
½	pint sour cream
¼	cup dry sherry

Saute mushrooms in butter. Add salt and pepper to taste. Add flour and blend. Add cream and cook, stirring constantly, until sauce is thickened. Add chutney, sour cream and sherry. Cook until heated thoroughly. Serve over Quiche.

Lemon Pastry Shell

10-inch pastry shell

1½	cups sifted flour
½	teaspoon salt
	scant ¼ cup ice water
9	tablespoons butter
1	heaping teaspoon shortening
	grated rind and juice of ½ lemon

Sift flour and salt, cut in butter and shortening until crumbly. Add lemon rind, juice and ice water. Mix lightly. Form a ball and roll out on lightly floured board. Roll 1½ inches larger than 10 inch pie pan. Trim to 1 inch beyond pan. Roll edge under. Form into rim and flute. Bake at 425 degrees for 10 minutes for partially baked shell for Chicken Quiche.

Quiche a la Suisse

6 servings

4	large eggs
1½	cups cream
½	pound Gruyere cheese, grated (about 2 cups)
1	teaspoon salt
¼	pound bacon
½	cup butter
2	medium onions, very thinly sliced
2	leeks, thinly sliced
1	teaspoon chopped chives
1	teaspoon marjoram
1	teaspoon chopped fresh parsley
1	9-inch unbaked pastry shell

Beat eggs with cream, add cheese and salt and set aside. Fry bacon until crisp, crumble and set aside. Melt butter in same skillet, add onions and leeks and saute until golden brown. Remove from heat and add chives, marjoram, parsley and bacon. Combine with egg mixture and pour into pastry shell. Bake at 400 degrees for about 40 minutes or until a knife inserted in the center comes out clean.

Artichoke Quiche

6 servings

1   9-inch pastry shell, partially
     baked
2   6-ounce jars marinated
     artichokes
1   small onion, finely chopped
1   clove garlic, minced
4   large eggs
¼   cup dry bread crumbs
¼   teaspoon salt
½   pound sharp Cheddar cheese,
     grated (about 2 cups)
2   tablespoons finely chopped
     parsley
⅛   teaspoon pepper
⅛   teaspoon oregano
⅛   teaspoon Tabasco sauce

Drain artichokes, reserving the marinade. Saute onion and garlic in marinade for 5 minutes. In a large bowl, beat eggs. Add bread crumbs, salt, pepper, oregano and Tabasco. Stir in cheese, parsley, artichokes and onion mixture. Pour into partially baked pastry shell and bake at 325 degrees for 45 minutes.

Note: This may also be served as a first course.

Quiche aux Fruits de Mer

4-6 servings

1   9-inch pastry shell, partially
     baked
2   tablespoons minced green
     onions
3   tablespoons butter
¼   pound (1 cup) cooked fresh or
     frozen shrimp, crab or lob-
     ster (or a combination)
     pinch of pepper
2   tablespoons Madeira
¼   cup grated Swiss cheese
3   large eggs
1   cup heavy cream
¼   teaspoon salt
     pinch of pepper

Cook onions in butter 1 or 2 minutes until tender but not brown. Add fish and stir 2 minutes. Add pepper and wine. Raise heat and boil a moment. Allow to cool slightly.

Beat eggs with cream and seasonings. Gradually add fish mixture. Pour egg and fish mixture into pastry shell and sprinkle with grated cheese. Bake in the upper ⅓ of oven at 375 degrees for 25 to 30 minutes or until done.

Note: This is lovely for luncheon served with fresh fruit, or fruit salad and small cinnamon rolls.

COLORADO CACHE COLORADO CACHE COLORADO CACHE COLORADO CACHE COLORADO CACHE COLORADO CACHE COLORADO CACHE COLORADO CACHE COLORADO

Crustless Quiche

8 servings

¼   **pound butter**
½   **cup flour**
6   **large eggs**
1   **cup milk**
1   **pound Monterey Jack cheese,**
      cubed
1   **3-ounce package cream**
      cheese, softened
2   **cups cottage cheese**
1   **teaspoon baking powder**
1   **teaspoon salt**
1   **teaspoon sugar**

Melt butter in small saucepan, add flour and cook until smooth. Beat eggs, add milk, cheeses, baking powder, salt, sugar and butter-flour mixture. Stir until well blended. Pour into a well greased 9 × 13 × 2 inch pan. Bake uncovered at 350 degrees for 45 minutes.

Note: Cut in small pieces and serve as an hors d'oeuvres.

Chicken Livers au Vin

8 servings

24   **chicken livers**
2   **large onions, chopped**
4   **tablespoons butter**
1   **pound mushrooms, halved**
1   **cup chopped cooked ham (or**
      chopped, fried bacon)
      salt and pepper
      flour
1   **cup stock**
1   **cup dry red wine**

Saute onion in butter until lightly browned. Cut chicken livers in half, roll in flour seasoned with salt and pepper, and cook in the same pan for 3 minutes. Remove the chicken livers from pan. In same pan, saute mushrooms and bacon (or ham) lightly. Stir in 1 teaspoon of the flour seasoned with salt and pepper, cooking until brown. Slowly add the stock and wine. Add chicken livers and simmer uncovered 2 to 3 minutes.

Note: This may be cooked in advance and gently reheated.

RADO CACHE COLORADO CACHE COLORADO CACHE COLORADO CACHE COLORADO CACHE COLORADO CACHE COLORADO CACHE COLORADO CACHE COLORADO CACH

Skiers' Sausage

6 servings

1 **pound link sausage**
6 **medium baking apples, pared
    and sliced**
  salt and pepper to taste
1 **tablespoon fresh lemon juice**
3 **tablespoons brown sugar**

Brown sausage and cut each link in half. Drain thoroughly. Butter a 1½ quart casserole. Combine apples and sausage links and put in casserole. Sprinkle with salt and pepper, lemon juice and brown sugar. Cover and bake at 350 degrees for 45 minutes.

Deviled Sausage

6 servings

2 **pounds Jimmy Dean's regular
    sausage**
1 **cup chopped green pepper**
1 **cup sliced mushrooms,
    sauteed**
2 **tablespoons butter**
2 **tablespoons flour**
1 **teaspoon curry powder**
1½ **cups milk**
  salt and pepper to taste
2 **tablespoons soft bread
    crumbs**
2 **tablespoons freshly grated
    Parmesan cheese**

Fry sausage until brown, separating with a fork. Drain off grease. Add green pepper and mushrooms and mix well. Melt butter, blend in flour and curry powder. Gradually add milk and cook, stirring until thickened. Add salt and pepper and cook 1 minute. Mix with the sausage combination and spoon into a 1½ quart casserole. Sprinkle with bread crumbs and Parmesan cheese. Bake uncovered at 350 degrees for 30 minutes.

Cheese and Sausage Grits

10 servings

1   **pound Jimmy Dean's regular sausage, browned**
    Tabasco sauce to taste
⅓   **clove garlic, minced**
½   **teaspoon salt**
⅛   **teaspoon pepper**
1   **cup instant grits**
2   **cups boiling water**
1   **cup grated extra-sharp Cheddar cheese (4 ounces)**
¼   **cup butter, melted**
2   **large eggs, well beaten**
1   **8-ounce can mild green chiles, seeded and chopped**

Brown sausage and drain. Add Tabasco sauce, garlic, salt and pepper to sausage. Set aside. Cook grits in 2 cups boiling water. Add all ingredients together, stirring until well mixed. Pour mixture into a well buttered 9 × 13 × 2 inch baking dish. Bake uncovered at 350 degrees for 1 hour.

Chipped Beef Pie

8 servings

2	**9-inch pastry shells, baked**
½	**pound chipped beef (can use dried, pressed beef in packages)**
1½	**cups tomatoes, chopped and drained**
3	**tablespoons butter**
2	**tablespoons flour**
1	**pint sour cream**
½	**cup mayonnaise**
8 - 10	**stuffed green olives, cut in half**
10 - 12	**ripe olives, cut in half**
2	**tablespoons chopped chives**

Pour boiling water over chipped beef and drain well. Melt butter and add flour, stirring until well blended. Add sour cream, mayonnaise, tomatoes, chipped beef, olives and chives, mixing well. Pour into baked pastry shells. Bake at 350 degrees for 30 minutes. Cool 10 minutes before cutting.

Barbara Conwell's Omelet Fillings

Shredded Monterey Jack cheese and chopped green chile peppers

Major Grey's chutney, chopped or slivered toasted almonds or cashews

Mixed minced fresh herbs such as tarragon, parsley, chives and marjoram

Caviar and sour cream

Smoked salmon, sour cream and chopped green onions

Sauteed mushrooms and sour cream

Crab meat or shrimp, quickly heated in butter

Cooked asparagus tips and sour cream

Sauteed chopped spinach and chopped green onions

Cooked diced artichoke hearts and Parmesan cheese

Sliced avocado and shredded Monterey Jack cheese with alfalfa sprouts

Sauteed chicken livers and mushrooms or green onions

Sour cream with fresh strawberries, blueberries or raspberries

Chopped mushrooms and watercress with sour cream and Tabasco sauce

Chopped tomatoes, avocados, green chiles in sour cream topped with shredded Monterey Jack cheese

Camembert or Brie

Cooked bacon, sauteed mushrooms, shredded fresh spinach and sour cream

HOT AIR BALLOONING NEAR THE AIR FORCE ACADEMY/SAILBOATS AT GRAND LAKE

Hints from the **Roaring Fork**

Always tear lettuce for tossed salads as cutting or slicing gives the lettuce a bitter taste.

Use your hands to toss green salads so the lettuce does not bruise, or toss gently with tongs.

Wrap rinsed salad greens in paper towels and refrigerate for an hour or more. Excess moisture will be absorbed.

To freshen wilted salad greens, douse them quickly in hot water, then in ice water to which a little vinegar has been added.

The proportions for a perfect oil and vinegar dressing are one part vinegar to two parts olive oil.

Try using rice vinegar instead of the old stand-bys in a vinaigrette dressing for a lovely, soft flavor.

Use salad dressings sparingly; a thin coating is all that is needed.

Tomatoes tend to thin salad dressings so add them at the last minute. Slice them in wedges to keep them from losing a lot of their juice.

Watercress and mint will keep well if washed and drained, then stored in air-tight containers in the refrigerator.

Parsley, mint and herbs can be easily dried by snipping the freshest part of the stalk and using a dish towel folded accordion-fashion in 3 or more parts. Lay the stalks side by side in the folds but not overlapping. Let them dry for three or four days. When dry, run fingers down the stalk to remove the leaves, crush them slightly and store in an air-tight container.

To make colorful onion rings to garnish salads, let them soak in pickled beets or beet juice.

Walnuts or pecans toasted in butter and garlic salt are delicious in a green salad.

Use kitchen shears or scissors to cut grapes in half. Remove the seeds with another snip.

To easily unmold a salad, run a spatula around the edge to loosen, invert on a serving platter and place a hot, damp dish towel over the mold. Shake gently.

For a fluffy fruit salad dressing, beat 3 tablespoons of mayonnaise with a cup of softened vanilla ice cream.

The **Roaring Fork River** was named for the sound created by a number of rapids made when the stream cut its way through the granite mountains. The river runs by the town of Aspen, where some of the best skiing in the world is available from November through April, and site of the distinguished cultural events conducted by the Aspen Institute for the Humanities.

79

Salads and Salad Dressings

COLORADO CACHE COLORADO CACHE COLORADO CACHE COLORADO CACHE COLORADO CACHE COLORADO CACHE COLORADO CACHE COLORADO CACHE COLORADO CACHE COLORADO C

Caesar Salad

8-10 servings

2 **heads romaine lettuce, torn and thoroughly chilled**
¾ **cup freshly grated Parmesan cheese**
1 **cup fresh croutons (see index)**

Place lettuce, cheese and croutons in a large salad bowl.

Dressing:
¼ **cup fresh lemon juice**
¼ **cup red wine vinegar**
¾ **cup good quality olive oil**
1 **large anchovy fillet**
  garlic, pressed, to taste
  pepper to taste
  dash of Worcestershire sauce
1 **egg, lightly beaten**

Blend together lemon juice, vinegar and oil. Set aside. In another small bowl, mash anchovy to a paste; add garlic, pepper and Worcestershire sauce. Add egg and mix well, then beat in lemon juice mixture until thoroughly blended.

Pour desired amount of dressing over salad greens, a little at a time. Toss and serve.

A Caesar of a Different Color

6-8 servings

2 **tablespoons olive oil**
1 **clove garlic, peeled**
2 **tomatoes, peeled**
2 **heads romaine, cut in 1 inch strips**
¼ **cup chopped green onions**
½ **cup freshly grated Romano cheese**
½ **cup crisply fried bacon, crumbled**
1 **avocado, diced**

Pour olive oil and a sprinkling of salt into a large wooden bowl. Rub the garlic clove firmly into bowl. Remove garlic clove and place tomatoes, green onions and avocado in the bottom of the bowl. Add romaine. Top with bacon, cheese and croutons.

Dressing:
¾ **cup olive oil**
  juice of 2½ lemons
1 **tablespoon chopped fresh mint**
¼ **teaspoon oregano**
½ **teaspoon freshly ground pepper**
1 **coddled egg**
½ **cup fresh croutons (see index)**

Mix all dressing ingredients in a jar. Shake vigorously making sure the egg yolk is broken and well blended. Make the dressing well in advance to impart the subtle hint of mint. Toss salad with dressing just before serving.

RADO CACHE COLORADO CACHE COLORADO CACHE COLORADO CACHE COLORADO CACHE COLORADO CACHE COLORADO CACHE COLORADO CACHE COLORADO CACHE COLORADO CACHE COLORADO CACH

Green, Green Salad

6 servings

- 1 **cup vegetable oil**
- ⅓ **cup fresh lime juice**
- 3 **tablespoons sugar**
- 1½ **teaspoons salt**
- ⅛ **teaspoon white pepper**
- ⅛ **teaspoon cayenne pepper**
- ¼ **teaspoon celery salt**
- 6 **paper-thin slices fresh lime, quartered (optional)**
- 1½ **quarts mixed salad greens**

Mix oil, lime juice, sugar, salt, pepper, cayenne and celery salt. Shake or beat until well blended. Just before serving add lime slices to salad greens in a bowl. Shake dressing again and pour over greens, using just enough to coat the leaves well. Mix lightly and serve.

Ripe Olive and Artichoke Salad

4-6 servings

- 1 **head Bibb or leaf lettuce, washed and dried**
- 1 **6-ounce jar marinated artichoke hearts, drained**
- ½ **10-ounce can pitted ripe olives**
  Parmesan cheese to taste
  croutons to taste

Dressing:
- **juice of ½ lemon**
- 1 **teaspoon dill weed**
- ¼ **cup olive oil**
- ¼ **teaspoon salt**
  dash of pepper

Tear lettuce into bite-sized pieces. Cut artichoke hearts into quarters. Cut olives into halves. Add lettuce pieces. Just before serving, toss with salad dressing. Top with croutons and sprinkle with Parmesan cheese. Gently toss again.

COLORADO CACHE COLORADO CACHE COLORADO CACHE COLORADO CACHE COLORADO CACHE COLORADO CACHE COLORADO CACHE COLORADO CACHE COLORADO CACHE COLORADO C

Watercress and Mushroom Salad

4 servings

16 fresh mushrooms
2 bunches watercress
    vinaigrette dressing
1 tablespoon chopped parsley
2 tablespoons chopped chives

Thinly slice mushroom caps and combine with the trimmed watercress. Toss with vinaigrette dressing and sprinkle with chopped parsley and chives.

Vinaigrette Dressing:
6 tablespoons olive or vegetable oil
2 tablespoons wine vinegar
½ · 1 teaspoon salt
12 grinds of the pepper mill

Blend all dressing ingredients in a jar and refrigerate.

Gazpacho Salad

8 servings

2 medium cucumbers, peeled and thinly sliced
1 teaspoon salt
⅔ cup olive oil
⅓ cup wine vinegar
1 garlic clove, minced
1 teaspoon basil
1 teaspoon salt
½ teaspoon freshly ground pepper
10 medium mushrooms, sliced
4 green onions, thinly sliced
½ cup minced parsley
3 large tomatoes, peeled and chopped
1 medium green pepper, chopped
½ pound Swiss cheese, cut into thin strips
4 hard cooked eggs, sliced

Place cucumber slices in bowl and sprinkle with 1 teaspoon salt. Let stand for 30 minutes. In a large bowl combine olive oil, wine vinegar, garlic, basil, salt and pepper. Add mushrooms and green onions. Drain cucumber slices and pat dry. Add to bowl. Top mixture with parsley and mix gently. Add a layer of tomatoes and top them with green pepper. Cover bowl and chill for at least 4 hours. Just before serving add Swiss cheese strips. Toss salad gently and garnish with hard cooked eggs.

Pepper Steak Salad

3 cups rare roast beef, cut in thin strips
2 tomatoes, cut in wedges
1 green pepper, cut in strips
1 cup sliced celery
⅓ cup sliced green onion
⅓ cup sliced fresh mushrooms
4 cups mixed greens, such as Bibb, leaf or romaine lettuce or Savoy cabbage

Choose One:
Marinade #1
½ cup teriyaki sauce
⅓ cup dry sherry
⅓ cup salad oil
3 tablespoons white vinegar
½ teaspoon ground ginger

Marinade #2
½ teaspoon salt
¼ teaspoon pepper
3 dashes Tabasco sauce
¼ teaspoon Worcestershire sauce
2 teaspoons lemon juice
¼ cup red wine vinegar
2 cups salad oil
2 tablespoons green peppercorns

6 servings

Combine beef, tomatoes, green pepper, celery, onion and mushrooms. In a screw top jar combine ingredients for marinade of your choice. Shake well. Pour over beef mixture. Toss to coat well. Cover and refrigerate 2 or 3 hours. Drain, reserving marinade. Place greens in large salad bowl; top with marinated meat and vegetables. Pass reserved marinade for dressing.

COLORADO CACHE COLORADO CACHE COLORADO CACHE COLORADO CACHE COLORADO CACHE COLORADO CACHE COLORADO CACHE COLORADO CACHE COLORADO C

Aspen Village Salad

romaine lettuce
1 chicken breast, cooked, skinned and boned
Monterey Jack cheese, cut into strips
several slices salami
3 - 4 orange slices
3 avocado slices
several pitted, ripe olives
several crisp tortilla wedges

Cumin Dressing:
¼ cup sour cream
¼ cup mayonnaise
1 tablespoon fresh lemon juice
⅛ teaspoon dry mustard
⅛ teaspoon garlic salt
¼ teaspoon ground cumin
2 tablespoons green chile salsa or chili sauce

1 serving

For each salad, arrange outer romaine leaves on plate. Finely chop a few inner leaves and arrange on top. Cut chicken breast into strips and place on lettuce. Add cheese, salami, orange slices, avocado and olives. Cover and chill. At serving time, add cumin dressing and garnish with tortilla wedges.

2-3 salad servings

Blend sour cream and mayonnaise, add remaining dressing ingredients and chill.

Curried Chicken Salad

2 cups diced, cooked chicken breasts
1 apple, peeled and diced
1 cup diced, fresh pineapple
¼ cup white raisins
⅓ cup chopped dates
2 tablespoons chopped chutney
½ teaspoon salt

Dressing:
2 teaspoons curry powder
2 tablespoons chicken broth
1 cup mayonnaise

6-8 servings

Combine ingredients and refrigerate.

Simmer curry powder in broth for 2 minutes, stirring to a smooth paste. Cool. Add paste to mayonnaise. Stir mayonnaise and curry powder mixture into chicken salad mixture 1 hour before serving.

Note: The amount of curry depends on the kind and freshness. This recipe is calculated for fresh curry, which is stronger than old curry.

Chicken Salad

6 servings

4   whole cooked and diced
    chicken breasts
½   cup water chestnuts, sliced
½   cup chopped pecans
½   cup seedless grapes
¼   cup finely chopped celery
1   teaspoon finely minced
    candied ginger
¾   cup mayonnaise
2   tablespoons wine vinegar
1   tablespoon soy sauce
2   teaspoons minced onion
½   teaspoon curry powder
6   slices canned pineapple
    lettuce leaves

Mix chicken and water chestnuts, pecans, grapes, celery and ginger. Blend mayonnaise, vinegar, soy sauce, onion and curry powder. Toss dressing with the chicken mixture. Chill. To serve, spoon onto pineapple slices arranged on lettuce leaves.

Million Dollar Salad

6 servings as a salad
4 servings as a meal

½   head iceberg lettuce, finely
    chopped
½   head romaine lettuce, finely
    chopped
½   bunch watercress, finely
    chopped
1   small bunch chicory, finely
    chopped
2   medium tomatoes, peeled and
    finely chopped
2   cooked chicken breasts, diced
6   strips bacon, crisply fried and
    crumbled
1   avocado, diced
3   hard cooked eggs, chopped
2   tablespoons fresh chives,
    chopped
3   ounces bleu cheese, crumbled

Arrange lettuce greens in a salad bowl. Scatter tomatoes, chicken, bacon and avocado over the greens. Garnish top with the eggs, chives and bleu cheese. Just before serving, toss salad with the dressing.

Dressing:

- 1⅓ cups vegetable oil
- ⅔ cup red wine vinegar
- 1 teaspoon sugar
- 1 clove garlic, minced
- 1 teaspoon salt
- ½ teaspoon pepper
- 1 teaspoon Dijon mustard
- 1 teaspoon Worcestershire sauce
- 1 teaspoon paprika

Combine dressing ingredients and refrigerate for 8 hours.

Mandarin Salad

- ½ cup sliced almonds
- 3 tablespoons sugar
- ½ head iceberg lettuce
- ½ head romaine lettuce
- 1 cup chopped celery
- 2 whole green onions, chopped
- 1 11-ounce can mandarin oranges, drained

Dressing:

- ½ teaspoon salt
  dash of pepper
- ¼ cup vegetable oil
- 1 tablespoon chopped parsley
- 2 tablespoons sugar
- 2 tablespoons vinegar
  dash of Tabasco sauce

4-6 servings

In a small pan over medium heat, cook almonds and sugar, stirring constantly until almonds are coated and sugar dissolved. Watch carefully as they will burn easily. Cool and store in air-tight container. Mix all dressing ingredients and chill. Mix lettuces, celery and onions. Just before serving add almonds and oranges. Toss with the dressing.

Layered Salad

10 servings

½ head iceberg lettuce
1 10-ounce bag fresh spinach
4 eggs, hard cooked and
    chopped
1 bunch green onions, chopped
    (including tops)
1 pound bacon, crisply fried
    and crumbled
1 10½-ounce package frozen
    tiny peas, thawed
2 teaspoons sugar
    salt and pepper
1 cup grated Swiss cheese

Optional ingredients:
    water chestnuts
    celery
    tomato slices

Dressing:
1½ cups sour cream
1½ cups mayonnaise

Wash, drain and tear lettuce and spinach into pieces. In a 10 × 13 inch glass baking dish, using only one half of the ingredients, layer the lettuce, spinach, egg, onion, bacon and peas. Sprinkle with 1 teaspoon sugar, and salt and pepper. Frost with half of the dressing mixture. Repeat the layers, using the remaining half of the ingredients. Frost the top with the rest of the dressing and garnish with Swiss cheese. Cover with plastic wrap and refrigerate overnight. Serve by cutting into squares.

Note: This salad stays fresh for several days because the dressing seals the lettuce mixture and keeps it crisp.

Puckerbrush Road Salad

6 servings

1 bunch red leaf lettuce
1 11-ounce can mandarin
    oranges, chilled and
    drained
1 cup sliced, fresh mushrooms
1 small bermuda onion, sliced
    and separated into rings
1 green pepper, sliced into rings
½ avocado, sliced

Mix salad ingredients and refrigerate. Toss with the dressing just before serving.

Note: A hearty salad that is very good with steak.

Dressing:

½ cup mayonnaise (or salad dressing)
½ cup sour cream
¼ cup dill pickle juice
½ avocado, mashed
1 tablespoon chopped parsley
2 teaspoons chopped chives
1 teaspoon dill weed

Mix dressing ingredients ahead and refrigerate.

Shanghai Salad

14-16 servings

1 20-ounce package fresh bean sprouts
1 16-ounce can water chestnuts, thinly sliced
½ cup toasted, slivered almonds
1 green pepper, sliced
2 quarts salad greens, washed and dried

Toss bean sprouts, water chestnuts, green pepper and almonds with greens. Toss again with dressing.

Dressing:

1½ cups mayonnaise
1½ teaspoons prepared mustard
½ teaspoon Tabasco sauce
2 teaspoons chili powder
1 tablespoon fresh, minced onion
2 tablespoons vinegar
1½ teaspoons marjoram
¾ teaspoon thyme
1½ teaspoons minced garlic

Combine and shake in covered jar until well blended.

Salads and Salad Dressings

Strauss Salad

1 10-ounce package fresh
   spinach, finely chopped
½ lemon
4 - 6 generous tablespoons
   chopped bacon
1 chopped hard cooked egg
1 egg
   salt and pepper to taste

Gooseneck Dressing:

½ cup vinegar
1 tablespoon celery salt
1 tablespoon cracked pepper
½ teaspoon dry mustard
1 tablespoon Maggi seasoning
2 teaspoons salt
   juice of 1 lemon
3 cups vegetable oil

4-6 servings

Sprinkle salt and pepper in wooden bowl; squeeze juice from ½ lemon and add raw egg. Stir well. Add bacon, chopped egg and spinach. Mix well. Sprinkle with a little lemon juice and serve. Must be served cold. Serve with gooseneck dressing.

Note: This recipe is from the Calgary Inn, Alberta, Canada.

1 quart

Dissolve all of the dressing ingredients in the vinegar except the oil. Add oil, slowly. Keep stirring until well blended. Refrigerate.

Korean Salad

1 10-ounce package fresh
   spinach
8 ounces fresh bean sprouts
1 6-ounce can water chestnuts,
   drained and sliced
4 hard cooked eggs, sliced
6 strips bacon, crisply fried and
   crumbled

Dressing:

1 cup vegetable oil
½ cup white vinegar
¾ cup sugar
¼ cup brown sugar, packed
⅓ cup catsup
1 tablespoon Worcestershire
   sauce
1 medium onion, quartered
   dash of salt

6-8 servings

Wash, dry and remove stems from spinach and tear into pieces. Add the bean sprouts, water chestnuts, eggs and bacon and toss lightly. Add the dressing and toss again, gently.

Combine all of the dressing ingredients in a blender and run on high speed for a few seconds.

89

Salads and Salad Dressings

COLORADO CACHE COLORADO CACHE COLORADO CACHE COLORADO CACHE COLORADO CACHE COLORADO CACHE COLORADO CACHE COLORADO CACHE COLORADO CACHE COLORADO

Crab and Rice Salad

1   7½-ounce can crabmeat (or 1
      6-ounce package frozen
      crab)
3   cups cooked rice
1   10-ounce package frozen
      small peas, cooked
4   stalks celery, finely chopped
⅓   cup sliced green onions
½   cup sour cream
1   cup mayonnaise
1   tablespoon Spice Island salad
      seasoning
1   tablespoon fresh lemon juice
      salt and pepper to taste
      bibb lettuce leaves
      curry powder for garnish

4 servings

Combine crab, rice, peas, celery, green onions, sour cream mayonnaise, salad seasoning, lemon juice and salt and pepper to taste. Chill 24 hours. Serve on leaf of lettuce and sprinkle lightly with curry powder.

Centennial Coleslaw

½   medium cabbage
½   small red cabbage
2   carrots, shredded
1   green pepper, chopped
½   cup raisins

Sauce:
3   tablespoons vinegar
⅓   cup sugar
1½ cups mayonnaise

8-10 servings

Shred cabbages. Add carrots, green pepper and raisins. Place ½ cabbage mixture in a bowl; pour ½ of the sauce over it. Add rest of cabbage mixture and rest of sauce. Press down with hand or large spoon, cover and refrigerate overnight.

Mix ingredients for sauce together.

Garden of the Gods Sublime Salad

8 servings

asparagus
beets, cut in julienne
carrots, cut in julienne
wax beans
green beans
artichoke hearts
avocado
cucumber slices
cherry tomatoes
hard cooked eggs
green onions
radishes

Arrange an assortment of chilled vegetables, fresh or canned, on a bed of lettuce on a large platter. Serve dressing in a bowl in the center of the platter.

Crabmeat Dressing:

2	cups mayonnaise
1½	cups sweet pickle relish
	juice of 1 lemon
	dash of Tabasco sauce
½	pint whipping cream, whipped
1	pound crabmeat and/or shrimp, fresh or frozen
3	hard cooked eggs, chopped

Mix dressing ingredients and keep well chilled until serving.

Note: Expensive! Serve to the most wonderful people you know. They are worth it and so is this salad.

Broccoli-Cauliflower Salad

6-8 servings

1	small head cauliflower
2	large stalks broccoli
1	small onion, chopped
1	cup mayonnaise
1	tablespoon vinegar
1	tablespoon sugar

Divide cauliflower and broccoli into bite-size flowerets. Some of the tender stalks of the broccoli can be used also. Combine the mayonnaise, vinegar and sugar. Add this dressing to the vegetables.

Note: This tastes much better when made at least 1 day ahead. It will also keep for several days in the refrigerator when sealed tightly.

91

Salads and Salad Dressings

COLORADO CACHE COLORADO CACHE COLORADO CACHE COLORADO CACHE COLORADO CACHE COLORADO CACHE COLORADO CACHE COLORADO CACHE COLORADO

Zucchini Appetizer Salad

6 servings

1¼	pounds zucchini, each about 5 inches long
1	14-ounce can regular strength beef broth
6	tablespoons olive oil
4	tablespoons tarragon flavored wine vinegar
2	tablespoons chopped green onion
1	tablespoon finely chopped green pepper
1	tablespoon finely chopped parsley
2	teaspoons Dijon mustard
½	teaspoon salt
⅛	teaspoon pepper
	cherry tomato halves to taste
	sliced ripe olives to taste

Rinse zucchini and cut off ends. Bring broth to boil. Add zucchini and simmer covered until just tender when pierced, 6 to 8 minutes. Drain and cut zucchini lengthwise into quarters, or smaller depending on size. Combine oil, vinegar, onion, green pepper, parsley, mustard, salt and pepper. Pour over zucchini. Cover and chill for 2 hours. To serve, divide zucchini into 6 portions and garnish with tomatoes and olives. Pour dressing over each serving.

Note: Good as an appetizer.

Sauerkraut Salad

12 servings

1½	cups sugar
¾	cup vinegar
¼	cup vegetable oil
1	1-quart jar sauerkraut
1	teaspoon celery seed
1½	cups diced celery
1	2-ounce jar pimento, diced
1	onion, thinly sliced
½	green pepper, diced
	pepper to taste

Mix sugar with vinegar and oil, and boil for 5 minutes. Mix remaining ingredients in a large bowl. Add the cooked dressing. Mix well and refrigerate for at least 24 hours.

Note: A delicious accompaniment to German meals; tangy and colorful.

Caliente Salad

8 servings

1 15½-ounce can kidney beans,
     drained
1 cucumber, diced
1 small onion, diced
1 green pepper, diced
3 large tomatoes, diced
4 slices bacon, crisply fried and
     crumbled
1 cup mayonnaise
1 teaspoon chili powder
     dash of cayenne pepper
     salt and pepper to taste
2 cups lettuce, torn into small
     pieces

Combine all ingredients except bacon and lettuce. Refrigerate. Add bacon and lettuce just before serving.

Marinated Bean and Celery Salad

8-10 servings

2 15½-ounce cans red kidney
     beans
2 cups sliced celery
6 green onions finely sliced
½ green pepper, coarsely
     chopped
1 cup chopped sweet pickle
     hard cooked eggs for garnish

Marinade:

½ cup olive oil
1 teaspoon garlic juice
2 teaspoons dill seed
½ teaspoon ground cardamom
1 teaspoon salt
½ cup red wine vinegar
6 drops of Tabasco sauce
1 teaspoon crushed tarragon
1 teaspoon curry powder

Drain kidney beans and rinse in cold water. Combine beans, celery, onion, green pepper and pickle and marinate for at least ½ day. Serve ice cold on crisp bed of lettuce. Garnish with hard cooked egg wedges.

Matchless Macaroni Salad

8-12 servings

2 - 3 cups seedless green grapes, halved
1 8-ounce package shell macaroni
1 8-ounce can pitted ripe olives, drained and halved
¾ cup chopped green onions
2 - 3 ounces bleu cheese, crumbled
  salt and pepper to taste
¼ teaspoon garlic powder
3 tablespoons fresh lemon juice
1 cup mayonnaise

Cook macaroni according to package directions. Drain. Combine hot macaroni with grapes, olives, onion, cheese, salt, pepper and garlic powder. Mix together lemon juice and mayonnaise until smooth. Combine macaroni and mayonnaise until evenly mixed. Refrigerate covered several hours or overnight. Add more mayonnaise if desired, before serving.

Vermicelli Salad

10-12 servings

1 14-ounce package vermicelli coils
1 medium red onion, chopped
1 medium green pepper, chopped
1 tablespoon chopped parsley
1½ teaspoons celery seed
½ teaspoon oregano
½ teaspoon chopped chives
¼ cup Italian dressing
1 cup mayonnaise
  salt and pepper to taste
1 pound shrimp or crabmeat, cooked, rinsed and marinated in ½ to 1 cup lemon juice (optional)

Cook vermicelli in boiling water, stirring constantly. Drain and blanch with cold water. Add onion, green pepper, parsley, celery seed, chives, oregano and Italian dressing. Moisten well with the mayonnaise, adding more if necessary. Add salt and pepper to taste.

Note: Delicious with ham and hamburgers. A refreshing change from potato salad.

Prospector's Potato Salad

8-10 servings

4   cups diced, boiled potatoes
1   cup diced cucumber
3   tablespoons minced green
    onions
1½ teaspoons salt
½   teaspoon pepper
3   hard cooked eggs, diced

Dressing:
1½ cups sour cream
½   cup mayonnaise
¼   cup vinegar
¾   teaspoon celery seed
¾   teaspoon dill weed
1   teaspoon prepared mustard

Combine dressing ingredients. Add dressing to warm potatoes and mix lightly. Add remaining salad ingredients and mix thoroughly. Refrigerate for several hours to blend flavors.

Lemon Lark Mold

1 quart mold

1   envelope unflavored gelatin
¼   cup cold water
6   ounces cream cheese
3   tablespoons sugar
1   cup milk
½   cup boiling water
1   6-ounce can frozen lemonade,
    thawed
1   quart strawberries

Soften gelatin in cold water, then dissolve in boiling water. In another bowl, blend cream cheese and sugar, gradually adding milk. Add gelatin to cream cheese mixture. Add lemonade and blend. Pour into a 1 quart mold and refrigerate until jelled. Unmold and fill center with strawberries.

95

Salads and Salad Dressings
COLORADO CACHE COLORADO CACHE COLORADO CACHE COLORADO CACHE COLORADO CACHE COLORADO CACHE COLORADO CACHE COLORADO CACHE COLORADO

Cherry Port Salad Mold

2 cups dark cherries, cooked,
    pitted and drained (or 1
    1-pound can pitted, dark
    cherries, drained, reserving
    juice)
1 cup cherry juice (or juice and
    water to make 1 cup)
1 3-ounce package cherry or
    orange gelatin
1 cup Port wine
1 cup chopped nuts
1 large banana, diced (optional)

8-12 servings

Heat cherry juice to boiling. Add gelatin and stir until dissolved. Cool. Add wine; chill until slightly thickened. Fold in cherries, nuts and banana. Turn into 1½ quart mold. Chill until firm.

Molded Cranberry Salad

2 cups cranberries
1 whole orange
1 cup sugar
2 3-ounce packages cherry
    gelatin
1½ cups hot water
1 cup diced celery
1 apple, diced

6-8 servings

Grind cranberries and orange together. Add sugar and allow to stand 2 hours. Dissolve the gelatin in boiling water. Cool. Add celery, apple and cranberry mixture. Pour into 1½ quart mold or 8 individual molds and refrigerate.

Cranberry-Wine Ring

6-8 servings

½ **cup walnuts**
2 **cups raw cranberries**
½ **teaspoon grated lemon rind**
¾ **cup sugar**
½ **cup cold water**
2 **envelopes unflavored gelatin**
1 **cup red wine**
2 **tablespoons fresh lemon juice**
½ **cup mayonnaise**

Place walnuts in a blender and chop. Set aside. Place cranberries in the blender and chop by turning on and off quickly, and stirring in between. Stir in lemon rind and sugar. Set aside. Pour cold water into blender. Sprinkle gelatin on water and soften for 10 minutes. Heat the wine and add to blender. Blend until gelatin has dissolved. Mix all ingredients together. Pour into a wet 1½ quart mold and refrigerate until set.

Food Processor Instructions:
Place walnuts in the container with the steel blade and chop. Set aside. Add cranberries, lemon rind and sugar and chop. Set aside. Pour cold water into the container. Sprinkle gelatin on the water and soften for 10 minutes. Add hot wine and process until the gelatin has dissolved. Mix all ingredients together. Pour into a wet mold and refrigerate until set.

Molded Spiced Peach Salad

8 servings

Spiced Peaches:
1 **1-pound can peaches**
½ **cup sugar**
10 **cloves**
¼ **cup vinegar**
2 **cinnamon sticks**
1 **whole star anise**

Combine all ingredients except peaches and heat until sugar is dissolved. Add fruit and simmer 8 minutes. Refrigerate overnight.

Salad:
1 **recipe spiced peaches, chopped**
1 **13-ounce can pineapple chunks, drained**
1 **envelope unflavored gelatin**
¼ **cup cold water**
1 **10-ounce jar watermelon pickles, drained**
2 **cups combined fruit juices (if necessary add water to make 2 cups)**

Heat and dissolve gelatin in the water. Add the juices and fruits and mix thoroughly. Pour into a 1½ quart mold and refrigerate until set.

COLORADO CACHE COLORADO CACHE COLORADO CACHE COLORADO CACHE COLORADO CACHE COLORADO CACHE COLORADO CACHE COLORADO CACHE COLORADO CACHE COLORADO

Ouray Parfait Salad

2 3-ounce packages orange
    gelatin
1½ cups boiling water
1 6-ounce can frozen orange
    juice, undiluted
1 pint orange sherbet
1 13-ounce can Mandarin
    oranges, drained (juice may
    be used as part of boiling
    water)

Dressing:
1 cup mayonnaise
¼ cup cream cheese,
    softened
    dash of ground ginger

8-10 servings

Dissolve gelatin in boiling water. Add frozen orange juice and sherbet and stir until melted. Stir in orange sections and pour into a 9 × 13 inch pan or individual molds and freeze. Serve as individual salads on lettuce leaf and top with the dressing.

    Note: This is an excellent salad to serve with game birds.

Molded Corned Beef Salad

1 3-ounce package lemon
    gelatin
1¼ cups hot water
1 can corned beef, cubed
1 cup diced celery
1 medium onion, diced
1 cup diced cucumber (or ½
    cup diced green pepper)
1 cup mayonnaise
1 teaspoon fresh lemon juice
2 teaspoons horseradish
    pinch of salt

6-8 servings

Dissolve gelatin in hot water. Mix mayonnaise, lemon juice, horseradish and salt. Beat mayonnaise mixture into the gelatin until smooth. Add remaining ingredients. Pour into 1½ quart mold and chill thoroughly.

    Note: Chill the can of corned beef for easier cubing.

Salads and Salad Dressings

Molded Gazpacho Salad with Avocado Dressing

6-8 servings

2   **envelopes unflavored gelatin**
3   **cups tomato juice**
⅓   **cup red wine vinegar**
1   **teaspoon salt**
    dash of Tabasco sauce
2   **small tomatoes, peeled and diced**
1   **medium cucumber, peeled and diced**
½   **medium bell pepper, diced**
¼   **cup chopped onion**
1   **tablespoon chopped chives**
¼   **cup chopped celery**

Sprinkle gelatin over tomato juice and stir over low heat until dissolved. Remove from heat and add vinegar, salt and Tabasco sauce. Stir. Chill until partially set. Add vegetables and stir. Pour into a 1½ quart mold or pan. Serve with avocado dressing.

Avocado Dressing:

1   **ripe avocado**
1   **tablespoon lemon juice**
½   **cup light cream**
½   **cup sour cream**
1   **clove garlic, minced**
⅛   **teaspoon sugar**
1½   **teaspoons salt**
1   **tablespoon grated onion**
    dash of cayenne pepper

Peel and mash avocado with lemon juice. Stir light cream into sour cream. Add seasonings. Stir in avocado and chill.

Salmon-Avocado Mousse

6 servings

- 1 **package unflavored gelatin**
- 1 **cup cold water**
- 2 **tablespoons sugar**
- 2 **tablespoons fresh lemon juice**
- 1 **tablespoon white wine vinegar**
- 2 **tablespoons grated onion**
- ½ **teaspoon salt**
- 2 **tablespoons horseradish**
- 1 **1-pound can red salmon**
- ½ **cup mayonnaise**
- ½ **cup finely chopped ripe olives**
- ½ **cup finely chopped celery**

Dressing:
- 1 **large avocado**
- ½ **cup sour cream**
   salt

Soften gelatin in cold water. Stir over low heat until dissolved. Add sugar, lemon juice, vinegar, onion, salt and horseradish. Chill until almost set. Fold in salmon, mayonnaise, olives and celery. Spoon into 1 quart mold. Chill until firm.

Peel and mash avocado. Blend with sour cream and salt. Serve with salmon salad.

Note: Omit or reduce amount of olives and celery to serve on crackers.

Aspic with Shrimp and Asparagus

8 servings

- 2 **cups water**
- 1 **cup water**
- 2 **packages unflavored gelatin**
- ¾ **cup cider vinegar**
- 1 **14-ounce bottle chili sauce**
- ½ **teaspoon salt**
- ¼ **teaspoon pepper**
- 8 **leaves Bibb lettuce**
- 2 **cups shrimp, cooked and chilled**
- 1 **avocado, sliced**
- 16 **asparagus spears, cooked and chilled**
- 16 **cherry tomatoes**
- ½ **cup vinaigrette dressing (see index)**

In a saucepan, boil 2 cups water. Soften 2 packages gelatin in 1 cup water. When water boils, pour in gelatin-water and vinegar. Stir until gelatin is dissolved. Add chili sauce, salt and pepper. Stir and let cool to warm. Put through strainer, then fine sieve. Pour into 2 quart buttered ring mold and chill. When firm unmold on serving plate lined with Bibb lettuce. Fill center of ring with shrimp. Garnish outside of ring with avocado slices, asparagus and cherry tomatoes. Lightly drizzle with vinaigrette dressing.

Creamy Tomato Salad Mold

8-10 servings

2 10½-ounce cans tomato soup
2 3-ounce packages cream cheese
2 packages unflavored gelatin
⅓ cup cold water
1 cup mayonnaise
1 cup finely diced celery
½ cup finely diced green onion
1 cup finely diced green pepper
½ cup diced pecans
   small cooked shrimp, amount according to taste (optional)

In a saucepan over low heat, combine cheese and soup. Dissolve gelatin in cold water and add to soup mixture. Mix well and let cool. Add mayonnaise, vegetables, nuts and shrimp. Pour into 2 quart mold and chill.

Egg Ring Mold

12 servings

16 eggs, hard cooked
1 cup cream
1 cup mayonnaise
3 envelopes unflavored gelatin
½ cup cold water
1 cup hot water
1 large onion, finely chopped
2 teaspoons salt
1 teaspoon Worcestershire sauce
½ cup finely chopped parsley

While still warm, force the eggs through a medium-fine sieve and set aside. Dissolve gelatin in cold water, then dissolve in the cup of hot water. Add the remaining ingredients to the gelatin and mix thoroughly. Pour into a 2 quart ring mold. Refrigerate for 4 hours. Garnish and serve with Louis dressing.

Louis Dressing:

1 pint mayonnaise
1 pint sour cream
⅔ cup chili sauce
1 tablespoon horseradish
6 celery stalks, minced
1 green pepper, minced
½ teaspoon celery seed
   generous dash of cayenne pepper
   salt and pepper to taste

6 cups

Mix all ingredients and chill.
    Note: Ring may be filled with shrimp or a combination of seafood. Cold asparagus is a great complement.

Mustard Ring

¾ **cup sugar**
3 **tablespoons Coleman's dry mustard**
½ **teaspoon salt**
⅔ **cup cider vinegar**
⅓ **cup water**
4 **eggs, well beaten**
1 **envelope unflavored gelatin**
2 **tablespoons cold water**
½ **pint whipping cream, whipped**

6-8 servings

Mix the dry ingredients. Add vinegar and eggs. Dissolve gelatin in the cold water and add to the vinegar and egg mixture. Cook to a soft custard in double boiler. Cool. Fold in whipped cream. Pour into 1 quart ring mold and chill.

Note: Excellent with ham. Most attractive when center of mold is filled with cole slaw and pineapple pieces.

Tropical Fruit Salad

2 **avocados, peeled and sliced diagonally**
1 **papaya, peeled and sliced diagonally**
   Bibb lettuce leaves

Papaya Dressing:
1 **cup salad oil**
⅓ **cup tarragon vinegar**
¼ **cup sugar**
1 **tablespoon lime juice**
¼ **teaspoon paprika**
½ **teaspoon salt**
½ **teaspoon dry mustard**
1 **tablespoon minced onion**
1½ **tablespoons papaya seeds**

4 servings

Arrange alternate slices of avocado and papaya on a lettuce leaf. Pour the dressing over the fruit just before serving.

1½ cups

Place salad oil, vinegar, sugar, lime juice, paprika, salt, mustard and onion in blender jar. Cover, blend thoroughly. Add papaya seeds to blender and blend until seeds are the size of coarsely ground pepper. Chill.

Salad by Committee

24 servings

2	pounds cooked chicken or turkey breast meat, diced
2	pounds cooked ham, diced
2	pounds Cheddar cheese, grated
2	pounds bacon, fried and crumbled
1	dozen hard boiled eggs, grated
3 - 4	ripe avocados, diced
1	pound fresh mushrooms, thinly sliced
1	7¾-ounce can pitted ripe olives, thinly sliced
2	bunches radishes, thinly sliced
2	bunches green onions, thinly sliced
1½	pints cherry tomatoes, halved
3	6-ounce jars marinated artichoke hearts, diced (reserve juice)
5 - 6	heads of lettuce, preferably mixed greens

Dressing:

1	cup salad oil
⅓	cup wine vinegar
	reserved artichoke juice from 3 6-ounce jars
½	teaspoon dry mustard
½	teaspoon garlic powder
1	teaspoon sugar
½	teaspoon salad herbs
	salt and pepper to taste

Mix oil, vinegar, artichoke juice and seasonsings to make dressing. Marinate mushrooms and artichoke hearts in dressing 3-4 hours. When ready to serve, mix all remaining ingredients together in a very large wooden bowl. Toss with dressing, mushrooms and artichoke hearts.

Note: This has become a favorite of a group who picnic at the quaint hilltop cemetery in Central City before the annual fashion show. Each person brings part of the many ingredients. It is served with Sangria, warm muffins and brownies.

COLORADO CACHE COLORADO CACHE COLORADO CACHE COLORADO CACHE COLORADO CACHE COLORADO CACHE COLORADO CACHE COLORADO CACHE COLORADO CACHE COLORADO

Bavarian Cucumber Dressing

1½ cups

½ onion, grated and drained
2 cucumbers, peeled, shredded
     and drained
1 tablespoon red wine vinegar
1 teaspoon chopped parsley
1 clove garlic, crushed
1½ teaspoons salt
1 teaspoon sugar
½ teaspoon coarsely ground
     black pepper

Combine the ingredients and let ripen at least 6 hours before using. Serve a dollop on a wedge of lettuce or toss generously with a combination of greens.

Hot Salad Dressing

1½ cups

12 slices bacon
6 tablespoons bacon grease
9 tablespoons vinegar
3 teaspoons flour
3 egg yolks
1 tablespoon water
6 tablespoons sour cream
½ teaspoon salt
3 tablespoons sugar

Cut the bacon into ½ inch squares and cook. Drain, reserving 6 tablespoons of bacon grease. Add the vinegar to the bacon grease and cool. Add water to the egg yolk and blend in the flour. Add this mixture to the pan combining the bacon and bacon grease with vinegar. Cook on medium temperature, stirring constantly, until the mixture thickens. Add cream, salt and sugar and bring to a boil. Pour over lettuce an serve at once.

Note: This dressing can be reheated.

Low Calorie Dressing

1½ cups

1 cup cottage cheese
¼ cup buttermilk
¼ cup bleu cheese, crumbled
½ teaspoon celery seed,
     rosemary or dill weed

Combine all the ingredients in a blender, except the bleu cheese, and blend. Add the bleu cheese and refrigerate until chilled.

Vinaigrette Dressing

½ cup

- 5 tablespoons vegetable oil
- 3 tablespoons vinegar (cider or white wine)
- 1 clove garlic, crushed
  scant ½ teaspoon salt
- ¼ teaspoon Beau Monde seasoning
  dash of cracked pepper
  dash of paprika
  generous pinch of oregano
- 1 green onion, finely chopped

Place all ingredients in a jar. Shake well to mix. Chill at least 1 hour. This salad dressing is a very good complement to a heavy meal but it does not keep well.

Creamy Lemon Dressing

1¼ cups

- 1 cup sour cream
- 2 tablespoons fresh lemon juice
- 2 teaspoons sugar
- 1 teaspoon salt
  pepper to taste

Stir lemon juice, sugar, salt and pepper into the sour cream with a wooden spoon. Beat well to blend.

Note: Good with Boston lettuce and sliced cucumbers or an assortment of greens.

Zesty Creamy Italian Dressing

3 cups

- 1 10½-ounce can beef consomme
- 1 16-ounce jar mayonnaise
- 4 cloves garlic, mashed
- 2 tablespoons red wine vinegar
- 1 tablespoon coarsely ground pepper

Mix the ingredients and chill in the refrigerator for at least 8 hours.

Sesame Seed Dressing

½ cup sesame seeds
1 tablespoon butter
½ cup freshly grated Parmesan
    cheese
1 cup sour cream
½ cup mayonnaise
1 tablespoon tarragon vinegar
1 tablespoon sugar
½ cup chopped green pepper
2 tablespoons minced onion
¾ teaspoon salt
½ teaspoon garlic salt

1¾ cups dressing

Saute sesame seeds in butter until brown. Cool and add cheese. Mix mayonnaise, sour cream, vinegar, sugar, green pepper, onion, salt and garlic salt. Add cooled sesame mixture.

Note: If the seed and cheese mixture is stored separately from the cream mixture, this dressing may be kept at least a week in the refrigerator.

Mint French Dressing

1 cup salad oil
1 cup red wine vinegar
1 clove garlic, split
¼ teaspoon oregano
¼ teaspoon salt
¼ teaspoon freshly ground
    pepper
¼ teaspoon chopped fresh mint

2 cups

Place all ingredients in a jar and refrigerate. Allow to stand 24 hours before using. Remove garlic. Shake vigorously before tossing with greens.

Creme Fraiche

1 cup heavy cream
2½ teaspoons buttermilk

1 cup

Combine the heavy cream and buttermilk in a jar. Cover the jar tightly and shake the mixture for at least 1 minute. Let the cream stand at room temperature for at least 8 hours, until thick. Store in the refrigerator. Will keep 4-6 weeks.

ADO CACHE COLORADO CACHE COLORADO CACHE COLORADO CACHE COLORADO CACHE COLORADO CACHE COLORADO CACHE COLORADO CACHE COLORADO CACHE COLORADO CACHE

Poppy Seed Dressing

4 cups

1½ cups sugar
2 teaspoons dry mustard
2 teaspoons salt
⅔ cup vinegar
1 small onion, chopped
2 cups vegetable oil
3 tablespoons poppy seeds

Combine sugar, dry mustard, salt, vinegar, onion and oil in blender. Blend for one minute. Add poppy seeds and blend a few seconds more. Refrigerate.

Note: Serving suggestions: fresh fruit salad, red cabbage with sliced avocados and green grapes, Bibb lettuce with grapefruit sections, sliced avocados and pomegranate seeds (optional as the season for these is very short).

Croutons

Cut the crusts from slices of day-old bread. Cut the bread into evenly sized squares. Saute bread cubes in a frying pan with a little clarified butter, turning to brown on all sides. Drain on paper toweling. Or toast cubes on a jelly roll sheet which has been lightly spread with a mixture of olive oil and vegetable oil. Toast at 250 degrees for 30 to 40 minutes.

Scarlet O'Horseradish Dressing

2 cups

1 cup thick sour cream
1 small onion, minced
1½ tablespoons sugar
1½ teaspoons salt
½ cup cooked beets, finely diced
5 tablespoons horseradish, undrained
1 clove garlic, crushed (optional)

Mix the ingredients thoroughly with a spoon. Chill. Serve tossed with assorted salad greens and slices of cucumber.

COLORADO CACHE COLORADO CACHE COLORADO CACHE COLORADO CACHE COLORADO CACHE COLORADO CACHE COLORADO CACHE COLORADO CACHE COLORADO CACHE COLORADO

Fresh Fruit Dressing

2 cups

1 cup sour cream
4 tablespoons honey
3 tablespoons orange juice
1 cup coconut granola

Mix sour cream, honey and orange juice. Sprinkle granola on top of choice of fresh fruits. Toss with sour cream mixture.

Blender Mayonnaise

1 cup

1 large egg
1 tablespoon fresh lemon juice
¼ teaspoon dry mustard
¼ teaspoon salt
½ teaspoon sugar
⅛ teaspoon cayenne pepper
   dash of onion salt or powder
   dash of garlic powder
      (optional)
¾ cup vegetable oil

In a blender place all ingredients except the oil. Start blending on low speed and slowly add oil through the center of the blender top until mixture is thick and creamy, about 30 seconds. Stir with rubber spatula and store covered in the refrigerator. If more than 1 cup is desired, make only one recipe at a time.

Note: This mayonnaise will keep at least 2 weeks. Delicious and economical.

Bleu Cheese Dressing

3 cups

¾ cup vegetable oil
¼ cup cider vinegar
2 cups sour cream
1 teaspoon salt
1 medium clove garlic, minced
4 ounces bleu cheese, crumbled
   freshly ground pepper to taste

In a blender pour ¼ cup of oil and ¼ cup vinegar. Blend. Add sour cream and blend. Add the remaining oil and the seasonings; blend. Add the crumbled bleu cheese to the above mixture and stir carefully. Refrigerate.

Note: This is also good as a dip with crudites as it is quite thick.

GINGERBREAD HOUSES IN GEORGETOWN

Fish and Game

Hints from **La Junta**

Food safety is very important in all stages of handling game. Clean and chill it as soon as possible. Make sure it is thoroughly cooked. Don't cross-contaminate by using the same platters and utensils for raw and cooked meat without washing between handlings.

Proper packaging is the key to freezing success. Fish keeps better when frozen in water. The cuts of game meat should be frozen quickly and kept at a temperature of 0 degrees.

Pounding the tougher steaks and chops before cooking helps break up the tougher meat fibers.

Trim the fat because it retains the game taste.

Knowing the age of the bird or big game will usually dictate the cooking method, The outer end of the breastbone is a good indicator; it is flexible in a young bird.

Aging game birds in the refrigerator 24-48 hours before cooking (as in a marinade) or freezing removes much of the wild flavor.

Since game birds are very lean, larding is necessary. Venison can be very dry also. Elk is more like beef. Strips of bacon will always enhance the flavor and moistness.

Always be appreciative to the hunter or fisherman. A sportsman is very concerned with the final presentation of his provisions.

La Junta is situated in the southeastern, arid prairie country. Sagebrush, cacti, yucca and mesquite cover the somber land, the habitat of prairie dogs, jack rabbits and lizards. The Yucca plant was used by the Indians to make rope from its fiber, and its roots make a lather in water.

111

Fish and Game

COLORADO CACHE COLORADO CACHE COLORADO CACHE COLORADO CACHE COLORADO CACHE COLORADO CACHE COLORADO CACHE COLORADO CACHE COLORADO C

Colorado Camper's Trout

1 serving

1 **pound bacon**
2 **white onions, thinly sliced**
1 - 2 **freshly caught, pan-sized trout, cleaned**
½ **cup yellow corn meal**
½ **cup flour**
1 **tablespoon salt**
1 **teaspoon pepper**

Fry, drain and nibble on bacon while doing next step! Saute onions in bacon grease, drain and salt, and nibble while preparing the fish. Coat fish well with mixture of corn meal, flour, salt and pepper. Fry fish in hot grease until done and very crisp. Garnish with onion and bacon.

Note: Serve with bread and campfire coffee. This is the best way to eat trout: when it is stream-fresh, it's hard to beat!

Smoked Trout or Salmon

8 or more trout

1 **cup Morton's Tender Quick**
8 **teaspoons Liquid Smoke**
½ **cup ice cream salt**
1 **gallon water**

Soak fish 24 hours in above mixture, using a crock or non-metallic container. Drain. Bake at 200 degrees for 4 hours on greased cookie sheet. Close door during baking. Turn once after 2 hours. Wrap in freezer paper and freeze to keep.

Note: Serve plain as an appetizer with unsalted crackers.

Trout Amandine

4 servings

8 **trout fillets**
1 **cup milk**
½ **cup flour**
   salt and pepper
⅓ **cup butter**
½ **cup slivered almonds**
6 **sprigs parsley**
12 **lemon wedges**
3 **tablespoons dry white wine**

Dip fillets in milk and roll in flour which has been seasoned with salt and pepper. In a skillet, brown fish on both sides in butter. Arrange fish on serving platter and keep warm. Saute almonds in butter, add wine and pour over fish. Garnish with parsley and lemon.

Trotelle alla Savoia (Baked Trout with Mushrooms)

4 servings

- 4 **trout, cleaned with heads and tails left on**
  salt and freshly ground pepper
  flour
- ½ **cup butter**
- 2 **tablespoons olive oil**
- 1 **pound fresh mushrooms, thinly sliced**
- 1 **teaspoon lemon juice**
- ¾ **cup thinly sliced green onions (include 2 to 3 inches of green part)**
- ¼ **cup fresh bread crumbs**

Season trout lightly with salt and pepper. Roll in flour and brush off excess. In a heavy 10 to 12 inch skillet, melt 2 tablespoons of butter with the olive oil over high heat. When foam subsides, add the trout and cook for 4 to 5 minutes on each side or until golden brown. Carefully transfer trout to a plate or platter. In a stainless steel or enameled skillet, melt about 4 tablespoons butter over moderate heat. Add mushrooms, sprinkle with lemon juice and cook about 3 minutes until slightly soft, stirring constantly with a wooden spoon. Remove mushrooms to a buttered 9 × 13 inch oven-proof baking dish. Melt 1 tablespoon butter in skillet and add green onions. Cook one minute. Remove to a bowl. Lightly brown bread crumbs in remaining butter. Place trout on mushrooms, then top with green onions and bread crumbs. Bake at 425 degrees for about 10 minutes or until trout is white and flakes.

Poached Salmon with Cucumber Sauce

6 servings

- 6 **fresh salmon steaks**
- 1 **quart water**
- 1½ **tablespoons salt**
- 2 **tablespoons lemon juice**
- 1 **bay leaf**
- 1 **lemon, quartered**
- 2 **tomatoes, quartered**

In a large skillet heat the water, salt, lemon juice and bay leaf to boiling. Simmer 3 of the steaks at a time for 10 minutes. Remove with a large slotted spoon or spatula. Chill the steaks well.

Cucumber Sauce:
- 1 **unpeeled cucumber**
- ½ **cup sour cream**
- ¼ **cup mayonnaise**
- 1 **tablespoon minced parsley**
- 2 **teaspoons grated onion**
- 2 **teaspoons cider vinegar**
- ¼ **teaspoon salt**
  pinch of black pepper

Grate enough cucumber to make 1 cup. Do not drain. Add the remaining ingredients and stir well. Chill.

At serving time, arrange the salmon on a platter or board. Garnish with lemon quarters and tomato quarters. Serve with cucumber sauce.

Pheasant a la Creme

4 servings

2   **pheasants**
    salt and pepper
    paprika
    flour
½   **cup butter**
2   **cups sour cream**
2   **tablespoons lemon juice**
½   **pound mushrooms, sliced**
1   **onion, finely chopped**
½   **cup finely chopped celery**
½   **cup sliced, pitted ripe olives**
2   **tablespoons chopped**
      pimentos

Split birds in half. Sprinkle with salt, pepper and paprika. Dredge lightly with flour. Brown in butter until golden. Remove birds and place in a small roasting pan. Add remaining ingredients to butter in which birds were browned. Pour over pheasants. Cover and bake at 300 degrees for 2 hours or until tender.

Note: Higher oven temperature may cause sour cream to curdle.

Pheasant Madeira

6 servings

6   **pheasant breasts**
½   **cup cream**
½   **cup butter**
    flour
    salt and paprika
½   **cup sliced green grapes**
1   **6-ounce can artichoke hearts**
1   **cup Madeira**

Remove skin from breasts. Dip in cream and dredge in flour, salt and paprika. Saute lightly in butter. Add wine and cover with foil. Bake at 325 degrees for 1 hour and 15 minutes or until tender. Remove breasts from baking dish and set aside. Add ½ cup cream to the sauce remaining in baking dish. Reheat. Stir in grapes and artichoke hearts. Pour over pheasant and serve with wild rice.

Pheasant Nebraska

pheasants
Bisquick mix
butter

Partially freeze or defrost pheasants and slice breast meat thinly. Dredge in Bisquick and fry quickly in lots of butter. Save rest of carcass to make broth for soup. Make twice as much as you think you'll need. It goes fast! This can be used for duck as well as thinly sliced venison steaks.

RADO CACHE COLORADO CACHE COLORADO CACHE COLORADO CACHE COLORADO CACHE COLORADO CACHE COLORADO CACHE COLORADO CACHE COLORADO CACHE COLORADO CACHE COLORADO CACHE

Smokey Hill Pheasant Pie

6 servings

1	**3 to 4 pound pheasant**
1	**bay leaf**
1	**stalk celery**
6	**peppercorns**
1	**tablespoon salt**
½	**cup butter or margarine**
½	**cup flour**
1	**cup light cream**
½	**teaspoon pepper**
½	**teaspoon salt**
½	**pound pearl onions, peeled**
¼	**pound fresh mushrooms, sliced**
1	**10-ounce package frozen peas**
1	**2-ounce jar chopped pimento**
	pastry for 9-inch crust

Place pheasant in a large saucepan and cover with water. Add bay leaf, celery, peppercorns and 1 tablespoon salt. Cover and cook over low heat about 2 hours or until tender. (A pressure cooker will cut the cooking time in half.) Remove meat from bone and strain broth.

Melt butter in medium saucepan. Add flour and stir until blended. Gradually add 2 cups of the broth, stirring constantly. Stir in light cream, pepper and salt. Cook until thickened. Arrange pheasant pieces, onions, mushrooms, peas and pimentos in a 2 quart casserole. Add sauce to within 1 inch of top. Arrange pastry shell over mixture; seal edges and cut steam vents. Bake in a preheated 450 degree oven for 25 minutes or until crust is golden brown.

Pheasant Casserole

6 servings

12	**ounces mild pork sausage**
½	**pound mushrooms, sliced**
8	**ounces water chestnuts, chopped**
1	**large onion, finely chopped**
1	**6-ounce box of Uncle Ben's wild rice mix**
¼	**cup flour**
¼	**cup butter**
½	**cup milk**
1¾	**cup chicken broth**
	juice of ½ lemon
1	**teaspoon salt**
⅛	**teaspoon pepper**
2	**cups boned pheasant (or turkey or chicken)**
½	**cup slivered, toasted almonds**

Saute sausage and drain off grease. Saute onion and mushrooms in sausage grease. When nearly done, add water chestnuts. Squeeze lemon juice over mixture. Cook rice according to instructions on the package. Make a white sauce with the flour, butter, milk, chicken broth, salt and pepper. Lightly toss together the pheasant, sausage, rice and mushroom mixture. Pour sauce over and toss again. Bake at 350 degrees for at least 1 hour. Sprinkle with almonds before serving.

Note: This is a good dish for company because after baking time, just turn off the over and let this sit in the warm oven until ready to serve. This even improves the flavor.

COLORADO CACHE COLORADO CACHE COLORADO CACHE COLORADO CACHE COLORADO CACHE COLORADO CACHE COLORADO CACHE COLORADO CACHE COLORADO

Baked Pheasant or Quail in Cream Sauce

4 servings

2 pheasants or 4 quail
   seasoned flour
3 tablespoons butter or
   margarine
½ pound fresh mushrooms
⅓ cup sliced almonds
½ small onion, chopped
3 celery stalks, chopped
1 pint cream
1 tablespoon salt
1 teaspoon pepper
1 cup dry sherry

Quarter pheasant or halve quail. Dip in seasoned flour and brown in butter. Set aside. Saute mushrooms, almonds, onion and celery in butter. Place game in Dutch oven and pour over sauteed mixture. Cover and bake at 350 degrees for 1½ hours. Add cream, salt, pepper and sherry. Cover and bake an additional 30 minutes or until birds are tender.

Pheasant with Brandy and Sour Cream

6 servings

3 pheasants
   celery and sliced apples to
    stuff birds
¼ cup butter
8 shallots, thinly sliced
¼ cup brandy
2 cups chicken stock
   salt and pepper
1 pint sour cream
¼ cup horseradish
   bacon

Stuff and truss birds. Brown in butter with shallots. Remove to Dutch oven or roaster and cover with bacon slices and pan juices. Pour brandy over and ignite. When flame subsides, add chicken stock and seasonings. Cover tightly and bake at 350 degrees for 1½ hours, basting occasionally. Remove cover to brown for 15 minutes at 375 degrees. Add cream and horseradish to juices. Baste well and roast 15 minutes, covered. Serve with juices over wild rice.

RADO CACHE COLORADO CACHE COLORADO CACHE COLORADO CACHE COLORADO CACHE COLORADO CACHE COLORADO CACHE COLORADO CACHE COLORADO CACHE COLORADO CACHE COLORADO CACHE

Barbecued Pheasant

4-6 servings

2 pheasants
1 teaspoon salt
½ teaspoon black pepper
¾ cup flour
  shortening
1 tablespoon butter or
  margarine
1 medium onion, chopped
1 tablespoon brown sugar
1 tablespoon cornstarch
¼ cup catsup
2 tablespoons vinegar
2 tablespoons Worcestershire
  sauce
½ teaspoon dry mustard
1 16-ounce can tomatoes,
  chopped
¼ teaspoon salt
½ teaspoon pepper

Cut pheasant into serving pieces. Combine salt, pepper and flour. Coat pheasant with seasoned flour and brown in hot shortening. Remove from skillet and drain grease. Add butter or margarine to skillet and saute onions until tender. Combine sugar and cornstarch and blend into onions. Add remaining ingredients. Cook slowly, stirring frequently, for 20 to 25 minutes or until slightly thickened. Arrange pheasant in baking dish and cover with sauce. Bake covered in a 300 degree oven for 1½ to 2 hours, or until tender. Baste occasionally with the sauce.

Pheasant with Sauerkraut

6 servings

2 2½- to 3-pound pheasants
  onions and celery to stuff
    pheasants
  seasoned flour
¼ cup butter
2 - 3 cups sauerkraut
  juniper berries or caraway
    seed

Rub pheasant cavities with salt and pepper. Stuff with onion and celery as desired. Coat with flour. Saute in butter until golden. Place on a bed of sauerkraut in a clay pot cooker (Rumtopf) or a Dutch oven. Cover with sauerkraut and berries or caraway seeds. Cover and bake at 325 degrees for about 2 hours, or until tender. The pheasants will be moist and the sauerkraut is outstanding.

COLORADO CACHE COLORADO CACHE COLORADO CACHE COLORADO CACHE COLORADO CACHE COLORADO CACHE COLORADO CACHE COLORADO CACHE COLORADO

Roast Pheasant with Wild Rice Stuffing

4 servings

2 **pheasants**
salt and pepper
2 **tablespoons butter**
4 **slices bacon**

Season the cavities of pheasants with salt and pepper and coat with butter.

Wild Rice Stuffing:

½ **cup wild rice, cooked in**
chicken stock
½ **cup brown rice, cooked in**
chicken stock
4 **tablespoons butter, divided**
1 **medium onion, chopped**
½ **pound mushrooms, sliced**
¼ **cup chopped celery**
½ **cup chopped pecans**
2 **tablespoons chopped fresh**
parsley
¼ **teaspoon thyme**
¼ **teaspoon marjoram**
salt and pepper to taste

Combine the rice to cook. When done, add 2 tablespoons of the butter and toss with a fork to fluff. Saute onion, mushrooms and celery in remaining butter. Add to rice and toss with remaining ingredients. Stuff birds and truss lightly. Cover breast with bacon strips and bake in a heavy Dutch oven covered at 350 degrees for about 1½ to 2 hours or until done. Serve with Cream Sauce for Pheasant (see index).

Breasts of Partridge

4 servings

breasts of 2 partridges,
cleaned
1 **teaspoon salt**
¼ **teaspoon cayenne pepper**
½ **cup butter**
2 **tablespoons chopped onion**
½ **teaspoon rosemary**
4 **small slices ham,**
cut ½ inch thick
½ **pound mushrooms, sliced**
2 **tablespoons flour**
1 **cup chicken broth**
2 **tablespoons dry white wine**

Cut breasts away from bone (partially frozen breasts will cut better) leaving skin on. Sprinkle with salt and cayenne pepper. In a large skillet, melt butter and add onion and rosemary. Brown breasts on both sides for 10 minutes or until cooked., Place ½ breast on each slice of ham on platter and keep warm. Saute mushrooms in pan for 3 minutes. Push mushrooms aside and add flour, blending with a whisk while adding chicken broth. Continue heating, stirring until smooth and thickened. Season with salt and pepper to taste. Add wine and pour over birds.

Note: This is good served with corn pudding and a green salad.

118

Fish and Game

RADO CACHE COLORADO CACHE COLORADO CACHE COLORADO CACHE COLORADO CACHE COLORADO CACHE COLORADO CACHE COLORADO CACHE COLORADO CACHE

Colorado Blue Grouse en Casserole

4 servings

4 medium potatoes
4 tablespoons butter
2 tablespoons oil
½ pound small white onions, peeled
4 1-pound grouse, dressed (save giblets)
  salt and pepper to taste
½ cup dry white wine
½ cup bourbon
2 teaspoons instant beef boullion
½ pound fresh mushrooms, sliced
1 15-ounce can small whole carrots
2 tablespoons flour

Cut potatoes lengthwise into 4 sections. Melt butter and oil in flame proof skillet or casserole over direct heat. Add potatoes and onions and saute until golden. Remove vegetables and set aside. Brown grouse. Sprinkle with salt and pepper. Add wine and bourbon and ignite. When flames subside, add instant boullion and blend well. Add mushrooms, onions and potatoes. Cover tightly and bake at 350 degrees for 1 hour or until tender, basting occasionally with juices in casserole. Drain carrots and add to casserole; heat. Drain pan juices into saucepan. Stir in flour to make a thick gravy, if desired. Pour sauce over grouse before serving.

Note: Cooking time should be increased for larger grouse.

Windsor Canadian Goose

6-8 servings

1 goose, 6 to 8 pounds
1 quart buttermilk
1 8-ounce package dried prunes
2 apples, sliced
5 slices bacon
  butter

Sauce:

½ cup butter
¼ cup flour
¾ cup beef or chicken broth
  salt to taste
1 cup sour cream
4 tablespoons currant jelly

Soak goose in buttermilk at least 4 hours in refrigerator. Wash bird and drain. Stuff with prunes and apples. Truss and wrap in bacon. Cover tightly with heavy duty foil. Bake until tender at 325 degrees for about 3 hours. Baste with butter to brown.

Melt butter in saucepan. Stir in flour with whisk. Add broth and heat, stirring constantly. Just before serving add sour cream and jelly. Heat and serve.

Remove fruit from goose before serving and arrange on platter around it.

COLORADO CACHE COLORADO CACHE COLORADO CACHE COLORADO CACHE COLORADO CACHE COLORADO CACHE COLORADO CACHE COLORADO CACHE COLORADO

Quail on Croutons

6 servings

6	**quail with giblets**
¾	**cup flour**
1	**teaspoon salt**
½	**teaspoon pepper**
¾	**cup butter or margarine**
1	**large onion, finely chopped**
1	**cup sherry**
½	**cup dry white wine**
12	**slices thick-sliced bread**
1	**cup red currant jelly**
	grated rind and juice of 1 lemon and 1 orange
½	**teaspoon dry mustard**
	parsley for garnish

Clean quail. Remove and set aside giblets. Preheat oven to 350 degrees. Split birds in half. Mix flour, salt, pepper and put in large paper bag. Put quail in bag and shake well to coat. Heat 4 tablespoons butter or margarine in large skillet and saute onions and giblets for about 5 minutes. Remove onions and transfer giblets to a bowl. Mash giblets with remaining butter, ½ cup sherry, salt and pepper to taste. Brown split birds well on both sides in remaining grease. Transfer birds to roasting pan. Add white wine to skillet, scraping sides and bottom with spatula to loosen particles. Bring to a boil and pour over birds. Place birds in oven, covered, and bake for 45 minutes to 1 hour.

Toast bread slightly and spread with giblet paste. Arrange on a large platter and place half bird on each. In a small saucepan, melt jelly over high heat, add rind and juice of lemon and orange and dry mustard. Bring to a rapid boil. Pour in a sauce boat. Garnish birds with sprig of parsley and serve immediately.

Dove or Duck Breast Appetizer

dove or duck breasts
fresh orange juice
bacon

Split and bone bird breast, saving remainder for soup broth. Marinate breasts in fresh orange juice overnight. Wrap each breast in a strip of bacon and fasten with a toothpick. (Duck breasts will need slicing into individual serving pieces.) Roast over open charcoal fire about 10 minutes, or until bacon is cooked.

Indian Garden Duck

6 servings

3	**duck breasts, split and boned**
½	**cup dry red wine**
¼	**cup soy sauce**
½	**teaspoon sugar**
	garlic salt to taste

Marinate duck breasts in wine, soy sauce and spices for at least 24 hours. Broil 5 minutes on each side. Return to marinade. This will keep in the refrigerator for up to 2 weeks. Take meat out as you like and slice very thin. Serve as an hors d'oeuvre with melba toast or plain crackers.

RADO CACHE COLORADO CACHE COLORADO CACHE COLORADO CACHE COLORADO CACHE COLORADO CACHE COLORADO CACHE COLORADO CACHE COLORADO CACHE COLORADO CACHE

Wild Duck la Porte

1　**duck**
　　salt
1　**apple, finely chopped**
½　**onion, finely chopped**
1　**celery stalk, chopped**
½　**cup butter, melted**
1　**cup chicken broth**

2 servings

Clean duck inside and out. Salt inside and out. Fill cavity with apple, onion and celery. Cover with melted butter and chicken broth. Bake at 350 degrees, covered, with breast side down for 2½ hours. Turn and cook with breast side up 15 to 20 minutes, basting with chicken broth. Uncover and cook 10 to 15 minutes. Make a gravy with the drippings.

　　Note: This is a very simple and sure method of cooking duck. It can be dressed up with different sauces.

Platte River Duck

1　**duck**
1　**small onion**
1　**small orange**
6　**tablespoons barbecue sauce**
6　**tablespoons dry sherry**
　　salt and pepper

2 servings

Stuff duck with orange and onion. Rub well with salt and pepper. Place breast down in heavy duty aluminum foil large enough to completely seal duck. Pour barbecue sauce and sherry over duck and seal. Bake at 275 degrees for 3 hours.

　　Note: This is so easy for a family dinner. Everything is in the pantry!

Wild Duck Deluxe

¼　**cup margarine**
2　**tablespoons flour**
1 - 2　**cloves garlic, minced**
4　**duck breasts, if large**
　　(more if not)
　　salt and pepper
2　**onions, finely chopped**
2　**carrots, sliced**
¼　**cup parsley, chopped**
2　**cups tomato juice**
1　**cup orange juice**
1　**can consomme**
½　**cup dry sherry**

6-8 servings

Make a paste of the margarine, flour and garlic and spread on the ducks which have been washed, dried, salted and peppered. Place in 450 degree oven, breast side up, for 15 minutes, uncovered. Meanwhile, combine onions, carrots, parsley, juices and consomme. Bring to boil and simmer 20 minutes. Pour over ducks, turn breast side down and cover. Reduce heat to 350 degrees and cook 2 hours. Uncover last 20 minutes and add sherry.

Duck a la Lake Olaf

breast of 2 ducks, split and boned (may include legs)
1 **onion, chopped**
1 **cup chopped fresh mushrooms**
3 **celery stalks, chopped**
1 **6½-ounce can water chestnuts, chopped**
½ **pound butter**
1 **jar currant jelly**
1 **ounce dry sherry**
1½ **cups bourbon**
dash of Worcestershire sauce
salt and pepper

4 servings

Saute onion, mushrooms, celery and water chestnuts. Set aside. In a large pan, melt butter and jelly. Add sherry, bourbon and Worcestershire sauce. Bring to a boil. Slip in the duck, lower heat, but keep at a boil. Cook 10 to 15 minutes, then turn meat for another 10 to 15 minutes. Combine mushrooms, onion, celery and water chestnuts with duck and juices. Serve over wild rice.

Wild Duck Stuckey

2 **ducks**
butter or bacon grease
salt and pepper
1 **10½-ounce can beef consomme**
¼ **pound mushrooms, sliced and sauteed**
4 **cups cooked wild rice**
1 **cup cooked brown rice**
Tokay grapes, for garnish

Currant Jelly Sauce:
1 **jar currant jelly**
⅓ **cup Worcestershire sauce**
½ **cup butter**

4 servings

Rub ducks with butter or bacon grease, salt and pepper inside and out. Brown in a 500 degree oven for 30 minutes. Smother with rest of ingredients. Cover tightly and return to 350 degree oven for 2 hours. This can stay in low oven for an hour or more without drying out. Serve with currant jelly sauce.

Simmer ingredients in double boiler covered for 1 hour. Beat with wire whisk before serving.

Quarter ducks to serve. Mound rice in center of platter. Surround with duck quarters and garnish with Tokay grape clusters.

122

Fish and Game

RADO CACHE COLORADO CACHE COLORADO CACHE COLORADO CACHE COLORADO CACHE COLORADO CACHE COLORADO CACHE COLORADO CACHE COLORADO CACHE COLORADO CACHE COLORADO CACHE

Wild Duck in Apple Juice and Brandy

6-8 servings

4 **ducks**
  salt and pepper
4 **small onions**
4 **small apples**
  celery
  rosemary
  garlic salt
  celery salt
½ **cup sherry**
½ **cup apple juice**
¼ **cup peach brandy**

Rub inside duck cavities with salt and pepper. Place onion, apple and celery inside each duck. Sprinkle with rosemary, garlic salt and celery salt. Put in deep roasting pan and add sherry, apple juice and brandy. Roast covered at 375 degrees for 2 hours, basting frequently. Remove top during last 30 minutes to insure browning. Quarter or halve ducks to serve.

Note: This can be done with just the duck breasts, lowering the heat to 300 degrees. Save the remainder of the bird to use as broth for soup.

Duck or Pheasant Soup

8 servings

  carcass of 2 birds (use breasts in other recipes, save thighs and legs for soup)
3 **quarts water, salted**
2 **onions, chopped**
2 **carrots, chopped**
2 **celery stalks, chopped**
1 **10-ounce package frozen chopped broccoli**
2 **tablespoons chicken broth crystals**
1 **tablespoon curry powder**
2 **tablespoons dry sherry**
2 **tablespoons uncooked rice**
  lemon slices, for garnish

Stew birds in salted water with onions, carrots and celery for about 1 to 2 hours, or until meat falls off the bones easily. Remove birds and take the meat off the bone and chop coarsely. Add broccoli and cook about 5 minutes. Season and puree if desired. Return to pot and add sherry, rice and meat. Simmer for about 20 minutes. Serve in heated bowls with lemon slices. Soup is better the second day. If desired, chill and reheat at serving time.

COLORADO CACHE COLORADO CACHE COLORADO CACHE COLORADO CACHE COLORADO CACHE COLORADO CACHE COLORADO CACHE COLORADO CACHE COLORADO CACHE COLORADO CACHE COLORADO

Mount Evans Elk Sausage

5-6 rolls

2½ teaspoons garlic salt
1 teaspoon hickory smoked salt
5 teaspoons Tender Quick
(meat curing salt)
2½ teaspoons coarsely ground
pepper
2½ teaspoons mustard seed
4 pounds ground elk meat
1 pound ground pork

Combine garlic salt, smoked salt, curing salt, pepper and mustard seed. Gradually add to meat. Mix well with hands. Refrigerate, covered, overnight. Mix again. Refrigerate again, covered, overnight. On third day form mixture into five or six rolls about 2 inches in diameter. Place rolls about two inches apart on rack in large, shallow pan. Place on center shelf of preheated 350 degree oven. Bake 10 minutes. Reduce heat to 200 degrees. Bake 8 hours, turning every 2 hours. Drain off grease when necessary. (Outside will be dark and glossy; inside will be pink.) Cool. Wrap in foil. Store in refrigerator up to two weeks. Store in freezer about one month.

Elk Salami

5 rolls

2 cups water
1 tablespoon liquid smoke
4 pounds ground elk meat
1 pound ground pork
1½ teaspoons garlic salt
1 teaspoon onion salt
½ teaspoon mustard seed
6 tablespoons Tender Quick
(meat curing salt)
¼ teaspoon pepper

Combine water and liquid smoke. Add to meat. Mix well. Combine garlic salt, onion salt, mustard seed, curing salt and pepper. Add to meat and mix well with hands. Shape into long rolls about 2½ inches in diameter. Wrap each roll separately in heavy duty foil. Fold foil, closing tightly, down center and on ends. Refrigerate rolls 24 hours. With meat fork, make holes through foil about one inch apart on bottom of rolls (opposite fold). Place rolls on rack in large, shallow pan. Place a shallow pan with hot water on lower oven shelf to create steam. Bake rolls on center oven shelf at 325 degrees for 2 hours. Remove foil. (Salami will be a fairly bright pink on both the outside and inside.) Set rolls on rack to drain and cool. Wrap in foil or plastic wrap. Store in refrigerator up to 10 days. Store in freezer about one month.
Note: Taste will improve with storage.

Daddy's Venison Chili

6 quarts, plus

1½	**teaspoons cumin powder**
1½	**teaspoons oregano**
1½	**teaspoons cayenne pepper**
1½	**teaspoons black pepper**
1	**teaspoon salt**
2	**teaspoons garlic powder**
3	**tablespoons sugar**
6 - 8	**ounces Gebhardt's chili powder**
3	**cups cold water**
1	**ounce juice from top of can of jalapeno peppers**
1	**gallon can peeled tomatoes**
1	**1-pound can peeled tomatoes**
2	**15-ounce cans tomato sauce**
6	**large green peppers**
6	**large Bermuda onions**
½	**pound hot pork sausage**
5	**pounds venison meat, ground**
1	**pint high quality olive oil**

Garnishes:
shredded lettuce
chopped tomato
grated cheese

Dissolve spices and sugar in the cold water. Top with the jalapeno juice. If a hotter chili is desired, dice a few of the jalapenos in the spices. Set aside. In an 8 quart heavy pot, put in tomatoes, squashing them by hand. Add tomato sauce and turn to medium heat. Meanwhile, dice the green peppers and onions. When tomatoes have heated, add spices, stirring well. In a large, high-sided skillet saute the chopped peppers and onions in olive oil until quite tender but not brown. This may take two skillets. Add to the chili pot. Saute sausage in olive oil, then meat, until an even grey, not brown. Add meats to pot and simmer, covered, on low to warm fire for 4 hours, stirring every 30 minutes, making sure it will not burn. Turn off heat and let cool on stove. Pour in about 2 cups of boiling water and let cool. Cover and place in refrigerator overnight. Next day, skim off all grease which has hardened and skim again while heating on medium burner. Ladle into quart containers and freeze.

Note: If you like beans in chili, heat a quart of the chili with 1 10-ounce can of ranch style beans. Serve with shredded lettuce, chopped tomatoes and grated cheese for each person to sprinkle on top.

Elk or Venison Liver

elk or venison liver
bacon

If you are so fortunate to have access to fresh liver, it is best then. Frozen it is still better than the best calf's liver.

Slice paper thin. Fry diced bacon in skillet. When almost done, add liver and fry until it is seared on the outside and pink in the center. An elk liver is so large you will have plenty left over to slice and freeze in individual packages.

Sweet and Sour Elk Meatballs

4 servings

1	**pound ground elk**
½	**pound ground pork**
½	**teaspoon salt**
¼	**teaspoon garlic powder**
¼	**teaspoon pepper**
¼	**teaspoon dried mustard**
1	**12-ounce jar chili sauce**
1	**10-ounce jar grape jelly**

Place the meats in a large mixing bowl. Add salt, garlic, pepper and mustard and knead with a fork or your hands. Shape into cocktail size balls about 1½ inches in diameter. Place on a cookie sheet and bake at 350 degrees until brown, about 15 minutes. Pour the chili sauce and jelly into a large saucepan over medium heat and stir until jelly melts. Add the meatballs, a few at a time, carefully stirring to cover the meat with sauce. Continue cooking over medium heat for about 20 minutes.

Note: This improves when prepared a few days in advance and refrigerated or frozen. Reheat at serving time in a chafing dish or serve over brown rice with a green salad as a Sunday night supper.

Venison Meat Loaf

4 servings

1	**pound ground venison**
½	**pound bulk pork sausage**
1	**egg**
¼	**cup tomato sauce**
¾	**cup dry bread crumbs**
½	**teaspoon sage**
	salt and pepper to taste
½	**onion, chopped**
½	**cup catsup**
½	**cup brown sugar, packed**
	orange slices for garnish

Combine all ingredients except catsup and brown sugar, blending thoroughly. Shape into loaf. Combine catsup and brown sugar and spread on meat loaf. Bake at 350 degrees for about 1 hour. Garnish with orange slices.

ADO CACHE COLORADO CACHE COLORADO CACHE COLORADO CACHE COLORADO CACHE COLORADO CACHE COLORADO CACHE COLORADO CACHE COLORADO CACHE COLORADO CACHE COLORADO CACHE

Marinated Venison Roast

8 servings

1 venison roast, 6 to 8 pounds
  salt pork, thinly sliced
2 tablespoons garlic powder
  salt to taste
  freshly ground pepper
2 cups dry red wine
2 bay leaves
5 slices bacon

Make slits about 1 inch deep at regular intervals in the roast. Force slices of pork into each slit. Rub the roast with garlic powder, salt and pepper. Place in heavy duty foil in a roasting pan and pour wine over meat. Add bay leaves to the pan and let marinate in refrigerator 8 to 10 hours, turning occasionally. Arrange bacon over top of meat. Seal the foil. Bake in a 300 degree oven for 2½ to 3 hours. Uncover the last 30 minutes of cooking to brown.

Oven Barbecued Venison

8 servings

1 5-pound venison roast
  salt and pepper
½ cup bacon grease
1 clove garlic, minced
3 cups water
2 cups barbecue sauce
  salt and pepper
1 cup catsup
8 ounces tomato sauce
1 teaspoon sugar
2 medium onions, coarsely
    chopped
1 cup celery, cut in large pieces
2 green peppers, cut in large
    pieces
3 - 4 drops Tabasco sauce
8 hard rolls

Season roast with salt and pepper. Brown on all sides with garlic in bacon grease. Drain off excess grease. Add water, bring to boil and cook covered in 325 degree oven about 3 hours or until done. Remove meat from pan and cut into slices ¼ inch thick. Add remaining ingredients to pan drippings. Mix and cook covered about 1 hour or until sauce is thickened in a 325 degree oven. Add meat slices to sauce and continue to cook about 30 minutes. Serve on split hard rolls.

Elk Sauerkraut Rolls

4   elk or venison steaks
3   slices bacon
1   onion, chopped
2   teaspoons sugar
½   teaspoon pepper
1   teaspoon salt
1   cup sauerkraut
½   cup beef broth

4 servings

Pound meat quite thin and cut into pieces about 3 × 4 inches. Dice bacon and fry. Add onion and cook 5 minutes. Add sugar, salt, pepper and sauerkraut. Heat thoroughly. Place a portion of sauerkraut mixture in center of each piece of meat. Roll and tie securely with thread or fine string. Place rolls in a buttered 8 × 12 × 2 inch casserole and add beef broth. Bake in a moderate oven at 350 degrees for about 1 hour or until tender.

Mexican Elk Steak

2   pounds elk or venison,
        trimmed and cut into
        1 inch cubes
4   tablespoons vegetable oil
2   onions, cut in rings
2   large green peppers,
        cut in strips
1   1-pound 12-ounce can
        tomatoes
1   6-ounce can tomato paste
1   teaspoon chili powder
½   teaspoon paprika
1   10-ounce can enchilada sauce
1   clove garlic, minced
2   bay leaves
1   teaspoon ground cumin
½   teaspoon oregano
1   7-ounce can taco sauce
2   large potatoes, cubed
1   7-ounce can chopped
        green chiles

6 servings

Brown meat in oil. Add onions and green peppers and simmer about 30 minutes. Add remaining ingredients and simmer slowly until meat is tender, about 1½ hours. Watch labels on enchilada sauce and taco sauce. This can be hot!

Note: This is a favorite of hearty eaters served with a green salad and sopaipillas. Fresh pineapple for dessert is refreshing.

ADO CACHE COLORADO CACHE COLORADO CACHE COLORADO CACHE COLORADO CACHE COLORADO CACHE COLORADO CACHE COLORADO CACHE COLORADO CACHE

Venison Swiss Steak

4 servings

2 pounds venison steaks, cut in
   serving pieces
flour
cooking oil
1 package dry onion soup mix
2 bay leaves
2 teaspoons packaged
   spaghetti sauce seasoning
salt and pepper
1 cup Burgundy or other
   dry red wine
1 16-ounce can tomato sauce

Dredge meat in flour. Brown on both sides in oil. Drain off grease. Combine soup mix, seasoning, wine and tomato sauce. Pour over meat. Bring to a boil, reduce heat and simmer covered about 1½ hours or until tender. If sauce gets too thick, add more wine or water.

Note: This works well in the oven at 300 degrees for 2 hours or in a crock pot according to instructions.

Venison Piquant

6 servings

2 pounds venison, cut in
   2 inch cubes
½ cup butter or cooking oil
salt and pepper
flour
¼ teaspoon caraway seeds
1 onion, finely chopped
   juice of ½ lemon
2 cups sour cream
2 bouillon cubes

Season meat with salt and pepper and dredge with flour. Brown in heavy skillet in butter or oil. Add caraway seeds, onion, lemon juice, sour cream and crushed boullion cubes. Cook slowly covered for 1½ hours. It can be cooked in a pressure cooker at 5 pounds pressure for 25 minutes after it has been browned. Serve on seasoned lemon rice or wild rice.

Note: This can be used for Swiss steak.

Venison Steak with Sausage Filling

4 servings

2 venison round steaks,
      pounded
1 pound Mr. Green's sausage
3 green onions, chopped
2 tablespoons chopped parsley
1 egg, lightly beaten
½ pound fresh mushrooms,
      sliced
2 tablespoons raw rice
      pepper to taste
½ - 1 cup Burgundy

Arrange 1 steak in bottom of buttered casserole. Combine sausage, mushrooms, parsley, rice, pepper and egg. Spread ½ of this mixture over steak in casserole. Place second steak on top and spread remaining mixture over this. Add wine. Cover and bake at 300 degrees for 3 hours or until meat is tender.

Venison Chops Polonaise

6 servings

6 venison chops
1 onion, sliced
2 carrots, sliced
4 shallots, chopped
4 sprigs parsley
½ teaspoon thyme
1 teaspoon salt
6 crushed peppercorns
6 juniper berries
½ cup vinegar
¼ cup oil
      red wine
¼ cup butter
1 cup sour cream

Combine meat, vegetables, seasonings, vinegar, oil and enough red wine to cover the chops. Let stand in refrigerator about 24 hours. Drain chops, reserving ½ cup of the marinade. Wipe the meat dry. Cook it 4 minutes on each side in butter. Remove marinade to the skillet and bring to a boil. Stir in sour cream and heat. Adjust seasonings. Serve the sauce separately. Serve with wild rice.

Note: Sauteed mushrooms are excellent with most venison recipes.

Orange Sauce for Game Birds

2½ cups

1 cup sugar
½ cup butter
½ cup frozen orange juice
    concentrate
1 11-ounce can mandarin
    oranges, drained
½ cup lemon juice
    juice and grated rind of 1
    orange
1 tablespoon Galliano or
    Neapolitan liqueur

Bring sugar, butter and orange juice concentrate to a boil. Add other ingredients. Heat and serve.

   Note: So simple and melts in your mouth! This is especially good with duck or dove.

Orange Ginger Relish for Game Birds

1 cup

2 tablespoons mustard
½ teaspoon ground ginger
1 cup orange marmalade

Mix ingredients thoroughly. Will keep indefinitely in a jar in the refrigerator.

Roast Wild Duck Glaze

1½ cups

1 cup apricot preserves
½ cup honey
1 tablespoon brandy
1 tablespoon Cointreau
1 teaspoon freshly grated
    lemon rind

Mix ingredients together. Pour over oven-roasted wild ducks about 15 minutes before they are done according to your specific recipe.

Cream Sauce for Pheasant

pan juices from pheasant
½ **cup minced carrot**
¼ **cup minced onion**
3 **tablespoons flour**
½ **teaspoon thyme**
2½ **cups chicken broth**
3 **tablespoons dry sherry or white wine**
½ **cup heavy cream**
watercress or parsley for garnish

Remove all but 3 tablespoons of pan juices. Heat remaining juices and saute carrot and onion for 5 minutes. Add flour and thyme and stir for 2 minutes. Add chicken broth. Puree this mixture in blender and return to pan. Add sherry and cream and heat just to boiling point. Garnish pheasants with watercress or parsley and serve with sauce.

TELLURIDE FALLS/WHEELER NATIONAL MONUMENT

ADO CACHE COLORADO CACHE COLORADO CACHE COLORADO CACHE COLORADO CACHE COLORADO CACHE COLORADO CACHE COLORADO CACHE COLORADO CACHE

Hints from **Central City**

To reduce an excessively salty taste in stews, soups or casseroles, add several slices of raw potato and cook for about 10 minutes. Remove potato slices before serving.

While browning small pieces of meat, do not allow them to touch. This will retain the meat juices in each piece.

Use clarified butter when browning or frying as it does not burn. If you use regular butter add 1 tablespoon vegetable oil to 2 tablespoons butter to prevent burning.

When coating meat or chicken with flour or breading mix for frying, chill the meat for an hour or two. The coating will adhere better.

Sprinkle a frying pan with salt before adding meat to prevent fat from splattering.

When frying, broiling or charcoal cooking meats, turn only once to insure maximum juiciness.

Never prick meats when cooking. Pricking allows juices to escape.

Oven-cook meats uncovered for maximum juice retention, or cook covered for rich gravy.

Always let roasted meats rest for 15 to 20 minutes for easier carving.

Partially freeze raw meats before slicing thinly.

When making white sauce or gravy, add boiling liquid to prevent lumping or use a cook's best friend, a wire whisk.

To easily remove a garlic clove from stews, spaghetti sauce, etc., spear the garlic with a toothpick before placing in the pot.

For a beautifully browned turkey, make a tent from a grocery bag by cutting out the bottom of the bag. Then cut the sides just long enough to extend an inch below the top or your roasting pan with the turkey in it. The natural fold in the bag makes the top of the tent. No basting is necessary as the turkey bastes itself.

Central City is located in an area known as the richest square mile on earth because of a reputed ½ billion dollars in ore found during the gold rush. It was the site of the first legal execution under Colorado Territorial Government. It currently hosts the Central City Festival in the Opera House and attracts many great guest artists during the brief summer opera and play season.

COLORADO CACHE COLORADO CACHE COLORADO CACHE COLORADO CACHE COLORADO CACHE COLORADO CACHE COLORADO CACHE COLORADO CACHE COLORADO CACHE COLORADO CACHE COLORADO

Chicken Nicoise

6 servings

2 tablespoons olive oil
1 5-pound roasting chicken (or
    2 2½- to 3-pound chickens)
    cut into serving pieces
2 tablespoons butter
12 small white onions, peeled
2 large green peppers, sliced
    into rings
2 cloves garlic, minced
1 pint cherry tomatoes (or 3
    tomatoes, peeled, seeded
    and chopped)
1 tablespoon tomato paste
1 tablespoon minced parsley
½ teaspoon thyme
1 bay leaf
    salt and pepper to taste
¾ cup dry white wine
1 cup strong chicken stock
¾ cup ripe olives, pitted
2 tablespoons minced parsley

Heat olive oil in a large flameproof casserole and brown the chicken on all sides. Remove chicken. Add butter and onions to casserole and brown slowly. Add green peppers and garlic and cook for 1 minute. Add tomatoes and stir until coated with oil. Stir in tomato paste, parsley, thyme, bay leaf, salt, pepper and wine. Simmer for 5 minutes, then add chicken stock. Return chicken to casserole, cover and bake at 350 degrees for 1½ hours or until tender, basting several times with the pan liquids. Remove chicken to a heated platter. Reduce cooking liquids over high heat for 5 minutes. Skim grease. Stir in the olives. Pour sauce and vegetables over the chicken. Sprinkle with parsley.

Note: This is especially good served with saffron rice.

Chicken Alfredo

4 servings

¼ cup vegetable oil
¼ cup lemon juice
¼ cup freshly grated Parmesan
    cheese
1 teaspoon oregano
4 teaspoons salt
1 teaspoon pepper
2 chicken broiler-fryers, halved
1 cup flour
4 teaspoons paprika
2 teaspoons salt
½ teaspoon pepper
2 teaspoons freshly grated
    Parmesan cheese
½ cup butter

Combine oil, lemon juice, Parmesan cheese, oregano, 2 teaspoons salt and 1 teaspoon pepper. Beat well. Pour over chicken halves, cover and refrigerate for 2 hours or longer. Combine remaining ingredients except butter. Remove chicken from marinade and roll in the flour mixture. Saute chicken in butter until browned on both sides. Place each chicken half, skin side up, in center of a double thick square of heavy duty aluminum foil. Bring up sides and ends and seal with tight double folds. Place packets on a baking sheet and bake at 425 degrees for 1 hour.

Coq au Vin

4 servings

4	strips bacon, cut into small pieces
2	tablespoons chopped onion
1	broiler-fryer chicken, cut in serving pieces
8	small, whole onions
½	cup coarsely chopped carrots
1	clove garlic, minced
2	tablespoons Cognac
1	pound fresh mushrooms, sliced
2	tablespoons butter
4	sprigs parsley
1	medium bay leaf
¼	teaspoon dried thyme leaves
3	sprigs celery leaves
2	cups Burgundy

In a skillet, brown bacon pieces and chopped onion; remove. Add chicken pieces and brown slowly in bacon grease; remove. To same skillet add onions, carrots, garlic and Cognac and cook until tender, about 3 minutes. Remove vegetables from skillet and pour off grease. Saute mushrooms in 2 tablespoons butter. Make a bouquet garni by placing the parsley, bay leaf, thyme and celery leaves in a tea ball or cheesecloth. Place in a 2 quart casserole. Arrange the chicken pieces, vegetables, onions, bacon and sliced mushrooms in layers. Add Burgundy to the browning skillet. Heat to boiling and stir to loosen the crusty brown pieces. Pour mixture over casserole. Cover and bake in 350 degree oven for 2½ hours. Remove the bouquet garni from casserole before serving.

Twelve-Boy Curry

6 servings

6	tablespoons butter
1	cup minced onion
1	cup chopped celery
4-5	cloves garlic, minced
½	cup flour
1-2	tablespoons curry powder, or to taste
1	teaspoon dry mustard
½	teaspoon salt
¼	teaspoon pepper
1	teaspoon paprika
	dash of cayenne pepper
1¼	cups strong beef stock
1	cup light cream
3	tablespoons catsup
1	3-pound chicken, stewed, meat cut into bite-size pieces

Melt butter in a large skillet. Add onion, celery and garlic and cook over medium heat until onion is limp. Combine all of the dry ingredients and add to the onion mixture, stirring over low heat until blended. Slowly add beef stock and cream and stir until smooth. Add catsup. Cook for 2 minutes then add chicken and heat to boiling point. Let stand 1 hour then reheat. Serve over hot buttered rice with any, or better yet, all of the condiments.

Note: This curry is best if made a day ahead and reheated.

Condiments:
> chopped hard cooked eggs
> chopped onion
> shredded coconut
> chopped salted peanuts
> sweet pickle relish
> chutney
> chopped green pepper
> chopped green or ripe olives
> orange marmalade
> chopped, cooked crisp bacon
> raisins
> crushed pineapple

Chicken Cacciatore

8 servings

2	broiler-fryer chickens, cut into serving pieces
½	cup flour
1	teaspoon salt
¼	cup butter
¼	cup olive oil
2	medium onions, sliced
1	green pepper, sliced
1	pound mushrooms, sliced
2	small cloves garlic, minced
1	1-pound, 12-ounce can Italian plum tomatoes, drained and chopped (reserve juice)
2	chicken bouillon cubes
2	tablespoons chopped, fresh parsley
1½	teaspoons salt
¼	teaspoon pepper
½	teaspoon oregano
½	teaspoon marjoram
½	teaspoon thyme
½	cup dry white wine
½	cup sliced ripe olives
	Parmesan cheese

Dredge chicken pieces in salt and flour. Brown chicken in mixture of oil and butter. Remove to a casserole. Saute onion, garlic, green pepper and mushrooms. Stir in tomatoes, bouillon cubes, parsley, seasonings, white wine and ½ cup reserved juice. Cook a few minutes to blend. Add to chicken in casserole. Cover and bake at 350 degrees for 45 minutes, or until chicken is almost tender. Uncover, add olives and bake 15 to 20 minutes longer. Remove chicken and vegetables to a warm platter. Rapidly boil liquid until slightly reduced and thickened. Pour over chicken. Sprinkle with Parmesan cheese. Serve with spaghetti.

ADO CACHE COLORADO CACHE COLORADO CACHE COLORADO CACHE COLORADO CACHE COLORADO CACHE COLORADO CACHE COLORADO CACHE COLORADO CACHE COLORADO CACHE

Country Captain

6-8 servings

1	**tablespoon butter**
1	**medium onion, chopped**
1	**large green pepper, chopped**
1	**stalk celery, chopped**
2 - 3	**cloves garlic, minced**
½	**pound fresh mushrooms, sliced**
2	**1-pound cans tomatoes**
1	**teaspoon salt**
1	**teaspoon white pepper**
½	**teaspoon curry powder, or to taste**
1	**teaspoon thyme**
1	**tablespoon minced parsley**
1	**4 to 5 pound chicken, stewed, meat removed from bones and chopped**
1	**1-pound can tiny peas cooked rice, brown or white slivered almonds currants or raisins**

Melt butter in large pan. Add onion, green pepper and celery and saute until soft. Add garlic and mushrooms and cook 5 minutes. Add tomatoes and seasonings, including parsley. Simmer 10 minutes. Add chicken and simmer 20 minutes. At this point you may remove pan from heat, refrigerate and reheat just before serving. Add peas and some of their liquid if the mixture seems too thick. It should be stew-like. Surround with rice on a platter and sprinkle with almonds and currants or raisins.

Chicken "Divine"

4-6 servings

3	**whole chicken breasts**
	rosemary to taste
	salt to taste
	pepper to taste
1	**slice onion**
1	**pound fresh or frozen broccoli**
¾	**cup raw rice, cooked**

Sprinkle chicken with rosemary, salt and pepper. Bake chicken at 350 degrees for 1 hour. Cool. Skin, bone and slice. Cook broccoli in water with salt and onion. Drain. Layer chicken, then broccoli, then rice in buttered casserole. Pour cheese sauce over entire dish. Add more grated Parmesan on top if desired. Bake uncovered at 350 degrees for 30 minutes or until bubbly.

Cheese Sauce:

¼ cup butter
¼ cup flour
2 cups milk
½ teaspoon salt
⅛ teaspoon pepper
1 cup grated, sharp
   Cheddar cheese
½ cup freshly grated
   Parmesan cheese

Melt butter, add flour and stir until smooth. Cook 2 minutes. Gradually add milk, stirring constantly until thickened. Add cheeses and seasonings.

Almond Chicken

4 servings

3 chicken breasts, skinned,
   boned and thinly sliced
3 tablespoons peanut oil
2 5-ounce cans bamboo shoots,
   drained and diced
2 cups celery, sliced diagonally
2 5-ounce cans water chestnuts,
   drained and sliced
½ cup slivered blanched
   almonds
2 tablespoons soy sauce
3 cups chicken broth
3 tablespoons cornstarch
½ cup water

Heat oil in wok over high heat. Add chicken and stir-fry until browned. Add bamboo shoots, celery, water chestnuts, almonds, soy sauce and chicken broth. Cover and cook gently for 5 minutes. Blend together cornstarch and water. Add to chicken mixture and cook, stirring, until thickened. Serve with rice.

Chicken Spaghetti

12-15 servings

1	**5-pound chicken, stewed**
1	**pound bacon, diced**
2	**large onions, thinly sliced**
2	**pounds tomatoes**
½	**pound fresh mushrooms, sliced**
1	**cup stuffed olives, sliced**
1	**pound spaghetti, cooked**
4	**cups grated Cheddar cheese**

Remove meat from the stewed chicken, cut into bite-sized pieces and set aside. Fry bacon in a large skillet until brown. Remove bacon from pan and all but 2 tablespoons grease. Brown onions in the grease, then add bacon, tomatoes, mushrooms and olives. Bring to a boil and simmer for 5 minutes. Add chicken to the skillet and simmer about 10 minutes. Butter a large casserole and layer the spaghetti, chicken mixture and cheese. The casserole may be put in the refrigerator overnight. Bake uncovered at 350 degrees for 1 hour, or until thoroughly heated and bubbling.

Note: Great for potluck dinner. Children love it!

Stir-Fry Chicken and Broccoli

4 servings

2	**chicken breasts, skinned, boned and thinly sliced**
3	**tablespoons cornstarch**
4	**tablespoons soy sauce**
2	**tablespoons peanut oil**
½	**pound broccoli, broken into small pieces**
1	**medium onion, sliced or chopped**
¼	**pound mushrooms, sliced**
2	**cups fresh bean sprouts**
1	**cup chicken broth**

Place chicken, cornstarch and soy sauce in a bowl and stir until chicken is thoroughly coated. Let stand 15 minutes. Heat oil in wok over high heat. Add chicken and stir-fry until browned. Remove chicken from wok. Add broccoli and onion to wok and stir-fry 2 minutes. Add mushrooms and bean sprouts. Return chicken to pan. Stir in chicken broth. Cover and cook gently for 5 minutes or until vegetables are crisp-tender. Serve with rice.

Note: Make plenty. The left-overs are great.

COLORADO CACHE COLORADO CACHE COLORADO CACHE COLORADO CACHE COLORADO CACHE COLORADO CACHE COLORADO CACHE COLORADO CACHE COLORADO

Chicken Puffs with Sausage

8 servings

9 frozen patty shells
8 chicken thighs
   salt and pepper to taste
¼ cup butter
½ cup chicken broth
½ pound fresh mushrooms, minced
¼ cup flour
1 teaspoon salt
¼ teaspoon pepper
1 cup light cream
½ cup white wine
8 pork sausage links, cooked
1 egg yolk
2 tablespoons light cream

Place package of patty shells in refrigerator for at least 8 hours to defrost. Season chicken thighs with salt and pepper to taste. Brown well in butter in a large skillet over medium heat. Add broth, cover and simmer for 30 minutes or until tender. Remove chicken from pan and cool. Add mushrooms to pan and simmer for 3 minutes. Blend flour, salt and pepper into mushroom mixture. Add 1 cup light cream and wine and stir over medium heat until thickened. Cool. Remove bones, skin and cartilage from chicken, leaving meat in whole piece. Place a sausage in each thigh. Roll each patty shell on a lightly floured pastry cloth into a 6 inch square. Place about 2 tablespoons of mushroom mixture in center of each pastry square and top with a stuffed chicken thigh. Fold pastry over chicken and place seam side down on a greased baking sheet. At this point the packets can be refrigerated for several hours. Brush each packet with egg yolk mixed with cream and decorate with tiny pieces of pastry cut from remaining patty shell. Brush again with yolk mixture and bake at 400 degrees for 30 minutes or until golden. Serve with Sauce Madere.

Chicken Durango

4-6 servings

½ cup butter, melted
   juice of 2 lemons
1 teaspoon garlic salt
1 tablespoon paprika
1 tablespoon oregano
   salt and pepper to taste
4 chicken breasts, split
   (or 1 frying chicken cut in serving pieces)

Mix together all ingredients except chicken. Marinate chicken in sauce for 3 to 4 hours. Place chicken in baking dish, skin side up, and bake uncovered at 325 degrees for 45 minutes or until done.

Chicken in Sour Cream

4-6 servings

2 **cups sour cream**
¼ **cup fresh lemon juice**
4 **teaspoons Worcestershire**
   sauce
2 **teaspoons celery salt**
2 **teaspoons paprika**
1 **clove garlic, pressed**
2 **teaspoons pepper**
3 **chicken breasts, split**
   and skinned
¾ **cup bread crumbs**
½ **cup butter, melted**

Combine sour cream, lemon juice, Worcestershire sauce, celery salt, paprika, garlic and pepper in a large, deep bowl. Add chicken pieces and coat well. Allow to marinate in the sour cream mixture overnight in the refrigerator, covered. When ready to cook, remove pieces of chicken from the sauce and roll in the crumbs. Arrange in a large baking dish and sprinkle with butter. Bake uncovered at 350 degrees for 45 minutes or until done.

Note: Excellent cold for picnics.

Chicken Dijon

4 servings

3 **tablespoons butter**
4 **chicken breasts, split,**
   skinned and boned
2 **tablespoons flour**
1 **cup chicken broth**
½ **cup light cream**
2 **tablespoons Dijon mustard**
2 **tomatoes, cut in wedges**
2 **tablespoons minced**
   fresh parsley

Melt butter in a large skillet. Add chicken breasts and cook until done and lightly browned, about 20 minutes. Remove chicken to a warm serving platter. Stir flour into drippings in the skillet and cook for 1 minute. Add the chicken broth and light cream. Stir and cook until the sauce thickens and bubbles. Stir in the mustard. Return the chicken to the skillet, cover and heat for 10 minutes. Garnish with tomatoes and sprinkle with parsley.

COLORADO CACHE COLORADO CACHE COLORADO CACHE COLORADO CACHE COLORADO CACHE COLORADO CACHE COLORADO CACHE COLORADO CACHE COLORADO (

Fruit Stuffed Chicken Breasts

6 servings

- ¾ **cup butter or margarine**
- 1 **cup diced apple**
- ½ **cup coarsely chopped nuts**
- ½ **cup white raisins**
- 1 **1¼-pound can crushed pineapple**
- 1 **cup soft bread crumbs, toasted**
- 1 **teaspoon salt**
- 1 **teaspoon ground cinnamon**
- ½ **teaspoon ground nutmeg**
- ¼ **teaspoon ground ginger**
- ¼ **teaspoon ground cloves**
- 6 **whole chicken breasts, boned fruit sauce**

Melt ½ cup butter in skillet. Add apple and nuts and cook 10 minutes. Remove from heat. Add raisins, ½ cup drained pineapple (save remaining pineapple and syrup for sauce), bread crumbs, ½ teaspoon salt, cinnamon, nutmeg, ginger and cloves and mix well. Sprinkle insides of chicken breasts with remaining salt. Place ⅓ cup stuffing on inside of each breast. Fold over sides and fasten with skewers or string. Place remaining ¼ cup butter in foil-lined 9 × 13 inch baking pan. Place pan in oven at 350 degrees until butter melts, about 5 minutes. Place breasts, skin side down in melted butter. Return to oven and bake 25 minutes. Turn chicken and bake 20 minutes more. Serve with fruit sauce.

Fruit Sauce:

- 1 **tablespoon sugar**
- 1 **tablespoon cornstarch**
- ⅛ **teaspoon salt**
- ½ **teaspoon ground cinnamon**
- ¼ **teaspoon ground nutmeg**
- ⅛ **teaspoon ground ginger**
- 1 **cup orange juice**
  crushed pineapple and syrup
- ¼ **cup white raisins**
- 1 **tablespoon butter or margarine**
  slivered peel from one orange
  sections from one orange

Combine sugar, cornstarch, salt, cinnamon, nutmeg and ginger and blend well. Mix in orange juice. Add pineapple and syrup left from stuffing, raisins, butter and orange peel and mix. Cook and stir over medium heat until sauce comes to a boil and thickens. Add orange sections and heat.

Chicken Boursin

2-3 servings

1 **5-ounce package garlic and herb flavored Boursin cheese**
2 **chicken breasts, split, skinned and boned**
   lemon or lime juice
   salt and pepper to taste
1 **egg, well beaten**
   flour
   dry bread crumbs
½ **cup butter**
¼ **cup oil**

Two hours, or up to 2 days before serving, quarter the package of cheese and roll each quarter into a finger ½ inch thick. Wrap each finger in plastic wrap and chill well. Flatten chicken between 2 sheets of waxed paper and pound until 1/8 inch thick. Sprinkle lightly with juice, salt and pepper. Place cheese fingers lengthwise on long sides of breasts. Roll chicken around cheese to enclose it and secure with toothpicks. Dust chicken rolls with flour, dip in egg and roll in bread crumbs. Chill 1 hour or longer. In a heavy skillet just large enough to hold chicken in 1 layer, saute the rolls in butter and oil over medium high heat for 10 minutes per side. Drain on paper towels and serve immediately.

Blackhawk Chicken

8 servings

8   **chicken breasts, split, skinned and boned**
16 **slices Gruyere or Emmenthaler cheese, each 1 × 2½ × ¼ thick**
16 **slices prosciutto or Virginia ham**
    seasoned flour
3   **eggs, beaten**
3   **cups bread crumbs**
½   **cup butter**
6   **tablespoons Cognac**
1   **cup heavy cream**

Wrap each slice of Gruyere in a slice of prosciutto. Put boned breasts between 2 pieces of waxed paper and pound them with the flat side of a cleaver or heavy knife. Wrap each chicken breast piece securely around a ham packet, covering it completely. Dust with seasoned flour then dip in beaten egg and roll in fine bread crumbs. Refrigerate at least 1 hour. Brown breasts carefully on both sides in butter, then arrange on a heat-proof platter and finish cooking in oven at 350 degrees for 10 minutes or until fork tender. Do not allow them to dry out. Into the pan in which they were browned, pour Cognac, ignite, and when the flame dies down, add cream. Simmer until thickened. Add salt and pepper to taste. Pour sauce over chicken just before serving.

Chicken Rochambeau

8 servings

2 tablespoons fat
1 onion, finely chopped
2 tablespoons flour
2 cups brown sauce or canned
   beef gravy
3 tablespoons tomato puree
   salt and pepper to taste
2 shallots, minced
½ cup dry red wine
½ teaspoon chopped
   fresh parsley
4 chicken breasts, split,
   skinned and boned
   flour
⅓ cup vegetable oil
8 slices cooked ham
8 slices bread, crusts trimmed,
   brushed with butter and
   baked in a slow oven
   until crisp
1 cup Bearnaise sauce
   (see index)
   fresh parsley for garnish

Heat fat in skillet, add onion and saute until lightly browned. Blend in flour and cook until brown. Add brown sauce and tomato puree and cook, stirring, until sauce thickens and is reduced to about 1 cup. Season with salt and pepper. In a saucepan combine shallots, parsley and red wine and cook over high heat until the mixture is reduced to 1/8 cup. Blend together the onion and wine mixtures, stir in the parsley and set aside. Sprinkle chicken breasts with salt and pepper and dust with flour. Brown chicken in oil over medium heat. Transfer to a baking dish and bake uncovered at 250 degrees for 20 to 30 minutes or until tender. Just before serving, place 1 slice of ham on each slice of toast. Spread 2 tablespoons sauce over each ham slice. Place a chicken breast on top, cover with more sauce and finish with 2 tablespoons of Bearnaise sauce on each. Garnish with parsley.

Chicken Livers in Sour Cream

3-4 servings

½ cup butter
⅓ pound fresh mushrooms, sliced
1 large onion, sliced or chopped
1 pound chicken livers
   salt and pepper to taste
⅓ cup dry sherry
1 cup sour cream

Melt butter in skillet. Add mushrooms and onion and saute until onion is limp. Add chicken livers and saute for 1 minute. Cover and cook slowly for 15 minutes. Stir in sherry and sour cream and heat, but do not boil. Serve over rice or patty shells.

Dodine de Poulet (Veal Stuffed Boned Chicken)

6-8 servings

1 - 5 **pound roasting chicken**
1 **pound lean ground veal**
1 **egg, beaten**
3 **tablespoons chopped chives**
3 **tablespoons minced parsley**
3 **carrots, cooked and coarsely chopped**
1 **teaspoon tarragon**
1 **large clove garlic, minced**
1 **teaspoon salt**
1 **teaspoon pepper**
4 **tablespoons butter, softened pan sauce**

Bone the chicken, leaving the skin intact (or have the butcher do this for you). Place boned chicken, skin side down, on a piece of waxed paper. If the meat is not evenly distributed on the skin, do it yourself by cutting away pieces of meat and placing them on the bare spots. With the side of a heavy plate pound the chicken to a uniform thickness. Cover and refrigerate while making stuffing. In a large bowl combine the veal, egg, chives, parsley, carrots, tarragon, garlic, salt and pepper. Mix together lightly but thoroughly. Test for seasonings by frying a small amount of the stuffing and tasting. Correct the seasonings. Spoon the veal mixture onto the boned chicken, forming it into a cylinder, then pull the skin up around the stuffing so that it meets down the center. Sew the skin together with a needle and dark colored button thread. Place the stuffed chicken roll, seam side down, in a shallow roasting pan and coat the skin with softened butter. At this point the roll may be refrigerated for several hours. Remove from refrigerator and allow to come to room temperature. Roast in an oven preheated to 375 degrees for 1 hour and 15 minutes, basting every 15 minutes with the pan juices. Increase heat to 425 degrees and roast an additional 10 minutes, or until evenly brown. Remove from oven, remove thread and slice. Serve on a platter garnished with bunches of parsley or nasturtium blossoms. Serve with pan sauce.

Pan Sauce:

    pan drippings
1 **cup chopped mushrooms**
1 **tablespoon minced onion**
4 **tablespoons flour**
1½ **cups chicken stock**
½ **cup dry white wine**
1 **tablespoon minced fresh parsley**

Remove all but 4 tablespoons of grease from the pan drippings and place the roasting pan on the stove over low heat. Add mushrooms and onion to the pan and saute for 2 minutes. Blend in flour and cook, stirring, over medium heat for 3 minutes. Gradually stir in chicken stock and wine and cook until thickened. Season with salt and pepper, stir in parsley and serve.

    Note: This is beautiful when sliced. A spectacular presentation!

Glazed Cornish Game Hens

4 servings

wild rice stuffing
(see index)
4 **Cornish game hens**
2 **tablespoons butter, softened**
currant sauce

Prepare wild rice stuffing. Stuff game hens. Rub skin with softened butter. Bake at 350 degrees for ½ hour, then baste every 15 minutes with currant sauce until hens have baked for 1½ hours.

Currant Sauce:

1 **tablespoon butter**
½ **cup currant jelly**
2 **tablespoons fresh lemon juice**
¼ **cup cider vinegar**
1 **tablespoon cornstarch**
1 **teaspoon salt**
3 **whole cloves**

Melt butter and add jelly and lemon juice. After jelly has melted, add vinegar, cornstarch, salt and cloves. Cook until thickened.

Turkey and Wild Rice Casserole

4-6 servings

1 **cup wild rice, washed**
water
6 **tablespoons butter**
1 **pound fresh mushrooms, sliced**
½ **cup chopped onion**
2 **teaspoons salt**
¼ **teaspoon freshly ground**
pepper
3 **cups cooked turkey, cut into**
small pieces
½ **cup sliced almonds**
3 **cups turkey or chicken broth**
1½ **cups heavy cream**
2 **tablespoons dry sherry or**
white wine or 1 tablespoon
fresh lemon juice

Cover rice with water in a saucepan and bring to a boil. Remove from heat. Let soak 1 hour, then drain. Melt 3 tablespoons of butter in a skillet. Add mushrooms and onion and saute over medium heat until lightly browned. In a large bowl combine rice, mushroom mixture and all remaining ingredients except butter. Turn into a buttered 2 quart casserole. Cover and bake at 350 degrees for 1¼ hours. Remove the cover, dot with remaining butter and bake uncovered an additional 20 minutes.

Note: This makes leftover turkey as good as the first time around.

Colorado Casserole

4 servings

8 ounces brown and serve
    sausage links
2 tablespoons flour
2 cups cooked, cubed chicken
4 large tomatoes, peeled and
    chopped
1 cup strong chicken broth
½ cup sliced green onions
¼ teaspoon savory
¼ teaspoon thyme
¼ teaspoon Tabasco sauce
1 pound fresh asparagus
½ cup slivered almonds

Cut sausages into quarters and fry in skillet until golden brown. Add flour and cook a few minutes more. Combine with chicken, tomatoes, broth, onions and seasonings in a buttered 2 quart baking dish. Trim asparagus and drop into boiling salted water and boil until crisp-tender, from 3 to 10 minutes, depending on size. Drain and arrange in a row on top of casserole. Sprinkle almonds in a row along center. Bake covered at 375 degrees for 35 minutes, or until hot and bubbly.

Sugar Steak Sebastian

6-8 servings

1 sirloin steak, 2½ to 4 inches
    thick
1 pound superfine sugar
¼ cup brown sugar, packed

Bring the steak to room temperature. Completely cover the steak on all sides with the sugars, working it into the meat with the fingers. Broil over a hot charcoal fire for 15 minutes per side. Remove from fire and place in a preheated 350 degree oven on a baking sheet for 10 minutes per inch of thickness.

    Note: Don't call the fire department! The sugar burns off and produces a juicy, medium rare steak.

COLORADO CACHE COLORADO CACHE COLORADO CACHE COLORADO CACHE COLORADO CACHE COLORADO CACHE COLORADO CACHE COLORADO CACHE COLORADO (

Salt-Broiled Steak

4 servings

1 **sirloin steak, 2 to 3 inches thick, trimmed**
   freshly ground pepper
1 **clove garlic, minced**
2 **tablespoons brandy**
4 **cups coarse salt**
   water
½ **cup butter, melted**
2 **tablespoons fresh lemon juice**
1 **tablespoon minced fresh parsley**
   French bread slices

Sprinkle both sides of steak with pepper, garlic and brandy. Set aside for 15 minutes. Moisten salt with enough water to make it pack together. Place steak on a hinged broiling rack and pack down half of the salt on top of the steak. Cover with a single paper towel (which will burn off), close rack, turn over, open and prepare the second side in the same manner. Grill over hot charcoal for 15 minutes per side for rare. Brush salt off the steak. Slice on a platter. Add butter, lemon juice and parsley to the meat juices in the platter and spoon over meat. Serve over French bread slices.

Sauteed Steak with Green Peppercorns

4 servings

2-2½ **pounds steak, ¾ to 1 inch thick**
   green peppercorns
2 **tablespoons butter**
2 **tablespoons oil**
   salt and pepper to taste
½ **cup beef stock, red wine, dry white wine or vermouth**
2 - 3 **tablespoons softened butter**

Press peppercorns onto both sides of meat. Let sit one hour. Put butter and oil into heavy skillet over medium-high heat until the butter foam begins to subside. With grease very hot but not burning, saute the steak on each side for 3 to 4 minutes. The steak will be medium-rare when a bit of red juice begins to ooze at the surface of the steak. Remove steak to a hot platter and season to taste with salt and pepper. Keep warm while completing the sauce. Pour grease out of skillet. Add the liquid and set skillet over high heat. Scrape up juices with wooden spoon while rapidly boiling down the liquid until it is reduced almost to a syrup. Remove from heat and swirl the softened butter into the liquid until it is absorbed. The butter will thicken the liquid into a light sauce. Pour sauce over steak and serve.

Note: A subtle version of a pepper steak.

RADO CACHE COLORADO CACHE COLORADO CACHE COLORADO CACHE COLORADO CACHE COLORADO CACHE COLORADO CACHE COLORADO CACHE COLORADO CACHE

Steak Hong Kong

4 servings

4 6 to 8 ounce rib eye steaks,
      cut ½ inch thick
      pepper to taste
6 tablespoons brandy
1 tablespoon soy sauce
1 teaspoon Worcestershire sauce
1½ teaspoons Dijon mustard
1 tablespoon steak sauce
1 tablespoon chili sauce
1 teaspoon beef stock base
½ cup water
      salt and pepper to taste
2 tablespoons butter

Sprinkle steaks with pepper and 2 tablespoons brandy and set aside for 15 minutes. Grill the steaks in a greased skillet over high heat for 3 minutes per side for rare. Remove from pan and keep warm. Pour remaining brandy into the skillet and ignite. When flames die down, stir in all remaining ingredients except butter. Stir over high heat until reduced and thickened. Swirl in butter. Return steaks to skillet and baste with sauce.

Tournedos Charlemagne

4 servings

2 tablespoons butter
4 large shallots, minced
¾ pound fresh mushrooms,
      minced
      salt and pepper to taste
1 teaspoon tomato paste
1 tablespoon oil
4 tournedos, cut 1¼ inches thick
1 cup Bearnaise sauce
      (see index)

Melt butter in skillet. Add shallots and mushrooms and saute over high heat until most of the moisture has evaporated. Season with salt and pepper. Remove from heat and stir in tomato paste. Set aside. Heat oil in a large skillet. Add tournedos to pan and cook over high heat for 3 minutes per side for rare. Place tournedos on a heated serving platter. Divide mushroom mixture and place on top of each tournedo. Cover each with Bearnaise sauce.

Note: Serve with roasted or sauteed potatoes and watercress.

...let and in it sear the filets over high heat ...e. Season with salt and pepper and set ...skillet saute the mushrooms, ham and ...oons of butter for about 5 minutes. Add ...rry. Cook and stir a few more minutes to ...Set aside. Brush 1 sheet filo dough with ...other sheet on top. Repeat this 3 more ...ck of filo, place 2 tablespoons of mush-...center and top with 1 filet. Wrap the filo ...d place seam side down on a greased ...h with melted butter and bake at 450 ...tes or until lightly browned. Meat will be

...m meat with broth, Madeira and Bovril. ...ce heat, add lemon juice and let simmer ...ing occasionally. Remove skillet from ...tter. Spoon 2 tablespoons of sauce over ...e. Pour remaining sauce in a sauce boat. ...essive variation of beef Wellington.

½ **cup soy sauce**
¼ **cup or more dry red wine**
3 **tablespoons vegetable oil**
2 **tablespoons Worcestershire
    sauce**
1 **large clove garlic, sliced
    pepper to taste
    chopped green onion
      or chives (optional)
    chopped dill weed (optional)
    celery seed (optional)**
1 **1½ pound flank steak,
    trimmed**

...s in the pan in which meat is to be marinated. Marinate flank steak, turning occasionally, for 2 to 12 hours in the refrigerator. Broil meat over hot coals for 5 minutes per side for rare meat. Slice meat on the diagonal across the grain and serve.

French Steak

4 servings

2   **pounds round steak**
    flour
    salt and pepper to taste
2   **tablespoons butter**
2   **large onions, thinly sliced**
1   **clove garlic, minced**
1   **cup white wine**
1   **tablespoon olive oil**
1   **cup beef broth**
1   **teaspoon Worcestershire sauce**
1   **teaspoon soy sauce**
⅛   **teaspoon pepper**
1   **cup grated Cheddar cheese**
½   **cup sour cream or yogurt**

Cut steak into serving pieces. Dredge steak with flour seasoned with salt and pepper. Brown on both sides in butter and oil in a heavy pan. Remove steak from pan, add onions to the pan and saute until golden. Stir in garlic, wine, broth, Worcestershire sauce, soy sauce and pepper, being careful to stir up all the browned bits from the bottom of the pan. Return steak to pan, cover and simmer slowly for 1½ hours or until meat is very tender. Remove meat to a platter and keep warm. Stir the cheese into the onions and pan juices until melted, then stir in sour cream and heat but do not boil. Pour the sauce over the meat and serve.

Miner's Steak

4 servings

1½   **pounds round steak,**
      cut into strips
¼   **cup flour**
1   **teaspoon salt**
¼   **teaspoon pepper**
1   **large onion, sliced**
1   **tablespoon molasses**
3   **tablespoons soy sauce**
1   **cup beef broth**
1   **1-pound can tomatoes,**
      or tomato puree
1   **green pepper, sliced**
¼   **pound fresh mushrooms, sliced**

Dredge steak strips in a mixture of flour, salt and pepper. Put into Dutch oven and add all remaining ingredients. Bake covered at 325 degrees for 2½ to 3 hours.
    Note: Serve with noodles or rice.

COLORADO CACHE COLORADO CACHE COLORADO CACHE COLORADO CACHE COLORADO CACHE COLORADO CACHE COLORADO CACHE COLORADO CACHE COLORADO CACHE COLORADO

Braised Short Ribs

4-6 servings

6   **pounds beef short ribs,
     cut into serving pieces
     and trimmed**
1   **large onion, coarsely chopped**
⅓   **cup dry red wine**
2   **teaspoons horseradish**
1   **teaspoon paprika**
¼   **teaspoon pepper**
2   **tablespoons fresh lemon juice**
1   **10½-ounce can consomme**
1   **cup water**
¼   **cup flour**
1   **teaspoon sugar**
2   **teaspoons dill weed**
½   **cup water**

Lightly butter a large Dutch oven. Brown meat on all sides over medium heat. Remove meat from pan and pour off grease. Add onion to pan and saute until limp. Add wine, horseradish, paprika, pepper, lemon juice, consomme and water. Return meat to pan, cover and bake at 325 degrees for 2½ to 3 hours or until tender. Remove meat from pan. Trim away any remaining visible fat and discard the bones which should be loose and easily removed. Remove all grease from liquid in pan. Measure liquid and add water to make 2½ cups. Pour back into pan. In a bowl combine flour and ½ cup water and mix until smooth. Stir into pan liquid with sugar and dill weed. Bring mixture to a boil, stirring. Return meat to pan, cover and bake an additional 30 minutes.

Roast Beef Perfection

1 roast

1   **standing rib roast, any size**

Start at 3:00 p.m. Preheat oven to 375 degrees. Place roast in oven and cook 1 hour. Turn oven off. Keep the oven door closed! 45 minutes before serving, turn the oven to 300 degrees. The temperatures given are for sea level cooking. For high altitude cooking, add 25 degrees to each temperature.

    Note: Cooked this way, the roast beef will be a juicy medium-rare and perfect every time.

Spicy Pot Roast

6-8 servings

2 tablespoons olive oil
1 4 to 5 pound pot roast
1 cup tomato sauce
1 cup dry red wine
2 pieces orange peel,
      orange part only, each
      about 1 × 2 inches
5 whole cloves
2 cinnamon sticks
1 clove garlic, minced
12 small white onions, peeled
¼ teaspoon sugar

Heat olive oil in a large Dutch oven, add pot roast and brown on all sides. Add tomato sauce, ½ cup of wine, orange peel, cloves, cinnamon and garlic. Cover and bake at 300 degrees for 3 hours. Add remaining ingredients, cover and cook 1 hour longer, or until meat is tender. Remove meat to a warm platter and let stand for 15 minutes before slicing. Skim grease from pan juices and serve as sauce over meat slices.

Pot Roast Breckenridge

4-6 servings

1 3-pound bottom round
      beef roast
¼ cup butter
3 carrots, chopped
4 stalks celery, chopped
½ cup chopped onion
1 clove garlic, minced
¼ pound mushrooms, chopped
1 10½-ounce can consomme
½ cup dry red wine
2 teaspoons salt
⅛ teaspoon pepper
½ teaspoon paprika
1 tablespoon capers
¼ cup flour (optional)
1 cup sour cream

Brown roast in butter in a large Dutch oven. Add carrots, celery, onion and garlic to pan and cook until onion is limp. Add mushrooms. Combine half of the consomme with the wine, salt, pepper, paprika and capers. Add to beef. Cover and bake at 350 degrees for 2 hours, or until meat is tender. Remove meat to a heated platter. With a slotted spoon remove most of the vegetables from the pan liquids and puree them in a food processor or blender. Return the puree to the pan. Combine flour, if desired, with remaining consomme and stir into pan liquids. (If not using flour, just add consomme.) Cook until sauce boils and thickens. Stir in sour cream and heat but do not boil. Serve the sauce over the sliced meat.

Rocky Mountain Brisket with Barbecue Sauce

6 servings

1½   **teaspoons salt**
1½   **teaspoons pepper**
2   **tablespoons chili powder**
1   **teaspoon crushed bay leaves**
2   **tablespoons Liquid Smoke**
4   **pounds beef brisket**

Combine salt, pepper, chili powder and bay leaves. Rub meat completely with Liquid Smoke. Place meat, fat side up, in a large roasting pan. Sprinkle dry seasoning mixture on top. Cover tightly. Bake for 4 hours at 325 degrees. Scrape seasoning off meat and cut in very thin slices across the grain. Serve with barbecue sauce.

Barbecue Sauce:

3   **tablespoons brown sugar**
1   **14-ounce bottle catsup**
½   **cup water**
2   **tablespoons Liquid Smoke**
    salt and pepper to taste
4   **tablespoons Worcestershire sauce**
3   **teaspoons dry mustard**
2   **teaspoons celery seed**
6   **tablespoons butter**
¼   **teaspoon cayenne pepper**

Combine all ingredients. Bring to a boil, stirring occasionally. Cook for 10 minutes. Serve with sliced brisket.
    Note: Good by itself or on onion rolls.

Glazed Corned Beef

4-6 servings

1   **3 to 4 pound corned beef**
    water
4   **bay leaves**
4   **small, hot, whole red chiles**
3   **pieces stick cinnamon, broken up**
12   **peppercorns**
3   **cloves garlic, cut in half**
1   **large onion, sliced**
½   **cup brown sugar, packed**
½   **teaspoon ground cloves**
½   **teaspoon ground ginger**
½   **teaspoon dry mustard**
¼   **teaspoon celery salt**
¼   **teaspoon cracked caraway seed**

Place corned beef in a large pot and cover with water. Add bay leaves, chiles, cinnamon, peppercorns, garlic and onion. Bring to a boil, cover, lower heat and simmer slowly for 4 to 4½ hours or until meat is tender. Drain, then blot dry. Blend together all remaining ingredients and rub into meat while meat is still warm. Fasten in a rotary basket or on a spit and let rotate over a slow charcoal fire for 1 hour. You may also roast the corned beef directly over a charcoal fire for 10 to 15 minutes per side instead of using spit.

Beef Bourguignon

6 servings

1	**cup chopped bacon**
3	**pounds lean beef, cut into 2 inch cubes**
1	**tablespoon salt**
2	**tablespoons flour**
¼	**teaspoon pepper**
3	**cups sliced onion**
6	**medium carrots, cut into chunks**
½	**cup Cognac**
1	**clove garlic, minced**
3	**cups Burgundy**
2	**cups beef stock**
1	**tablespoon tomato paste**
1	**bay leaf, crumbled**
½	**teaspoon thyme**
¾	**pound fresh mushrooms, quartered**
15 - 18	**small white onions, peeled and parboiled**
2	**tablespoons butter**
1	**tablespoon vegetable oil**
1	**teaspoon lemon juice**
⅛	**teaspoon salt pepper to taste**
½	**cup chopped parsley**

Saute bacon in a large skillet until brown. Remove with a slotted spoon. Season beef cubes with salt, pepper and flour and fry in the bacon grease a few at a time until thoroughly browned. Combine beef cubes with bacon in a large casserole. In the same skillet in which the bacon and beef were browned, saute sliced onions, carrots and garlic until golden brown. Add Cognac, heat and flame. Add sliced onions and carrots to the casserole. Mix well. Stir in Burgundy, beef stock, tomato paste, bay leaf and thyme. Bring to a boil on top of stove, cover, place in oven and bake at 325 degrees for 2½ to 3 hours, or until meat is very tender. Skim grease. Meanwhile, saute the mushrooms in butter and oil. Add lemon juice, salt, pepper and onions and cook for 2 minutes. Just before serving add mushrooms and parsley to the top of the casserole.

Note: This can be prepared a day in advance. Flavor is enhanced by reheating.

Katie Stapleton's Ballymaloe Irish Stew

4 servings

3	**pounds lamb**
4	**onions**
4	**carrots**
3	**cups stock, water or red wine salt and pepper**
4	**whole potatoes parsley, chopped**

Cut fat from lamb and cube. Render fat in Dutch casserole. Brown lamb cubes in hot fat. Peel onions and carrots and cut into chunks. Add onions, carrots, liquid and seasonings. Peel whole potatoes and place them on top. Simmer gently for 1½-2 hours; turn occasionally to prevent sticking. Skim fat. Serve with a sprinkling of parsley and thicken liquid with arrowroot or flour.

Cassoulet

4-6 servings

2 pounds sweet Italian sausage
2 pounds beef chuck, cut in
    1 inch cubes
1 large onion, sliced
2 medium cloves garlic, minced
2 green peppers, seeded and
    cut in eighths
1 pound white beans, cooked
1 teaspoon basil
½ teaspoon salt
1 teaspoon paprika
¼ teaspoon pepper
2 beef bouillon cubes dissolved
    in 1 cup boiling water
¼ cup chopped fresh parsley

Brown sausages, cut in thirds and place in a 2½ to 3 quart casserole. Drain grease from skillet, reserving 2 tablespoons. Brown beef in 1 tablespoon grease and add to casserole. Saute onion and garlic in remaining 1 tablespoon grease until tender. Add green peppers and cook 1 minute longer, stirring. Add to casserole, along with the cooked beans. Sprinkle with seasonings and mix lightly. Add bouillon, cover and bake in 350 degree oven for 1 hour and 15 minutes or until beef is tender.

Mother Lode Beef Stew

6 servings

2 pounds beef stew meat, cut
    into 1½ inch cubes
½ cup flour
3 tablespoons shortening
1 medium onion, sliced
1 clove garlic
2 bay leaves
1 teaspoon salt
1 teaspoon sugar
½ teaspoon pepper
½ teaspoon paprika
⅛ teaspoon ground cloves
1 teaspoon fresh lemon juice
1 teaspoon Worcestershire
    sauce
4 cups boiling water
6 carrots, sliced
8 whole, small boiling onions
5 stalks celery, sliced

Dredge meat in flour. Melt shortening in heavy skillet or Dutch oven. Add beef cubes, a few at a time and saute until meat is evenly browned. Do not allow the pieces of meat to touch one another while browning. Add onion, garlic, seasonings and boiling water. Cover tightly and cook over low heat 2 to 3 hours, until meat is tender. Add vegetables, continue cooking 30 minutes longer or until vegetables are tender.

158
Entrees

ADO CACHE COLORADO CACHE COLORADO CACHE COLORADO CACHE COLORADO CACHE COLORADO CACHE COLORADO CACHE COLORADO CACHE COLORADO CACHE COLORADO CACHE COLORADO CACHE

Feijoada (Brazilian Black Bean Stew)

4 servings

1   pound black beans, washed
       and picked over
water
1   large onion, chopped
2   cloves garlic, pressed
¼   pound salt pork,
       blanched and sliced
1   bay leaf
¼   teaspoon pepper
1   tablespoon beef stock base
1½ - 2   pounds meat, cooked (use any
       combination of the following:
       pork sausage, smoked or not,
       lean beef, cut into 1 inch
       cubes, tongue, meaty ham
       hocks or ham cubes, lean pork
       cut into 1 inch cubes)
1   tablespoon olive oil
2   tomatoes, peeled and
       chopped
1   medium onion, chopped
1   clove garlic, minced
3   tablespoons minced parsley
2   tomatoes, peeled and sliced
2   oranges, peeled and sliced
Tabasco sauce
Brazilian rice (see index)

Soak beans overnight in enough cold water to cover. Next day drain water, place beans in a large kettle and add enough cold water to cover beans by 2 inches. Add large onion, 2 cloves garlic, salt pork, bay leaf, pepper and beef stock base. Bring to a boil, lower heat, cover and simmer for 2 hours or until beans are almost tender. Stir occasionally to prevent beans from sticking. Add more water if necessary. Add meats and cook 1 hour. Remove 1 cup of beans from pot and set aside. Heat olive oil in a small skillet. Add onion and saute until soft. Add tomatoes, garlic and parsley and saute 1 minute. Add reserved beans and mash into onion-tomato mixture. Add this mixture to the kettle and cook 1 hour. Serve with Brazilian rice, sliced tomatoes, sliced oranges and Tabasco sauce.

Beef and Tomatoes

4 servings

1   pound tender beef,
       thinly sliced
3   tablespoons cornstarch
3   tablespoons soy sauce
2   tablespoons peanut oil
1   large onion, sliced or chopped
1   clove garlic, minced
2   tomatoes, sliced into thin
       wedges

Combine beef, cornstarch and soy sauce in a bowl and stir to coat meat evenly. Let stand 15 minutes. Heat oil in wok over high heat. Add meat and stir-fry until browned. Remove meat and add vegetables to pan, adding tomatoes last. Stir-fry 2 minutes. Return meat to wok. Add broth, cover and cook gently 5 minutes. Serve with rice.

COLORADO CACHE COLORADO CACHE COLORADO CACHE COLORADO CACHE COLORADO CACHE COLORADO CACHE COLORADO CACHE COLORADO CACHE COLORADO CACHE COLORADO

Any of the following ingredients:
- 1 **green pepper, thinly sliced**
- 2 **cups bean sprouts**
- 1 **cup sliced celery**
- ¼ **pound mushrooms, sliced**
  bamboo shoots
  water chestnuts, sliced
- 1 **cup beef or chicken broth**

Chinese Curried Beef and Vegetables

6 servings

1½	**pounds flank steak**
2	**small onions**
3	**medium sized tomatoes**
1	**green pepper**
¼	**teaspoon ground ginger**
½	**teaspoon sugar**
1	**tablespoon soy sauce**
1	**tablespoon curry powder**
½	**cup beef stock**
2	**tablespoons vegetable oil**
2	**teaspoons cornstarch**
1	**tablespoon water**

Cut the flank steak in half, lengthwise, then slice thinly on the diagonal. Cut onions in quarters and separate the layers. Remove stem ends from tomatoes. Halve pepper and remove seeds. Cut tomatoes and pepper into bite-sized triangular shaped pieces. Combine ginger, sugar, soy sauce, curry powder and beef stock and set aside. Heat oil in a large skillet. Saute meat quickly in hot oil, shaking pan to turn meat until it is almost completely browned. Push meat to the side of the pan. Add onions, tomatoes and green pepper and saute about 1 minute. Mix meat with vegetables and pour stock mixture over all. Cook, stirring, about 1 minute. Stir cornstarch and water together and blend into liquid. Cook, stirring until smooth and slightly thickened. Serve over rice.

Beef and Snow Peas

4 servings

¼	**cup soy sauce**
1	**tablespoon corn starch**
1	**tablespoon dry sherry**
1	**teaspoon sugar**
1	**pound flank steak, trimmed and thinly sliced against the grain**
2 - 4	**tablespoons vegetable oil**
½	**teaspoon salt**
¼	**pound snow peas**

Combine soy sauce, corn starch, sherry and sugar in a large bowl. Add meat, stirring to coat with marinade. Set aside. Heat 2 tablespoons oil in wok or large skillet over high heat. Add salt. Add snow peas to wok and stir-fry 1 minute. Remove to a platter. Add more oil to wok if necessary, then add beef mixture and stir-fry 3 minutes or until meat loses its red color. Return snow peas to wok and heat gently. Serve with rice.

Braciola

6 servings

3	slices white bread
½	cup water
1½	pounds lean ground beef
1	egg, lightly beaten
2	tablespoons minced parsley
1	clove garlic, minced
	salt and pepper
6 - 8	thin slices Westphalian ham or prosciutto
3	tablespoons raisins
3	tablespoons minced onion
2	tablespoons pine nuts
2	tablespoons Romano cheese
1	tablespoon olive oil
3	6-ounce cans tomato paste
2½	cups water
1½	cups dry red wine
½	teaspoon basil
½	teaspoon salt
	pepper to taste

Place bread slices in a large bowl. Add water and crumble bread with fingertips. Mix in ground beef, egg, parsley, garlic, salt and pepper. On a piece of waxed paper, pat beef mixture into a ½ inch thick rectangle. On top of beef, arrange in layers the ham, raisins, onion, pine nuts and Romano cheese. Starting at the narrow end of the rectangle, roll meat up and seal the seam. Wrap tightly in waxed paper and chill at least 3 hours. Brown meat in olive oil over moderate heat in a large skillet. Remove meat from pan. Into meat drippings in skillet stir tomato paste, water, wine, basil, salt and pepper. Stir and simmer for 15 minutes. Return meat to pan, baste with sauce, cover and simmer over low heat for 1 hour. Remove meat to a heated platter. Pour sauce into a sauceboat and serve with green noodles.

Hamburger Eggplant Parmesan

6-8 servings

12	slices eggplant, ½ inch thick, peeled
2	pounds ground beef
3	tablespoons olive oil
¼	cup chopped onion
¼	cup chopped green pepper
2	tablespoons flour
2	teaspoons salt
¼	teaspoon pepper
½	teaspoon oregano
2	cups canned tomato sauce
2	cups grated Mozzarella cheese
½	cup freshly grated Parmesan cheese

Cook the eggplant slices in boiling salted water until tender, about 5 minutes. Brown meat in 2 tablespoons of the oil, stirring occasionally. Drain. Cook onion and green pepper in remaining oil until the vegetables are wilted. Combine meat and vegetables in the skillet and stir in flour, salt, pepper and oregano. Add tomato sauce and cook until thickened. Arrange half the eggplant slices in a shallow 2 quart buttered baking dish. Spoon over half the meat mixture and half the cheese. Repeat the layers and bake uncovered at 300 degrees for 30 minutes.

Canneloni with Meat and Spinach

4 servings

- 1 cup ground left-over pot roast
- 1 cup left-over gravy
- 1 10-ounce package frozen chopped spinach, cooked and squeezed dry
- ½ teaspoon oregano (optional)
- 3 tablespoons freshly grated Parmesan cheese
- 1 tablespoon minced onion
- 1 small clove garlic, minced dash of nutmeg salt and pepper to taste
- 4 wide lasagna noodles, cooked and cut in half

Combine all ingredients except noodles. Place 3 tablespoons of filling in the center of each noodle half, wrapping noodle around filling until slightly overlapping. Place seam-side down in a well greased casserole, cover with sauce and sprinkle with additional Parmesan cheese. Bake at 375 degrees for 30 minutes or until bubbly and lightly browned.

Sauce:

- 2 tablespoons butter
- 2 tablespoons flour
- 1 cup milk
- ¼ teaspoon salt dash of nutmeg dash of Tabasco sauce
- 1 cup grated Swiss cheese

Melt butter in saucepan. Stir in flour and cook over low heat for 2 minutes. Slowly stir in milk. Cook, stirring constantly until thickened. Add seasonings and stir in cheese until smooth.

Note: Special treatment for leftover pot roast.

Reuben Casserole

6-8 servings

- 8 ounces wide noodles, cooked
- 3 tablespoons butter
- 1 pound sauerkraut, drained
- 2 cups chopped corned beef
- 2 medium tomatoes, peeled and sliced
- ¼ cup Thousand Island dressing
- 8 ounces shredded Swiss cheese (2 cups)
- 4 crisp rye crackers, crushed
- ½ teaspoon caraway seed

In a greased 9 × 13 inch pan layer buttered noodles, sauerkraut, corned beef and tomatoes. Dot with salad dressing and sprinkle with cheese. Top with cracker crumbs and caraway seed. Bake covered at 350 degrees for 40 minutes. Uncover and bake about 15 minutes more or until bubbly.

Note: A treat for Reuben sandwich lovers.

Canneloni Crepes

Filling:
- 2 tablespoons olive oil
- ¼ cup finely chopped onions
- 1 teaspoon minced garlic
- 1 10-ounce package frozen, chopped spinach, defrosted, squeezed dry and chopped again
- 2 tablespoons butter
- 1 pound beef round steak, ground twice
- ¼ pound ground pork sausage
- 5 tablespoons freshly grated Parmesan cheese
- 2 tablespoons heavy cream
- 2 eggs, lightly beaten
- ½ teaspoon oregano
  salt to taste
  freshly ground pepper to taste

Bechamel Sauce:
- 4 tablespoons butter
- 4 tablespoons flour
- 1 cup milk
- 1 cup heavy cream
- 1 teaspoon salt
- ⅛ teaspoon white pepper

Tomato Sauce:
- 2 tablespoons olive oil
- ½ cup finely chopped onions
- 2 cups Italian plum or whole pack tomatoes, coarsely chopped, undrained
- 3 tablespoons tomato paste
- ½ teaspoon basil
- 1 teaspoon sugar
- ½ teaspoon salt
  freshly ground pepper to taste

8 servings

Make 1 recipe crepes (see index) and set aside.

Cook onions and garlic in olive oil until soft. Stir in spinach and cook 3 to 4 minutes, stirring constantly. When all moisture has boiled away, transfer to a large bowl. Melt butter in skillet, add meats and brown. Add to mixture in bowl and add remaining ingredients for filling.

Melt butter, stir in flour. Gradually add milk and cream, whisking constantly. With pan on high heat, stir constantly until mixture comes to a boil and is smooth. Simmer, still stirring 2 to 3 minutes longer or until sauce coats wires of the whisk heavily. Remove from heat and season with salt and pepper.

Cook onion in olive oil until tender. Add rest of ingredients. Reduce heat and simmer with pan partially covered for 40 minutes. Stir occasionally. Press sauce through a fine sieve.

Assembly: Place a heaping tablespoon of filling on each crepe and roll up. Pour a film of tomato sauce in two 10 x 14 inch baking dishes. Make one layer of canneloni. Pour Bechamel sauce over canneloni and spoon rest of tomato sauce on top. Sprinkle with Parmesan cheese and bake uncovered for 20 minutes at 375 degrees. Broil 30 seconds to brown top.

Super Deluxe Pizza

2 14-inch pizzas

Crust:

2	packages dry yeast
1¼	cups warm water
1	teaspoon honey
¼	cup vegetable oil
1	teaspoon salt
2½	cups unbleached flour
1	cup whole wheat flour

Dissolve yeast in water, add honey. Combine oil, salt and flours in a large bowl. Add yeast mixture and stir hard to combine all ingredients. Knead until smooth and satiny on a floured board. Place in a greased bowl, cover with a tea towel and let rise in a warm place until doubled in bulk. Punch down dough and knead again lightly. Divide into 2 pieces, roll out dough and fit into 2 14-inch pizza pans or shape on baking sheets.

Sauce:

3	tablespoons olive oil
1	large onion, chopped
3	cloves garlic, minced
1	1-pound 12-ounce can tomatoes and juice, chopped
1	6-ounce can tomato paste
1	tablespoon oregano
1	teaspoon basil
1	bay leaf
1	tablespoon honey
1	tablespoon salt
¼	teaspoon pepper

Heat oil in a large pan. Add onions and saute until limp. Add garlic and cook for 1 minute. Add remaining ingredients. Bring to a boil, lower heat and simmer uncovered for 1 hour, stirring occasionally. Remove bay leaf.

Pizza Toppings:

Mozzarella cheese
Italian sausage, crumbled or
  sliced, and browned
mushrooms, lightly sauteed
green pepper, sliced into rings
pepperoni, sliced
onions, chopped
other cheeses
red peppers, dried or fresh
ground beef, cooked and
  crumbled

Cover pizza dough with sauce, then add any combination of toppings you like. Bake at 500 degrees for 10 to 15 minutes. To test for doneness, lift up a corner of the crust. It should be evenly browned on the bottom.

Deep Dish Pizza

6-8 servings

Dough:

- 1 package dry yeast
- 1 cup lukewarm water
- 1 tablespoon sugar
- 1 teaspoon salt
- 2 tablespoons oil
- 2½ - 3 cups flour

Dissolve yeast in water in bowl. Add sugar, salt and oil. Mix well. Gradually add flour to form stiff dough. Knead on a floured surface until smooth and elastic. Place in greased bowl, cover with a tea towel and let rise in a warm place until doubled in bulk.

Meat Sauce:

- 1 pound Italian sausage
- ¼ cup chopped onion
- 1 clove garlic, minced
- 1 pound tomatoes, chopped
- 1 6-ounce can tomato paste
- ½ pound mushrooms, sliced
- 1 teaspoon oregano
- 1 teaspoon salt
- ⅛ teaspoon pepper

Brown meat in a large skillet with onion and garlic. Drain grease. Add remaining ingredients and simmer for 30 minutes. Cool.

Cheese Filling:

- 1 pound Ricotta cheese
- ¼ pound Mozzarella cheese, grated
- 2 eggs, lightly beaten
- ¼ cup minced parsley
- ⅛ teaspoon salt

Combine all ingredients and mix well.

Topping:

- ½ pound Mozzarella cheese, grated
- ½ teaspoon oregano
- ¼ cup grated Parmesan cheese

Roll out half of dough on floured surface into a large rectangle. Place in a greased 11 × 17 inch jelly roll pan or a 9 × 13 inch glass baking dish, easing dough gently to fit up the sides. Spread with cheese filling. Roll out remaining dough and fit over cheese filling. Cover with meat sauce. Bake at 400 degrees for 15 minutes. Sprinkle with Mozzarella cheese, oregano and Parmesan cheese and bake an additional 15 minutes or until golden.

Pedro's Delight

6 servings

- 1 **pound ground beef**
- 1 **large onion, chopped**
- 3½ **cups canned tomatoes**
- 2 **4-ounce cans green chiles**
- 1 **pound Monterey Jack cheese, grated**
- 1 **10-ounce bag tortilla chips**
- 1 **cup whipping cream with 1 tablespoon vinegar added**
  whole tortilla chips
  sliced tomatoes

Saute onion and ground beef together. Add tomatoes and green chiles. Layer tortilla chips, meat mixture and cheese. Pour soured cream over top. Bake uncovered at 350 degrees for 30 minutes. If prepared ahead and refrigerated, lengthen baking time 15 minutes. Garnish with whole tortilla chips and sliced tomatoes.

Spaghetti Pie

6 servings

- 6 **ounces spaghetti**
- 2 **eggs, beaten**
- ¼ **cup freshly grated Parmesan cheese**
- 2 **tablespoons butter**
- ⅓ **cup chopped onion**
- 1 **cup sour cream**
- 1 **pound Italian sausage**
- 1 **6-ounce can tomato paste**
- 1 **cup water**
- 4 **ounces Mozzarella cheese, sliced**

Break spaghetti in half. Cook in boiling salted water until done. Drain. While still warm combine spaghetti with eggs and Parmesan. Pour into a well greased 10 inch pie plate and pat mixture up and around sides with a spoon. Melt butter, add onion and saute until limp. Stir in sour cream and spoon over spaghetti. Remove sausage from casing, crumble and cook in skillet until done. Drain. Add tomato paste and water. Simmer 10 minutes. Spoon sausage on top of sour cream mixture. Bake at 350 degrees for 25 minutes. Arrange Mozzarella on top and return to oven until cheese melts.

Note: This freezes well before baking so make 2 at a time.

Scandinavian Meatballs

4 servings

½ **pound lean ground pork**
½ **pound ground beef**
1 **medium onion, minced**
⅔ **cup milk**
½ **cup bread crumbs**
1 **egg**
1 **clove garlic, minced**
¼ **teaspoon thyme**
  salt and pepper to taste
1 **cup water**
2 **teaspoons chicken stock base**
  or
2 **chicken bouillon cubes**
1 **tablespoon flour**
½ **cup water**
3 **rounded tablespoons sour cream**
¼ **teaspoon dill weed**

Mix together first 9 ingredients, kneading lightly but thoroughly with hands. Shape into small round balls using 1 rounded teaspoon for each. Brown on all sides in a lightly greased skillet, shaking frequently so that meatballs keep their round shape. Pour off excess grease from skillet, add water and chicken stock base or bouillon cubes. Cover and simmer 1 hour. When done, remove meatballs from pan and keep warm. Add flour to pan, stir until smooth and cook for 1 minute. Add ½ cup water or more if gravy seems too thick. Heat to boiling point and boil 1 minute. Stir in sour cream and dill and return meatballs to pan. Heat thoroughly but do not boil. Serve with rice or noodles.

Spear's Charcoaled Pork Roast

1 roast

1 **pork loin (have butcher crack ribs so that it will be easy to slice into chops)**
  garlic salt
  Lawry's seasoned salt

Sprinkle the pork roast with garlic salt until it looks like a white coating, then rub with seasoned salt. Roast for 2 hours, or until meat thermometer registers done, in a covered barbeque grill with coals on 2 sides and the roast in the middle. Serve with chunky applesauce flavored with grated horseradish.

Javanese Pork

4 servings

1½ **pounds pork, trimmed and cut into 1 inch cubes**
1 **12-ounce can beer**
½ **cup orange marmalade**
¼ **cup sugar**
½ **cup soy sauce**
1 **clove garlic, minced**
16 **large mushrooms**
8 **pearl onions, peeled and blanched**
1 **large green pepper, cut into eighths**

Place pork in a deep bowl. Combine next 5 ingredients thoroughly and pour over pork. Refrigerate overnight. Stir several times. One hour before cooking add vegetables to marinade. String pork and vegetables on skewers and cook over medium hot charcoal fire, basting frequently with marinade.

South Park Pork Casserole

4-6 servings

2 **pounds lean pork, cut into 1 inch cubes**
2 **pounds sauerkraut**
2 **cups sliced onions**
6 **slices bacon, cut in half**
3 **cups water**

Brown pork cubes in a large greased skillet. Set aside. Spread 1 pound of sauerkraut in the bottom of a 2 quart casserole. Cover with 1 cup of sliced onions. Distribute pork cubes on top. Layer the remaining onions and sauerkraut and top with bacon slices. Pour water over all. Bake uncovered at 325 degrees for 5 to 6 hours.

Sweet and Sour Pork

6 servings

2 pounds boneless pork loin, cut into ½ inch cubes
¼ cup soy sauce
  cornstarch
2 or more eggs, beaten
  flour
  oil for frying
1 large onion, cut into eighths
1 large green pepper, cut into 1 inch squares
1 cup pineapple chunks, drained (reserve juice)
2 small tomatoes, cut into thin wedges
  sweet and sour sauce

Toss pork cubes with soy sauce. Roll the cubes in cornstarch, then in beaten egg, then in flour. Fry in hot oil until golden brown. Drain on paper towels and keep warm in 350 degree oven. Heat 1 tablespoon oil in wok over high heat. Add onion and stir-fry for 2 minutes. Add green pepper and stir-fry an additional 2 minutes. Add pineapple and tomatoes and stir-fry 1 minute. Return pork cubes to wok, add sauce and stir until thoroughly heated. Serve with hot, steamed rice.

Sweet and Sour Sauce:

½ cup pineapple juice (use juice from canned pineapple chunks)
¼ cup wine vinegar
2 tablespoons oil
2 tablespoons brown sugar
1 tablespoon soy sauce
½ teaspoon pepper
1 teaspoon cornstarch
2 teaspoons water

Combine pineapple juice, vinegar, oil, brown sugar, soy sauce and pepper in saucepan. Bring to a boil and add cornstarch which has been mixed with water. Stir until clear and slightly thickened.

Hogback Pork Chops

4-6 servings

8 pork chops, ¾ inch thick
½ cup apple juice
½ cup light raisins
1 teaspoon salt
¼ cup brown sugar, packed
¼ teaspoon ground nutmeg
¼ teaspoon ground cinnamon
3 large red apples, each cut into 6 to 8 wedges
½ cup water

Brown chops in a greased skillet over medium heat. Arrange chops in a shallow 2 quart baking dish. Pour apple juice over chops and sprinkle with raisins and salt. Cover and bake at 350 degrees for 45 minutes. Turn chops. Combine brown sugar, nutmeg and cinnamon and coat apple wedges with this mixture. Arrange apples around chops. Sprinkle apples with the remaining sugar mixture and pour water over all. Cover and bake an additional 15 minutes.
  Note: A children's favorite.

Piquant Pork Chops

8 servings

3	cloves garlic, mashed
½	teaspoon salt
½	teaspoon thyme
⅛	teaspoon pepper
8	loin pork chops, 1 inch thick
3	tablespoons butter
2	cloves garlic, minced
1	large onion, minced
1½	cups dry white wine
1½	cups beef broth
5	tablespoons tomato paste
3	tablespoons minced parsley
1	tablespoon Dijon mustard
⅓	cup chopped sour pickle
3	tablespoons butter, softened

Combine 3 cloves garlic, salt, thyme and pepper and rub this mixture into both sides of pork chops. Cover and refrigerate several hours or overnight. Grease a large, oven-proof skillet. Wipe the garlic mixture from the chops and brown them in the skillet on 1 side only for 15 minutes over moderate heat. Preheat oven to 350 degrees. Turn chops and transfer the skillet to the oven. Bake uncovered for 20 minutes or until tender. While chops are baking, melt 3 tablespoons butter in a saucepan. Add onion and 2 cloves garlic and saute until the onion is limp. Add the wine, broth, tomato paste, parsley and mustard to the onion mixture. Bring this to a boil and continue to cook until the sauce is slightly thickened. Stir in the chopped pickle. Remove chops from the oven and place on a large platter. Skim grease from the pan juices. Pour the onion sauce into the skillet and heat sauce, stirring up the brown bits from the bottom of the skillet. Return chops to the pan and heat, spooning sauce over them. Remove chops to a platter, swirl butter into sauce, and pour over chops. Garnish with parsley.

Pork Chops Florentine

6 servings

6	loin pork chops ½ to ¾ inch thick
1½	pounds fresh spinach, washed, chopped and lightly steamed
2	tablespoons grated onion
6	tablespoons butter
6	tablespoons flour
1¼	cups strong chicken stock
1¾	cups milk
	salt and white pepper to taste
	dash of nutmeg
2	egg yolks, lightly beaten
1	cup grated Swiss cheese
3	tablespoons freshly grated Parmesan cheese

Brown pork chops in a lightly greased skillet. Lower heat, cover and cook about 30 minutes or until tender. Keep warm. Combine the cooked spinach with the grated onion and set aside. In a medium saucepan melt butter. Stir in the flour and cook over low heat for 3 minutes. Slowly stir in chicken stock and milk and continue to stir until thickened. Add salt, pepper and nutmeg. Stir a little of this sauce into egg yolks and then return the yolk mixture to the sauce, stirring until smooth and thick. Mix 1 cup sauce with spinach mixture and spread it over the bottom of a large, greased shallow casserole. Arrange pork chops on top of spinach. Meanwhile, stir the Swiss cheese into the sauce and stir over low heat until cheese is melted. Pour sauce over pork chops, sprinkle with Parmesan cheese and bake uncovered at 400 degrees for 15 minutes or until bubbling and the cheese is lightly browned.

Pork Chops with Spaghetti

4 servings

3 **tablespoons butter**
3 **tablespoons olive oil**
2 **cloves garlic, pressed**
¼ **teaspoon pepper**
⅛ **teaspoon crushed red pepper**
1 **teaspoon rosemary**
4 **pork chops, 1 inch thick**
2 **cups chopped tomatoes**
3 **tablespoons minced parsley**
½ **teaspoon salt**
¾ **pound spaghetti**
4 **tablespoons butter**
4 **tablespoons freshly grated
   Parmesan cheese**

Melt butter with olive oil in a large heavy skillet. Add garlic, pepper and red pepper. Sprinkle rosemary on pork chops then brown chops slowly in the skillet. Add tomatoes, parsley, and salt. Cover and cook slowly for 20 minutes. Uncover and cook an additional 20 minutes or until tender. Cook the spaghetti, drain and toss with butter and Parmesan. Add ½ cup sauce to the spaghetti. Place spaghetti on a hot platter, arrange the chops on the spaghetti and pour sauce over all.

Russian Pork Chops

4 servings

4 **pork chops, 1½ inches thick**
1 **tablespoon oil**
1 **tablespoon flour**
2 **tablespoons wine vinegar**
2 **teaspoons sugar**
½ **cup sour cream**
1 **bay leaf
   salt and pepper to taste**

Brown pork chops in oil and remove from pan. Add flour and stir to loosen crusty bits from bottom of pan. Add remaining ingredients and stir until blended. Return pork chops to pan, cover and cook slowly about 50 minutes, or until tender.

Caraway Mustard Leg of Lamb

8-10 servings

1 **6 to 8 pound leg of lamb**
3 **cloves garlic, slivered**
½ **cup prepared mustard
   (or more)**
¼ **cup caraway seeds**

Make tiny slits all over the surface of the leg of lamb. Insert slivers of garlic. Generously coat the lamb with mustard then sprinkle with caraway seeds. Place in a shallow roasting pan. Roast at 325 degrees for 18 to 20 minutes per pound for medium.

Gift Wrapped Ham

12 servings

1 9½-ounce package
    pie crust mix
1 teaspoon dry mustard
½ teaspoon sage
1 8-pound canned ham
1 egg, beaten
   paprika

Combine dry pie crust mix with mustard and sage, then prepare according to package directions. Roll pastry out to a 17 inch square. Place drained and wiped ham in center of pastry. Wrap edges as you would a package. Moisten edges with cold water and press together firmly to seal. Place seam side down on a greased baking sheet. Decorate with tiny pastry cutouts from extra dough. Brush with egg, sprinkle with paprika and bake at 450 degrees for 1 hour or until browned.

Barbara Conwell's Ham Stuffed with Fruit and Nuts

12 servings

1 8-pound boneless baked ham
1 6-ounce package chopped,
    dried mixed fruit
2 cloves garlic, minced
½ cup slivered almonds
1 shallot, minced
2 tablespoons chopped parsley
   salt and pepper to taste
⅛ teaspoon dry mustard
⅛ teaspoon ground cloves
⅛ teaspoon ground nutmeg
⅛ teaspoon ground cinnamon
   Madeira
   white wine
   brown sugar, dry mustard and
    sherry for the glaze

Using a zucchini knife or long corer, core out several tunnels horizontally in the ham. Mix the chopped dried fruit with the spices and enough Madeira to bind, about ½ cup. Stuff the tunnels using the zucchini knife to push in the stuffing. Tie the ham with string to keep the stuffing in place while baking. Score the top of the ham and bake according to the ham directions, basting frequently with white wine. About 20 minutes before done, glaze with a mixture of brown sugar, dry mustard and sherry. Allow ham to cool about 15 minutes before carving. Use an electric knife to ease carving.

172

Entrees

ADO CACHE COLORADO CACHE COLORADO CACHE COLORADO CACHE COLORADO CACHE COLORADO CACHE COLORADO CACHE COLORADO CACHE COLORADO CACHE

Herb Roasted Lamb

6-8 servings

1	leg of lamb, trimmed
½	teaspoon garlic slivers
1	teaspoon salt
½	teaspoon coarsely ground black pepper
½	teaspoon ground ginger
1	bay leaf, crumbled
¾	teaspoon thyme
½	teaspoon sage
½	teaspoon marjoram
1½	tablespoons soy sauce
1	tablespoon vegetable oil

Preheat oven to 300 degrees. Cut small slits in the lamb and insert garlic slivers with tip of knife. Combine remaining ingredients and rub thoroughly over and into the meat. Roast on a rack in a roasting pan, uncovered. Cook 18 minutes per pound for medium. Let stand 20 minutes before carving.

Grilled Herbed Leg of Lamb

6-8 servings

1	4 to 5 pound leg of lamb, boned and butterflied
1	onion, sliced
1	clove garlic, minced
	juice of 1 lemon
½	cup red wine vinegar
¾	cup safflower oil
¼	teaspoon oregano
¼	teaspoon thyme
½	teaspoon rosemary
½	teaspoon basil
1	teaspoon salt
	dash of pepper

Place lamb, flattened, in a glass dish just large enough to hold it. Combine remaining ingredients and pour over meat. Marinate for several hours in the refrigerator, turning occasionally. Roast meat over a hot charcoal fire for 25 to 30 minutes per side for medium rare.

COLORADO *CACHE* COLORADO *CACHE* COLORADO *CACHE* COLORADO *CACHE* COLORADO *CACHE* COLORADO *CACHE* COLORADO *CACHE* COLORADO *CACHE* COLORADO

Marinated Lamb Chops

4 servings

8   **loin lamb chops, cut 1 inch thick and trimmed**
2   **tablespoons wine vinegar**
1   **tablespoon lemon juice**
2   **teaspoons mustard**
3   **tablespoons olive oil**
1   **clove garlic, minced**
¼   **teaspoon ground ginger**
1   **teaspoon rosemary**
¼   **teaspoon salt**
1   **small onion, sliced**

Place lamb chops in a deep ceramic or glass bowl. Combine remaining ingredients and pour over chops. Marinate in the refrigerator, covered for 4 to 5 hours. Broil over a hot charcoal fire or under an oven broiler for 5 minutes per side for medium rare.

Dilled Lamb Shanks

4 servings

2   **tablespoons butter**
6   **meaty lamb shanks**
2   **large onions, thinly sliced**
1   **cup dry white wine**
1   **cup strong beef stock**
1   **tablespoon dill weed**
    juice of ½ lemon
    salt and pepper to taste
1   **cup sour cream**

Melt butter in Dutch oven. Add the lamb shanks and brown them thoroughly over medium heat. Remove from pan, then remove all but 1 tablespoon grease from pan. Add onions and cook until limp. Return the meat to the pan, pour wine and stock over all. Stir in dill weed. Cover and simmer over low heat for 2 hours or until meat is tender. Skim grease from the pan juices. Stir in salt and pepper, lemon juice and sour cream and heat but do not boil. Serve with boiled potatoes and cucumber salad.

Note: You may cover and bake the lamb shanks at 350 degrees for 2 hours or until tender.

ADO CACHE COLORADO CACHE COLORADO CACHE COLORADO CACHE COLORADO CACHE COLORADO CACHE COLORADO CACHE COLORADO CACHE COLORADO CACHE

Veal Marsala with Cream

4 servings

2 tablespoons vegetable oil
3 tablespoons butter
1¼ pounds thin veal scallops
5 tablespoons flour
   salt and pepper to taste
½ cup dry Marsala
⅓ cup heavy cream

Heat oil and butter in large skillet over high heat. Dredge veal scallops, one at a time, on both sides in flour. As butter foam begins to subside, put veal in skillet. Don't put any more in skillet than will fit without overlapping. Brown the veal quickly on both sides; about 30 seconds per side is enough if the cooking grease is hot. When browned on both sides, transfer to a large platter. Season meat on platter with salt and pepper to taste. Add Marsala to skillet, stir, scraping the cooking residues loose from the bottom of the pan. When Marsala has begun to boil away, add cream, stir constantly over high heat until cream is bound with juices in pan into a thick, dark sauce. Turn heat to medium and add veal. Simmer for 5 minutes and serve with sauce.

Veal Scallops with Mushrooms and Ham

4 servings

4 veal scallops, ¼ inch thick
   flour
4 tablespoons butter
   salt and pepper to taste
2 medium onions, chopped
2 shallots, minced
½ pound fresh mushrooms, chopped
1 4-ounce ham slice, cut in julienne strips
2 tablespoons flour
1 cup milk
¾ cup grated Gruyere or other Swiss cheese
2 tablespoons cream, warmed

Dust the scallops with flour. Heat butter in a skillet over moderately high heat. Add scallops and brown lightly. Season with salt and pepper and place in an ovenproof baking dish. Add onions and shallots to the skillet and saute for 5 minutes. Add mushrooms and cook an additional 2 minutes. Add ham to the skillet. Stir in flour and slowly add milk. Bring the sauce to a boil, stirring constantly, then lower heat and cook until thick. Sprinkle half of the cheese on the veal scallops, cover with sauce and top with the remaining cheese. Bake uncovered at 425 degrees for 15 minutes. Just before serving, sprinkle with cream.

Veal Oscar

4 servings

4   **veal cutlets, flattened or pounded very thin**
2   **tablespoons fresh lemon juice**
    pepper to taste
    seasoned flour
16 **spears fresh asparagus, cooked**
4   **crab legs, cooked, shells removed**
1   **cup Hollandaise sauce (see index)**

Sprinkle cutlets with lemon juice and pepper on both sides. Dust with seasoned flour. Heat butter in a large skillet. Saute cutlets over moderately high heat for 4 minutes on each side, until lightly browned. Remove to a warm platter. On each cutlet place 4 spears of asparagus and one crab leg. Cover with Hollandaise sauce.

Veal Piccata

4 servings

1½ **pounds veal round or sirloin, cut ¼ to ½ inch thick**
    salt and pepper to taste
    flour
3   **tablespoons butter**
1   **tablespoon olive oil**
2   **cloves garlic, minced**
½   **pound fresh mushrooms, sliced**
2   **tablespoons fresh lemon juice**
½   **cup dry white wine**
2   **teaspoons capers plus 1 teaspoon caper juice (optional)**
3   **tablespoons minced parsley**
½   **lemon, thinly sliced**

Sprinkle veal with salt and pepper on both sides and dust lightly with flour. Heat butter and olive oil in a large skillet. Add veal and brown on both sides. Remove veal from skillet. Add garlic and mushrooms to pan and cook one minute. Return veal to pan. Add lemon juice, white wine, cover and simmer for 20 minutes or until veal is tender. Add capers. Remove to a warm platter, sprinkle with parsley and garnish with lemon slices.

Blanquette of Veal with Water Chestnuts

12 servings

1 cup butter
4 pounds boneless veal, cut into 1 inch cubes
2 onions, minced
2 cloves garlic, minced
½ teaspoon pepper
2 teaspoons salt
3 dashes of cayenne pepper
2 pounds fresh mushrooms, quartered
2 cups beef broth
¼ teaspoon ground nutmeg
1½ bay leaves
4 5-ounce cans water chestnuts, drained and sliced
¾ cup heavy cream
½ cup Cognac
¼ cup chopped parsley

Melt ½ cup butter in heavy skillet and brown the veal in batches on all sides, adding the onion and garlic with the last batch to brown along with the veal. Add pepper, salt and cayenne. Place meat and onions in a 4 quart casserole. Melt the remaining butter in the same skillet and saute mushrooms quickly. Add mushrooms to meat. Deglaze the pan with a little broth and add to casserole with the remaining broth. Add nutmeg, bay leaves and water chestnuts. Cover and bake at 375 degrees for 1½ hours or until meat is tender. Stir in cream and bake an additional 15 minutes uncovered. Stir in Cognac and reheat. Sprinkle with parsley and serve.

Fillet of Sole a la Loire

8 servings

8 large fillets of sole
1 pound bay shrimp
2 teaspoons chopped shallots
3 cups dry white wine
2 tablespoons butter
2 egg yolks
½ cup heavy cream
2 tablespoons sweet butter parsley, minced
½ teaspoon dill weed or to taste

Cut each fillet in half, making the cut across the width. Place several shrimp in the center of each fillet and roll the fillets around the shrimp. In a buttered saucepan, add the shallots and white wine. Very carefully lay the fillet rolls in the saucepan, cover with a buttered round of waxed paper and cook covered. Poach them very gently for about 10 minutes. Remove the rolls to a heated serving dish, reserving the poaching liquid. Reduce poaching liquid by ⅓. In another saucepan combine egg yolks and cream and a little of the poaching liquid. Stir into the remaining hot poaching liquid. Add dill and correct the seasoning. Cook gently but do not boil. Swirl in the sweet butter and pour over the fillet rolls. Sprinkle with parsley and more dill if desired.

Katie Stapleton's Sole Veronique

4 servings

1 **cup green grapes, halved and seeded**
2 **tablespoons dry white wine**
1 **pound sole fillets**
1 **tablespoon lemon juice**
   salt and pepper to taste
½ **teaspoon grated orange peel**
1 **teaspoon diet margarine**
1 **orange, cut in slices**
   watercress sprigs

Place grapes in a bowl and drizzle with wine. Arrange fish on a sheet of foil on a broiling pan, and sprinkle with lemon juice. Season with salt, pepper and grated orange peel. Dot with diet margarine. Broil until golden brown, about 5 minutes. Arrange the wine-marinated grapes, cut side down, over the top of the sole fillets, and broil about 1 minute longer. Garnish each serving with an orange slice and watercress.

Shrimp, Crab and Artichokes Au Gratin

6 servings

¼ **cup butter**
½ **pound fresh mushrooms, sliced**
1 **clove garlic, minced**
2 **tablespoons finely minced shallots**
¼ **cup flour**
½ **teaspoon pepper**
¾ **cup milk**
2½ **cups grated, sharp Cheddar cheese (8 ounces)**
⅔ **cup dry white wine**
2 **7½-ounce cans king crab, flaked and drained**
1 **pound shrimp, cooked**
1 **10-ounce package frozen artichoke hearts, cooked and drained**
2 **tablespoons bread crumbs**
1 **tablespoon butter, melted**

Melt butter in skillet; add mushrooms, garlic and shallots and saute for 5 minutes. Remove from heat and stir in flour, pepper and milk. Slowly bring to a boil, stirring and remove from heat. Add ½ cup of cheese and stir until melted. Stir in wine. Combine sauce, crab, shrimp, artichokes and remaining cheese. Pour into buttered 2 quart casserole. Combine bread crumbs and melted butter and sprinkle on top of casserole. Top with remaining cheese. Bake uncovered at 375 degrees for 30 minutes or until bubbly and lightly browned.

RADO CACHE COLORADO CACHE COLORADO CACHE COLORADO CACHE COLORADO CACHE COLORADO CACHE COLORADO CACHE COLORADO CACHE COLORADO CACHE COLORADO CACH

Snapper Amandine

4-6 servings

8 - 12	**fillets red snapper or trout**
	milk to cover
2	**teaspoons salt**
4	**drops Tabasco sauce**
1½	**cups flour**
1	**teaspoon white pepper**
¼	**pound butter**
2	**tablespoons oil**
½	**pound butter**
½	**cup sliced almonds**
2	**tablespoons lemon juice**
2	**teaspoons Worcestershire sauce**
1	**teaspoon salt**
¼	**cup chopped parsley**

Soak fillets in a mixture of milk, 1 teaspoon salt and Tabasco sauce for at least 30 minutes. Season flour with 1 teaspoon salt and pepper. Remove fillets from milk, pat dry and coat lightly with seasoned flour, shaking off excess. In saucepan, melt ¼ pound butter and add oil. In a large skillet pour butter mixture to a depth of 1/8 inch. When very hot, fry fillets, a few at a time, turning once. Do not crowd fillets. Keep grease very hot and at proper depth by adding more from saucepan as necessary. Place cooked fillets on a warm platter and keep warm. When all are cooked, wipe out skillet. Prepare sauce in same skillet by melting ½ pound butter and lightly browning almonds. Add lemon juice, Worcestershire sauce, salt and parsley. Mix and heat well. Just before serving, pour some sauce over fillets and serve remaining sauce in pitcher.

Red Snapper with Fresh Tomatoes

4 servings

2	**pounds red snapper fillets**
	salt and pepper to taste
3	**tablespoons butter**
1	**medium onion, chopped**
1	**clove garlic, minced**
1½	**tablespoons flour**
2	**green onions, chopped**
½	**cup dry white wine**
4	**tomatoes, peeled, seeded and coarsely chopped**
1	**teaspoon chopped parsley**
	pinch of tarragon, thyme, and basil
¼	**cup fine bread crumbs**
2	**tablespoons freshly grated Parmesan cheese**

Place fillets in well buttered baking dish and season with salt and freshly ground pepper. Melt butter in saucepan. Add onion and garlic and saute for 5 minutes without browning. Stir in flour and add wine. Bring to a boil and simmer for 5 minutes. Season with salt and pepper. Add tomatoes and herbs. Pour sauce over fish and sprinkle with bread crumbs and cheese. Bake uncovered at 350 degrees for approximately 30 minutes.

Deviled Crab and Shrimp

6 servings

1 **medium green pepper, chopped**
1 **medium onion, chopped**
1 **cup chopped celery**
1 **cup crabmeat (or more as desired)**
1 **cup shrimp, cleaned and chopped (or more as desired)**
½ **teaspoon salt**
⅛ **teaspoon pepper**
1 **tablespoon Worcestershire sauce**
1 **cup mayonnaise**
1 **cup buttered bread crumbs**

Combine all ingredients except crumbs. Place in individual au gratin dishes or ramekins. Sprinkle with crumbs and bake at 350 degrees for 30 minutes.

Shrimp de Jonghe

6-8 servings

2 **pounds medium-large shrimp, cooked**
¼ **cup butter**
1½ **cups hot milk**
1 **cup toasted bread crumbs**
½ **cup finely minced parsley**
1 **clove garlic, minced**
1½ **teaspoons salt**
⅛ **teaspoon freshly ground pepper**
½ **cup butter, softened**
4 **tablespoons freshly grated Parmesan cheese**
¼ **cup butter, melted**

Saute shrimp in ¼ cup butter over medium heat for 2 minutes. Place in a shallow 2 quart casserole. Pour hot milk over bread crumbs and mix well with a fork. Let stand until mixture is the consistency of thick custard. If too thick add more milk. Add parsley, garlic, salt, pepper and soft butter. Mix thoroughly and spread over shrimp. Sprinkle with Parmesan cheese, drizzle with melted butter and bake at 350 degrees for 30 minutes. Place under broiler for several minutes to brown lightly. Watch carefully so that it does not burn.

ADO CACHE COLORADO CACHE COLORADO CACHE COLORADO CACHE COLORADO CACHE COLORADO CACHE COLORADO CACHE COLORADO CACHE COLORADO CACHE COLORADO CACH

Barbecued Shrimp

4 servings

2 **pounds fresh jumbo shrimp, in shell**
1 **cup olive or vegetable oil**
1 **cup dry sherry**
1 **cup soy sauce**
1 **clove garlic, mashed**

Combine all ingredients and marinate in the refrigerator for 3 to 4 hours. Shell and devein shrimp and cook over a hot charcoal fire for 2 to 3 minutes per side or until just barely cooked. Serve with butter sauce.

Butter Sauce:
½ **pound butter**
  juice of 1 lemon
½ **teaspoon salt**
1 **tablespoon Worcestershire sauce**
1 **tablespoon soy sauce**
3 · 4 **dashes Tabasco sauce**

Melt butter in small saucepan, add remaining ingredients and keep warm.

Hollandaise and Bearnaise Sauces

Hollandaise Sauce:
2 **egg yolks**
½ **cup butter, divided into 3 pieces**
1 **tablespoon fresh lemon juice**

¾ cup

Combine egg yolks and lemon juice in the top of a double boiler over hot, not boiling water. Add butter, 1 piece at a time, stirring constantly until melted. Continue stirring until thickened.

Bearnaise Sauce:
1 **recipe Hollandaise sauce**
¾ **teaspoon grated onion**
1 **teaspoon minced parsley**
2 **teaspoons tarragon or white vinegar**
¼ **teaspoon tarragon**

Combine all ingredients.
    Note: Can make ahead and keep covered. No need to reheat because it will be served over hot meat, fish, poultry, or vegetables. If desired, place in a preheated thermos (rinsed with boiling water) for up to 2 hours.

OLORADO CACHE COLORADO CACHE COLORADO CACHE COLORADO CACHE COLORADO CACHE COLORADO CACHE COLORADO CACHE COLORADO CACHE COLORADO C

Green Peppercorn Sauce

1½ cups

3 **tablespoons butter**
3 **tablespoons minced shallots**
3 **tablespoons brandy**
1 **tablespoon green peppercorns, chopped or mashed**
2 **teaspoons Dijon mustard**
1 **bouillon cube, crushed**
1 **cup heavy cream**
1 **tablespoon butter, softened**

Melt butter in a small saucepan, add shallots and saute until golden. Stir in brandy and reduce over high heat by half. Add remaining ingredients except butter and cook until thickened, stirring constantly. Swirl in remaining butter.
   Note: Serve with broiled fish or meat.

Teriyaki Marinade I

1 cup

½ **cup soy sauce**
½ **cup dry sherry, saki, or
   bourbon**
2 **tablespoons sugar**
1 **large clove garlic, sliced**
½ **teaspoon ground ginger (or ½
   inch fresh ginger, peeled
   and chopped)**

Blend all ingredients until sugar is dissolved. Use this marinade for beef, pork, chicken or any kind of meat.

Teriyaki Marinade II

1 cup

⅓ **cup soy sauce**
⅓ **cup pineapple juice**
⅓ **cup red wine**

Combine all ingredients. This unusual marinade imparts a unique flavor to any meat or fowl.

Mustard Ham Sauce

2 cups

½ **cup sugar**
2 **tablespoons flour**
2 **eggs, lightly beaten**
½ **cup prepared mustard**
½ **cup vinegar**
½ **cup beef bouillon**
¼ **cup butter**

Sift flour and sugar together. Add eggs and mix well. Add remaining ingredients. Cook over low heat, stirring constantly until thick. Serve hot. Refrigerate leftover sauce to use for sandwiches.

Note: A delicious sweet-sour sauce.

Fairly Wonderful Fish Sauce

1½ cups

1½ **tablespoons butter**
2 **tablespoons flour**
2¼ **cups boiling, salted water**
1 **egg yolk**
1 **tablespoon cold water**
6 **tablespoons butter**
   juice of 2 lemons, or to taste

Melt 1½ tablespoons butter in a skillet. Stir in flour until well blended. Add boiling water and whisk until thickened. Beat the egg yolk with the cold water. Remove skillet from heat and stir in the egg yolk. Add 6 tablespoons butter and stir until melted. Strain the sauce and add the juice of the lemons, or to taste.

Note: Serve over your favorite broiled fish.

Mustard-Mayonnaise Sauce

About 2 cups

1 **cup mayonnaise**
½ **cup Dijon mustard**
2 **tablespoons green peppercorn**
   mustard
1 **teaspoon dry mustard**
1 **tablespoon finely minced**
   parsley
   pinch of cayenne pepper
2 **hard cooked eggs, finely**
   chopped
   juice of 1 small lemon

Mix all ingredients well in a bowl and let sit 30 minutes before serving.

Note: this is good on cold meats and as a dip for crudites.

Dill Sauce for Fish

2 cups

1 **pint sour cream**
1 **teaspoon Dijon mustard**
½ **teaspoon salt**
¼ **teaspoon white pepper**
½ **or more teaspoons dill weed**
1 **tablespoon fresh lemon juice**
2 **teaspoons capers**

Combine all ingredients. Serve with broiled fish.

Cumberland Sauce

3 cups

1 **orange**
1 **cup water**
6 **ounces currant jelly**
   dash of cayenne pepper
1 **teaspoon lemon juice**
1 **cup Port**

Cut peel of orange into pin-like slivers and cook in water over high heat for 5 minutes. Remove peel with slotted spoon. Add remaining ingredients and heat until jelly melts. Serve hot with beef fondue, lamb, duck, venison or other meats. Refrigerate leftover sauce.

Note: Try it on cold roast beef or cooled slices of fillet.

Mock Bordelaise

⅓ cup

1½ **cups red table wine**
1 **generous tablespoon Bovril**

Combine wine and meat seasoning base in a saucepan and cook over medium heat until reduced by at least ⅔. Serve with steak.

Note: Better than the sauce served in most restaurants.

SAND DUNES

Hints from the **Garden of the Gods**

A general rule for cooking vegetables covered or uncovered: vegetables that grow underground should be cooked covered, those that grow above ground should be cooked uncovered.

Any vegetable, fresh or frozen, may be cooked in the oven. Place in a covered dish, add salt and 2 tablespoons butter. Cook at 350 degrees to desired tenderness.

For flavor variation, cook vegetables in chicken stock, beef stock or consomme.

Peas become more than ordinary with the addition of crushed mint leaves, slivers of orange rind, nutmeg, or sauteed mushrooms during cooking.

To peel tomatoes easily, place them in boiling water for a few seconds.
Add a little sugar when cooking tomatoes to bring out their flavor and cut acidity.

To prevent eyes from watering when peeling onions, hold onion under running water or try holding two matches, striking end out, in your teeth while peeling. It works!

Use extra ears of corn by slicing off the kernals and heating them in a little milk and butter.

When replacing dried herbs with fresh herbs, use twice the amount.

When sauteeing fresh mushrooms, sprinkle with a little lemon juice to prevent discoloration.
Fresh mushrooms freeze well if washed, dried and stored whole or sliced in plastic bags. Use without defrosting in any cooked dish. Save the trimmed stems and store in the same manner for use in stocks, soups, etc.
Mushrooms should be stored in the refrigerator in paper bags to keep them from "weeping".

To dewax any vegetable or fruit, immerse for 5 minutes in a quart of tap water containing 10 to 15 drops liquid detergent. Wash with one tablespoon vinegar and rinse under running water. Rub with a towel.

Fresh parsley will keep well if stored in a screwtop jar in the refrigerator.

Use hot milk when mashing potatoes to keep them from becoming heavy or soggy.

When the tomato plants in your garden are still producing and frost or snow threatens, carefully pull up the plants, roots and all, and hang them upside down in your basement or store room. The remaining green tomatoes will ripen and give you fresh ones for another month.

The **Garden of the Gods** is an area of massive, irregular, strange red sandstone rock formations resembling human figures and animals. Found at the foot of Pike's Peak, it is near Colorado Springs, sister town of Manitou Springs, sacred ground where the Ute and Comanche met in peace.

Artichoke Hearts Au Gratin

6 servings

2	14-ounce cans artichoke hearts
½	clove garlic, minced
¼	cup butter
½	teaspoon salt
¼	teaspoon pepper
⅓	cup flour, sifted
1½	cups milk
1	egg, slightly beaten
½	cup grated Swiss cheese
1	tablespoon dry bread crumbs, finely crushed
1	teaspoon paprika

Cut artichoke hearts into thin slices. Saute artichokes and garlic in butter until tender. Remove artichoke hearts to a shallow baking dish. Stir seasonings and flour into remaining butter. Slowly add milk, stirring constantly. Cook over low heat until thickened. Remove from heat. Slowly add liquid to egg and ¼ cup of the cheese. Blend until smooth. Pour sauce over artichoke hearts and sprinkle with remaining ¼ cup cheese, crumbs and paprika. Bake at 450 degrees for 15 minutes.

Artichokes and Mushrooms Supreme

6 servings

1	pound large mushrooms
4	tablespoons butter
2	14-ounce cans artichoke hearts
1¼	teaspoons salt
¼	teaspoon pepper
¼	teaspoon thyme
½	cup dry sherry

Wash mushrooms and trim stems. Saute mushrooms in butter until barely tender. Add artichokes, seasonings, and sherry and cook over high heat to reduce liquid, approximately 2 minutes. Do not overcook. Serve immediately.

188
Vegetables

DRADO CACHE COLORADO CACHE COLORADO CACHE COLORADO CACHE COLORADO CACHE COLORADO CACHE COLORADO CACHE COLORADO CACHE COLORADO CACH

Asparagus and Sauces

6 - 10 **asparagus spears per person**
enough water to generously
cover asparagus spears
laying horizontally in a
large pot.
1½ **teaspoons salt per quart of**
water

Bring the water to a boil and lay in the spears. Bring the water to a boil as quickly as possible, reduce heat and boil slowly, uncovered for 12 to 15 minutes. Asparagus is done when a knife pierces the butt-end easily. Lift spears carefully from the pot and place on a serving platter. If you do not plan to serve it immediately, cover the platter with a folded napkin and place platter over pot of hot cooking water. It will keep warm for 20 to 30 minutes. Serve with butter or one of the following sauces.

Hollandaise sauce:
(see index)

Sauce Mousseline:
½ **cup whipping cream, whipped**
1½ **cups Hollandaise sauce**

Fold the whipped cream into the Hollandaise just before serving.

Special Green Beans

6-8 servings

2 **10-ounce packages frozen,**
French-cut green beans
2 **tablespoons margarine**
1 **small onion, minced**
1 **tablespoon chopped fresh**
parsley
1 **teaspoon salt**
¼ **teaspoon white pepper**
1 **tablespoon flour**
¼ **teaspoon freshly grated lemon**
rind
1 **cup sour cream**
1 **tablespoon dry sherry**
1 **cup grated sharp Cheddar**
cheese
½ **cup buttered bread crumbs**

Cook beans according to package directions. Set aside. In a saucepan, melt margarine and saute onion and parsley for 5 minutes. Add salt, pepper, flour, lemon rind, sour cream and sherry and cook another 3 minutes. Add beans to mixture. Pour into buttered 1½ quart casserole. Sprinkle with cheese and bread crumbs. Bake uncovered at 350 degrees for 30 minutes.

Dutch Snap Beans

6 servings

½   **pound bacon, cut into small pieces**
2   **onions, chopped**
2   **cloves garlic, chopped**
1   **tablespoon butter**
2   **pounds fresh green beans, snapped or cut**
4   **medium tomatoes, blanched, peeled, and chopped saving the juice**
1   **cup dry white wine**
    salt and pepper to taste
1   **teaspoon basil**

Cook bacon until limp and curling, saving the grease. In a large pan or Dutch oven, saute onions and garlic in butter over low heat. Add green beans, tomatoes, tomato juice, bacon, bacon grease and white wine. Season with salt, pepper and basil. Cover and let the mixture simmer for 30 minutes, or until beans are tender. Add small amounts of wine or water if the sauce reduces too much during the cooking. There should be about ½ cup liquid remaining when the beans are cooked.

Note: This is a wonderful complement to any grilled meats and a welcome change from baked beans!

Green Beans with Water Chestnuts

4 servings

½   **pound green beans, sliced diagonally (may use 1 10-ounce package frozen beans)**
½   **cup water chestnuts, sliced**
½   **cup fresh mushrooms, sliced**
½   **clove garlic, crushed**
1   **teaspoon vegetable oil**
1   **teaspoon sesame oil**
2½   **teaspoons soy sauce**
½   **teaspoon salt**
¼   **teaspoon pepper**
1   **teaspoon sugar**
2   **teaspoons sesame seeds, crushed**

Stir-fry beans, water chestnuts, mushrooms and garlic in oils. Add the remaining ingredients. Cover and cook until beans are tender, about 4 to 5 minutes.

Picnic Beans

4 servings

¼ pound bacon, cubed
1 small onion, chopped
1 1-pound can butter beans
  and juice
8 ounces chili sauce
  salt and pepper to taste

Brown bacon with the onion in a skillet. Pour the bacon, onion, and bacon grease into a 1 quart casserole with beans, chili sauce, salt and pepper. Bake at 350 degrees for 1 hour.

Lima Beans with Tomatoes

6 servings

1 cup sliced celery
½ cup chopped onion
3 tablespoons bacon grease
1 1-pound can tomatoes
¾ teaspoon salt
½ teaspoon sugar
½ teaspoon pepper
2 10-ounce packages frozen
  lima beans

Saute celery and onion in hot bacon grease for 3 minutes. Add tomatoes, salt, pepper and sugar. Bring to a boil, lower heat and simmer 10 minutes. Add lima beans, cover and simmer 20 to 35 minutes until tender.

Broccoli with Gruyere Cheese

8 servings

2 pounds fresh broccoli
6 tablespoons dry white wine
  salt and pepper to taste
6 tablespoons melted butter
⅔ cup grated Gruyere cheese

Divide thick stems of broccoli by cutting from the flowerets down through stems to make thin stemmed stalks of broccoli about ½ inch in diameter. Peel stems and score ends. Cook broccoli until crisp but tender. Drain, put in 9 × 13 inch baking dish. Add wine to melted butter, pour over broccoli. Sprinkle with cheese. Place in preheated 300 degree oven for 10 minutes or until cheese melts.

COLORADO CACHE COLORADO CACHE COLORADO CACHE COLORADO CACHE COLORADO CACHE COLORADO CACHE COLORADO CACHE COLORADO CACHE COLORADO CACHE COLORADO

Creamed Broccoli with Almonds

8 servings

3 cups chopped broccoli,
   cooked and drained
¼ cup butter
¼ cup flour
1 cup light cream (half and half)
¾ cup hot water
1 beef boullion cube
2 tablespoons dry sherry
2 tablespoons fresh lemon juice
   pepper to taste
¼ cup grated Parmesan cheese
¼ cup slivered almonds,
   toasted

Arrange broccoli in 8 x 12 inch shallow baking dish. Melt butter and blend in flour. When mixture is smooth, add cream and hot water in which boullion cube has been dissolved. Stir constantly until mixture is smooth and thickened. Add sherry, lemon juice and pepper. When all are well blended, pour sauce over cooked broccoli and sprinkle with cheese and almonds. Bake at 350 degrees for 20 minutes.

Broccoli with Cashews

6 servings

1 large bunch fresh broccoli
   (or 2 10-ounce packages
   frozen broccoli)
2 tablespoons minced onion
2 tablespoons butter
1 cup sour cream
2 teaspoons sugar
1 teaspoon vinegar
½ teaspoon poppyseeds
¼ teaspoon salt
½ teaspoon paprika
1 cup roasted cashews

Cook broccoli in water until crisp. Saute onion in butter. Stir in sour cream and remaining ingredients, except cashews. Layer broccoli in a buttered 1½ quart baking dish and cover with sauce. Sprinkle with cashews and bake uncovered at 325 degrees for 25 minutes.

Brussel Sprouts in Brown Butter

6 servings

3 tablespoons butter
1 tablespoon fresh lemon juice
1 quart fresh Brussel sprouts,
   cooked

Heat butter over low heat until it begins to brown. Add lemon juice and pour over hot cooked Brussel sprouts.

RADO CACHE COLORADO CACHE COLORADO CACHE COLORADO CACHE COLORADO CACHE COLORADO CACHE COLORADO CACHE COLORADO CACHE COLORADO CACH

Brussel Sprouts Dijon

8-10 servings

3 **10-ounce packages frozen Brussel sprouts**
¼ **pound butter**
¼ **cup dry white wine**
3 **tablespoons Dijon mustard**
¼ **teaspoon sage**
1 **cup heavy cream**
   slivered almonds, toasted and blanched

Cook Brussel sprouts in butter and wine until tender, but still slightly crisp. Stir in mustard, sage and cream. Cook until thickened, shaking pan occasionally so that each sprout is well coated. Serve sprinkled with warm toasted almonds.

Sour Cream Cabbage

6-8 servings

1 **firm cabbage**
1 **egg, well beaten**
2 **tablespoons sugar**
¼ - ½ **teaspoon ground nutmeg**
   salt and pepper to taste
1 **cup sour cream**

Cut cabbage in half, core and slice. Cook it in as little water as possible until it is tender, 5 to 10 minutes. Drain, then add the other ingredients, blend and heat through on a low burner. Serve immediately.

Swedish Red Cabbage

4-6 servings

1 **medium red cabbage, 2 to 2½ pounds**
4 **tablespoons butter**
1 **tablespoon sugar**
1 **teaspoon salt**
⅓ **cup water**
⅓ **cup white vinegar**
¼ **cup red currant jelly**
2 **tablespoons grated apple**

Wash cabbage in cold water. Cut in half, core and slice finely. Combine butter, sugar, salt, water and vinegar in a large pot or Dutch oven and bring to a boil. Add cabbage and stir to coat. Bring to a second boil and cover tightly. Bake at 350 degrees for 2 hours. Do not allow to dry out. Add more water if necessary. 10 minutes before the cabbage is completely cooked, mix in jelly and grated apple.

Note: Serve with cornish game hens or, for a family dinner, add 1 pound cooked and drained pork sausage patties or links.

Oriental Carrot Souffle

8-10 servings

1   10½-ounce package frozen
    peas
1   handful Mung bean sprouts
    pinch of marjoram
    parsley flakes
    salt
    pepper
    butter
    soy sauce to taste
1½ cups carrots, about 2 pounds,
    cooked and pureed
    pinch of cloves
2   tablespoons honey
1   teaspoon salt
½   cup butter
6   tablespoons flour
1½ cups cream
6   egg yolks
8   egg whites, stiffly beaten
    mushroom caps, for garnish
    butter
    lemon juice

Saute peas and bean sprouts slightly, just to soften. Season with marjoram, parsley flakes, salt, pepper, butter and soy sauce. Set aside.

Season carrots with cloves, honey and salt. Butter a souffle dish or Bundt pan. Melt remaining butter, add flour and cook 1 minute. Add cream and cook until thick, stirring constantly. Remove from heat. Add egg yolks and carrots. Cool. Fold in egg whites. Bake at 350 degrees for 35 minutes. Unmold on platter. Place peas and bean sprout mixture in center and surround with a row of mushroom caps that have been lightly sauteed in butter and lemon juice.

Apricot-Glazed Carrots

4-6 servings

2   pounds carrots, cut on
    diagonal
3   tablespoons butter or
    margarine
⅓   cup apricot preserves
¼   teaspoon ground nutmeg
¼   teaspoon salt
½-1 teaspoon freshly grated
    orange peel
2   teaspoons fresh lemon juice
    parsley, for garnish

Cook scraped and cut carrots in salted water until just tender, about 20 minutes. Drain. Melt butter and stir in preserves until blended. Add nutmeg, salt, orange peel and lemon juice. Toss carrots with apricot mixture until well coated. Garnish with parsley and serve at once.

Note: Good with poultry or pork.

ADO CACHE COLORADO CACHE COLORADO CACHE COLORADO CACHE COLORADO CACHE COLORADO CACHE COLORADO CACHE COLORADO CACHE COLORADO CACHE COLORADO CACHE COLORADO CACHE (

Barbara Conwell's Carrots and Parsnips

4 servings

4 **medium carrots**
4 **medium parsnips**
  butter
  salt and pepper
  tarragon

Shred equal amounts of carrots and parsnips with shredding blade of food processor or by hand. Poach briefly in salted water and drain. Quickly saute in butter and season to taste with salt, pepper and tarragon.
  Note: Not only wonderful but quick.

Glazed Carrots

4 servings

2 **tablespoons chopped onion**
2 **tablespoons chopped parsley**
2 **tablespoons butter**
8 **medium carrots, peeled and quartered**
1 **10½-ounce can consomme**
¼ **teaspoon sugar**
  dash of nutmeg

Cook onion and parsley in butter for 5 minutes. Add carrots, consomme, sugar and nutmeg. Cover and cook 15 minutes. Uncover, cook 15 minutes more or until carrots are tender and sauce is slightly thickened.

Nutty Carrots

8 servings

5 **cups carrot sticks, cut into 3 inch pieces**
1½ **cups water**
½ **teaspoons salt**
½ **cup melted butter**
2 **teaspoons honey**
1 **teaspoon salt**
¼ **teaspoon coarsely ground pepper**
2 **tablespoons fresh lemon juice**
¼ **teaspoon freshly grated lemon peel**
½ **cup coarsely broken walnuts**

Cook carrots in water with ½ teaspoon salt until just tender. Drain thoroughly. Meanwhile, heat remaining ingredients, except walnuts. Pour sauce over hot carrots. Toss with walnuts.

Carrots and Grapes

6 servings

2 pounds carrots, scraped and
    cut in thick diagonal pieces
butter
⅛ teaspoon sugar
1 tablespoon vodka
½ cup water
1 cup Tokay grapes, seeded
    salt and pepper to taste

Saute carrots in butter for a few minutes. Sprinkle carrots with sugar and cook, stirring, for a minute or two. Add vodka and water, and cook until carrots are almost tender. Add grapes and cover the pan. Cook until carrots are very tender. Add salt and pepper to taste.

Note: A colorful complement to a fall dinner.

Cauliflower au Gratin

6 servings

1 medium head cauliflower
    salt and pepper to taste
1 cup sour cream
1 cup grated sharp Cheddar
    cheese
2 teaspoons toasted sesame
    seeds

Break cauliflower into flowerets. Cook covered in a small amount of boiling salted water until tender, about 10 to 15 minutes. Drain well. Place half of flowerets in a 1 quart casserole, season with salt and pepper. Spread with ½ cup sour cream and ½ cup cheese. Top with 1 teaspoon sesame seeds. Repeat layers. Bake uncovered at 350 degrees until cheese melts and sour cream is heated through, about 10 minutes.

Corn and Zucchini Mexicana

8-10 servings

2 pounds zucchini, sliced
1 large onion, chopped
2 tablespoons butter
2 10-ounce packages frozen,
    whole kernel corn
½ pound Old English processed
    cheese, cubed or grated
1 4-ounce can green chiles,
    seeded and chopped
    salt and pepper to taste

Saute squash and onion in butter until just tender. Cook corn until just tender. Add corn, cheese and green chiles to squash and onions. Cook over low heat until cheese is melted, stirring occasionally. Season with salt and pepper. Pour into a 2 quart casserole and bake uncovered at 350 degrees for 30 minutes.

ADO CACHE COLORADO CACHE COLORADO CACHE COLORADO CACHE COLORADO CACHE COLORADO CACHE COLORADO CACHE COLORADO CACHE COLORADO CACHE

Cauliflower Souffle

4 servings

1 small head cauliflower, broken into flowerets
½ teaspoon salt
freshly ground pepper
freshly ground nutmeg
cayenne pepper
⅛ teaspoon rosemary
3 tablespoons butter
3 tablespoons flour
1½ cups hot milk
5 eggs, separated
pinch of salt
1½ cups grated Swiss cheese
2 tablespoons dry bread crumbs
parsley, for garnish

Cook cauliflower in boiling, salted water until tender, about 10 minutes. Puree and season with salt, pepper, nutmeg, cayenne pepper and rosemary. Melt butter in a saucepan, stir in flour and cook for 2 minutes. Add milk and stir until thickened. Remove pan from heat and blend in 4 of the egg yolks, one at a time. Add cauliflower puree and all but 2 tablespoons grated cheese. Beat the 5 egg whites with a pinch of salt until stiff. Carefully fold into the cheese mixture. Pour into a buttered souffle dish and sprinkle with the remaining grated cheese, bread crumbs and garnish with parsley. Bake at 400 degrees for 35 to 40 minutes.

Corn-Broccoli Bake

6 servings

1 10-ounce package frozen, chopped broccoli, defrosted
1 1-pound can creamed corn
¼ cup crushed saltine crackers
1 egg, beaten
2 tablespoons butter, melted
1 tablespoon instant minced onion
½ teaspoon salt
dash of pepper
¼ cup cracker crumbs
2 tablespoons butter, melted

Combine first eight ingredients and place in buttered 1 quart casserole dish. Mix cracker crumbs with remaining 2 tablespoons butter and sprinkle on top. Bake covered at 350 degrees for 45 minutes.

Escalloped Corn

butter
2 10-ounce packages frozen
    corn
½ teaspoon salt
    pepper to taste
¾ cup fine cracker crumbs
1 cup grated Cheddar cheese
6 tablespoons butter
1 egg
1 generous tablespoon sugar
2 cups milk
    paprika

8 servings

Butter a 2½ quart round casserole. Layer corn, salt, pepper, cracker crumbs and cheese. Dot with butter; repeat. Beat egg and add sugar and milk. Pour over mixture. Bake at 350 degrees for 45 minutes to 1 hour. Cover the casserole for the first ½ hour, then uncover and sprinkle top with paprika. Let stand at least 5 minutes before serving.

Caponata

1 large eggplant, unpeeled
⅔ cup olive oil
2 medium onions, diced
1 cup diced celery
1 pound Italian tomatoes and
    juice
⅓ cup wine vinegar
1 tablespoon sugar
2 teaspoons salt
¼ teaspoon pepper
3 dashes of cayenne pepper
1 14-ounce can green or ripe
    olives, diced
2 tablespoons capers with
    1 tablespoon juice
2 tablespoons pine nuts
    juice of 1 lemon

8 servings

Cut eggplant into ½ inch cubes. Heat ⅓ cup olive oil in large skillet. Saute eggplant for 5 minutes, stirring often. It will absorb oil and change color slightly; remove from heat. Add remaining oil to skillet and saute onions until transparent. Add celery and tomatoes with liquid. Cook over medium heat about 15 minutes, stirring often, until sauce has reduced and thickened. Stir in vinegar, sugar, and seasonings and eggplant. Cook covered for 10 minutes. Add olives, capers and pine nuts and cook uncovered 10 minutes longer. Check seasoning and add lemon juice to taste. Chill well before serving. Make 24 hours in advance. Refrigerates well for 2 weeks and freezes well.

Note: Serve as an antipasto with chopped parsley, as a hot or cold side dish with meat or fowl, or as a sandwich filling on French rolls.

198
Vegetables

ADO CACHE COLORADO CACHE COLORADO CACHE COLORADO CACHE COLORADO CACHE COLORADO CACHE COLORADO CACHE COLORADO CACHE COLORADO CACHE COLORADO CACHE COLORADO CACHE C

Ratatouille

6-8 servings

½ **pound eggplant**
½ **pound zucchini**
1 **teaspoon salt**
4 **tablespoons olive oil, or more if needed**
½ **pound yellow onions, thinly sliced**
2 **green peppers, sliced**
2 **cloves garlic, mashed**
  salt to taste
  pepper to taste
1 **pound fresh tomatoes, peeled, seeded and juiced**
3 **tablespoons minced parsley**

Peel eggplant and cut into slices about ¼ inch thick, 3 inches long and 1 inch wide. Scrub zucchini and slice off each end. Cut zucchini into slices about the same size as the eggplant slices. Place vegetables in a bowl and toss with salt. Let stand for 30 minutes. Drain and dry on paper towels. In a skillet, heat olive oil and saute one layer of eggplant at a time for about a minute on each side to brown lightly. Remove to a side dish. In the same pan, cook the onions and peppers slowly, adding a little more olive oil if neded, until tender but not browned. Stir in garlic and season with salt and pepper to taste.

Slice the tomato pulp in ½ inch strips. Lay them over the onions and peppers. Season tomatoes with salt and pepper. Cover the pan and cook over low heat for 5 minutes, or until tomatoes have begun to render their juice. Uncover, baste the tomatoes with the juices, raise heat and boil for several minutes until juice has almost evaporated. Put ⅓ of the tomato, onion and green pepper mixture in the bottom of a 2½ quart casserole and sprinkle it with 1 tablespoon parsley. Add half the eggplant and zucchini mixture on top of tomato layer, then half the remaining tomatoes and parsley. Put in the rest of the eggplant and zucchini, and finish with the remaining tomatoes and parsley. Cover the casserole and simmer over low heat for 10 minutes. Uncover, tip casserole and baste with the juices. Raise heat slightly and cook uncovered for 15 minutes more, basting several times, until juices have evaporated, leaving just a spoonful or two. Do not let the vegetables scorch on the bottom of the casserole. Refrigerate and let flavors blend for a day.

Note: This may be reheated and served as a vegetable or served cold as a dinner accompaniment or served at room temperature with crackers for hors d'oeuvres. For a main dish, add cooked slices of mild or sweet Italian sausage. Serve with chopped fresh parsley.

Rum Flambeed Mushrooms

6-8 servings

1	pound fresh mushrooms
6	tablespoons butter
1	teaspoon fresh lemon juice
¼	teaspoon salt
1/	teaspoon pepper
3	tablespoons light rum, heated
½	cup heavy cream, heated

Wash mushrooms and trim stems. Melt butter, add lemon juice, salt and pepper. Heat and add mushrooms. Saute until browned. Drain. Pour rum over mushrooms and ignite. When flame dies, stir in heated heavy cream.

Note: Serve as a vegetable or pour over steaks as a sauce.

Glazed Onions

4-6 servings

6	large onions
5	tablespoons butter
½	teaspoon salt
½	teaspoon black pepper
½	teaspoon celery salt
1	tablespoon sugar
½	cup dry sherry
2	tablespoons freshly grated Parmesan cheese

Peel and slice onions in ¼-inch slices; separate into rings. In a skillet, combine butter, onion, salt, pepper and sugar. Simmer onions unti limp. Add sherry and cook 2 to 3 minutes. Sprinkle with Parmesan cheese and serve immediately.

Cold Dill Peas

4 servings

1	10-ounce package frozen tiny peas
1	cup sour cream
½ - 1	tablespoon dill weed
1	teaspoon chopped chives
	salt and pepper to taste
½ - 1	teaspoon curry powder
	fresh lemon juice to taste

Cook and drain peas thoroughly. Mix together other ingredients very thoroughly. Carefully combine with peas. Chill and garnish with more dill or chives.

Note: May be used in place of a salad.

Savory Green Peas

6-8 servings

2 **10-ounce packages frozen peas (or one pint fresh peas)**
2 **sprigs parsley**
6 **small green onions**
1 **heart of lettuce**
4 **tablespoons butter, cut in pieces**
1 **teaspoon salt**
1 **teaspoon sugar**
4 **slices bacon, cooked and crumbled (optional)**

Combine all ingredients except bacon in a bowl and refrigerate for at least 8 hours. Place in a pan with three tablespoons water and cook covered until tender. Discard the parsley, onions, and lettuce. Add bacon if desired.

Oriental Peas

8 servings

2 **10-ounce packages frozen peas, cooked**
1 **cup sliced water chestnuts**
1 **cup fresh bean sprouts**
½ **pound mushrooms, sauteed**
1 **cup Bechamel sauce (see index)**
   soy sauce to taste
   French fried onion rings, frozen and baked separately

Mix all ingredients except onion rings and bake at 350 degrees for 30 minutes. Add onion rings and bake 10 minutes more.

Spinach Roll with Mushrooms

6-8 servings

3 **10-ounce packages
   frozen spinach**
¼ **cup bread crumbs**
2 **teaspoons salt**
¾ **teaspoon pepper
   pinch of ground nutmeg**
6 **tablespoons butter, melted**
4 **eggs, separated**
4 **tablespoons grated
   Parmesan cheese**
1½ **pounds mushrooms, sliced**
¼ **cup butter**
1½ **tablespoons flour**
1 **cup Hollandaise sauce
   (see index)**

Thaw spinach, squeeze out all excess moisture. Chop. Butter a 15 × 10 × 1 inch jelly roll pan; line with wax paper. Butter wax paper and sprinkle with bread crumbs. Place spinach in bowl, add 1 teaspoon salt, ¼ teaspoon pepper, nutmeg and melted butter. Beat in egg yolks one at a time. Beat egg whites in a small bowl until they hold soft peaks—if not using a copper bowl, add 1/8 teaspoon cream of tartar when egg whites reach foamy stage. Fold into spinach mixture. Spoon mixture into prepared pan and smooth the top evenly with a spatula. Sprinkle with Parmesan cheese. Bake at 350 degrees for 15 minutes or until the center feels barely firm when touched. While the spinach roll is baking, saute mushrooms quickly in ¼ cup butter. Sprinkle mushrooms with 1½ tablespoons flour, remaining 1 teaspoon salt, and ¼ teaspoon pepper. When roll is done baking, place a sheet of buttered wax paper or foil, butter side down, over the roll and invert onto a warm cookie sheet. Carefully remove bottom paper. Spread mushroom mixture over hot spinach roll. Roll up, jelly roll fashion, then ease roll onto warm platter. Spread Hollandaise sauce over top. Serve immediately.

Note: This can be made ahead up to the point where you spread Hollandaise sauce over the top. Cover with foil and heat until warmed through, then spread sauce.

Spinach Quiche

6 servings

1 **cup grated Swiss cheese**
1 **10-ounce package spinach,
   cooked and drained**
1 **partially cooked 9 inch
   pie shell**
1¼ **cups half and half**
3 **eggs**
1 **teaspoon salt**
2 **tablespoons butter**

Spread ¾ of the cheese and spinach on the bottom of the pie shell. Beat the cream, egg and salt together until frothy. Pour over the cheese and spinach. Sprinkle with remaining cheese and dot with butter. Bake at 375 degrees for 25 to 30 minutes or until pie is set.

Spinach on Artichoke Bottoms with Mock Hollandaise

6 servings

2 10-ounce packages frozen, chopped spinach (or use fresh spinach)
½ pound fresh mushrooms
6 tablespoons butter
1 tablespoon flour
½ cup milk
½ teaspoon salt
½ teaspoon garlic powder
1 14-ounce can artichoke bottoms (not marinated)
1 cup sour cream
1 cup mayonnaise
¼ cup lemon juice

Cook spinach and drain well. Reserve 16 mushroom caps. Chop remaining caps and stems and saute in 2 tablespoons butter. Saute the 16 mushroom caps in another tablespoon butter. Melt 2 tablespoons butter in saucepan. Add flour and cook until bubbling. Add milk, stirring constantly, until smooth. Add seasonings, then the chopped mushrooms and spinach. Drain artichoke bottoms. Place in a 2 quart baking dish and cover with creamed spinach. Combine sour cream, mayonnaise and lemon juice and heat slowly until blended before adding to casserole. Top with sauce and mushroom caps. Bake at 375 degrees for 15 minutes.

Note: This can be made a day ahead and reheated.

Honey-Glazed Acorn Squash

4-6 servings

2 or 3 acorn squash
salt and pepper to taste
¼ cup honey
2 tablespoons butter, softened
1 tablespoon Worcestershire sauce
¼ cup chopped walnuts
¼ cup raisins

Cut squash in half, remove seeds. Place cut-side down in shallow pan. Add ½ inch hot water to pan. Bake uncovered at 350 degrees for 40 to 50 minutes, or until almost tender. Turn cut-side up, season with salt and pepper. Combine other ingredients and spoon into cavities of squash. Bake uncovered at 350 degrees for 15 minutes or until filling is heated.

Layered Squash

4-6 servings

3 small yellow squash or
    zucchini (or mixed), sliced
4 tomatoes, sliced
1 onion, thinly sliced
    salt and pepper to taste
½ teaspoon tarragon
6 ounces grated Emmenthaler
    cheese

Butter a deep 2 quart casserole. Using half the vegetables, make a layer of zucchini, tomatoes and onion. Sprinkle with salt, pepper and tarragon. Add half the cheese and repeat the layers. Bake covered at 350 degrees for 45 minutes to 1 hour.

Tomatoes Vinaigrette

4 servings

12 thick tomato slices
¼ cup chopped green onions
1 cup olive oil
⅓ cup wine vinegar
2 teaspoons oregano leaves,
    crushed
1 teaspoon salt
½ teaspoon pepper
½ teaspoon dry mustard
2 cloves garlic, crushed
1 tablespoon minced parsley

Combine all ingredients in a bowl and marinate 4 hours. Serve on lettuce leaves.
    Note: This may be served as a salad.

Tomato Pie

6-8 servings

1 9-inch unbaked pastry shell
3 medium tomatoes, peeled and
    thickly sliced
½ teaspoon salt
¼ teaspoon pepper
½ teaspoon basil
¼ cup chopped, fresh chives
¼ cup mayonnaise
1 cup grated, sharp
    Cheddar cheese

Bake pie crust at 425 degrees for 5 minutes. Remove from oven, reduce heat to 400 degrees. Cover the bottom of pie crust with tomato slices, sprinkle with salt, pepper, basil and chives. Thoroughly combine the mayonnaise and cheese. Carefully spread this mixture evenly over the tomato slices, making sure to seal the edges of the pie crust completely. Bake for 35 minutes.

204
Vegetables

DO CACHE COLORADO CACHE COLORADO CACHE COLORADO CACHE COLORADO CACHE COLORADO CACHE COLORADO CACHE COLORADO CACHE COLORADO CACHE COLORADO CACHE COLORADO CACHE C

Escalloped Tomatoes

6 servings

½ **cup chopped onion**
3 **tablespoons butter, melted**
2¼ **cups fresh, soft breadcrumbs**
2 **tablespoons chopped parsley**
3½ **teaspoons Worcestershire sauce**
1½ **teaspoons salt**
1½ **pounds fresh tomatoes, peeled, or 1 1-pound 15½ ounce can Italian tomatoes, drained and chopped**
2 **tablespoons olive oil**

Saute onion in butter for 5 minutes. Stir in breadcrumbs, parsley, 1½ teaspoons Worcestershire sauce, salt and set aside. Slice tomatoes into ¼-inch thick slices. Arrange a layer in a lightly buttered 1½ quart casserole. Combine oil and rest of Worcestershire sauce and pour a little over tomatoes. Sprinkle lightly with breadcrumb mix. Repeat layers, ending with breadcrumbs. Bake covered at 375 degrees for 30 minutes. Uncover and bake an additional 15 minutes or until breadcrumbs are lightly browned.

Tomato and Onion Surprise

8 servings

2 **cups seasoned bread crumbs**
5 **tomatoes, sliced**
1 **medium white onion, thinly sliced and separated into rings**
½ **cup butter**
2 - 3 **tablespoons chives**
1 **12-ounce carton sour cream**

Line a buttered 9 × 9 inch casserole dish with half of the bread crumbs. Alternate tomato and onion slices. Dot with half the butter. Mix chives with sour cream. Spread over tomato and onion rings. Sprinkle with remaining bread crumbs. Dot with remaining butter. Bake uncovered at 350 degrees for 45 minutes or until lightly browned and cooked through.

Tomatoes Somerset

4 servings

3 - 4	tomatoes, peeled and sliced
½	cup finely cut, mild Cheddar cheese
½	cup finely cut, sharp Cheddar cheese
2	tablespoons chopped green pepper
3	tablespoons chopped onion
¼	cup butter, melted
1	cup Ritz cracker crumbs
½	cup diced celery
1	teaspoon salt
¼	teaspoon paprika
3 - 4	green pepper rings

Mix all ingredients except pepper rings and pour into buttered baking dish. Top with green pepper rings. Bake at 350 degrees for 20 minutes.

Deviled Tomatoes

8 servings

4	tomatoes, halved
	salt and freshly ground pepper
	cayenne pepper to taste
2	tablespoons buttered bread crumbs
2	tablespoons butter
½	teaspoon prepared mustard
	dash of Tabasco sauce
2	teaspoons Worcestershire sauce
1	teaspoon sugar
1½	tablespoons vinegar
1	egg yolk
	chopped parsley for garnish

Place tomato halves in a shallow baking dish. Sprinkle lightly with salt, pepper and cayenne, and then with buttered bread crumbs. Set aside. Melt butter in a small saucepan. Add mustard, Tabasco sauce, Worcestershire sauce, sugar, vinegar and a sprinkling of salt. Bring to a boil. Beat egg yolk and add a little of the vinegar mixture while stirring. Return to saucepan and cook over low heat until thickened, stirring constantly. Broil tomatoes until the crumbs are brown. Serve with a spoonful of sauce on each half and garnish with parsley.

ADO CACHE COLORADO CACHE COLORADO CACHE COLORADO CACHE COLORADO CACHE COLORADO CACHE COLORADO CACHE COLORADO CACHE COLORADO CACHE COLORADO CACHE

Tomatoes Duxelles

4 servings

2	medium tomatoes
12	medium mushrooms
2	small sweet onions
4	tablespoons butter
¼	cup dry sherry
1	teaspoon fresh lemon juice
¼	teaspoon salt
	dash of pepper
1	egg yolk
1	tablespoons grated
	Parmesan cheese

Cut tomatoes in half. Place the 4 halves in a buttered pie plate. Finely chop mushrooms. Peel and finely chop onions. Saute mushrooms and onions in butter, then add sherry, lemon juice, salt and pepper. Simmer 5 to 10 minutes until liquid is absorbed. Remove pan from heat and stir in egg yolk. Spread mixture over tomato halves. Sprinkle halves with Parmesan cheese. Bake at 350 degrees for 10 minutes, then slide under broiler for a minute or so, until tops are brown.

Cheese Stuffed Tomatoes

8 servings

4	medium tomatoes
2	cups grated Swiss cheese
½	cup light cream
2	egg yolks, slightly beaten
2	tablespoons chopped chives
3	tablespoons grated onion
½	teaspoon dried marjoram
	leaves
1	teaspoon dried mustard
1½	teaspoons salt
⅓	cup seasoned bread crumbs
2	tablespoons butter

Halve tomatoes crosswise. Scoop out pulp leaving shells intact and chop pulp coarsely. Combine tomato pulp with cheese, cream, egg yolks, chives, onion, marjoram, mustard and salt. Mix well. Spoon cheese mixture into tomato shells. Toss bread crumbs with melted buter, and sprinkle over cheese mixture. Arrange tomato halves in buttered baking dish. Bake uncovered at 350 degrees for 25 minutes.

Note: May be prepared early in the day and refrigerated until ready to bake.

Telluride Tomatoes

6 servings

- 6 medium tomatoes
- 1 pint fresh mushrooms, chopped (about 1½ cups)
- 2 tablespoons butter
- ½ cup sour cream
- 2 egg yolks, beaten
- ½ cup bread crumbs
- 1 teaspoon salt
  dash of pepper
  pinch of thyme
- 1 tablespoon butter
- 3 tablespoons bread crumbs

Cut stem end from tomatoes and scoop out pulp. Turn shells upside down to drain. Finely chop the pulp to measure 1 cup. Set aside. Cook mushrooms in butter. Combine sour cream and egg yolks. Add to mushrooms and tomato pulp and mix well. Stir in crumbs, salt, pepper and thyme. Cook and stir until mixture thickens and boils. Place tomato shells in 8 × 8 inch baking dish. Spoon mushroom mixture into tomatoes. Combine 1 tablespoon butter and 3 tablespoons bread crumbs and sprinkle on tomatoes. Bake at 375 degrees for 25 minutes.

Zucchini Souffle

6-8 servings

- 2 pounds sliced zucchini
- 1 tablespoon butter
- ⅔ cup sour cream
- ⅓ cup grated Cheddar cheese
- ½ teaspoon salt
- ⅛ teaspoon paprika
- 1 egg yolk, beaten
- 1 tablespoon chopped chives
- 1 egg white, stiffly beaten
- ½ cup cracker crumbs
- 2 tablespoons melted butter

Cook zucchini in boiling water until tender, but slightly crisp. Drain. Melt 1 tablespoon butter, stir in sour cream, cheese, salt and paprika. Cook over low heat, stirring constantly, until cheese is melted. Remove from heat and stir in egg yolk and chives. Stir into zucchini and fold in beaten egg white. Place in a souffle dish. Toss crumbs with melted butter and sprinkle on top. Bake at 350 degrees for 20 minutes.

Note: Similar to a corn pudding.

Zucchini Roulade

4 servings as entree
6 servings as vegetable

1	**cup milk**
1	**tablespoon chopped carrots**
1	**tablespoon chopped celery**
1	**tablespoon chopped onion**
2	**sprigs parsley**
1	**bay leaf**
	pinch of thyme
1	**pound zucchini**
1½	**teaspoons salt**
1	**shallot, minced**
1½	**tablespoons butter**
¼	**cup flour**
4	**egg yolks**
	nutmeg
	salt
	pepper
6	**egg whites**
	pinch of salt
	butter
⅓	**cup freshly grated Parmesan cheese**
1½	**cups Mornay sauce (see index)**

Scald milk with carrots, celery, onion, parsley, bay leaf and thyme. Remove pan from heat and let mixture stand covered for 10 minutes. Strain flavored milk into a bowl and let cool. Scrub, trim and grate zucchini and place in a colander. Toss with 1½ teaspoons salt and let stand for 10 minutes. Rinse zucchini and squeeze out excess moisture. In a skillet, saute shallot in butter until it is softened. Add zucchini and saute mixture for 5 minutes or until zucchini is tender. Transfer mixture to a large bowl. In a saucepan, slowly add ¼ cup of the flavored milk to the flour, stirring with a wire whisk, and continue to stir mixture until it is a smooth paste. Add remaining milk, bring mixture to a boil over high heat, stirring constantly, and cook for 30 minutes. Remove pan from heat and add egg yolks, one at a time, beating well after each addition. Add yolk mixture to zucchini mixture and season with nutmeg, salt and pepper. In a bowl, beat egg whites with a pinch of salt until they hold stiff peaks. Stir ¼ of the beaten egg whites into zucchini mixture and fold in remaining whites, gently but thoroughly. Butter an 11 × 16 inch jelly roll pan and line it with foil. Butter and flour the foil. Pour zucchini mixture into the pan and spread it evenly with a spatula. Bake at 375 degrees for 15 minutes. Turn roulade out on a tea towel and sprinkle with Parmesan cheese. Make Mornay sauce. Spread roulade with 1 cup of sauce and roll lengthwise, using the towel to help roll it. Transfer roulade to a heated serving dish and pour over the remaining sauce.

Stuffed Zucchini

4 servings

2	**medium zucchini**
½	**cup chopped onion**
1	**garlic clove, minced**
4	**tablespoons butter**
1	**large tomato, peeled, seeded and chopped**
	salt and pepper
½	**cup soft bread crumbs**
2	**tablespoons freshly grated Parmesan cheese**

Wash zucchini and cut in half lengthwise. Hollow out shells, reserving pulp. In 2 tablespoons butter, saute garlic and onion until soft. Add zucchini pulp and tomatoes and mix together. Fill shells with mixture, rounding the top. Melt remaining butter and mix with breadcrumbs and cheese. Sprinkle on top of stuffed shells and place in a shallow buttered baking dish. Cover with foil and bake at 350 degrees for about 30 minutes.

Sweet and Sour Zucchini

2 quarts

1½	**tablespoons dry onions**
½	**cup white wine vinegar**
½	**cup chopped green pepper**
½	**cup chopped celery**
7	**small zucchini, thinly sliced**
¾	**cup sugar**
1	**teaspoon pepper**
⅓	**cup oil**
⅔	**cup cider vinegar**
1	**teaspoon salt**

Soak onions in wine vinegar in a large bowl. Add remaining ingredients and refrigerate overnight. Drain well and serve chilled or at room temperature.

Note: This may be used as a salad.

Indonesian Melange

8 servings

1	**green pepper, cut into strips**
1	**1-pound 10-ounce can pineapple chunks (packed in own juice) reserve liquid**
2	**large tomatoes, peeled and cut into eighths**
2	**apples, peeled, cored and sliced**
1	**large banana**

(continued on following page)

RADO CACHE COLORADO CACHE COLORADO CACHE COLORADO CACHE COLORADO CACHE COLORADO CACHE COLORADO CACHE COLORADO CACHE COLORADO CACHE COLORADO CACHE COLORADO CACHE COLORADO CACH

Sweet and sour sauce:

- ½ **cup pineapple juice, from the pineapple chunks**
- ¼ **cup wine vinegar**
- 2 **tablespoons oil**
- 2 **tablespoons brown sugar**
- 1 **tablespoon soy sauce**
- ½ **teaspoon pepper**
- 1 **teaspoon cornstarch**
- 2 **teaspoons water**
  cayenne pepper to taste

(continued from previous page)

Make sweet and sour sauce by combining pineapple juice, vinegar, oil, brown sugar, soy sauce and pepper in a saucepan. Mix cornstarch in the water. Heat the pineapple juice mixture and add the cornstarch and water. Cook over medium heat until thickened. Add cayenne pepper carefully. The sauce should be hot to the taste with seasoning and temperature. Add fruits and vegetables and heat just until they begin to soften but are still slightly crisp.

Note: Wonderful with any curry, broiled chicken, lamb chops or paella.

Sunshine Casserole

- 1 **medium onion, chopped**
  butter
- 4 - 6 **yellow squash, sliced**
- ½ **teaspoon garlic salt**
- ¼ **teaspoon ground cumin**
- 1 **teaspoon salt**
- ¼ **teaspoon pepper**
- 2 **10-ounce packages frozen whole kernel corn, cooked and drained**
- 2 **cups grated sharp cheese (preferably New York sharp Cheddar)**
  seasoned buttered bread crumbs

6-8 servings

Saute onion in butter in a large skillet. Add squash, cover and steam until squash is tender. Drain and add seasonings and corn. Cover and cook 5 minutes more. Stir in cheese and place in a 1½ quart casserole and top with bread crumbs. Bake at 350 degrees for 25 to 30 minutes.

Fresh Garden Delight

4 servings

1 medium zucchini, sliced
1 medium yellow crookneck squash, sliced
1 medium onion, sliced
6 - 12 Chinese pea pods (if frozen, partially thaw)
1 cup fresh green beans, sliced
1 small green pepper, chopped
4 tablespoons butter
¾ teaspoon seasoning salt
2 teaspoons seasoning pepper
½ teaspoon dill weed

Saute all vegetables lightly in melted butter. Cover tightly for 10 to 12 minutes and stir occasionally. Sprinkle with seasoning salt, seasoning pepper, and dill weed.

Stir-Fry Harvest Vegetables

6-8 servings

1 bunch broccoli
1 small cauliflower
2 cups fresh sliced mushrooms
2 tablespoons lemon juice
2 tablespoons peanut oil
1 small slice ginger root
½ cup sliced green pepper
2 cups diagonally sliced celery
1 clove garlic, minced
1 teaspoon salt
1 teaspoon onion salt
1 teaspoon black pepper
2 tablespoons soy sauce
½ cup grated sharp Cheddar cheese

Trim stems and leaves from broccoli and cauliflower. Divide into small flowerets. Pour lemon juice over mushrooms and set aide. Measure oil into wok, rub ginger root around sides of wok and discard. Arrange broccoli and cauliflower on bottom and sides of wok. Layer mushrooms, green pepper and celery in wok. Add garlic and all seasonings except soy sauce. Cover and cook for about 10 minutes or until vegetables are cooked, but still crisp. Add soy sauce and grated cheese. Cook until cheese is melted.

PAWNEE BUTTE NATIONAL GRASSLANDS

Hints from **Golden**

Always stir rice with a fork, or toss it with 2 forks. Using a spoon bruises the grains and makes them sticky.

Rice will be fluffier and drier if a slice of dry bread is put on top of it after cooking and draining.

To keep noodles from boiling over add 1 tablespoon butter to the cooking water.

For fluffier mashed potatoes add a pinch of baking soda along with the milk and butter.

Soak raw potatoes in cold water at least 30 minutes before frying to improve crispness.

To keep cooked rice warm, place rice in colander over simmering water and cover with cloth or paper towels.

Add a little white wine, Marsala or sherry to uncooked rice that has been stirred into some melted butter in the saucepan. Add regular amount of liquid and cook for a superb tasting rice.

Golden is located just west of Denver at the foot of Lookout Mountain, site of Buffalo Bill's grave. For a time Golden and Denver claimed the site of the state capitol and the legislature moved each session from one to the other. Named for an early miner, this small town rivaled Denver as the chief settlement in Colorado Territory.

Pasta Walnetto

6-8 servings

1   **12-ounce package noodles
    (Kluski or egg noodles)**
¼   **cup heavy cream**
¼   **cup sour cream**
    **salt and freshly ground black
    pepper**
3   **tablespoons butter**
2   **cloves garlic, finely minced**
1   **cup finely chopped walnuts**
1   **cup freshly grated Parmesan
    cheese**
½   **cup chicken broth**

Boil the noodles al dente. Drain well. Mix heavy cream and sour cream, add to noodles with salt and pepper to taste and 2 tablespoons of the butter. Cover and keep warm. Heat the remaining tablespoon of butter in a small pan. Saute the garlic for 3 minutes, being careful not to let it brown. Remove from heat, stir in walnuts, Parmesan and chicken broth. Toss with the noodles. Serve immediately.

Linguine with Artichokes in White Sauce

4 servings

¼   **cup olive oil**
¼   **cup butter**
1   **teaspoon flour**
1   **cup chicken stock**
1   **clove garlic, crushed**
2   **teaspoons fresh lemon juice**
1   **teaspoon minced parsley**
    salt and pepper to taste
8   **artichoke hearts, cooked and
    drained**
2   **tablespoons freshly grated
    Parmesan cheese**
1   **teaspoon drained capers**
1   **pound linguine, cooked**
2   **tablespoons olive oil**
1   **tablespoon freshly grated
    Parmesan cheese**
1   **tablespoon softened butter**
¼   **teaspoon salt**

In a large heavy skillet heat ¼ cup olive oil and ¼ cup butter over moderately low heat. Add flour and cook mixture, stirring, for 3 minutes. Stir in chicken stock, and cook over moderately high heat for 1 minute. Add garlic, lemon juice, parsley, and salt and pepper to taste. Cook for 5 minutes over low heat, stirring occasionally. Add artichoke hearts, 2 tablespoons Parmesan cheese, and drained capers and cook, covered, for 8 minutes. In large casserole, combine 2 tablespoons olive oil, 1 tablespoon Parmesan cheese, softened butter, and ¼ teaspoon salt. Add the drained linguine to the casserole and toss with the cheese mixture. Divide pasta among 4 heated bowls, top with sauce and garnish each serving with additional grated Parmesan cheese.

6

Pasta, Rice and Potatoes

ADO CACHE COLORADO CACHE COLORADO CACHE COLORADO CACHE COLORADO CACHE COLORADO CACHE COLORADO CACHE COLORADO CACHE COLORADO CACHE

Linguine with Tomatoes and Zucchini

6 servings

- 4 **ounces linguine, cooked and drained**
- ⅓ **cup butter**
- ⅓ **cup chopped onion**
- 1 **green pepper, seeded and cut into strips**
- 2 - 3 **cups sliced zucchini**
- 4 **medium tomatoes, peeled, seeded and cut into strips**
- ¼ **cup chopped parsley**
- ½ **cup freshly grated Parmesan cheese**
- ½ **cup Gruyere or other Swiss cheese**

Melt butter in a skillet and saute onion for about 5 minutes. Add green pepper and cook a few minutes more. Combine with remaining ingredients, reserving a few tablespoons Parmesan cheese for top. Place in buttered 2 quart casserole and top with cheese. Bake covered at 350 degrees for 30 to 40 minutes, or until cheese is bubbling. Do not overcook.

Fettuccine Alfredo

6 servings

- 1 **pound fettuccine noodles, cooked al dente**
- ¼ **pound butter**
- 1 **egg yolk**
- ¼ **cup heavy cream**
- ½ **cup freshly grated Parmesan cheese**
  salt and pepper to taste

Cream butter until fluffy. Add egg yolk and cream and beat constantly while adding cheese a tablespoon at a time. Put drained noodles in large heated serving bowl. Add cheese mixture to fettuccine and season as desired with salt and pepper. Prepare just before serving as it should be served immediately.

COLORADO CACHE COLORADO CACHE COLORADO CACHE COLORADO CACHE COLORADO CACHE COLORADO CACHE COLORADO CACHE COLORADO CACHE COLORADO CACHE COLORADO

Fettuccine a la Papalina

4 servings

- 2 tablespoons butter
- 2 cups sliced mushrooms
- 2 cups cooked ham, cut in julienne
- 1 small onion, minced
- 1 clove garlic, pressed
  salt and pepper to taste
- 4 egg yolks
- ¼ cup freshly grated Parmesan cheese
- 6 tablespoons butter
- 1 tablespoon fresh lemon juice (optional)
- 8 ounces fettuccine noodles, cooked
- 3 tablespoons minced parsley
- 3 tablespoons Parmesan cheese

Melt butter in a large skillet. Add mushrooms, ham, onion, garlic and saute over medium heat for 5 minutes. Add salt and pepper to taste. Meanwhile, in the top of a double boiler over hot, but not boiling, water, combine egg yolks and Parmesan cheese thoroughly. Add butter to the yolk mixture, 1 tablespoon at a time, stirring constantly and allowing each piece of butter to melt before each addition. Add lemon juice and continue to cook until sauce is slightly thickened. Pour sauce over hot noodles and toss lightly, add ham mixture and toss to combine. Sprinkle the dish with the minced parsley and Parmesan cheese and serve immediately.

Note: Serve as an accompaniment or as an after theatre supper with a tossed green salad.

Rice with Green Chiles

6-8 servings

- 3 cups sour cream (24 ounces)
- 2 4-ounce cans chopped, mild green chiles
- 4 cups cooked rice
- 2½ cups grated Monterey Jack cheese (8 ounces)
- 2½ cups grated Cheddar cheese (8 ounces)
  salt and pepper to taste

Mix together sour cream and chiles and set aside. Toss cheeses together. Butter a 1½ quart casserole dish. Put half of rice in casserole, spread half of sour cream mixture on rice, top with half of cheeses and sprinkle with salt and pepper. Repeat these layers a second time. Cover casserole and bake for 25 minutes at 375 degrees. Remove cover and bake an additional 10 minutes, or until bubbly.

Note: This may be easily halved or doubled, and may be assembled early in the day, refrigerated, and baked later. Allow more baking time if casserole is chilled.

Pasta, Rice and Potatoes

Feathered Rice

4 servings

1 cup raw long-grain rice
1½ teaspoons salt
2½ cups boiling water

Spread the rice in a shallow pan, place in preheated 375 degree oven. Bake, stirring occasionally until golden brown, about 10 minutes. Put into casserole, add salt and boiling water. Cover tightly. Bake 20 minutes at 400 degrees or 30 minutes at 350 degrees until rice absorbs the water and puffs up light and fluffy. Remove cover at the end of the suggested time, run a fork through it and if moisture is not all absorbed return to oven uncovered for a few minutes.
Note: Has a wonderful, toasted flavor.

Rice, Cheese and Corn Bake

6 servings

1½ cups chopped celery
3 tablespoons chopped onion
¼ cup butter
3½ cups fresh or frozen corn
1 cup raw rice, cooked
3 cups grated Cheddar cheese
(12 ounces)
1½ cups milk
1 teaspoon salt
⅛ teaspoon paprika

Saute celery and onion in butter for about 5 minutes. Mix with remaining ingredients and place in a buttered 2 quart casserole. Cover and bake at 300 degrees for 1 hour.
Note: Easy to make ahead for a patio party.

Brazilian Rice

4-6 servings

2 tablespoons olive oil
1 medium onion, chopped
1 clove garlic, pressed
2 tomatoes, peeled
and chopped
4 cups water
1 teaspoon salt
2 cups long-grain raw rice

Heat olive oil in skillet. Add onion and garlic and saute until golden brown. Add rice and tomatoes and cook over medium heat, stirring constantly, for 3 minutes. Add water and salt, bring to a boil, cover, lower heat, and cook for 20 to 30 minutes, or until rice is dry and fluffy.
Note: Serve with Feijoada. (See index)

219

Pasta, Rice and Potatoes

COLORADO CACHE COLORADO CACHE COLORADO CACHE COLORADO CACHE COLORADO CACHE COLORADO CACHE COLORADO CACHE COLORADO CACHE COLORADO C

Spaghetti alla Carbonara

4 servings

- 1 **pound bacon, diced (or 1 pound Italian sausage, crumbled)**
- 1 **onion, chopped**
- 1 **8-ounce package spaghetti, cooked and kept hot**
- 3 **eggs, well beaten**
- 8 **ounces freshly grated Romano cheese**

In a skillet fry bacon or sausage with onions until meat is cooked. Drain off most of the grease, leaving about 3 tablespoons. When ready to serve, mix eggs and cheese with spaghetti. Add meat mixture and toss together carefully. Serve immediately in large portions.

Risi e Bisi

6 servings

- 5 **cups chicken stock**
- 4 **tablespoons butter**
- ½ **cup finely chopped onions**
- 2 **cups fresh peas**
- ¼ **pound cooked, smoked diced ham**
- 1½ **cups raw rice**
- 2 **tablespoons softened butter**
- ½ **cup freshly grated Parmesan cheese**

Slowly simmer chicken stock in a 2 to 3 quart saucepan over low heat. In a heavy 3 quart casserole, melt 4 tablespoons butter over moderate heat. Add the onions and cook, stirring frequently until they are transparent but not browned. Add the peas, rice and diced ham. Cook for 2 minutes, or until the rice grains are buttery and somewhat opaque. Add 2 cups of simmering stock and cook uncovered, stirring occasionally, until almost all of the liquid is absorbed. Add another cup of stock. When this is absorbed, the rice and peas should be tender. If not, add more stock, ½ cup at a time and continue cooking and stirring. Gently stir in softened butter and grated cheese. Serve at once while the rice is creamy and hot.

Note: An interesting risotto variation.

Rice and Mushrooms

6-8 servings

3 cups cooked, long-grain rice
½ pounds mushrooms, sliced
4 green onions, chopped,
    including ½ of the tops
3 tablespoons butter
1 tablespoon fresh lemon juice
3 tablespoons dry white wine
¼ cup chopped parsley
¼ teaspoon salt

In a small skillet, saute onions and mushrooms in melted butter. Remove from heat. Add lemon juice, wine, parsley and salt. Combine with cooked rice. Add additional butter, if desired.

Orange Pilaf

6 servings

¼ cup butter
½ cup chopped celery
¼ cup chopped green onions
1 cup long-grain raw rice
1 cup orange juice
1 teaspoon salt
1 orange, peeled and cut into
    small pieces
¼ cup slivered almonds

In a large saucepan over medium-high heat, cook celery and green onions in butter until tender, about 4 to 5 minutes. Add the rice and brown lightly, stirring frequently, for another 4 to 5 minutes. Add orange juice, salt and 1 cup water, heat to boiling. Cover and reduce heat, simmering the rice for 25 minutes until it is tender and the liquid is absorbed. Gently stir in the orange pieces and almonds.

    Note: Serve hot with lamb, poultry or game birds.

Fried Rice

4 servings

2 tablespoons peanut oil
½ teaspoon salt
2 eggs
⅓ cup chopped onions
⅓ cup chopped green onions
1 cup fresh bean sprouts
1 tablespoon chicken
    stock base
3 tablespoons soy sauce
3 cups cooked rice
    pepper to taste

Heat oil in wok or large skillet over high heat. Add salt. Break eggs into wok and scramble quickly until egg is cooked and in small particles. Add onions and green onions and stir-fry for 2 minutes. Add bean sprouts and stir-fry for 1 minute. Add remaining ingredients and stir-fry until thoroughly hot. Serve with any oriental entree.

221

Pasta, Rice and Potatoes

COLORADO CACHE COLORADO CACHE COLORADO CACHE COLORADO CACHE COLORADO CACHE COLORADO CACHE COLORADO CACHE COLORADO CACHE COLORADO CACHE COLORADO

Kentucky Spoonbread

4-5 servings

1 **cup white corn meal**
3 **cups milk**
1 **teaspoon salt**
1 **teaspoon baking powder**
2 **tablespoons melted butter**
3 **eggs, separated**

Cook corn meal and 2 cups of the milk until stiff, about 10 minutes. Stir frequently to prevent scorching. Remove from heat. Add salt, baking powder, melted butter and remaining 1 cup milk. Beat egg yolks well. Add to cornmeal mixture. Beat egg whites until stiff and fold in carefully. Bake in greased 2 quart round casserole in 375 degree oven for 35 to 45 minutes, or until brown on top. Spoon out and serve with butter.

Barbara Conwell's Stuffed Baked Potato

1 serving

1 **baking potato**
  grated zucchini
  butter
  salt and pepper
  Gruyere cheese, grated

Bake potato until done; slice off top and scoop out, leaving shell intact. Grate enough zucchini to equal the amount of potato and saute it in butter. Mix potato with zucchini and salt and pepper to taste. Stuff potato shell with potato-zucchini mixture and top with grated cheese. Bake at 450 degrees just long enough to reheat and melt cheese, about 5 minutes.

Parmesan Potato Sticks

6 servings

6 **medium potatoes (pared or not, as desired)**
6 **tablespoons butter**
  salt to taste
6 **tablespoons freshly grated Parmesan cheese**

Cut potatoes into 6 or 8 wedges lengthwise. Place shallow baking pan in 425 degree oven with butter to melt. Add potato sticks and bake for 20 to 30 minutes, turning occasionally. Sprinkle with salt and cheese. Return to oven for 2 to 3 minutes.
  Note: The French fry without the fry.

222

Pasta, Rice and Potatoes

RADO CACHE COLORADO CACHE COLORADO CACHE COLORADO CACHE COLORADO CACHE COLORADO CACHE COLORADO CACHE COLORADO CACHE COLORADO CACHE COLORADO CACHE

Baked Potatoes and Onion Pie

8 servings

4   **pounds potatoes, pared and
    very thinly sliced (8 cups)**
2   **large onions thinly sliced
    (3 cups)**
½   **cup butter**
½   **cup freshly grated
    Parmesan cheese**
    cayenne pepper
    salt and pepper

Preheat oven to 400 degrees. In a buttered 13 × 9 inch baking dish place ⅓ of the potatoes and ⅓ of the onions; sprinkle with salt and pepper and dot with ⅓ of the butter. Do this twice more. Cover and bake for 45 minutes or until tender. Uncover and bake until the top is lightly browned. Remove from oven, let cool for 5 minutes. Loosen around edge and invert on a heat-proof serving platter. Sprinkle cheese and cayenne on top and return to oven to brown cheese.

Mushroom Potato Pie

4-6 servings

3   **cups mashed potatoes**
1 - 1½ **cups fresh mushrooms, sliced**
¼   **cup minced onion**
1   **teaspoon fresh lemon juice**
2   **tablespoons butter**
½   **teaspoon salt**
       pepper to taste
½   **cup sour cream (4 ounces)**

Saute mushrooms and onion in butter. Stir in lemon juice, salt and pepper. Place half the mashed potatoes in a layer in a buttered 9 inch pie plate or casserole. Top potatoes with mushrooms, then sour cream. Cover with remaining potatoes. (It can be refrigerated at this point). Bake at 350 degrees for 35 to 45 minutes. Cut in wedges to serve.
   Note: Easy to make ahead or double.

Pickaroon Potatoes

6 servings

6   **large potatoes**
2   **tablespoons butter**
¼   **cup milk**
    salt and pepper to taste
½   **cup whipping cream, whipped
    until stiff**
¼   **cup grated Cheddar or
    Parmesan cheese**
1   **tablespoon hot horseradish
    paprika**

Peel and wash potatoes and cook in salted boiling water until tender. Drain and mash with the butter and milk. Beat until light and fluffy. Season with salt and pepper and fold in the horseradish. Pour into a buttered casserole, cover with whipped cream, sprinkle with the cheese and paprika. Bake in a preheated 350 degree oven until brown on top.
   Note: A super accompaniment to a grilled steak after a day on the slopes.

COLORADO CACHE COLORADO CACHE COLORADO CACHE COLORADO CACHE COLORADO CACHE COLORADO CACHE COLORADO CACHE COLORADO CACHE COLORADO

Hominy San Juan

6 servings

1   16-ounce can white hominy
1   cup sour cream (8 ounces)
1   4-ounce can chopped, mild
    green chiles
1   cup grated Cheddar cheese
    (4 ounces)
    salt to taste

Drain hominy and place in a saucepan. Add sour cream, chiles and cheese and mix over low heat. Add salt. Place in an ungreased 1 quart casserole and bake uncovered at 375 degrees for 20 minutes.

Note: Great with any broiled meat.

Pinon Nut Barley Bake

8 servings

½   cup chopped celery
    (or sliced mushrooms)
½   cup chopped green onions
5   tablespoons margarine
1   cup barley
⅓   cup chopped parsley
2 - 3   cups chicken broth
½   cup pine nuts
    salt and pepper

Saute celery or mushrooms and onion in margarine until soft. Add barley and cook until golden. In a 2 quart casserole, combine barley mixture, parsley and 1 cup chicken broth. Bake covered at 350 degrees for 30 minutes. Stir in pine nuts and 1 cup chicken broth. Bake uncovered for 45 minutes or until barley is tender. If necessary, add more broth. Season with salt and pepper to taste.

Note: Travels well.

Individual Yorkshire Pudding

4-6 servings

2   extra large eggs
1   cup milk
1   cup flour, sifted
¼   teaspoon salt
½   cup meat drippings
    (or vegetable oil)

Preheat oven to 450 degrees. Beat eggs with milk. Thoroughly whisk in flour and salt. (You may blend all ingredients in food processor.) Pour 1 tablespoon meat drippings or oil into muffin tins and place in 450 degree oven until grease begins to smoke. Remove pan and fill each cup ⅔ full. Bake for 20 minutes or until browned and puffed. All ingredients must be at room temperature so they will puff.

GREEN RIVER AT DINOSAUR NATIONAL MONUMENT

ADO CACHE COLORADO CACHE COLORADO CACHE COLORADO CACHE COLORADO CACHE COLORADO CACHE COLORADO CACHE COLORADO CACHE COLORADO CACHE COLORADO CACHE COLORADO CACHE

Hints from **Baker Peak**

To be sure the yeast you are using is still active "proof" it. To do this, pour 1 package dry yeast into ½ cup warm water (100-115 degrees), add 2 teaspoons granulated sugar. Stir well and set aside for a few minutes until mixture swells and bubbles appear on the surface.

To test whether the dough has been kneaded enough, make an indentation in dough with 2 fingers; it should spring back if kneaded enough.

To test when dough is properly risen, make an indentation in it with 2 fingers. It is ready if the dough **does not** spring back.

When using glass pans for baking, set the temperature 25 degrees lower than specified. Glass heats faster than metal and holds the heat longer.

Half butter and half lard is an ideal combination for bread. Butter is a silkier shortening, while lard produces a flakier texture.

Before slicing fresh bread, run serrated bread knife under hot water, dry, then slice bread.

Place a small dish of warm water in the oven while bread is baking to keep crust from getting too hard.

If you want a glossy crust on your bread brush the top lightly with a mixture of 1 egg and 1½ tablespoons of water immediately before baking. To insure a soft crust, brush lightly with melted butter as soon as you remove bread from oven.

To make lighter muffins, place greased pans into the oven for a few minutes before adding batter.

Nut and fruit quick breads should be baked the day before serving; the flavors mellow and the bread slices easier.

Baker Peak, a mountain in the Yampa valley, is near the resort town of Steamboat Springs. At one time "Steamboat" offered 150 medicinal springs with a combined flow of 2,000 gallons a minute and temperatures varying from 60 to 150 degrees. The town was named for the chugging sound resembling that of a river boat, made by one of the springs.

Honey Wheat Germ Bread

2 large loaves or 3 small loaves

2	packages dry yeast
1	cup warm water
2	tablespoons brown sugar
½	teaspoon salt
½	cup flour
1¼	cups scalded milk, cooled to warm
¼	cup honey
2	teaspoons salt
1¾	cups whole wheat flour
¼	cup wheat germ
3½	cups white flour

In a large mixing bowl combine yeast, water, brown sugar, salt and the ½ cup of flour. Beat until smooth. Cover and let stand in warm place 15 minutes. Add to this mixture the scalded milk, honey, salt, whole wheat flour and wheat germ. Beat 2 minutes with electric mixer and gradually stir in about 3½ cups white flour. Form into smooth ball on floured surface. Cover with bowl and let rest 10 minutes. Knead thoroughly and divide into 2 or 3 balls. Cover with bowl and let rest again. Shape each ball into a loaf and place in 2 well-greased standard loaf pans or 3 8×4 inch pans. Cover and let rise in warm place 45 to 60 minutes, or until doubled in bulk. Bake at 375 degrees for 35 to 40 minutes.

Note: A quick, easy, all-purpose bread—great toasted!

Honey Whole Wheat Casserole Bread

1 loaf

1	cup milk
¾	cup shortening
½	cup honey
2	teaspoons salt
¾	cup warm water (105 to 115 degrees)
2	packages dry yeast
3	eggs lightly beaten
4½	cups unsifted flour
1½	cups whole wheat flour
1	teaspoon soft butter

In a small saucepan, heat milk until bubbles form around edge of pan. Remove from heat. Add shortening, honey and salt, stirring until shortening is melted. Cool to lukewarm. Sprinkle yeast over water in large bowl and stir until yeast is dissolved. Stir in milk mixture and eggs. Combine flours. Add 4 cups flour mixture to yeast mixture. With electric mixer at low speed beat until blended. Beat at medium speed until smooth, about 2 minutes. With wooden spoon gradually beat in remaining flour mixture. Then beat, stretching dough 20 to 30 times. Cover with waxed paper and a moist towel. Let rise in warm place, free from drafts, until double in bulk, about 1 hour. Lightly grease a 2½ to 3 quart casserole. Punch dough down, and beat with spoon until smooth, about 30 seconds. Turn into casserole, cover and let rise until double in bulk, 20 to 30 minutes. With a sharp knife, cut a 4-inch cross, ½ inch deep, in top of dough. Bake at 375 degrees for 45 to 50 minutes, or until bread is nicely browned and sounds hollow when rapped with knuckle. Remove to wire rack. Rub butter over top of bread. Serve warm.

Fantastic Beer Rye Bread

2 long loaves or 3 round loaves

2	packages dry yeast
½	cup warm water
2½	cups beer
½	cup shortening
1	cup molasses (preferably dark)
1	tablespoon salt
1	tablespoon caraway seeds
5	cups rye flour
4	cups white, all-purpose flour
1	egg

Sprinkle dry yeast in warm water. Stir until dissolved. Heat beer until it just starts to bubble. Remove from heat and add shortening. Add molasses, salt and caraway seeds to beer and stir. Cool until lukewarm and stir in dissolved yeast. Beat in rye flour. Beat in white flour until dough is too firm to beat (you may not need it all). Turn out onto floured board. Knead until smooth and elastic, 6 to 10 minutes. Put into greased bowl and butter top of dough. Cover and let rise in warm place until doubled in bulk, about 1½ hours. On a lightly floured board, knead again until smooth. Shape into 2 long loaves or 3 round loaves. Slash top with very sharp knife several times. Brush with egg that has been beaten with 1 tablespoon water. Let loaves stand until doubled in bulk. Brush again with beaten egg. Bake in preheated 350 degree oven for 40 to 45 minutes.

Note: This is a delicious party bread served with roast beef, cheese, mustards and mayonnaise.

Irish Freckle Bread

2 loaves

4¾ - 5¾	cups unsifted flour
½	cup sugar
1	teaspoon salt
2	packages dry yeast
1	cup potato water
½	cup margarine
2	eggs at room temperature
¼	cup mashed potatoes at room temperature
1	cup seedless raisins

In a large bowl thoroughly mix 1½ cups flour, sugar, salt and undissolved yeast. Combine potato water and margarine in saucepan. Heat over low heat until liquid is warm—the margarine does not need to melt. Gradually add to dry ingredients and beat for 2 minutes at medium speed with electric mixer, scraping bowl occasionally. Add eggs, potatoes and ½ cup flour, or enough flour to make a thick batter. Stir in raisins and enough additional flour to make a soft dough. Turn out onto floured board. Knead until smooth and elastic, about 10 minutes. Place in greased bowl, turning dough to grease. Cover and let rise until doubled in bulk. Punch dough down. Turn out onto lightly floured board. Divide dough into 4 equal pieces. Shape each piece into a slender loaf, about 8½ inches long. Put 2 loaves, side by side, in each of 2 greased 8½ × 4½ × 2½ inch loaf pans. Cover. Let rise in warm place, free from draft until doubled in bulk. Bake in preheated 375 degree oven for 35 minutes, or until done. Remove from pans and cool on wire racks.

Anise Seed Bread

2 loaves

2	cups milk
¼	pound butter
6	tablespoons sugar
1	teaspoon salt
1	package dry yeast
¼	cup very warm water
1	teaspoon sugar
1	cup flour
1	large egg, well beaten
2	tablespoons anise seed
7	cups flour
1	egg, well beaten
	sesame seeds (optional)

Scald milk with butter; stir in sugar and salt. Cool. Dissolve yeast and 1 teaspoon sugar in warm water. Let sit for about 5 minutes until it bubbles—this proofs the yeast. Blend the 1 cup of flour into the milk. Add yeast, egg and anise seed. Gradually add enough flour to form dough; this may take slightly more or less than the 7 cups. Knead until dough is smooth and elastic. Let rise to double, punch down and knead again about 2 minutes. Form 2 braided loaves and put on cookie sheet, or form 2 regular loaves and put into greased 9 × 5 inch loaf pans. Paint with beaten egg, sprinkle with sesame seeds if desired. Let rise to almost double. Bake in a preheated 350 degree oven about 35 minutes until golden brown.

Anadama Bread

2 loaves

2	cups water
½	cup light molasses
¼	cup butter
½	cup cornmeal, preferably coarse, water-milled
4½ - 5	cups unbleached flour
1½	teaspoons salt
1	package dry yeast
½	cup warm water

Bring to boil in medium saucepan 2 cups water, molasses and butter. Lightly sprinkle in cornmeal. Cook 2½ minutes, stirring constantly to prevent lumping. Remove from heat. Cool mixture about 30 minutes to 120 degrees. Combine 2 cups of the flour and the salt. Add yeast to warm water and let rest for 10 minutes; stir. Gradually pour cooled cornmeal mixture into flour and salt mixture. Beat with electric mixer at low speed to blend. Add yeast and beat 2 minutes at medium speed to make a thick batter. Stir in rest of the flour to make a soft dough. Knead on floured surface about 10 minutes, adding flour if needed until dough is smooth and elastic. Place in greased bowl, turning to grease all the dough. Cover with a sheet of greased, waxed paper and a towel. Let rise until double in bulk. Punch down and divide in half; let rest covered for 10 to 15 minutes. Shape loaves and place in 2 greased 9 × 5 inch loaf pans. Cover again with greased, waxed paper and let rise until double, about 1 hour. Bake in preheated 400 degree oven for 30 to 40 minutes. Cool well on racks before slicing.

DO CACHE COLORADO CACHE COLORADO CACHE COLORADO CACHE COLORADO CACHE COLORADO CACHE COLORADO CACHE COLORADO CACHE COLORADO CACHE C

Sourdough Bread and Starter

Starter:
- 1 **package dry yeast**
- 2 **cups warm water**
- 2 **cups unbleached flour**

3 cups of starter and 2 loaves

Empty yeast into a warm mixing bowl and stir in water. Stir until yeast is dissolved. Add flour and stir until well blended. Cover with plastic wrap and let stand at room temperature for about 48 hours. (When ready, the starter will be bubbly with a somewhat yellowish liquid on top.) Store starter in the refrigerator in a jar with a loose-fitting lid. Every time part of the starter is removed to make bread, it must be replenished and at least once a week mix together sourdough starter, 1 cup of flour, 1 cup milk, ⅓ cup sugar. Keep 1 cup of this mixture at all times.

Sourdough Bread:
- 1 **package dry yeast**
- ¼ **cup warm water**
- 1 **teaspoon sugar**
- 1 **egg**
- ¼ **cup vegetable oil**
- ½ **cup water**
- 1 **teaspoon salt**
- ⅓ **cup sugar**
- 1 **cup sourdough starter**
- 3½ **cups flour**

Dissolve yeast in warm water, stirring in the sugar. Let this sit 15 minutes. Mix the egg, vegetable oil, water, salt and sugar in a large mixing bowl. Add the sourdough starter to the egg mixture along with the yeast mixture. With electric mixer thoroughly blend in 2 cups of the flour. Add remaining flour and mix with a wooden spoon. Turn onto floured board and knead 10 to 20 times. Add a bit more flour if still sticky. Spray mixing bowl with a non-stick spray oil. Put dough in bowl turning it to make sure the top of the dough is oiled. Cover bowl with cloth and let rise 2 hours in a warm place. After dough has risen to double in bulk punch down and pour onto floured board and knead again for 2 minutes. Divide into 2 balls and place in 2 well-greased loaf pans. Cover and let rise 2 more hours in a warm place Bake at 350 degrees for about 20 to 25 minutes.

COLORADO CACHE COLORADO CACHE COLORADO CACHE COLORADO CACHE COLORADO CACHE COLORADO CACHE COLORADO CACHE COLORADO CACHE COLORADO

Honey Whole Wheat Bread

3 loaves

3 cups whole wheat flour
1 tablespoon salt
2 packages dry yeast
3 cups milk
½ cup honey
2 tablespoons oil
1 egg, lightly beaten
1 cup whole wheat flour
4½ - 5 cups white flour

Combine the 3 cups of whole wheat flour, salt and yeast in a large bowl. In a saucepan over low heat combine milk, honey and oil. Heat until warm. Pour over flour mixture and blend well. Add egg and beat well. Add 1 cup wheat flour and 4½ to 5 cups white flour. Knead dough for 5 minutes. Place in a greased bowl. Cover with damp cloth and let rise 45 to 60 minutes, or until doubled in bulk. Punch down dough and divide into thirds. Put into greased loaf pans, cover with damp cloth and let rise until double. Put into COLD oven, set at 400 degrees and bake for 10 minutes. Reduce heat to 375 degrees and bake for 30 minutes or until golden brown.

Shredded Wheat Bread

2 loaves

2 shredded wheat biscuits
2 cups boiling water
2 tablespoons margarine
1 package dry yeast
½ cup warm water
¼ cup sugar
¼ cup molasses
    (or dark corn syrup)
1½ teaspoons salt
6 cups flour

Crumble shredded wheat into bowl. Add boiling water and margarine. Let cool. Dissolve yeast in warm water and add to wheat mixture. Add sugar, molasses, salt and flour. Mix well. Knead on a floured board until smooth. Place in greased bowl and let rise until double. Shape into 2 loaves, put in greased loaf pan and let rise again. Bake at 375 degrees for 40 to 45 minutes.

COLORADO CACHE COLORADO CACHE COLORADO CACHE COLORADO CACHE COLORADO CACHE COLORADO CACHE COLORADO CACHE COLORADO CACHE COLORADO CACHE

Oatmeal Bread

2 or 3 loaves

2	**packages dry yeast**
1	**cup warm water**
¼	**cup dark molasses**
½	**teaspoon salt**
½	**cup flour**
1¼	**cups scalded milk, cooled to lukewarm**
¼	**cup honey or molasses**
1	**egg**
2	**teaspoons salt**
2	**cups flour**
2	**tablespoons softened shortening**
1	**cup quick-cooking rolled oats**
3½	**cups flour**

In a large bowl combine yeast, warm water, dark molasses, salt and ½ cup flour. Beat until smooth and let stand in a warm place about 15 minutes. Add scalded milk, honey or molasses, egg, salt, 2 cups flour, shortening and oatmeal. Beat 2 minutes with an electric mixer. Gradually add about 3½ cups more flour. Form into smooth ball, cover with bowl and let stand 10 minutes. Knead dough for 5 minutes and shape into 2 or 3 balls. Cover with bowl and let rest 10 minutes more. Shape into 2 or 3 loaves and place in 2 standard loaf pans or 3 8×4 inch pans. Cover and let rise in warm place 45 to 60 minutes, or until doubled in bulk. Bake at 375 degrees for 35 to 40 minutes.

Bronco Bread

1 loaf

2	**tablespoons softened butter**
¼	**cup hot water**
½	**cup orange juice**
1½	**tablespoons freshly grated orange rind**
1	**egg**
1	**cup sugar**
2	**cups flour**
1	**teaspoon baking powder**
½	**teaspoon salt**
¼	**teaspoon baking soda**
1	**cup fresh blueberries, or frozen or canned, well-drained**

Combine butter, water, orange juice and rind in a bowl. Add egg and mix well. Add dry ingredients and fold in blueberries by hand. Bake at 325 degrees in greased 9×5 inch baking pan for 1 hour and 10 minutes. Cool on rack.

Note: Freezes well.

Croissants

2 **packages dry yeast**
1 **cup warm water**
¾ **cup evaporated milk**
1½ **teaspoons salt**
1 **egg**
⅓ **cup sugar**
¼ **cup melted butter**
1 **cup chilled butter**
5 **cups unsifted flour**
1 **egg beaten with**
   1 tablespoon water

32 large rolls or 64 small rolls

In a large bowl sprinkle yeast over warm water to soften. Stir in 1 cup flour, evaporated milk, egg, sugar, melted butter and salt. Beat to make a smooth batter. Set aside. Cut the chilled butter into the remaining flour until butter particles are the size of dried kidney beans. Pour yeast batter over top and carefully turn the mixture over with a spatula to blend just until all the flour is moistened. Cover bowl tightly with plastic wrap and refrigerate until well chilled, at least 4 hours and up to 4 days. Remove dough to floured board and press into a compact ball. Knead about 6 turns to release air bubbles. Divide dough into 4 equal parts. Shape one part at a time leaving remaining dough wrapped in plastic wrap in refrigerator. To shape, roll one quarter dough on floured board into circle 17 inches in diameter. With a sharp knife cut circle into 8 (16 for small rolls) pie-shaped wedges. For each croissant, loosely roll wedges toward point. Shape each roll into a crescent and place on ungreased cookie sheet with the point down. Allow at least 1½ inches space around each croissant. Cover lightly and let rise at room temperature in a draft-free place. Do not speed the rising of the rolls by placing them in a warm spot. When almost doubled in bulk, brush with egg and water mixture. Bake in preheated 400 degree oven for 12 to 15 minutes.
   Note: These rolls freeze well.

No Knead Rolls

3 **eggs**
3 **tablespoons sugar**
1 **package dry yeast**
1 **teaspoon salt**
1 **cup warm water**
½ **cup cold margarine**
4 **cups flour**

50 rolls

Dissolve yeast in 1 cup warm water and allow to stand 5 minutes. Beat eggs until light in color with electric mixer. Add sugar, salt and dissolved yeast. Stir to combine. Cut cold margarine into small chips and gently stir into egg mixture. Stir in flour until thoroughly combined. Cover bowl with plastic wrap. Let rise in draft-free place for 2 hours. Shape into dinner rolls or cinnamon or pecan rolls, as desired. Place in greased pans for sweet rolls, or on greased baking sheets for dinner crescents. Cover with tea towel. Let rise 1 more hour. Bake at 350 degrees until lightly browned.

Onion Lover's Twist

1 large loaf or 2 small loaves

1	package dry yeast
¼	cup warm water
4	cups flour
¼	cup sugar
1½	teaspoons salt
½	cup hot water
½	cup milk
¼	cup softened butter or margarine
1	egg

Filling:

¼	cup butter or margarine
1	cup finely chopped onion (or ¼ cup instant minced onions)
1	tablespoon grated Parmesan cheese
1	tablespoon sesame or poppy seed
¼	teaspoon garlic powder
¾	teaspoon salt
1	teaspoon paprika

Grease cookie sheet. In a large bowl dissolve yeast in warm water. Add 2 cups flour, sugar, salt, water, milk, butter and egg. With electric mixer, blend at low speed until moistened. Beat 2 minutes at medium speed. By hand, stir in remaining flour to form a soft dough. Cover and let rise in a warm place until light and doubled in size, 45 to 60 minutes.

To prepare filling, melt butter in saucepan and add remaining ingredients.

When dough has doubled in size stir down and place on a floured board. Knead until no longer sticky. Roll out to an 18 × 12 inch rectangle. Spread with filling, then cut lengthwise into three 18 × 4 inch strips. Beginning with the 18-inch side, roll up each strip. Seal edges and ends. On the prepared cookie sheet braid the three rolls together. Cover and allow to rise until doubled, about 45 to 60 minutes. Bake at 350 degrees for 30 to 35 minutes, or until golden brown. Serve warm or cool.

Note: To make 2 small loaves, cut the 3 filled rolls in half crosswise before braiding. Braid each set of rolls separately on greased cookie sheet; bake as directed.

Diamond Head Bread

1 loaf

¼	cup butter or margarine
¾	cup brown sugar, packed
1	egg
2	cups flour
1	teaspoon baking soda
½	teaspoon salt
⅓	cup frozen orange juice concentrate, thawed
1	cup crushed pineapple, spooned from can with juice included
½	cup chopped pecans

In a bowl cream butter and sugar, add egg and beat well. Add dry ingredients alternately with orange juice. Add pineapple including juice. Add nuts. Pour into a well greased loaf pan and bake at 350 degrees for 55 to 60 minutes. Cool on wire rack.

Karat Bread

2 loaves

3 eggs
1 cup vegetable oil
2 cups grated carrots
2 cups white sugar (or 1½ cups white sugar and ½ cup packed brown sugar)
3 cups flour
¼ teaspoon baking powder
1 teaspoon salt
1 teaspoon baking soda
1 teaspoon ground cinnamon
1 cup chopped pecans
8 ounces crushed pineapple, drained

In a large mixing bowl beat eggs until foamy. Add oil, carrots and sugar. Beat well. Sift together flour, baking soda, salt, baking powder and cinnamon. Add to egg mixture and blend well. Stir in nuts and pineapple. Grease and flour 2 loaf pans. Divide batter between the pans. Bake in a preheated 350 degree oven for 1 hour, or until done. Cool and remove from pans.

Note: Freezes well.

Applesauce Nut Bread

1 loaf

1 cup sugar
1 cup applesauce
⅓ cup vegetable oil
1 teaspoon baking soda
½ teaspoon baking powder
½ teaspoon ground cinnamon
2 eggs
3 teaspoons milk
2 cups sifted flour
¼ teaspoon salt
¼ teaspoon ground nutmeg
¾ cup chopped pecans

Topping:
¼ cup brown sugar, packed
¼ cup chopped pecans
¼ teaspoon ground cinnamon

In a large mixing bowl, thoroughly combine sugar, applesauce, oil, eggs and milk. Sift together flour, soda, baking powder, cinnamon, salt and nutmeg. Add to applesauce mixture and beat until well combined. Stir in pecans. Turn batter into well greased loaf baking pan. For topping, combine brown sugar, cinnamon and pecans. Sprinkle evenly over batter. Bake at 350 degrees for 1 hour. Cap loosely with foil after first 30 minutes of baking. Remove from pan and cool on rack.

Lemon Bread

1 loaf

6	tablespoons butter
¾	cup sugar
2	eggs
3	tablespoons lemon juice
2	teaspoons freshly grated lemon peel
1½	cups flour, sifted
1	teaspoon baking powder
1	teaspoon salt
½	cup milk
½	cup chopped walnuts
3	tablespoons lemon juice
½	cup sugar

Cream the butter and ¾ cup sugar. until fluffy. Beat in the eggs one at a time. Beat in 3 tablespoons lemon juice and the lemon peel. Combine sifted flour, baking powder and salt. To the butter mixture, add the flour mixture alternately with the milk, beating just enough to blend. Fold in walnuts. Line the bottom of a greased 8 × 4 inch loaf pan with waxed paper. Butter the waxed paper and turn batter into the pan. Bang pan down hard on the work surface to settle the batter evenly. Bake at 350 degrees 1 hour or until a toothpick inserted in the middle comes out clean. Blend the remaining 3 tablespoons of lemon juice and ½ cup sugar. Pour this mixture slowly over the hot bread. Let the bread remain in the pan until the glaze is absorbed, at least 15 minutes. Remove bread from pan, leaving on the waxed paper. Let stand on a rack until completely cooled. Remove waxed paper; wrap bread in foil and let sit for 24 hours before slicing.

Irish Brown Bread Royal Hibernian

1 or 2 loaves

5	cups whole wheat flour
2½	cups white flour
⅓	cup sugar
2	teaspoons sugar
2	teaspoons soda
1	teaspoon salt
2	eggs
2¼	cups buttermilk
1	cup softened butter or margarine

In a large mixing bowl, combine the whole wheat flour, sugar, soda and salt. In a separate bowl beat eggs until frothy and add buttermilk. Combine milk mixture and softened butter with the flour mixture and beat with an electric mixer for 2 minutes. Add white flour gradually and turn dough out onto a floured board. Knead thoroughly. Divide dough in half and shape into 2 round balls. Flatten the tops slightly and, with a knife, cut an "X" about ½ inch deep. Put loaves on a greased cookie sheet or into 2 9×5 inch loaf pans. (For loaf pans, cut slash down center lengthwise.) Bake at 400 degrees for 50 minutes. Cool before cutting into thin slices.

Note: It makes terrific toast.

Herb Buttered Bread

8 servings

1   **large loaf of uncut, white bread**
½   **pound butter**
½   **teaspoon whole savory, crushed**
1   **teaspoon thyme**
½   **teaspoon salt**
⅛   **teaspoon cayenne pepper**

Cut loaf of bread diagonally but not all the way through. Cream together all other ingredients until very soft. Spread mixture on all sides of each piece of bread. Tie string around loaf to hold shape. Brush top and all sides with butter mixture. Place in uncovered pan in refrigerator for 24 hours. Bake at 250 to 300 degrees for 30 to 40 minutes or until lightly browned.

Cheesy Herb Bread

8 servings

1   **loaf French bread**
1   **clove garlic, crushed**
1   **teaspoon marjoram leaves**
½   **cup softened butter**
¼   **cup finely chopped parsley**
1   **cup Parmesan cheese**

Slice bread into 1-inch slices. In a small bowl combine all but cheese and mix well. Spread mixture on bread. Sprinkle with Parmesan cheese. Wrap in foil and bake at 400 degrees for 20 minutes. Unwrap and bake an additional 5 minutes.

Quick Cheese Loaf

10 slices

1   **loaf Vienna or French bread**
½   **cup softened butter**
⅓   **cup onions, minced**
3   **tablespoons prepared mustard**
1   **tablespoon poppy seeds**
2   **teaspoons lemon juice**
   few drops of Tabasco sauce
12   **slices processed Swiss cheese**
4 - 6   **slices bacon, crisply fried and crumbled**

Peel off top and side crusts from loaf of bread. Mix butter, onions, mustard, poppy seeds, lemon juice and Tabasco. Make 8 to 10 slices in bread. Cut each cheese slice into 2 triangles and place one triangle, long-side down, in each cut of bread. Place the next triangle so that the point falls over the top of the cut in the bread. Continue until each cut has 2 triangles of cheese. Spread rest of butter mixture over top of loaf and sprinkle with crumbled bacon. Heat on a foil-covered cookie sheet at 350 degrees for 30 minutes.
   Note: Great with steak or barbecued ribs.

Orange Muffins

1 cup sugar
juice of one orange
(about ½ cup)
½ cup butter
1 cup sugar
¾ cup sour cream
2 cups flour, sifted
1 teaspoon baking soda
1 teaspoon salt
1 teaspoon grated orange rind
½ cup raisins
½ cup chopped nuts

36 miniatures

Mix sugar and orange juice. Set aside for dipping after muffins are cooked. Cream butter and sugar. Add sour cream alternately with the dry ingredients. Fold in orange rind, raisins and nuts. This is a stiff batter. Use well greased muffin tins that are small so that these are bite-sized. Bake at 375 degrees for 12 to 15 minutes. While still warm, dip them in the sugar-orange juice mixture. Cool on a wire rack.

Nutritious Bran Muffins

2 cups All Bran cereal
1 cup Bran Buds cereal
1 cup water, boiling
2 cups buttermilk
2½ teaspoons baking soda
1 cup honey
2 eggs, beaten
½ cup vegetable oil
2 cups miller's bran
1 cup flour
½ teaspoon salt
raisins or chopped dates
(optional)

48 muffins

Mix All Bran and Bran Buds together with boiling water and set aside. Pour buttermilk into a large mixing bowl. Stir in soda, honey, eggs, oil and cereal mixture and beat thoroughly. In another bowl combine the miller's bran, flour and salt. Add the flour mixture to the wet ingredients and beat. Pour into greased muffin tins and bake at 375 degrees for 20 to 25 minutes, or until a toothpick inserted in the center comes out clean. Serve warm.

Note: Batter will keep refrigerated for 6 weeks so you can bake just as many as you need at a time.

French Breakfast Muffins

18 servings

1½ cups plus 2 tablespoons flour
¾ cup sugar
2 teaspoons baking powder
¼ teaspoon salt
¼ teaspoon ground nutmeg
½ cup milk
1 egg, beaten
⅓ cup butter, melted
1 teaspoon ground cinnamon
½ cup sugar
½ teaspoon vanilla extract
⅓ cup butter, melted

Combine first five ingredients. Add milk, egg and ⅓ cup melted butter. Mix thoroughly. Grease and flour small muffin tins. Fill ½ full and bake at 400 degrees for 20 minutes, or until lightly browned. Remove from pan immediately and dip in remaining ⅓ cup melted butter and roll in a mixture of the sugar, cinnamon and vanilla. Serve warm.

Note: The flavor of fresh doughnuts without the work!

Sesame Cheese Muffins

12 servings

1½ cups Bisquick biscuit mix
¾ cup grated sharp Colby cheese
¼ cup minced onion
1 egg, well beaten
½ cup milk
1 tablespoon sesame seeds, toasted

Saute onions in 1 tablespoon butter until transparent. Mix Bisquick mix and ½ cup cheese together. Combine egg, milk and onion. Add all at once to Bisquick mixture and beat vigorously for 30 seconds. Fill well greased muffin tins ⅔ full. Sprinkle tops with some of the grated cheese and sesame seeds. Bake at 400 degrees for 12 to 15 minutes.

True Blue Muffins

12 muffins

1¼ cups flour, sifted
2 teaspoons baking powder
½ cup sugar
½ teaspoon salt
¼ cup melted butter
1 egg
¼ cup milk
¾ cup blueberries (drain and save ¼ cup of juice)

Cream butter and sugar; add egg. Add flour and baking powder alternating with milk and juice of blueberries. Fold in berries carefully. Bake at 400 degrees for 20 minutes.

ADO CACHE COLORADO CACHE COLORADO CACHE COLORADO CACHE COLORADO CACHE COLORADO CACHE COLORADO CACHE COLORADO CACHE COLORADO CACHE

Oatmeal Muffins

8 muffins

1 cup quick-cooking rolled oats
1 cup buttermilk
1 egg
½ cup brown sugar, packed
½ cup vegetable oil
1 cup flour
1 teaspoon baking powder
½ teaspoon salt
½ teaspoon baking soda
½ cup chopped dates (optional)
½ cup chopped walnuts
     (optional)

Mix all ingredients and spoon into greased muffin tins. Bake at 400 degrees for 15 to 20 minutes.

Gougere

6 servings

1 cup water
½ cup butter
¼ teaspoon salt
1 cup flour
4 eggs
1 cup grated Swiss cheese
¼ teaspoon ground nutmeg

Combine water, butter and salt in heavy saucepan. Add flour all at once, then beat with wooden spoon over low heat until mixture clings together and leaves sides of pan. Remove mixture from heat and cool slightly. Add eggs one at a time, beating vigorously until mixture has a satiny sheen. Stir cheese and nutmeg into batter. On a greased cookie sheet spoon batter into 8 equal mounds, arranged in a circle and touching each other. Bake at 400 degrees for 35 minutes or until puffs are golden. Serve hot with butter.

Southern Cornbread

6-9 servings

2 cups buttermilk
2 eggs
1 scant teaspoon baking soda
1 teaspoon salt
1½ cups cornmeal (preferably
     water ground)
3 tablespoons bacon grease

Put 3 tablespoons bacon grease in large iron skillet and heat slightly. While grease is getting hot, mix all of the other ingredients together. Pour batter into hot skillet. Bake at 400 degrees until firm, about 40 minutes. Serve hot with butter.

Johnnycake

8 servings

½ cup butter or margarine
1 tablespoon vinegar
   (or lemon juice)
1 cup, minus 1 tablespoon, milk
1½ cups cornmeal
¾ cup flour, unsifted
¾ cup sugar
½ teaspoon salt
2 eggs
1¼ teaspoons baking soda

Melt butter and set aside. Pour vinegar into measuring cup, add milk and set aside. In a large mixing bowl combine cornmeal, flour, sugar and salt. Make a well in the center and pour in eggs and butter. Add soda to milk, stir and add to mixture in the bowl. Mix well. Pour into greased pan or muffin tins. Bake at 375 degrees about 25 minutes or until a toothpick inserted in the center comes out clean.

   Note: This is best when served warm. Excellent when served with butter and maple syrup.

Yogurt Poppy Seed Coffee Cake

12-15 servings

1 2-ounce package poppy seeds
1 cup yogurt
1 cup butter
1½ cups sugar
2 cups plus 2 tablespoons
   sifted flour
2 teaspoons vanilla extract
2 teaspoons baking soda
4 eggs, separated

Grease angel food cake pan and dust lightly with flour. Soak poppy seeds in yogurt. Cream butter and add sugar. Blend into yogurt mixture. Beat egg yolks and add to mixture. Add vanilla, sifted flour and baking soda. Beat egg whites until stiff and fold in. Pour batter into prepared pan. Bake in preheated 375 degree oven for 45 minutes. Sprinkle with powdered sugar or drizzle with lemon glaze. Serve warm.

   Note: Great for meetings and coffees.

ADO CACHE COLORADO CACHE COLORADO CACHE COLORADO CACHE COLORADO CACHE COLORADO CACHE COLORADO CACHE COLORADO CACHE COLORADO CACHE

Sour Cream Coffee Cake

8-10 servings

1 cup butter at room temperature
3 cups sugar
6 eggs at room temperature
¼ teaspoon salt
¼ teaspoon soda
3 cups flour
1 cup sour cream
1 teaspoon vanilla extract

Topping:
2 cups chopped pecans
8 tablespoons dark brown sugar
4 teaspoons ground cinnamon

Cream butter and sugar. Add eggs, one at a time, beating well after each addition. Sift salt, soda and flour together 3 times. Alternately add sour cream and flour mixture, ending with flour mixture. Add vanilla. Grease a tube pan. Mix topping ingredients and sprinkle a small amount on the bottom of the pan; add ½ of batter. Sprinkle on more topping and add rest of batter. Sprinkle on remaining topping. Bake at 300 degrees for 1½ hours. Do not open oven door for the first hour of baking.

Sour Cream Pineapple Coffee Cake

8-10 servings

¾ cup butter
1½ cups sugar
2 eggs
1½ teaspoons vanilla extract
2½ cups flour
2½ teaspoons baking powder
¼ cup pineapple juice
1 cup crushed pineapple, drained
1 cup sour cream
1 cup powdered sugar
2 tablespoons pineapple juice
½ cup sliced almonds

Cream together butter, sugar, eggs and vanilla. Add flour, baking powder, pineapple juice, crushed pineapple and sour cream. Mix well and turn into a well greased and floured, fluted tube pan. Bake at 350 degrees for 55 to 60 minutes. Cool in pan 10 minutes. Remove from pan. Drizzle 1 cup powdered sugar and 2 tablespoons pineapple juice on top. Sprinkle with sliced almonds.

Cream Cheese Coffee Cake

3 round coffee cakes

¼ cup butter
1 8-ounce package cream cheese
1½ cups sugar
2 eggs
2 cups flour
2 teaspoons baking powder
½ teaspoon salt
1 teaspoon baking soda
½ cup milk
1 teaspoon vanilla extract

Cream together butter, cream cheese, sugar and eggs. In another bowl sift together flour, baking powder, salt and baking soda. Combine milk and vanilla and add to creamed butter mixture, stirring constantly until well blended. Add sifted flour mixture to the creamed ingredients, blending for 3 minutes or until all ingredients are well mixed. Spoon mixture into 3 greased and floured round cake pans.

Topping:

¼ cup butter
¼ cup flour
1 cup brown sugar

Mix topping ingredients together and sprinkle over dough mixture. Bake at 350 degrees for 20 minutes.

Note: Makes 3 coffee cakes and can be easily frozen.

Cheese Filled Coffee Cake

10-15 servings

1 package dry yeast
¼ cup lukewarm water
1 teaspoon sugar
1 egg, lightly beaten
2 cups flour, sifted
¼ teaspoon salt
¾ cup margarine
2 8-ounce packages cream cheese
1 cup sugar
1 teaspoon fresh lemon juice
powdered sugar

Mix yeast, water and sugar. Let stand for 10 minutes. Add egg. Cut margarine into flour and salt and mix well. Add yeast mixture. Divide into two balls and roll each into 8 × 10 inch rectangles. Make filling by combining cream cheese, lemon juice and sugar. Spread ½ of the filling on each rectangle and fold by taking each long side toward the middle, making sure the sides overlap a little. Fold the ends up about 1½ inches. Bake immediately at 375 degrees for 25 minutes. When cool, sprinkle with powdered sugar.

ADO CACHE COLORADO CACHE COLORADO CACHE COLORADO CACHE COLORADO CACHE COLORADO CACHE COLORADO CACHE COLORADO CACHE COLORADO CACHE

Swirl Coffee Cake

10 servings

⅔ **cup butter**
⅔ **cup sugar**
2 **cups flour, unsifted**
½ **teaspoon salt**
½ **teaspoon soda**
½ **teaspoon ground cinnamon**
¼ **teaspoon ground nutmeg**
1 **teaspoon baking powder**
2 **eggs**
⅔ **cup buttermilk**
½ **cup seedless preserves**

Cream butter and sugar; add ¾ cup flour. Blend mixture until it resembles crumbs. Reserve ⅔ of this mixture. To remaining portion, add baking powder, salt, soda, cinnamon, nutmeg and eggs. Beat until blended. Alternately, add remaining 1¼ cups flour and buttermilk, blending after each addition. Pour into a greased 9 × 9 pan. Drop the preserves by tablespoons in about 4 spots on top of batter. Cut preserves in with a knife. Sprinkle reserved mixture over top. (You may have to work with your fingers to break it up so it sprinkles fairly evenly.) Bake at 375 degrees for 35 minutes.

Swedish Buttermilk Coffee Cake

8-12 servings

1½ **cups flour, sifted**
1 **cup sugar**
1 **teaspoon ground cinnamon**
1 **teaspoon ground nutmeg**
½ **cup shortening**
1 **cup buttermilk**
1 **teaspoon baking soda**
¼ **teaspoon salt**
1 **egg, well beaten**
½ **cup white raisins**

Sift flour, sugar and spices. Cut in shortening. Save ¼ cup of this mixture for the topping. Add buttermilk, soda and salt to remainder and blend well. Add raisins and beaten egg. Mix well. Grease an 8 × 8 inch pan. Pour in batter and sprinkle with topping. Bake at 350 degrees for 35 minutes. You may make extra topping for more crunch!
   Note: Recipe can easily be doubled.

COLORADO CACHE COLORADO CACHE COLORADO CACHE COLORADO CACHE COLORADO CACHE COLORADO CACHE COLORADO CACHE COLORADO CACHE COLORADO

Danish Puff

2 coffee cakes

1 **cup flour**
1 **cup butter, divided**
2 **tablespoons water**
1 **cup water**
1 **teaspoon vanilla or almond extract**
1 **cup flour**
3 **eggs**
1½ **cups powdered sugar**
2 **tablespoons softened butter**
1½ **teaspoons vanilla extract**
1 - 2 **tablespoons water**

Measure 1 cup flour into bowl and cut in ½ cup butter. Sprinkle 2 tablespoons water over mixture. Mix with fork. Form into ball and divide in half. On ungreased cookie sheet, pat each half with hands into a strip, 12 x 3 inches. Strips should be about 3 inches apart. In a saucepan combine ½ cup butter and 1 cup water. Heat to boiling. Remove from heat and stir in vanilla extract. Beat in 1 cup flour, stirring to keep it from lumping. When smooth, add eggs one at a time, beating until smooth after each addition. Divide batter in half and spread each half evenly over strips. Bake 60 minutes at 350 degrees or until topping is crisp and browned. Mix powdered sugar, 2 tablespoons soft butter, 1½ teaspoons vanilla and water until smooth. Frost baked strips with the glaze.

Note: May be spread with jelly before glazing.

Quick Tea Ring

6-8 servings

¼ **cup brown sugar**
1½ **tablespoons cream**
¼ **cup melted butter**
   nuts and/or cherries
2 **cans refrigerated biscuits (12 to 16 biscuits)**
3 **tablespoons melted butter**
1 **teaspoon ground cinnamon**
½ **cup sugar**

Mix brown sugar, cream, melted butter, nuts and cherries. Place in bottom of 1½ quart salad mold. Dip each biscuit in melted butter, then in cinnamon sugar mixture. Bake at 425 degrees for 20 to 25 minutes.

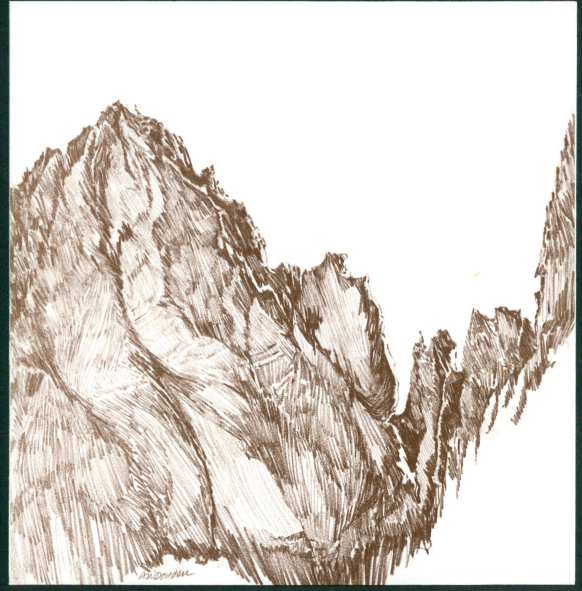

GARDEN OF THE GODS

Hints from **Montezuma**

Mexican food is a great favorite in Colorado, available in the many excellent restaurants and served often at home. Our preference is for the milder variety and so we have concentrated on this kind of recipe. We have included only recipes made with ingredients that are readily available.

In these recipes, corn tortilla are to be used unless flour tortillas are specified. Both kinds may be bought refrigerated or made at home. Tortillas may be frozen if tightly wrapped.

"Green chiles" referred to are the mild, canned variety. These are sold whole or chopped. If green Jalapeno chiles are substituted, you will have a hot surprise. If another type of chile is required in a recipe, it will be indicated. The types of chiles used in these recipes are:
- Canned, mild green chiles, also called chile Poblano.
- Jalapeno chiles, a very hot variety, especially the seeds. They are available both canned and fresh.
- Chile Piquene, a small, dried red chile, also very hot. They are sold in small boxes in the spice section of markets. They are sometimes labeled "small, red chiles".

Always wash your hands after handling chiles. It can be very painful if accidently rubbed in the eyes.

Always remove the seeds from chiles before using.

Refried beans, "frijoles refritos", are dried, pink or red beans that have been boiled until very soft, mashed and fried in hot lard or shortening. They are a staple in Mexican cooking and may be bought canned or made at home. They freeze well.

The cheeses used in the following recipes are sharp Cheddar, mild Cheddar and Monterey Jack. Muenster cheese may be substituted for Monterey Jack.

Sour cream is a favorite garnish for Mexican dishes. Dairy sour cream may be used, or a more authentic version can be made at home by combining 2 tablespoons buttermilk with 1 cup heavy cream and allowing it to ripen in a covered bowl at warm room temperature for 6 hours or until thickened.

The shortening used in Mexican cooking may be vegetable oil or solid vegetable shortening, but lard is most authentic in most recipes.

Beer is a favorite drink with Mexican food. There are several Mexican brands imported to this country. A delicious, customary way to drink it is to squeeze a wedge of lime onto the top of the open can and sprinkle with salt. Sip the beer through the lime and salt.

Montezuma, a once proud silver camp, was the site of the first silver discovery in Colorado Territory. Named for the last Aztec emperor of Mexico, it is located near A-Basin and Keystone ski areas. A few miles away lie Dillon Reservoir and the rejuvenated mining town of Breckenridge, offering year round recreation.

Margarita

1 drink

¼ fresh lime
1½ ounces Tequila
1 scant ounce Triple Sec
3 ounces sweet-and-sour bar mix
½ teaspoon brown sugar
salt

Rub lime around rim of each glass and dip rim of glass into salt to coat. Squeeze juice of lime wedge into each glass. Mix Tequila, Triple Sec, sweet-and-sour mix and brown sugar in a blender with ice. Strain and serve.

Pina Colada

4-6 servings

1 cup light rum
¾ cup canned cream of coconut
1½ cups unsweetened
    pineapple juice
cracked ice
fresh pineapple spears
    for garnish

Mix rum, cream of coconut and pineapple juice in blender for 30 seconds. Pour into glasses filled with cracked ice and garnish with pineapple spears.

Note: Cream of coconut is a nonalcoholic product found in the gourmet section of supermarkets as well as in liquor stores.

Sangria Blanca

4-6 servings

3½ cups dry white wine, chilled
    (1 bottle)
½ cup Cointreau
¼ cup sugar
ice cubes
1 10-ounce bottle club soda,
    chilled
1 orange, sliced
1 lemon, sliced
2 limes, cut in wedges

Combine wine, Cointreau and sugar until well blended in glass pitcher. When ready to serve, stir in ice and club soda. Add fruit and serve.

250

Mexican Food

ADO CACHE COLORADO CACHE COLORADO CACHE COLORADO CACHE COLORADO CACHE COLORADO CACHE COLORADO CACHE COLORADO CACHE COLORADO CACHE COLORADO CACHE

Salsa Fria

6 cups

4 tomatoes, peeled and
    finely chopped
½ cup minced onion
½ cup minced celery
¼ cup minced green pepper
¼ cup olive oil
3 tablespoons chopped,
    mild green chiles
2 tablespoons red wine vinegar
1 teaspoon mustard seed
1 teaspoon ground coriander
1 teaspoon salt
   dash pepper
   corn tortillas, cut in quarters
    and crisply fried

Combine all ingredients except tortillas. Cover and chill for at least several hours. Serve as a dip for fried tortilla quarters, or as a mild sauce for other dishes.

Taco Dip

5½ cups

1 28-ounce can tomatoes,
    mashed
2 4-ounce cans mild green chiles
¼ cup vegetable oil
⅓ cup red wine vinegar
2 bunches green onions,
    thinly sliced
5 -15 chile piquenes

In a blender mix the green chiles, oil and vinegar. Remove mixture from blender and add chile piquenes, green onions and mashed tomatoes. 5 chile piquenes will make the dip medium hot; 10 will make it hot; 15 will make it very hot. Serve as a dip for fried tortilla chips. This may also be used as a spicy-hot salsa with other dishes.

Ceviche

6-8 servings

1 pound firm, white fish filets
   juice of 12 limes
3 bay leaves
¼ teaspoon white pepper
1 teaspoon seasoned salt
1 clove garlic, minced
⅓ cup chopped onion
1 teaspoon crushed red pepper
1 teaspoon salt
¼ cup sliced, stuffed olives
¼ cup juice from olives
1 tablespoon vegetable oil
¼ cup catsup
2 tomatoes, finely chopped
1 hot green chile (Jalapeno),
   chopped

Remove tissue-like skin and cut fish into very thin strips, 1 inch long. Put fish in a glass jar and cover with lime juice. Refrigerate overnight. Drain and combine fish with remaining ingredients. Store in refrigerator for at least 1 hour. This will keep well for several days. To serve, remove bay leaves and serve in individual dishes with a garnish of lettuce, or serve as a dip with fried tortilla chips.

Guacamole

4 cups

4 ripe avocados
2 tablespoons fresh lemon juice
1 tomato, peeled and
   finely chopped
1 whole, mild green chile,
   chopped (or more to taste)
2 green onions, chopped
   salt and pepper to taste
   garlic powder to taste
   (optional)

Peel, seed and mash avocados. Add lemon juice, tomato, green chile, onions, salt, pepper and garlic powder. The dip may be served at this point, and will be chunky, or it may be processed in the blender if a smoother texture is desired.

To prevent the guacamole from turning dark, place the avocado seeds on top of the dip, cover tightly with plastic wrap, and refrigerate until serving time. This should not be made more than 4 hours before serving.

Serve as a dip for fried tortilla chips. Endive leaves may also be used to scoop the dip.

RADO CACHE COLORADO CACHE COLORADO CACHE COLORADO CACHE COLORADO CACHE COLORADO CACHE COLORADO CACHE COLORADO CACHE COLORADO CACHE COLORADO CACHE COLORADO CACHE COLORADO CACHE

Appetizer Empanadas

20 empanadas

1   **10-ounce package frozen patty shells, thawed**
½   **pound lean ground beef**
¼   **cup minced onion**
3   **tablespoons red chile salsa, hot or mild**
1   **teaspoon chili powder**
½   **teaspoon ground cumin**
½   **teaspoon garlic powder**
½   **teaspoon ground coriander salt and pepper to taste**

To make beef filling, crumble and saute beef and onion in a skillet until beef is cooked and onion is soft. Drain. Stir in red chile salsa, chile powder, cumin, garlic powder, coriander, salt and pepper. Set aside.

Place thawed patty shell dough on a floured board and roll out all in one piece to about 1/16 inch thickness. Cut dough into rounds with a 3 inch round cookie cutter or a large drinking glass. Put 2 teaspoons of filling on each dough circle. Fold each over into a half-circle. Moisten edges with water and press edges together with a fork. Place empanadas slightly apart on an ungreased cookie sheet. Prick tops with a fork. Bake at 400 degrees for 20 minutes or until golden brown. Serve hot. These may be wrapped carefully after baking and frozen. To reheat, bake frozen empanadas uncovered at 400 degrees for 7 to 8 minutes.

Nachos Para Sopear (Nacho Appetizer)

12 servings

12   **corn tortillas oil for deep frying**
½   **pound lean ground beef**
½   **pound chorizo sausage**
1   **large onion, chopped**
2   **16-ounce cans refried beans**
1   **4-ounce can chopped, mild green chiles**
3   **cups grated Monterey Jack cheese (12 ounces)**
¾   **cup bottled taco sauce**
¼   **cup chopped green onion**
1   **avocado, peeled, seeded and mashed**
1   **cup sour cream (8 ounces)**

Cut tortillas into sixths. Fry in deep hot oil until crisp. Drain on paper towels and salt to taste.

Remove casing from sausage and crumble into a skillet. Saute sausage, ground beef and onion until meat is lightly browned. Drain off grease and add salt to taste.

Use a large oven-proof baking dish or platter, about 10 × 15 inches or equivalent area. Spread refried beans on baking dish and top evenly with meat mixture. Cover with chiles, sprinkle with grated cheese. Drizzle taco sauce over cheese. This may be covered and refrigerated at this point for later use. Bake uncovered at 400 degrees for 20 to 25 minutes or until hot. Remove from oven and sprinkle with green onions. Put a mound of mashed avocado in the center. Put dollops of sour cream over all. Tuck fried tortilla pieces all around edges of platter and serve.

This may be served as an appetizer when baked in a large ovenproof platter. Keep it warm over a warming tray while serving. It may also be served as a casual main dish for four to six people.

Mexican Quiche Appetizer

½ cup butter
10 eggs
½ cup flour
1 teaspoon baking powder
   dash of salt
8 - 12 ounces canned, chopped
   mild green chiles
2 cups cottage cheese
   (16 ounces)
4 cups grated Monterey Jack
   cheese (1 pound)

24 servings

Melt butter in a 9 × 13 inch baking pan. Set aside. In a large mixing bowl beat eggs and add flour, baking powder and salt and mix well. Add melted butter, leaving the pan buttered. Add chiles and cheese. Mix together and pour into baking pan. Bake uncovered at 350 degrees for 45 to 60 minutes. Test for doneness with a knife. Be sure quiche is set and knife blade comes out clean when inserted in center. Cut into bite size squares while hot, but allow to cool slightly before removing from pan.

Note: This may be baked and frozen; reheat covered with foil.

Green Chile Bites

6 eggs, beaten
4 cups grated sharp
   Cheddar cheese (1 pound)
1 4-ounce can chopped,
   mild green chiles
   butter

64 pieces

Butter the bottom of an 8 × 8 inch baking pan. Spread green chiles on bottom of pan. Sprinkle grated cheese over chiles, and pour eggs over all. Bake uncovered at 350 degrees for 30 minutes, or until firm when pan is shaken. Cut in 1 inch squares. Serve hot on a warming tray.

Tostaditas with Cheese

6 corn tortillas
   shortening for deep frying
   salt to taste
1 cup grated mild Cheddar
   cheese (4 ounces)
2 tablespoons chopped, mild
   green chiles

6 servings

Cut tortillas into quarters and fry in deep hot fat until crisp. Drain on paper towels and place on ungreased cookie sheets. Sprinkle with salt to taste. Sprinkle cheese over tortilla pieces. Scatter chopped chiles over all. Bake uncovered at 375 degrees for 8 to 10 minutes. Serve immediately as an appetizer or snack.

ADO CACHE COLORADO CACHE COLORADO CACHE COLORADO CACHE COLORADO CACHE COLORADO CACHE COLORADO CACHE COLORADO CACHE COLORADO CACHE COLORADO CACHE

Mexican Salad

12 servings

1	**head iceberg lettuce**
½	**cup grated sharp Cheddar cheese (2 ounces)**
½	**cup chopped green onions**
½	**cup sliced ripe olives**
4	**tomatoes, sliced**
1	**cup crushed tortilla chips**

Avocado dressing:

1	**avocado, mashed**
1	**tablespoon lemon juice**
½	**cup sour cream (4 ounces)**
⅓	**cup vegetable oil**
½	**teaspoon sugar**
½	**teaspoon garlic salt**
½	**teaspoon chili powder**

Tear lettuce into bite-sized pieces. Combine lettuce, cheese, onions, olives, and tomatoes in a salad bowl. To make dressing, combine avocado, lemon juice, sour cream, oil, sugar, garlic salt, and chili powder and mix until smooth. This may be done in a blender. Toss salad with dressing and add crushed chips last.

Taco Salad

6 servings

1	**pound ground beef**
½	**clove garlic, crushed**
1	**4-ounce can chopped, mild green chiles**
1	**16-ounce can tomatoes, undrained**
1	**teaspoon salt**
⅛	**teaspoon pepper**
1	**head iceberg lettuce, torn into bite-size pieces**
1	**cup grated Cheddar cheese (4 ounces)**
6	**ounces fried tortilla chips, crushed**
½	**cup chopped green onion**
1	**tomato, sliced**

Saute beef and garlic until beef is browned. Drain. Add green chiles, tomatoes, salt and pepper and mix well. Cook over low heat uncovered for 30 minutes. Just before serving, arrange lettuce, cheese, chips and green onion in a chilled salad bowl. Add meat mixture and toss lightly. Garnish with sliced tomato and serve immediately. This is a good main course luncheon salad.

Cauliflower Salad with Guacamole Dressing

12 servings

1 head raw cauliflower,
(about 2 pounds)
½ cup thinly sliced green pepper
½ cup thinly sliced red pepper
¾ cup homemade oil and
vinegar dressing
1 head romaine lettuce
1 large cucumber, sliced
4 tomatoes, sliced

Thinly slice cauliflower; combine with green pepper and red pepper. Add oil and vinegar dressing and toss gently. Refrigerate at least 2 hours. To serve, line a large platter with crisp romaine leaves; mound cauliflower mixture in center; overlap alternate slices of tomatoes and cucumbers around the edge. Serve with Guacamole Dressing.

Dressing:
2 tablespoons oil and
vinegar dressing
2 ripe avocados,
peeled and chopped
1 small tomato,
peeled and chopped
2 tablespoons chopped,
mild green chiles
2 tablespoons grated onion
1 teaspoon salt

To make dressing, place avocados and oil and vinegar dressing in a blender and blend until smooth. Put mixture in a serving bowl and add remaining dressing ingredients and mix with a spoon. Place avocado pit on top of dressing to keep color green for a few hours. Cover surface with plastic wrap and chill until serving time.

Molded Guacamole Ring

12 servings

2 envelopes unflavored gelatin
½ cup cold water
1½ cups boiling water
6 tablespoons fresh lemon juice
1½ tablespoons grated onion
2½ teaspoons salt
dash of Tabasco sauce
3 cups mashed avocado
¾ cup mayonnaise
seafood or chicken salad
cherry tomatoes

Soften gelatin in cold water and dissolve in boiling water. Add lemon juice, onion and seasonings. While gelatin mixture is still liquid, stir in mashed avocado. Fold in mayonnaise, pour into a 10-inch ring mold and chill until firm. Unmold and fill center with chilled seafood or chicken salad. Surround with cherry tomatoes. This may also be served on a tray surrounded with fried tortilla chips for an appetizer.

ADO CACHE COLORADO CACHE COLORADO CACHE COLORADO CACHE COLORADO CACHE COLORADO CACHE COLORADO CACHE COLORADO CACHE COLORADO CACHE COLORADO CACHE

Cold Guacamole Soup

6 servings

- 1 **large ripe avocado**
- 1½ **cups good-quality chicken broth**
- 3 **tablespoons fresh lemon juice**
- 1 **cup half-and-half**
- 1 **teaspoon salt**
- ¼ **teaspoon pepper**
  dash of cayenne pepper
- 1 **cup sour cream (8 ounces)**

Peel avocado and remove seed. Cut into small pieces and place in a blender. Add chicken broth and lemon juice. Blend until smooth. Add cream, salt, pepper and cayenne pepper. Mix well and chill for 2 hours. Garnish each serving with a dollop of sour cream.

Gazpacho

8 servings

- 3 **large tomatoes, peeled and chopped**
- 1 **green bell pepper, chopped**
- 1 **cucumber, peeled and chopped**
- 1 **cup chopped celery**
- ½ **cup chopped green onion**
- 4 **cups tomato juice**
- 2 **avocados, chopped**
- 5 **tablespoons red wine vinegar**
- 4 **tablespoons olive oil**
- 2 **teaspoons salt**
- ½ **teaspoon black pepper**

Garnishes:
- **sour cream**
- **croutons**

Be sure all vegetables are very finely chopped. Combine all ingredients in a large non-metallic bowl and chill overnight. Serve soup cold with a dollop of sour cream on top of each serving. Pass croutons in a bowl.

Chile Relleno Casserole

8 servings

4   7-ounce cans whole, mild
      green chiles
1   pound Monterey Jack cheese
5   eggs
1¼ cups milk
¼   cup flour
½   teaspoon salt
      dash of black pepper
4   cups grated mild Cheddar
      cheese (1 pound)

Slit chiles lengthwise on one side. Remove seeds and drain. Slice Monterey Jack cheese into ¼-inch thick slices and place inside chiles. Place stuffed chiles in an ungreased 3 quart baking dish. Mix eggs, milk, flour, salt and pepper well, and pour over chiles. Sprinkle top with grated Cheddar. Bake uncovered at 350 degrees for 45 minutes.

Pastel de Elote (Mexican Corn Pie)

8 servings

3   large eggs
1   8¾-ounce can cream style
      corn
1   10-ounce package frozen corn,
      thawed and drained
½   cup butter, melted
½   cup yellow cornmeal
1   cup sour cream (8 ounces)
4   ounces Monterey Jack
      cheese, cut in ½ inch
      cubes
4   ounces sharp Cheddar
      cheese, cut in ½ inch
      cubes
1   4-ounce can chopped mild
      green chiles
½   teaspoon salt
¼   teaspoon Worcestershire
      sauce

Grease a 10 inch pie plate generously with shortening. In a large bowl, beat eggs. Add remaining ingredients and stir until thoroughtly mixed. Pour into pie plate and bake uncovered at 350 degrees for one hour.

The pie may be baked and then kept in the refrigerator for up to 3 days. Reheat refrigerated pie at 350 degrees for about 20 minutes. The pie may also be frozen after baking and kept frozen for up to 3 months. Thaw and reheat at 350 degrees for about 20 minutes.

Note: This may be served as a main luncheon dish or as a side dish for dinner.

Corn Tortillas

2 **cups Masa Harina
(made by Quaker)**
1¼ **cups water**
1 **tablespoon shortening**

16 tortillas

Heat water and shortening together until shortening melts. Stir into masa until well mixed. Heat two heavy skillets or griddles, one over low heat, one over medium-high heat. To make each tortilla, break off a piece of dough and shape it into a ball about 1½ inches in diameter. Place it between two plastic sandwich bags and roll out very thin with a rolling pin. For a more perfect round shape, tortillas may be made with a tortilla press. (A tortilla press may be purchased at many gourmet cookware stores.) Carefully remove the tortilla from the plastic bags. Place it on the cooler heated skillet and let cook until edges begin to dry out, about 30 seconds. Flip to other side on hot griddle and cook briefly until speckled. Cover cooked tortillas with a clean towel. These must be kept covered or they will become dry and hard. To reheat, wrap tortillas in foil and heat briefly in a 350 degree oven.

Note: These have a puffier texture than purchased tortillas. They are awkward to make at first, but become easier with practice.

White Flour Tortillas

2 **cups white flour**
1 **teaspoon salt**
1 **teaspoon baking powder**
1½ **tablespoons shortening**
¾ **cup cold water**

12 tortillas

Mix together dry ingredients. Cut in shortening. Add enough water to make a stiff dough (you may not need all of it). Divide dough into 12 pieces and roll each into a ball. Place each ball between two plastic sandwich bags and roll out very thin with a rolling pin. Use a tortilla press for a more perfect shape. Preheat a heavy skillet or griddle over medium-high heat. Bake each tortilla for about 2 minutes on each side. Cover baked tortillas with a clean towel. These may be reheated if wrapped in foil and placed in a 350 degree oven for a few minutes. These are used in some recipes or may be eaten plain with butter.

Huevos Rancheros

12 servings

6	cans Ortega Green Chile Salsa
1	15-ounce can tomato sauce
4	chorizo sausages, skinned and broken into pieces
1	bunch green onions, chopped
1	4-ounce can sliced ripe olives
2	teaspoons ground cumin
½	teaspoon garlic powder
12	corn tortillas
	oil for frying
12	eggs

Garnishes:
chopped green onion tops
chopped ripe olives
grated Monterey Jack cheese
chopped avocado
lime wedges

Heat ½ inch of oil in a small skillet. Dip each tortilla into hot oil for about 5 seconds, just to soften. Drain on paper towels. Set aside. Brown sausages, drain off grease and add green chile salsa, tomato sauce, green onions, sliced ripe olives, cumin and garlic powder. Simmer covered for 1 hour. Pour sauce into a large electric frying pan or top-of-the-stove skillet and heat through. Poach eggs in sauce, cooking as many as will comfortably fit in the pan at one time. Remove eggs carefully from sauce and place one on each softened tortilla. Spoon some sauce over each egg and sprinkle with garnishes, ending with a squeeze of lime over all.

Note: This sauce could also be used in omelettes.

Chicken Crepes Dolores

36 crepes

36	cooked crepes (see index)
1	3 to 4 pound chicken
1¼	pounds Swiss cheese, grated
2	cups heavy cream
1	teaspoon salt
1	teaspoon pepper
2	or more canned Jalapeno chiles, seeded, rinsed, and finely minced

Cook chicken, remove from bones, skin and dice meat. Reserve 1 cup cheese. Combine diced chicken, remaining cheese, salt, pepper and Jalapenos. Place a large spoonful of chicken mixture on each crepe and roll up. Place filled, rolled crepes in a shallow, ungreased baking dish and top with reserved cup of cheese. Pour cream over all. Bake at 325 degrees for 20 to 30 minutes or until thoroughly heated. These may be frozen without cream topping. Thaw, and add cream just before baking.

Cheese Enchiladas

6 servings

2	**cloves garlic, minced**
1	**medium onion, minced**
2	**tablespoons vegetable oil**
2	**tablespoons flour**
2	**cups chicken broth**
1	**4-ounce can chopped, mild green chiles**
2	**cups drained, chopped canned tomatoes**
12	**corn tortillas**
4	**cups grated Monterey Jack cheese (1 pound)**

Garnishes:

1	**avocado, sliced**
1	**cup chopped green onion**
2	**cups sour cream (16 ounces)**

Saute onion and garlic in oil until soft. Stir in flour and cook for 1 minute. Add broth and cook until thickened. Add chiles and tomatoes and simmer for 10 minutes. Cool slightly. Puree sauce in blender or food processor. Dip each tortilla in sauce, place a large spoonful of cheese and a spoonful of sauce in each, and roll up. Place filled, rolled tortillas in a large, flat ungreased baking pan. Pour remaining sauce over all and bake uncovered at 350 degrees for 15 minutes.

To serve, garnish with sliced avocado, sour cream, and chopped green onion.

Sour Cream Enchiladas

6 servings

12	**corn tortillas**
	vegetable oil for frying
4	**cups grated Longhorn cheese (1 pound)**
4	**cups grated Monterey Jack cheese (1 pound)**
½	**cup minced onion**
2	**cups sour cream (16 ounces)**

Green Chile Sauce:

3	**cups prepared white sauce**
1	**7-ounce can chopped, mild green chiles**
⅓	**cup minced onion**

To make Green Chile Sauce, combine white sauce, chiles and ⅓ cup minced onion in a saucepan and simmer until onion is tender, about 15 minutes. Set aside.

Mix cheese with ½ cup minced onion. Heat about ½ inch of oil in a small skillet. Dip each tortilla into the oil just to soften, about 5 seconds. Drain on paper towels. Place some cheese mixture on each tortilla and roll. Place filled, rolled tortillas in a large, flat ungreased baking dish. Top with Green Chile sauce and sprinkle with remaining cheese. Broil until bubbly and hot throughout. Top with sour cream just before serving.

Chicken Enchiladas

6 servings

- 2 **large, whole chicken breasts, poached**
- 1 **cup chopped onion**
- 1 **clove garlic, minced**
- 2 **tablespoons butter**
- 1 **16-ounce can tomatoes, chopped**
- 1 **8-ounce can tomato sauce**
- ¼ **cup chopped, mild green chiles**
- 1 **teaspoon sugar**
- 1 **teaspoon ground cumin**
- ½ **teaspoon salt**
- ½ **teaspoon oregano**
- ½ **teaspoon basil**
- 12 **corn tortillas**
- 2 **cups grated Monterey Jack cheese (8 ounces)**
- 1½ **cups sour cream (12 ounces)**

Cut chicken meat into 12 strips and salt to taste. Set aside. In a saucepan, saute onion and garlic in butter until soft. Add tomatoes, tomato sauce, chiles, sugar, cumin, salt, oregano and basil. Bring to a boil, reduce heat and simmer covered for 20 minutes. Remove from heat. Dip each tortilla in tomato mixture to soften. Place one piece of chicken and 2 tablespoons of cheese on each tortilla. Roll up and place seam side down in an ungreased 9×13 inch pan. Blend sour cream into remaining sauce mixture and pour over enchiladas. Sprinkle top with remaining cheese. Bake covered at 350 degrees for 40 minutes, or until heated through.

Chicken Enchiladas Supreme

6 servings

- 2 **cups cooked, chopped chicken or turkey meat**
- 1 **4-ounce can chopped, mild green chiles**
- 1 **7-ounce can green chile salsa**
- ½ **teaspoon salt**
- 2 **cups heavy cream**
- 12 **corn tortillas**
- 1½ **cups grated Monterey Jack cheese**

Combine chicken, green chiles and green chile salsa and mix well. Mix salt and heavy cream in a medium-sized bowl. Heat about ½ inch oil in a small skillet. Dip each tortilla into hot oil for about 5 seconds, just to soften. Drain on paper towels. Dip each fried tortilla into bowl containing cream and salt, coating each side. Fill each tortilla with chicken mixture. Roll and place in ungreased flat baking dish. Pour remaining cream over enchiladas and sprinkle with cheese. Bake uncovered at 350 degrees for 20 to 25 minutes.

Taos Chicken Chalupas

6 servings

- 2 **whole chicken breasts, poached and shredded**
- 2 **7-ounce cans Ortega green chile salsa**
- 12 **corn tortillas, crisply fried**
- 2 **cups refried beans (see index)**
- 2 **cups prepared guacamole (see index)**
- 2 **cups shredded lettuce**
- 2 **cups grated mild Cheddar cheese (8 ounces)**
- 2 **cups sour cream (16 ounces)**

Simmer chicken meat in green chile salsa over gentle heat for 15 minutes. To assemble each chalupa, begin with a crisp tortilla and layer on refried beans, guacamole, shredded lettuce, grated cheese, chicken with salsa, and sour cream. Serve two chalupas per person.

Note: These are easier to eat if you do not put too much of each ingredient on each tortilla.

Chalupas

8 servings

- 2 **pounds lean pork, cubed**
- 3 **tablespoons shortening**
- 2 **tablespoons flour**
- 1 **cup water**
- 1 - 2 **teaspoons ground cumin garlic salt to taste**
- 1 **14-ounce can tomatoes**
- 2 **7-ounce cans chopped, mild green chiles**
- 8 **crisply fried corn tortillas**
- 2 **whole chicken breasts, poached and shredded**
- 3 **cups refried beans (see index)**
- 2 **cups guacamole (see index)**
- 1½ **cups grated Cheddar cheese (6 ounces)**
- 1 **cup sour cream (8 ounces)**

Brown pork cubes in shortening. Stir in flour. Add water, cumin, garlic salt, tomatoes and green chiles. Simmer until thick, stirring occasionally. To assemble each chalupa, begin with a crisp tortilla and layer on refried beans, chicken, sauce, cheese, guacamole and sour cream.

Note: This is a very spicy-hot dish.

Carne Asada

8 servings

- 3 - 4 **pounds boneless beef sirloin steak**
- 2 **tablespoons olive oil**
  freshly ground black pepper to taste
- 2 **cups prepared guacamole (see index)**
- 2 **cups prepared refried beans (see index)**

Salsa Verde:

- ½ **cup minced green bell pepper**
- ½ **cup minced onion**
- ½ **cup chopped tomato**
- 2 **tablespoons chopped, mild green chiles**
- 1 **teaspoon ground cumin**
- 1 **clove garlic, mashed**
- ½ **teaspoon salt**
- 1 **teaspoon ground coriander**

To prepare Salsa Verde, in a saucepan combine green pepper, onion and tomato. Stir in chiles, cumin, garlic, salt and coriander. Heat sauce and simmer for 5 minutes just before serving.

Cut steaks into 8 serving-sized pieces and rub with olive oil and black pepper to taste. Leave at room temperature for 1 hour before cooking. Grill over very hot charcoal or on hottest setting of an electric skillet until cooked to desired degree of doneness. Outside of steaks should be crisply seared.

To serve, heat a large platter and arrange steaks in center. Place guacamole at one end of platter and heated refried beans at the other end. Spoon a narrow strip of Salsa Verde over steaks and pass more salsa at the table. Each person takes a serving of steak, guacamole, and refried beans and adds salsa to taste.

Note: This is good served with Sour Cream Enchiladas or Cheese Enchiladas (see index for recipes).

Green Chile Burritos

6 servings

- 2 **pounds lean pork, diced**
- 3 **10½-ounce cans chicken broth**
- 2 **7-ounce cans chopped, mild green chiles**
- 1 **16-ounce can tomatoes, chopped**
- 12 **white flour tortillas**
- 2 **16-ounce cans refried beans flour**
- 2 **cups grated Cheddar cheese (8 ounces)**
- 3 **cups shredded lettuce**
- 3 **tomatoes, chopped**

Simmer pork in broth until tender and thoroughly cooked. Add chiles and canned tomatoes. Simmer 15 to 20 minutes longer. Spread each tortilla with refried beans. Using a slotted spoon, put some pork mixture on each tortilla, reserving liquid to serve as sauce. Roll each tortilla and place in a shallow greased baking dish. Bake uncovered at 350 degrees for 15 minutes, or until hot. Thicken sauce with a little flour and spoon over burritos. Serve topped with grated Cheddar, shredded lettuce and chopped tomato.

264

Mexican Food

RADO CACHE COLORADO CACHE COLORADO CACHE COLORADO CACHE COLORADO CACHE COLORADO CACHE COLORADO CACHE COLORADO CACHE COLORADO CACHE COLORADO CACHE

Vegetarian Burritos

8-10 servings

1	large onion, thinly sliced
2	cloves garlic, minced
2	tablespoons vegetable oil
2	carrots, thinly sliced
1	large green bell pepper, sliced
4	medium zucchini, cut in ½ inch slices
2	large tomatoes, peeled and chopped
½	pound mushrooms, sliced
1	7-ounce can diced, mild green chiles
1	4-ounce can chopped, ripe olives
1	teaspoon chili powder
1	teaspoon salt
½	teaspoon oregano
½	teaspoon ground cumin
6	ounces Monterey Jack cheese with Jalapenos
12	ounces Cheddar cheese, grated
20	white flour tortillas

Guacamole Sauce:

6	ripe avocados
½	cup mayonnaise
¼	cup minced onion
¾	tablespoon salt
2	teaspoons chili powder
1	teaspoon garlic powder
½	teaspoon Tabasco sauce
3	tablespoons lemon juice
2	tomatoes, chopped

Garnishes:

sour cream
chopped onion
diced tomato
guacamole sauce

In a large kettle, saute onion and garlic in oil until soft. Add carrots, green pepper, zucchini, tomatoes, mushrooms, green chiles, olives, chili powder, salt, oregano and cumin. Bring to a boil and simmer for 10 minutes. While vegetables are simmering, make guacamole sauce by mashing avocado and stirring in all other guacamole sauce ingredients. Drain vegetables. Add both cheeses to drained vegetables and stir in pan to melt. Serve rolled in warm tortillas with guacamole sauce and garnishes.

Tostadas

6 servings

Meat Sauce:
- 1 **pound beef stew meat, cut in small cubes**
- 1 **tablespoon vegetable oil**
- 1 **small onion, finely chopped**
- 2 **cloves garlic, minced**
- 1 **4-ounce can chopped, mild green chiles**
- 1 **10-ounce can mild enchilada sauce**
- ¼ **cup tomato juice**

Refried Beans and Cheese:
- 1 **16-ounce can refried beans dash of Tabasco sauce**
- ¼ **cup sliced green onion**
- 4 **ounces Monterey Jack cheese, cut into strips**

Fried Tortillas:
- 6 **corn tortillas vegetable oil salt**

Salad Mixture:
- 6 **pitted ripe olives, sliced**
- 1 **tomato, finely chopped**
- 2 **tablespoons chopped, fresh parsley or cilantro**
- ¼ **teaspoon salt**
- 3 **cups shredded lettuce**
- 2 **tablespoons Italian salad dressing tops of 6 green onions, sliced**

Garnishes:
- 1 **avocado, chopped**
- 1 **cup grated Cheddar cheese (4 ounces) bottled taco sauce (optional)**

Brown meat in oil. Add onion and garlic and cook until soft. Add green chiles, enchilada sauce and tomato juice. Cover and simmer until meat is tender, about 1½ to 2 hours. This may be made in advance and reheated to serve.

Blend refried beans with Tabasco sauce and green onion. Place ⅓ of bean mixture in a greased 1 quart casserole dish. Top with ⅓ of cheese strips. Make two more layers each of remaining beans and cheese. Cover and bake for 30 minutes at 350 degrees.

Heat about ½ inch of oil in a small skillet over medium heat. Fry tortillas, one at a time, until crisp, turning once. Drain on paper towels and sprinkle with salt.

Mix all salad ingredients, adding dressing just before serving.

To serve tostadas, top a fried tortilla with hot refried bean mixture, then meat sauce and salad mixture. Garnish with chopped avocado, grated Cheddar cheese and taco sauce. Tostadas are easiest to serve buffet style, with each person "building" his own.

Flautas

1   **16-ounce can refried beans**
½   **teaspoon ground cumin**
¼   **teaspoon garlic salt**
1   **cup grated Monterey Jack cheese (4 ounces)**
¾   **pound chorizo sausage**
1½   **pounds ground beef**
3   **7-ounce cans Ortega green chile salsa**
8   **white flour tortillas**
3   **cups grated Colby Longhorn cheese (12 ounces)**
2   **large tomatoes, peeled and chopped**
¼   **cup sliced green onion tops**
4   **cups shredded lettuce**
1   **cup sour cream (8 ounces)**

8 servings

In a double boiler, combine refried beans, cumin, garlic salt and Monterey Jack cheese. Stir and heat over hot water until cheese melts. Crumble beef and sausage in a skillet and cook but do not brown. Drain grease. Add 2 cans green chile salsa and cook until most of the liquid has evaporated. Spread each tortilla with hot bean mixture. Spread meat over beans. Roll tortillas and place seam side down in a single layer in a large well greased baking pan. Pour remaining can of green chile salsa on top. Sprinkle with Colby cheese, tomatoes and green onion tops. Bake uncovered for 20 minutes at 350 degrees. Serve each flauta on a bed of shredded lettuce and top with a dollop of sour cream.

Tacoritos

1   **pound ground beef**
1   **tablespoon chili powder**
1   **clove garlic, minced**
½   **teaspoon salt**
½   **cup chopped onion**
3   **cups prepared white sauce**
½   **teaspoon ground sage**
½   **teaspoon oregano**
½   **teaspoon ground cumin**
2   **tablespoons chopped, mild green chiles**
2   **cups grated Cheddar cheese (8 ounces)**
2   **tomatoes, chopped**
12   **white flour tortillas**
½   **head iceberg lettuce, shredded**

12 servings

Brown ground beef and drain. Add chili powder, garlic, salt and onion. Combine white sauce, sage, oregano, cumin and chiles. Simmer over very low heat until warm. Reserve 1 cup sauce and 1 cup grated cheese. Mix remaining sauce and cheese with meat, lettuce and tomatoes. Place this mixture in tortillas, roll, and place seam side down in a flat ungreased baking dish. Top with reserved sauce and cheese. Cover with foil. Bake at 350 degrees for 15 minutes.

Pozole

8 servings

- 1 pork loin roast, about 3 pounds
- 5 cups water
- 3 cups strong chicken broth
- 2 cups chopped onion
- 2 teaspoons salt
- 1 whole chicken,
     about 2½ pounds
- 2 cloves garlic, crushed
- 1 tablespoon plus 1 teaspoon
     chili powder
- ½ teaspoon paprika
- 1½ tablespoons bacon grease
- 2 16-ounce cans white hominy,
     drained

Place pork roast, water and broth in a large soup kettle. Heat to boiling, add onions and salt. Cover and simmer gently for 30 minutes. Add chicken and heat to boiling, cover and simmer about 45 minutes. Remove pork and chicken from broth and allow to cool. Cover and refrigerate broth. Cut pork and chicken meat into small pieces and discard bones. Skim grease from broth. Stir garlic, chili powder and paprika into bacon grease over low heat just until blended. Stir a small amount of broth into mixture, add mixture to broth. Add hominy and heat to boiling. Cover and simmer gently for 20 minutes. Add pork and chicken and simmer until meat is hot, about 15 minutes. Serve soup in bowls and pass garnishes in individual bowls to add as desired.

Garnishes:
- chopped onions
- sliced radishes
- sliced avocado
- lime wedges

Mexican Eggplant

6 servings

- 1 large eggplant
- ¼ cup vegetable oil
- 1 15-ounce can tomato sauce
- 1 4-ounce can chopped, mild
     green chiles
- ¼ cup chopped green onion
- ½ teaspoon ground cumin
- ½ teaspoon garlic salt
- 1 cup grated Cheddar cheese
     (4 ounces)
- 6 ripe olives, sliced
- 1 cup sour cream (8 ounces)

Peel and slice eggplant. Brush both sides of each slice with oil. Place in a single layer on a greased baking sheet and bake at 450 degrees for 20 minutes. Combine tomato sauce, chiles, green onion, cumin and garlic salt in a saucepan. Simmer uncovered for 10 minutes. In a greased 9 × 13 inch casserole, layer eggplant, sauce and cheese. Top with sour cream and olives. Bake uncovered at 350 degrees for 20 minutes.

Montezuma Pie

8 servings

1½ pounds ground beef, browned
2 onions, chopped
1 clove garlic, minced
2 28-ounce cans tomatoes
   salt and pepper to taste
2 4-ounce cans chopped,
   mild green chiles
12 corn tortillas
8 cups grated Monterey Jack
   cheese (2 pounds)
2 cups sour cream (16 ounces)
   oil for frying

Saute onion and garlic in 2 tablespoons oil until transparent. Add tomatoes, salt and pepper and simmer for 10 minutes. Stir in chiles.

Heat about ½ inch of oil in a small skillet. Dip each tortilla into hot oil just to soften, about 5 seconds. Remove from oil and drain on paper towels.

In two 2½ quart casserole dishes, make layers of tortillas, sauce, beef, and grated cheese. Repeat layers, ending with cheese. Bake uncovered at 350 degrees for 30 minutes. Top with sour cream just before serving.

Mexican Chicken

8 servings

1 3-pound chicken, poached and
   shredded
1 onion, chopped
2 4-ounce cans diced, mild
   green chiles
2 tablespoons vegetable oil
1 12-ounce can mild enchilada
   sauce
1 cup chicken broth
1 cup half and half
2 cups grated Monterey Jack
   cheese (8 ounces)
18 corn tortillas
1 cup grated sharp Cheddar
   cheese (4 ounces)

Saute onion and green chiles in oil until onion is soft. Add cream, broth, Monterey Jack cheese and enchilada sauce and stir until melted. Add chicken meat. Put a layer of tortillas in the bottom of a greased 3 quart casserole dish. Spoon some chicken mixture over tortillas. Continue alternating layers of chicken mixture and tortillas. Top with Cheddar cheese. Bake uncovered at 300 degrees until heated through. This may be assembled in advance and frozen, to be thawed and reheated before serving.

COLORADO CACHE COLORADO CACHE COLORADO CACHE COLORADO CACHE COLORADO CACHE COLORADO CACHE COLORADO CACHE COLORADO CACHE COLORADO C

Chile Rellenos Harwood

12 servings

4	4-ounce cans Ortega, whole, mild green chiles
1½	pounds Monterey Jack cheese
6	large eggs, separated
1½	tablespoons flour
1½	teaspoons baking powder
2	16-ounce cans stewed tomatoes
1	quart cooking oil, heated to 375 degrees in an electric skillet

Put tomatoes in a saucepan over low heat and simmer gently for 45 minutes to reduce some liquid. Cut a rectangle of cheese and individually insert in each chile. Try to cut cheese to fit chiles. Blot chiles with paper towels. Beat egg whites with baking powder. Beat egg yolks with flour. Fold egg whites and yolks together gently. Dip each stuffed chile in egg mixture to coat and gently place in hot oil. Cook, turning once until chiles are golden all over. Place fried stuffed chiles in a large, flat ungreased baking dish, in one layer. Cover with tomatoes. Bake uncovered at 300 degrees for 20 to 30 minutes or until hot and bubbly.

Mexican Spoon Bread

9 servings

1	cup yellow corn meal
1	teaspoon salt
½	teaspoon baking soda
¾	cup milk
⅓	cup vegetable oil
2	eggs, beaten
1	17-ounce can cream-style corn
1	4-ounce can chopped, mild green chiles
1½	cups grated Monterey Jack cheese (6 ounces)

Mix cornmeal, salt and soda. Stir in milk and oil and mix well. Add eggs and corn and mix well. Spoon half of the mixture into a greased 9 x 9 inch baking pan. Sprinkle half of the chiles on top, then half of the cheese. Repeat layers, ending with cheese. Bake uncovered at 350 degrees for 45 minutes, or until wooden pick inserted in the center comes out clean. This should be spooned from the pan and eaten with a fork. It may be served as a substitute for potatoes with any kind of meat or poultry.

Sopa Seca (Mexican Rice)

4 servings

- 2 **teaspoons olive oil**
- ½ **teaspoon minced garlic**
- ½ **cup chopped onion**
- 1 **large tomato, chopped**
- 1 **cup uncooked, converted rice**
- 1 **small green bell pepper, seeded and diced**
- 1 **13-ounce can chicken broth dash of red pepper**
- ½ **teaspoon oregano**
- ½ **teaspoon salt**

Heat oil in a Dutch oven over moderate heat. Add garlic, onion and tomato. Cover and cook 3 minutes, or until onion is soft. Add rice and cook for 2 minutes, stirring, until rice is shiny and hot. Stir in green pepper, chicken broth, red pepper, oregano and salt. Bring to a boil. Cover and bake for 20 minutes at 400 degrees.

Green Chile Zucchini

10 servings

- 8 - 10 **zucchini**
- 1 **cup chopped onion**
- 1 **4-ounce can chopped, mild green chiles**
- 4 **cups grated Cheddar cheese (1 pound)**
- 4 **cups prepared white sauce salt and pepper to taste**
- 1 **cup dry bread crumbs crumbled bacon bits (optional)**

Wash and slice unpeeled zucchini and boil about 6 minutes or until barely tender. Drain and place in a buttered 9 × 13 inch baking dish. Add onion, chiles, salt and pepper. Stir grated cheese into hot white sauce until melted. Pour sauce over all and stir gently. Sprinkle top with bread crumbs and bacon bits. Bake uncovered at 350 degrees for 1 hour.

Sopaipillas

12 servings

- 4 **cups flour**
- 2 **teaspoons baking powder**
- 2 **teaspoons salt**
- 2 **teaspoons shortening**
- 1¼ **cups water shortening for deep frying**

Sift together dry ingredients. Add 2 teaspoons shortening and water and knead until smooth. Put into a plastic bag and let stand for 2 hours. Roll very thin and cut into small triangles. Fry in deep fat heated to 375 degrees until golden brown. Turn once. Drain on paper towels and serve with honey or sprinkled with cinnamon sugar. They are best made just before serving. They do not reheat well.

Chocolate Rum Dessert

8 servings

8   **eggs**
1   **cup sugar**
2   **envelopes unflavored gelatin,**
    dissolved in ¼ cup water
1   **tablespoon vanilla**
2   **cups heavy cream, whipped to**
    soft peaks
6   **ounces semisweet chocolate,**
    melted with ⅓ cup rum in a
    double boiler

Garnish:
½   **cup heavy cream, whipped**
    chocolate curls

Beat eggs and sugar in a bowl with an electric mixer for 10 minutes. Soften gelatin in cold water. Place gelatin in double boiler and stir over hot water until dissolved. Add egg mixture to dissolved gelatin very slowly. Add vanilla and fold in whipped cream. Divide mixture in half and fold melted and cooled chocolate into one half. Pour the two mixtures simultaneously into either side of a glass serving bowl and swirl slightly with a spatula to create a marbled effect. Freeze for 2 hours or refrigerate overnight. Decorate with chocolate curls and whipped cream put through a pastry tube.

Cold Rum Souffle

16 servings

8   **eggs, separated**
2   **cups sugar**
½   **cup fresh lime juice**
½   **cup fresh lemon juice**
    grated peel of 2 limes
    grated peel of 2 lemons
    salt
2   **tablespoons unflavored**
    gelatin
½   **cup dark rum**
2   **cups whipping cream**

Garnish:
    slivered lime and lemon peel

Beat egg yolks until light and fluffy. Add 1 cup sugar gradually and beat until smooth and light. Blend in fruit juices, grated peels and a pinch of salt. Stir in a saucepan over low heat until it thickens. Soak gelatin in rum and stir into hot custard until it dissolves. Cool. Beat egg whites until foamy and add remaining 1 cup sugar gradually. Beat until stiff. Beat whipping cream until stiff. Fold egg whites and whipped cream into cooled custard. Pour into a 12 cup Bundt pan, decorative mold or large souffle dish. Chill. To serve, unmold and garnish with slivered lime and lemon peel around edge.

Mexican Chocolate Cake

12-14 servings

- ¾ cup semi-sweet chocolate chips
- ½ cup walnuts
- 2½ teaspoons cinnamon
- 3 eggs
- ½ cup sugar
- ½ cup light brown sugar
- 2 tablespoons butter
- 1 cup buttermilk
- 1 teaspoon vanilla
- 2 cups sifted flour
- 1½ teaspoons baking powder
- ½ teaspoon baking soda
- ¼ teaspoon salt

Chocolate Frosting:
- 1 6-ounce package semi-sweet chocolate chips
- 1 cup sour cream (8 ounces)
- ¼ teaspoon ground cinnamon

Grease a 10 inch tube pan. In a blender, grate the chocolate chips and walnuts. In a large bowl, beat the eggs. Add sugar, brown sugar and butter, Beat well. Fold in the chocolate mixture and add cinnamon, buttermilk and vanilla. Gently fold in flour, baking powder, soda and salt until no dry ingredients are visible. Pour into prepared pan and bake at 350 degrees for 45 to 60 minutes. Cool in pan for 5 minutes. Turn out of the pan to cool completely. Split horizontally into 3 layers. Spread with chocolate frosting.

Melt chocolate chips over hot water in a double boiler. Stir in sour cream and cinnamon. Spread on cake.

Butter Pecan Sauce for Ice Cream

4 servings

- ½ cup dark brown sugar
- 1 tablespoon cornstarch
- ¾ cup water
- 1 tablespoon butter
- ¼ cup broken pecans
- 1 pint vanilla, chocolate or coffee ice cream

In a saucepan, mix together brown sugar and cornstarch. Add water and cook and stir over medium heat until thickened and bubbly, about 5 minutes. Stir in butter, add pecans. Serve warm over ice cream.

Pumpkin Flan

6-8 servings

1½ cups sugar
4 eggs
¼ teaspoon salt
1 teaspoon vanilla
2 teaspoons pumpkin pie spice
1 16-ounce can pumpkin
1 13-ounce can evaporated milk

Place 1 cup sugar in a small heavy skillet and stir over medium heat until melted and caramelized. Immediately pour into the bottom of a spring-form pan or a 10 inch metal pie pan. Tilt pan to coat inside with caramelized sugar.

Beat together remaining ½ cup sugar, eggs, salt, vanilla, spice, pumpkin and evaporated milk. Pour into prepared baking pan. Place pan in another shallow pan with ½ inch hot water in bottom. Bake at 350 degrees for 1½ hours. Cool and refrigerate until serving time. To serve, run a knife blade around edge of pan and invert onto serving plate.

Raspberry Flan

12 servings

½ cup sugar
2 10-ounce packages frozen
    raspberries, thawed
1½ cups half and half, scalded
5 eggs
1 egg yolk
¾ cup sugar
1 teaspoon vanilla
    fresh raspberries for garnish

Place a 2 quart baking dish in oven until warm. Heat ½ cup sugar in a small saucepan over low heat, stirring constantly, until sugar dissolves and turns golden. Pour melted sugar into the warm 2 quart baking dish and tilt to coat the bottom and ½ inch of sides. Invert baking dish on a plate and let stand to harden sugar.

Press raspberries through a sieve and discard the seeds. Reserve 1¼ cups of the strained raspberry liquid. Mix half and half, eggs, egg yolk, ¾ cup sugar and vanilla. Stir reserved raspberry liquid gradually into egg mixture. Pour into prepared baking dish. Place baking dish in shallow baking pan on oven rack and pour ½ inch hot water into baking pan. Bake uncovered for about 1 hour and 15 minutes at 350 degrees, or until knife inserted 1 inch from edge comes out clean. Remove baking dish from water and cool until lukewarm. Cover and refrigerate until cold. To serve, loosen edges with a spatula and invert onto a serving plate. Garnish with fresh raspberries.

THE WILLOWS AND BYERS PEAK

Hints from the **Matchless Mine**

General hints:

All recipes in this section are to be cooked on a high setting unless otherwise specified.

All recipes in this section are to be cooked uncovered unless otherwise specified.

No high altitude adjustments are necessary for the microwave. Occasionally you may need a little longer cooking time, a matter of seconds.

To retard any microwave cooking, place 8 ounces of water in a back corner of the oven to absorb some of the microwaves.

Microwave cooking times will always vary proportionally wih the amount of food cooked.

Any food that is dry or tough, except for stew meat, has been overcooked. Don't give up, try again and cook for a shorter period of time. If the shortened cooking time is not sufficient, let meat stand for 5 minutes before returing to microwave. The microwaves keep cooking internally even after the food is removed from the oven.

To test your microwave for accuracy, place 8 ounces of tap water in the oven and set time for 2½ minutes. Water should boil in this amount of time at Denver's altitude. Allow 3 minutes at sea level.

To convert regular recipes to microwave, cook ¼ of the given amount of time, and if necessary add time in increments of 30 seconds.

To clean your microwave, place a wet towel in the oven and microwave for 3 to 4 minutes. Let steam set for a few minutes and wipe out easily with the towel.

The best hint for your microwave is to have fun with it! Don't just thaw meat and boil water, experiment! Try and try again. It's such a time-saver that it is worth the effort. It is wonderful once you learn how, and you have to use it to learn!

To soften butter, place on a plate without metal trim and heat for 5 seconds, let stand for 15 seconds. Repeat if necessary.

To soften raisins, pour a little water over them, heat uncovered for 3 minutes and let stand for 2 minutes.

To toast almonds or other nuts, spread 1 cup nuts on a plate and heat 10 to 12 minutes, stirring every minute or so. Let stand for 2 minutes. Store in a covered glass jar.

To clarify sugared honey, remove metal top from jar and heat 1 minute. Watch carefully, as the time will vary with the amount of honey.

To dry fresh herbs, remove leaves from stem and spread on paper or cardboard. Cover with a paper towel and heat 2 to 3 minutes. If they are dry to the touch remove from the oven. If not, microwave a few more seconds. Let stand 10 minutes and store in a covered jar.

To freshen stale potato chips, crackers, etc., microwave 16 ounces for 30 to 45 seconds.

To melt butter, place in a bowl or cup and time as follows:

1 to 4 tablespoons–15 seconds	
¼ to ½ cup	–30 to 45 seconds
½ to 1 cup	–45 to 60 seconds

Microwave a lemon, lime or orange for 30 seconds before squeezing to get more juice.

COLORADO CACHE COLORADO CACHE COLORADO CACHE COLORADO CACHE COLORADO CACHE COLORADO CACHE COLORADO CACHE COLORADO CACHE COLORADO

To scald milk, heat for 1½ to 2 minutes per cup.

Use microwave to soften foods to a spreadable consistancy. Heat frostings, cheese spreads, honey, butter, cream cheese, icings, etc. 30 to 60 seconds per cup on medium setting.

For a hot compress for your aches and pains, heat a damp cloth for 15 to 20 seconds.

For T.V. dinners, "pop" frozen food from metal tray on to glass, plastic or paper plate and cook for 45 to 75 seconds.

Baby food:
- To warm refrigerated baby bottles, loosen the cap and heat 30 to 45 seconds for 8 ounces, 15 to 20 seconds for 4 ounces. Always test as these times are estimates.
- To warm a 4 ounce jar of baby food, remove metal lid, cover with waxed paper and heat for 30 seconds. Stir and test.

The **Matchless mine** was "Silver King" H.A.W. Tabor's most prized possession and one of the great bonanzas of the Leadville silver boom, paying $100,000 a month at times. Tabor amassed a fortune of several million dollars from his mining investments before the price of silver dropped and the Matchless ran dry. Baby Doe Tabor made a deathbed promise to her husband and kept the old worn-out mine, stubborn in her belief that the deep veins of the Matchless would again produce a fortune. She died in poverty and squalor, her dreams never realized.

Hors d' Oeuvres

Try any of your "meltables" in the microwave, chances are they will be wonderful. Most hors d'oeuvres can be successfully heated to serving temperature on a non-metallic serving dish. Prepare ahead and then just heat and serve.

Water Chestnut Bacon Wraps

40 pieces

- 2 **6½-ounce cans water chestnuts, drained**
- 1 **pound bacon**
- 1 **12-ounce bottle catsup**
- ½ **cup sugar**
- ½ **cup brown sugar, packed juice of 1 lemon**
- 2 **tablespoons Worcestershire sauce**
  Tabasco sauce to taste
- 2 **tablespoons dark molasses**

Cut bacon strips in half and wrap around whole chestnuts; secure with a toothpick. Place chestnuts on a roasting rack in a glass dish and cook until bacon is crisp, about 1 minute per chestnut. Mix the remaining ingredients and place in a shallow glass serving dish. Place chestnuts in the sauce and microwave for 1 minute until sauce is thoroughly heated.

Miniature Burritos

36 pieces

3	**tablespoons dry onion soup mix**
¼	**teaspoon paprika**
1½	**cup grated sharp cheese**
½	**cup sour cream**
¼	**cup freshly grated Parmesan cheese**
1	**package flour tortillas**
1	**8-ounce can chopped green chiles**

Combine onion soup mix, paprika, cheeses, chiles and sour cream. Spread about 3 tablespoons of the mixture on a tortilla and roll up. Cut each tortilla into 3 parts and secure each with a toothpick. Arrange in a circle on a pie plate and cook each plate 2 to 3 minutes until thoroughly heated and cheese is melted.

Teriyaki Steak Roll-ups

30 pieces

1	**tablespoon minced onion**
1	**clove garlic, minced**
1	**teaspoon Worcestershire sauce**
¼	**cup soy sauce**
1	**tablespoon sugar**
¼	**teaspoon ground ginger**
¼	**teaspoon salt**
½	**pound round steak or sirloin, cut diagonally into very thin strips**
1	**6-ounce can water chestnuts, halved**

Combine onion, garlic, Worcestershire sauce, soy sauce, sugar, ginger and salt. Coat meat strips evenly in this mixture and marinate for 30 minutes, stirring occasionally. Drain strips and wrap around water chestnuts, securing with a toothpick. Arrange on a shallow glass baking dish and cook in microwave for 3 to 4 minutes. Rest 5 minutes after cooking. Serve hot.

Note: If you are in a terrible hurry, ⅓ cup teriyaki sauce may be substituted for the marinade ingredients.

Bacon Bites

60 pieces

2	**pounds thick sliced bacon**
1½	**cups brown sugar, packed**
1½	**teaspoons dry mustard**

Place bacon slices in a single layer on microwave roasting rack in a glass baking dish. Combine brown sugar and mustard and sprinkle over bacon. Cook in microwave for 1 minute per bacon slice. Drain on paper towel and break into bite-sized pieces.

Roasted Chestnuts

1 pound raw chestnuts

Make an "x" slash on the rounded side of each nut, cutting through the shell to the nut. Arrange on a 9 or 10 inch glass plate. Cook in oven uncovered for 5 minutes or until shells pop open where slashed, stirring once. Serve warm by breaking open shells and removing nuts. If chestnuts become cold, return to oven for a few seconds until steaming hot.

Clamdigger Mushrooms

12 pieces

12 large fresh mushroom caps
1 3-ounce package cream cheese
1 7-ounce can clams, drained and minced
1 tablespoon parsley flakes
½ teaspoon garlic powder
12 canned French-fried onion rings, chopped

Wash mushrooms and remove stems. Soften cream cheese by placing in a mixing bowl and microwave ¼ to ½ minute. Mix all ingredients except mushrooms. Mound mixture lightly in mushroom cap. Place in a circle on a plate and sprinkle with chopped onion rings. Microwave 4 to 5 minutes turning halfway every 2 minutes. For smaller mushrooms, reduce time by ½ minute.

Walnut-Stuffed Mushrooms

50 pieces

2 tablespoons butter
¾ cup soft bread crumbs
¼ cup finely chopped walnuts
⅓ cup minced onion
2 tablespoons chili sauce
1 teaspoon salt
2 tablespoons fresh lemon juice dash of pepper
50 medium mushroom caps

In a 1 quart glass casserole melt butter 30 seconds. Combine with bread crumbs and walnuts and cook 2½ to 3½ minutes, stirring halfway through cooking time. Add onion, chili sauce, salt, lemon juice and pepper and blend evenly. Stuff mushrooms using about 1 tablespoon stuffing per cap. Arrange 10 to 12 mushrooms on a paper plate, cover with waxed paper and cook 8 to 10 minutes, rotating dish ¼ turn halfway through cooking time. Serve hot.

Seafarer's Delight

¼ **large green pepper, finely chopped**
½ **bunch green onions, minced**
2 **5-ounce jars very sharp cheese spread**
1 **7-ounce can minced clams, drained**
4 - 6 **dashes Tabasco sauce garlic salt to taste**

2 cups

Combine all ingredients in a 1½ quart casserole. Heat uncovered for 3 minutes or until cheese melts. Stir every minute.

Note: This may be served hot with corn chips, or better yet, chilled as a spread with crackers.

Crab Fondue

1 **6-ounce package king crab**
1 **5-ounce jar sharp cheese**
1 **8-ounce package cream cheese**
¼ **cup cream**
¼ **teaspoon garlic salt**
⅛ **teaspoon Tabasco sauce**
½ **teaspoon Worcestershire sauce**
French bread

6-8 servings

Melt cheeses for about 2 to 3 minutes in microwave, stirring often. Add other ingredients to cheeses and mix thoroughly. Serve with day-old French bread for dipping.

Celestial Crab

1 **6½-ounce can crab meat**
11 **ounces cream cheese**
3 - 4 **tablespoons finely chopped onion to taste**
½ - 1 **teaspoon fresh lemon juice to taste**
3 **tablespoons white wine**

4-6 servings

Soften cheese by cooking 1 minute. Mix in other ingredients and cook 1 to 2 minutes or until heated through. Serve with crackers. This can be served hot or cold.

COLORADO CACHE COLORADO CACHE COLORADO CACHE COLORADO CACHE COLORADO CACHE COLORADO CACHE COLORADO CACHE COLORADO CACHE COLORADO

Beer Cheese Spread

8 servings

- 1 **8-ounce package cream cheese**
- 4 **ounces processed sharp cheese (Old English)**
- 1 **tablespoon chopped green onion tops**
- ⅓ **cup beer**
- 1 **teaspoon horseradish**
- ½ **teaspoon dry mustard**

Melt cheeses in a glass dish in microwave for 2½ minutes. Gradually beat in the remaining ingredients. Cook covered for 2 minutes, stirring twice. Serve hot or cold with crackers or vegetables. We prefer it cold, but try both.

Pecan Spread

2 cups

- 1 **8-ounce package cream cheese**
- 2 **tablespoons milk**
- ¼ **cup finely chopped green pepper**
- ½ **teaspoon garlic salt**
- ¼ **teaspoon pepper**
- 2 **tablespoons dry onion flakes**
- ½ **cup sour cream**
- 1 **tablespoon butter, melted**
- ½ **cup coarsely chopped pecans**
- ½ **teaspoon salt**

Put cream cheese in a small casserole suitable for serving. Microwave for 45 seconds or just until softened. Add milk, green pepper, garlic salt, pepper, onion flakes and sour cream. Mix well. Place butter in a cup and microwave for 30 seconds to melt. Add nuts and salt. Stir well and drain on paper towel. Spoon nuts over cheese mixture. Serve with crackers or chips. This may be served hot or at room temperature.

RADO CACHE COLORADO CACHE COLORADO CACHE COLORADO CACHE COLORADO CACHE COLORADO CACHE COLORADO CACHE COLORADO CACHE COLORADO CACHE COLORADO CACHE

Beverages

For leftover tea or perked coffee, keep in refrigerator and heat as needed in a mug or cup for 1 to 2 minutes per serving.

Heat alcoholic beverages until warm enough to drink, do not boil. Time will vary with the quantity. Try all your hot drinks. Flavors will blend beautifully very quickly.

Thaw frozen orange juice in the pitcher. Remove from the can and microwave for 30 to 45 seconds, then add the water and mix.

Rum Toddy

1 serving

¾ **cup water**
   juice of 1 lemon (1 tablespoon)
1 **ounce rum**
1 **teaspoon honey**
   cinnamon stick

Combine ingredients except cinnamon in a mug or tea cup. Heat 1 to 1½ minutes and serve with cinnamon swizzle stick. This is wonderful for medicinal purposes to remedy any winter ailment!

Hot Spicy Grape Juice

4 cups

2 **cups grape juice**
1⅔ **cups water**
2 **tablespoons sugar**
2 **tablespoons fresh lemon juice**
1 **teaspoon ground cinnamon**
   pinch of ground ginger

In a 4 cup pitcher or bowl, combine all ingredients. Cook uncovered 6 to 7 minutes or until hot, stirring once. Serve hot or cold. To really zip this up you can add an ounce of vodka to each serving.

Gluwein

16 servings

- 2 **tablespoons whole cloves**
- 2 **tablespoons whole allspice**
- 2 **sticks cinnamon,**
      broken in pieces
- 4 **cups boiling water**
- 3 **tablespoons instant tea**
- 1 **6-ounce can frozen tangarine**
      or orange juice concentrate
- 1 **6-ounce can frozen Hawaiian**
      punch concentrate
- 6 **cups rosé wine**

Tie spices loosely in a piece of cheese cloth. Place in a deep casserole with the water. Cook for 5 minutes. Remove spices and add tea and juice concentrates. Cook 5 minutes more, stirring often. Stir in wine and serve immediately, or pour into a thermos and take to the game.

Soups and Sauces

For garlic butter, cook 1 cup butter or margarine with 3 cloves garlic, peeled and halved, for 1½ minutes until all butter is melted. Let stand for 20 minutes, remove garlic pieces and put butter in a glass container. Cover and refrigerate. This will keep for months.

A white sauce will keep for 4 to 5 weeks in the refrigerator. Reheat for 30 seconds to 2 minutes, stirring often. It is ready to use when it bubbles.

When you have a batch of soup, freeze some in "hot food" paper cups, well covered. Then take cups from freezer and have hot soup in 3 to 4 minutes with no clean up!

Tomato Soup

6 servings

- 6 **medium tomatoes**
- 1 **onion, chopped**
- 1 **stalk celery, chopped**
- 2 **cups chicken broth**
- 1 **tablespoon tomato paste**
- 1 **teaspoon basil**
      freshly ground pepper
- 1 **teaspoon salt**
- 1 **cup plain yogurt or sour cream**

Cut tomatoes in wedges to release juices. Place in a 3 quart glass casserole with onion and celery. Add chicken broth, tomato paste and basil. Season with pepper. Cook uncovered on highest setting for 20 minutes. Season with salt. Strain into serving bowls and garnish with spoonfuls of yogurt or sour cream.

Vegetable Cream Soup

4 servings

1	**cup chopped celery**
¼	**cup chopped onion**
2	**tablespoons water**
1	**can cream of mushroom soup**
1	**can vegetable soup**
1¼	**cups milk**
¼	**teaspoon seasoned salt**
½	**cup sour cream**
2	**tablespoons chopped parsley**

In a 1½ quart casserole combine celery, onion and water. Microwave, covered until vegetables are tender, about 5 minutes. Blend in soups, milk and seasoned salt. Cook covered until just boiling, 6½ to 7 minutes, stirring every 2 minutes. Blend in sour cream and cook covered about 30 seconds. Sprinkle each serving with a bit of chopped parsley when serving.

Cream of Zucchini Soup

8 servings

6	**cups sliced zucchini**
½	**tablespoon dried minced onion**
3	**chicken bouillon cubes**
¼	**cup margarine**
⅓	**cup flour**
1	**teaspoon seasoned salt**
3	**cups milk**
	sour cream (optional)

Place zucchini, onion and crumbled bouillon cubes in a 2½ quart glass casserole. Heat in oven 11 minutes or until zucchini is tender. Place in blender and puree. In same dish, melt margarine for 1 minute. Stir in flour and seasoned salt. Gradually stir in milk. Cook 8 minutes stirring often. Sauce should be thick and bubbling. Combine sauce and zucchini. Heat 2 minutes. Serve topped with sour cream if desired. If soup is too thick, add milk to achieve desired consistency. This can be frozen and reheated.

Hollandaise Sauce

1 cup

¼	**cup butter or margarine**
¼	**cup light cream**
3	**egg yolks, lightly beaten**
1	**tablespoon fresh lemon juice**
½	**teaspoon dry mustard**
¼	**teaspoon salt**
	dash of Cayenne pepper

Melt butter in a 4 cup glass measure in oven for 1 minute. Stir in remaining ingredients and cook 1 minute. Stir once while cooking. Stir briskly with wire whisk until light and fluffy. Don't overcook or sauce will curdle.

Note: For a quick Bearnaise sauce, add ¾ teaspoon crushed tarragon to Hollandaise sauce.

Vegetables

For a 10½-ounce package of frozen vegetables, open an end of the box and cook for 4½ minutes in the package. Put in a bowl, salt, butter and serve.

If you are cooking fresh vegetables ahead of time, undercook by 2 minutes, remove and cover. The steam will continue to cook the vegetables. You may warm them up later if necessary.

To peel a tomato easily, microwave 15 to 20 seconds, let stand 10 minutes and peel.

Corn on the cob from the microwave is the best ever! Place in a glass dish with ¼ cup water, cover and cook as follows: 2 ears - 4 to 5 minutes
4 ears - 7 to 8 minutes
6 ears - 9 to 10 minutes

Microwave chopped onion in butter until tender. Cool and freeze in ice cube trays. Once frozen, remove from trays and place in a plastic freezer bag. Each cube will be the equivalent of about 1 medium onion. Since it is already cooked, you need not be concerned about crunchy onions in your microwave dishes.

Mandarin Carrots

6 servings

- **4 cups carrots, cut into 2 inch pieces**
- **2 tablespoons butter or margarine**
- **1 11-ounce can mandarin orange sections, drained**
- **½ teaspoon salt**
- **⅛ teaspoon ground ginger**

Place carrots and butter in a 1½ quart casserole and cook covered for 10 to 12 minutes. Turn dish and stir halfway through cooking time. Add oranges, salt and ginger. Cook covered for 2 minutes. Let stand 2 to 3 minutes before serving.

CACHE COLORADO CACHE COLORADO CACHE COLORADO CACHE COLORADO CACHE COLORADO CACHE COLORADO CACHE COLORADO CACHE COLORADO CACHE COLORADO CACHE

Frosted Cauliflower

1   medium head cauliflower
½   cup mayonnaise
¼   teaspoon salt
1 - 2 teaspoons prepared mustard
¾   cup grated sharp Cheddar
      cheese
      paprika

4-6 servings

Remove woody base from cauliflower, leaving cauliflower whole. Cook cauliflower in 1½ quart glass dish with 2 tablespoons water and ½ teaspoon salt for 6 to 7 minutes per pound, covered. Rotate dish ¼ turn halfway through cooking time. Rest covered 5 minutes and season as desired. In a 2 cup glass measuring cup or mixing bowl, mix mayonnaise, salt and mustard and heat 1 minute. Spread over cooked cauliflower. Sprinkle with grated cheese and heat 1 minute until cheese melts. Sprinkle with paprika before serving.

Nutty Barley Bake

1   cup barley
½   cup margarine
1   medium onion, chopped
½   cup sliced almonds
1   5-ounce can water chestnuts,
      chopped
1   package dry onion soup mix
2   cups beef broth
1   8-ounce can mushrooms,
      sliced (or 5 to 7 medium-
      sized fresh mushrooms)

6 servings

In a 1½ quart glass casserole, melt margarine 30 seconds. Add chopped onion and barley and cook 6 minutes, stirring every 2 minutes. Add remaining ingredients and cook 6 minutes. Stir. Cook covered on low setting for 20 minutes. Add more water if liquid is absorbed before barley is cooked.

Almond Noodles

4 servings

- 8 **ounces fettuccine noodles, cooked**
- 6 **tablespoons butter**
- 2 **teaspoons olive oil**
- ½ **cup cream**
- 1 **clove garlic, minced**
- ½ **cup finely chopped parsley**
  pepper to taste
- ¼ **cup sesame seeds, toasted**
- ¼ **cup slivered almonds, toasted**
- ½ **cup grated Romano cheese**

Cook noodles according to package directions. Melt butter and oil for 1 minute in oven. Add cream, minced garlic and parsley and cook 1 minute. Combine butter mixture with noodles and stir to blend. Season with pepper to taste. Add sesame seeds, almonds and cheese and toss well so that cheese is well distributed throughout noodles. Return mixture to oven for 1 to 2 minutes until thoroughly heated.

Mushrooms and Peas

6 servings

- ½ **pound fresh mushrooms**
- 2 **tablespoons fresh lemon juice**
- 2 **tablespoons margarine**
- ¼ **teaspoon salt**
- ¼ **teaspoon seasoning salt**
  dash of pepper
- 1 **10-ounce package frozen peas**

Wash, dry and slice mushrooms. Sprinkle with lemon juice and stir to coat. Melt butter for 30 seconds and add seasonings. Stir in mushrooms and peas. Cook covered in a greased glass dish for 6 minutes, stirring twice.

Orange Sweet Potatoes

6 servings

- 3 **large oranges**
- 1 **1-pound 7-ounce can sweet potatoes**
- ½ **cup heavy cream**
- ½ **teaspoon salt**
- 1 **tablespoon brown sugar**
- 2 **cups miniature marshmallows**

Halve oranges, clean completely, removing all membranes and saving only the pulp and juice. Wash shells and set aside. Mash sweet potatoes and add cream, salt and brown sugar. Add orange pulp and juice. Fill orange halves with mixture and top with marshmallows. Set shells in glass casserole or pie plate. Microwave for 5 minutes.

Green Rice Casserole

8 servings

3	cups cooked long-grain rice
1	10-ounce package frozen spinach, thawed and drained
¾	cup finely chopped green onion with tops
½	cup minced parsley
½	cup slivered almonds
¼	cup butter or margarine
2	teaspoons fresh lemon juice
1	teaspoon salt
	dash of garlic powder
1	egg
1	cup milk

Combine rice, spinach, onion, parsley, almonds, butter, lemon juice, salt and garlic powder in a 2 quart casserole. Beat egg with milk. Stir into rice mixture. Cover and refrigerate. When thoroughly cooled, bake in microwave for 15 minutes. Turn dish every 4 minutes. Let casserole set for 10 minutes before serving.

Crunchy Tomato Halves

1 - 4	ripe, firm tomatoes, halved and arranged, cut side up, in a dish
½ - 2	tablespoons instant minced onion
¼ - 1	tablespoon sugar
½ - 2	teaspoons basil
¼ - 1	teaspoon salt
	dash of pepper
⅛ - ½	cup sharp cheese, grated
⅛ - ½	cup potato chips, finely crushed

Sprinkle tomato halves with ingredients, in order given. Cooking times:

    2 halves - 4 minutes
    4 halves - 8 minutes
    6 halves - 12 to 15 minutes
    8 halves - 16 to 20 minutes

Zucchini Parmesan

6 servings

- 4 **cups zucchini, sliced**
- 2 **eggs, beaten**
- 1 **cup mayonnaise**
- 1 **onion, chopped**
- ¼ **cup chopped green pepper**
- 1 **cup freshly grated Parmesan cheese**
  salt and pepper to taste
- 1 **teaspoon margarine, melted**
- 2 **tablespoons bread crumbs**

Place sliced zucchini in a 2 quart glass casserole and cook in the microwave for 5 minutes. Drain thoroughly. Beat eggs in a large bowl and stir in mayonnaise, onion, green pepper, cheese, salt and pepper. Add zucchini and return to casserole dish. Combine melted margarine and bread crumbs and sprinkle on casserole. Cook 5 minutes or until bubbly.

Broccoli Tomato Stacks

8 servings

- 1 **10-ounce package frozen, chopped broccoli**
- 2 **large tomatoes**
  salt
- ½ **cup grated Monterey Jack cheese**
- ½ **cup grated sharp Cheddar cheese**
- 2 **tablespoons dry minced onion**

Cook broccoli 6 minutes with ice side up. Do not add water. Slice tomatoes into 4 slices each, sprinkle with salt and place in a glass dish. Combine broccoli, ¼ cup of each cheese and onion. Spoon mixture on top of tomatoes and cook 4 minutes or until tomato is tender. Sprinkle with remaining cheese and cook 1 minute.

Bread and Breakfast

Cook extra pancakes or waffles and freeze wrapped in foil or plastic wrap. Bring from freezer, unwrap and rewrap in paper towel and cook. 2 pancakes - 45 seconds

2 waffles - 35 seconds

Heat syrup or honey in the bottle, removing metal top, for a much better flavor. For a 13 ounce bottle heat 35 to 40 seconds or until bubbles appear.

Poach an egg on toast. Crack an egg on toasted bread or an English muffin and cook for 45 to 55 seconds.

Caramel Coffee Cake

4-6 servings

- ⅓ **cup brown sugar, firmly packed**
- 3 **tablespoons butter or margarine**
- 1 **tablespoon water**
- ¼ - ½ **cup chopped walnuts (optional)**
- 1 **8-ounce can refrigerated biscuits**

Put brown sugar, butter and water in an 8 inch round glass dish and heat for 1 minute. Blend ingredients and stir in nuts. Separate biscuits and arrange in an overlapping ring. (For more servings, cut each biscuit in half or quarters). Spoon caramel mixture over the biscuits and place a small glass or custard cup in the center. Cook 2 to 3 minutes, rotating ¼ turn halfway through cooking time. Rest 2 to 3 minutes. Biscuits should be firm and not doughy, but not tough. Remove center glass and invert coffee cake on a serving plate.

Note: Cook this on defrost or slow cook, if available, for more volume, 4 to 5 minutes.

Peanut Butter-Applesauce French Toast

4 servings

6   ounces peanut butter
½   cup applesauce
8   slices frozen French toast
    soft butter or margarine

Blend peanut butter and applesauce. Spread mixture on 4 slices French toast. Top with remaining slices to make 4 sandwiches. Butter sandwiches lightly on both sides. Heat browning skillet in microwave for 4½ minutes. Place 2 sandwiches in skillet. Cook for 2 minutes, turn and cook again for 3 minutes. Repeat with remaining 2 sandwiches.

Note: Pour maple syrup over and serve for a super breakfast or brunch. Kids love it.

English Muffin Bread

2 loaves

5   cups flour
1   tablespoon sugar
2½   cups milk
2   packages yeast
2   teaspoons salt
¼   teaspoon soda
1   tablespoon water

Combine in a large glass bowl 3 cups flour, sugar and yeast. Heat milk in microwave for 1 minute until warmed. Add milk to flour mixture. Put mixture in oven and heat until smooth, 3 to 4 minutes. Add remaining flour to make a stiff batter. Cover bowl and put in a warm place until batter doubles in bulk, about 25 minutes. Stir down with a wooden spoon and add soda which has been dissolved in water. Place batter in 2 greased glass loaf pans and let double in bulk. Cook each loaf separately for about 7 to 8 minutes, until there are no doughy spots. Allow to cool out of pans so that doughy spots on bottom can dry.

Note: This bread must be toasted to obtain its full flavor.

Herb Bread

10 biscuits

1   tablespoon grated
     Parmesan cheese
1   teaspoon paprika
1   teaspoon instant
     minced garlic
1   teaspoon poppy seeds
10   refrigerator biscuits

Combine cheese, paprika, garlic and poppy seeds. Break biscuits in half. Roll in cheese and spice mixture. Drop in buttered 9 inch round cake dish with inverted glass custard cup in center of dish. Bake 5 to 5½ minutes on medium setting. Remove cup and invert ring on platter.

Carrot Pineapple Bread

2 loaves

3	**eggs**
1	**cup sugar**
1	**cup brown sugar, packed**
1	**cup vegetable oil**
1	**cup grated carrots**
1	**8¼-ounce can crushed pineapple**
2	**teaspoons vanilla extract**
3	**cups flour, sifted**
1½	**teaspoons ground cinnamon**
2	**teaspoons soda**
1	**teaspoon salt**

Beat eggs in a bowl, add sugars and oil and beat until smooth. Stir in carrots, undrained pineapple and vanilla. Sift dry ingredients and stir into batter. Pour into 2 greased glass loaf pans and cook each separately for 8 to 10 minutes. Test with a toothpick which should come out clean. This is more satisfactory if you fill loaf pans only ½ full.

Note: For additional color you may mix 2 tablespoons butter and 2 tablespoons brown sugar and spread on top of bread.

Halloween Bread

1 loaf

1½	**cups sugar**
2	**eggs, beaten**
½	**cup vegetable oil**
¾	**teaspoon salt**
½	**teaspoon ground nutmeg**
½	**teaspoon ground cloves**
1	**teaspoon ground cinnamon**
1	**teaspoon soda**
1¾	**cups flour**
1	**cup pumpkin**
⅓	**cup hot water**
	chopped pecans (optional)

Mix sugar and eggs with oil. Sift dry ingredients together and gradually add to egg mixture. Add pumpkin and water and stir until combined. Pour into a 1½ quart glass loaf pan and cook in microwave for 8 to 10 minutes, turning a quarter turn every 2 minutes. Toothpick should come out clean when inserted in several spots. You may add ½ to 1 cup chopped pecans if desired.

Main Dishes

For juicy barbecued chicken, precook in the microwave for 2 minutes per pound. Then place on hot coals and grill until well browned on both sides.

Barbecue extra steaks, or whatever is your specialty. When cool, wrap well and freeze. Then when the mood strikes you, bring out your steak and defrost in microwave to eating temperature. Instant barbecue!

When cooked chicken is called for in a recipe, use breasts, washed and shaken dry. Don't salt. Cover with waxed paper and cook for 7 minutes per pound until tender.

For hot sandwiches of almost any kind, heat right on the bread or roll on a paper towel so that the bottom won't be soggy. Or better yet, on a roasting rack so that the bottom is not trapped. Microwave 30 seconds per sandwich, 45 seconds for 2 sandwiches.

Skin all chicken before cooking, unless you are using a browning dish.

Burgundy Beef Stew

6 servings

1½ **pounds boneless chuck,**
    cut into 1½ inch cubes
2 **tablespoons butter**
1 **tablespoon vegetable oil**
1 **large turnip,**
    cut into 1 inch pieces
1 **pound small white onions,**
    peeled
1 **pound carrots,**
    cut into 1 inch pieces
3 **tablespoons flour**
1 **cup beef bouillon**
1 **cup Burgundy**
    dash of Worcestershire sauce
6 **peppercorns**
3 **bay leaves**

Heat butter and oil in a 3 quart glass casserole for 20 seconds. Brown beef, turnip, onions and carrots for 4 minutes. Add flour, stir and cook for 2 minutes. Add bouillon, wine, Worcestershire sauce, peppercorns and bay leaves. Cover and cook on low setting for 1 hour. Leave overnight and reheat 10 to 15 minutes the next day, or cook 20 minutes more if serving on the same day.

RADO CACHE COLORADO CACHE COLORADO CACHE COLORADO CACHE COLORADO CACHE COLORADO CACHE COLORADO CACHE COLORADO CACHE COLORADO CACHE COLORADO CACHE COLORADO CACHE

Stroganoff Pie

6 servings

1½ **pounds lean ground beef**
1 **cup chopped onion**
½ **cup sour cream**
1 **can cream of mushroom soup**
¼ **cup milk**
1 **teaspoon salt**
¼ **cup catsup**
1 **can refrigerated biscuits**
¼ **cup grated Parmesan or**
   Romano cheese

Crumble beef into a 2 quart casserole. Add onions and cook for 7 minutes, stirring occasionally, until beef is browned. Drain off grease. Combine sour cream, soup, milk and catsup. Add meat and onions to mixture and place in 2 quart casserole. Microwave for 5 minutes and add salt, mixing well. Place biscuits around edge of casserole and sprinkle with cheese. Return to oven and cook for 5 minutes. Run under a broiler to brown biscuits if desired.

Chinese Beef

4 servings

1 **7-ounce package frozen snow**
   peas (Chinese pea pods)
1 **pound lean ground beef**
½ **cup sliced green onions**
1 **can cream of mushroom soup**
1 **tablespoon soy sauce**
⅛ **teaspoon pepper**
1 **3-ounce can chow mein**
   noodles

Place package of frozen peas in oven for 1½ minutes to partially thaw. Crumble meat into a 1½ quart casserole. Slice onions and mix with meat. Layer peas over the meat mixture. Blend soup, soy sauce and pepper and spoon over the peas. Cook for 14 minutes until the meat mixture loses its pink color. Turn the dish every 4 minutes and let stand for 5 minutes before serving. Heat noodles on a paper plate in the microwave for 1½ minutes, turning the dish halfway through cooking time. Sprinkle noodles over the casserole and serve.

Tyrolean Rump Roast

8 servings

3½ - 4 **pound boneless
beef rump roast**
2 **teaspoons salt**
1 **teaspoon dry mustard**
¼ **teaspoon garlic powder**
¼ **teaspoon pepper**
1 **tablespoon catsup**
1 **teaspoon Worcestershire
sauce**
½ **cup dry red wine**

Sprinkle roast with seasonings. Place roast, fat side down, on a microwave roasting rack in a 2 quart baking dish. Microwave on medium setting for 20 minutes. Turn fat side up. Combine catsup, Worcestershire sauce and wine in a small mixing bowl. Pour the sauce over the roast and microwave on slow setting for 20 to 24 minutes or until rare. Let stand covered with foil for 10 minutes before serving.

Chili

8 servings

2 **pounds lean ground beef**
1 **large onion, diced**
1 **large green pepper, diced**
1 **1-pound 13-ounce can
tomatoes**
2 - 3 **tablespoons chili powder**
1 **teaspoon salt**
⅛ **teaspoon cayenne pepper**
⅛ **teaspoon paprika**
1 **15-ounce can kidney beans,
drained**
2 **8-ounce cans tomato sauce**

Brown beef in microwave for 7 minutes stirring twice. Drain. Saute onion and green pepper in 2 tablespoons water for 2 minutes. In a large bowl, combine all ingredients and cook covered for 12 minutes, stirring halfway through cooking time. Rest covered for 5 minutes before serving.

French Dip Sandwiches

1 **2 to 4 pound sirloin tip roast**
1 **package au jus mix**
   water
   small crusty dinner rolls
   butter
   mustard
   mayonnaise
   horseradish

8-12 servings

Early in the day, or the day before, prepare the roast. Place roast on roasting rack in a glass pan. Microwave 6 minutes per pound for medium rare. Rest. Cool completely, reserving drippings. Slice roast very thinly when cold. Prior to serving pour au jus mix and drippings into a 4 cup glass measure. Fill to the 3 cup mark with water. When ready to serve butter rolls and fill with meat. Microwave au jus mixture 5 minutes. Place filled rolls in a clean kitchen towel and cook, allowing 10 to 15 seconds for each small roll. Pour au jus into individual serving bowls, giving one to each person. Pass mustard, mayonnaise and horseradish.
Serve with a big green salad.

   Note: Easy for a group after the football game—or during.

Pizza Fondue

1 **pound ground beef**
½ **cup chopped onion**
2 **10½-ounce cans pizza sauce
    with cheese**
1 **tablespoon cornstarch**
½ **teaspoon basil**
2 **teaspoons oregano**
¼ **teaspoon garlic powder**
2 **cups grated Cheddar cheese**
1 **cup grated Mozzarella cheese**
1 **loaf French bread, cubed**

4-6 servings

Crumble beef in a 2 quart casserole. Add onion and cook for 5 minutes, stirring after 3 minutes. Drain off grease. Add cornstarch and seasonings to the pizza sauce. Stir well and add to the meat. Microwave for 4 minutes. Mix cheeses and add to the sauce mixture, ⅓ at a time. Microwave for 1 minute after each addition. Stir well. Serve with bread cubes for dipping.

   Note: This reheats beautifully. An easy dinner that the kids will love when served with a big tossed salad.

Cheesy Chicken Spinach

6 servings

- 1 10-ounce package frozen spinach
- 1 8-ounce package cream cheese
- 1 cup milk
- 1 cup grated Monterey Jack cheese
- ½ teaspoon salt
- ¼ teaspoon garlic salt
- ½ cup grated Parmesan cheese
- 2 cups chicken, cooked and cubed
- ½ cup crushed cornflakes

Defrost spinach in the box by opening an end and microwaving for 4 to 6 minutes. Squeeze dry or drain well. Spread spinach in a 9 inch greased casserole or an 8 inch glass pan. Make sauce by blending cream cheese, milk, Jack cheese, salt, garlic salt and ¼ cup Parmesan cheese together in a small glass bowl. Microwave for 2 minutes, stirring often. Spread half the sauce over the spinach and spread chicken over this layer. Top with remaining sauce. Sprinkle remaining ¼ cup Parmesan cheese and the cereal on top. Microwave for 6 minutes until bubbly. This can be browned under the broiler for added color.

Chicken Cortez

4 servings

- 6 chicken breasts, cooked and diced
- 1 5⅓-ounce can evaporated milk
- ½ cup sour cream
- 1 10-ounce can cream of chicken soup
- ½ cup Mexican hot sauce
- 1 medium onion, chopped
- ½ cup chopped celery
- 1 8-ounce can green chiles
- 6 corn tortillas, torn into 1 inch pieces
- ½ cup grated Monterey Jack cheese (2 ounces)
- ½ cup grated Cheddar cheese (2 ounces)

Cook chicken breasts in a glass dish covered with waxed paper for 16 to 18 minutes. Cool and tear into bite-sized pieces. Combine chicken, sour cream, evaporated milk, soup, hot sauce, onion, celery, chiles, tortillas and cheeses. Blend well. Microwave for 12 to 14 minutes, turning halfway through cooking time.

Party Chicken

4 servings

2½ - 3 **pounds chicken pieces, skinned**
¼ **cup mayonnaise**
1 **envelope dry onion soup mix**
½ **cup Russian salad dressing**
1 **cup apricot preserves**

Arrange chicken in a 9 × 13 inch glass baking dish, placing thickest meaty pieces to the outside of dish. Combine mayonnaise, soup mix, dressing and preserves and spread over chicken, coating each piece. Cover the dish with waxed paper and cook for 20 minutes, turning dish halfway through cooking time.

Buffet Ham

4-6 servings

3 **pounds pre-cooked ham**
1 **cup brown sugar, firmly packed**
¼ **cup pineapple juice**
1 **8-ounce can sliced pineapple**
8 **maraschino cherries**

Place ham on a roasting rack, fat side down, and cover with waxed paper. Cook in microwave on medium setting for 8 minutes per pound. Turn ham over halfway through cooking time. Mix brown sugar with pineapple juice and pour over ham to glaze. Decorate with sliced pineapple and cherries and continue to cook for last half of the time.

Salmon with Mock Hollandaise

2 servings

2 **tablespoons butter**
2 **6-ounce salmon steaks**
2 **teaspoons fresh lemon juice**
  salt
  pepper
  parsley

Preheat browning dish for 3 minutes. Add 1 tablespoon butter. Place the salmon in the dish and place remaining butter on top. Sprinkle with lemon juice. Cook for 3 minutes on first side, turn over and cook for 2 minutes on second side. Serve with mock Hollandaise sauce, boiled potatoes and buttered peas.

Mock Hollandaise Sauce:

8 **tablespoons butter**
3 **egg yolks**
2 **tablespoons fresh lemon juice**
¼ **cup mayonnaise**
  salt and pepper
  dash of cayenne pepper

Heat butter in a 4 cup glass measuring cup for 50 seconds until hot and bubbling. Stir in egg yolks, lemon juice and mayonnaise, stirring rapidly with wire whisk. Return to oven for 50 seconds. Stir halfway through and after taking from the oven, season with salt, pepper and cayenne.

Fish Fillets Amandine

6 servings

⅓ cup slivered almonds toasted
3 tablespoons butter
6 serving size fish fillets (1½ pounds)
½ teaspoon seasoned salt
1½ tablespoons fresh lemon juice lemon, cut in thin wedges
1 teaspoon Lawry's pepper

Toast almonds in microwave 5 to 7 minutes. Melt butter and blend with salt and pepper. Coat fillets in butter and arrange around the outside of a 2 quart glass dish. Sprinkle with lemon juice and cover with waxed paper. Cook 6 to 8 minutes, rotating dish ¼ turn halfway through cooking time. Rest for 5 minutes. Top with toasted almonds and serve with lemon wedges.

Shrimp Jambalaya

4-6 servings

2 tablespoons butter or margarine
1 large onion, chopped
½ cup chopped green pepper
1 clove garlic, minced or pressed
1 1-pound can tomato wedges in juice
1 14-ounce can regular strength chicken broth
1 cup diced cooked ham
4 ounces hot sausage, chopped and browned
¾ teaspoon salt
¼ teaspoon thyme, crumbled dash of pepper
1 bay leaf
2 cups quick cooking rice
1 pound medium-sized shrimp, shelled and deveined, or 1 pound cooked, frozen shrimp

In a 3 quart casserole, melt butter for 1 minute until bubbly. Stir in onion, green pepper and garlic. Cover and cook 7 minutes or until vegetables are limp. Stir in tomatoes and their liquid, broth, ham, parsley, sausage, salt, thyme, pepper, bay leaf and rice. Cover and cook 12 to 14 minutes, stirring 2 or 3 times, until rice is nearly tender. Arrange raw shrimp over top of rice, cover and cook 3 to 4 minutes or until shrimp turn pink. For precooked shrimp, arrange on top and cook 2 minutes. Let stand covered for 5 minutes. Remove bay leaf, stir well and serve in shallow bowls.

Desserts

For cookies, add 20% more flour if you want to try them in the microwave.

Use frozen pie crusts; "Pet Ritz Deep" is the best. Pop frozen crust from the foil pan and place in your glass microwave pie plate. Prick well with a fork and cook for 2½ minutes. To brown, brush with vanilla and egg white for a sweet pie, or with Worcestershire sauce for a quiche.

To make caramel topping for apples or ice cream, place 20 to 25 caramels in a bowl with 3 tablespoons cream or water, or rum. Heat for 3 minutes or until melted, stirring after 1½ minutes.

To melt chocolate for desserts, place a 1 ounce square of chocolate on waxed paper with the seam up and microwave for 1½ to 2 minutes. Then scrape into your bowl and have no extra clean up.

For quick mint icing, place a chocolate coated mint patty over a cookie or cake. 16 patties cover a single layer cake. Microwave for 2 minutes, let stand a minute and swirl to cover the top. Delicious on brownies or chocolate cake. For 1 cupcake, use 1 patty and melt for 30 seconds.

Heat brandy for flaming desserts for 15 seconds in a glass measuring cup, pour over dessert and ignite.

For hot pie, heat 30 to 45 seconds per piece.

Strawberry Pie

8 servings

- 1 **9-inch baked pastry shell**
- 1½ **quarts fresh strawberries**
- 3 **tablespoons corn starch**
- 1 **cup sugar**
- 1 **cup water**
- 1 **teaspoon butter or margarine**
- 1 **8-ounce package cream cheese, softened**

Clean and hull berries. Measure ⅔ cup of berries and mash in a 1 quart measuring cup. Add water and sugar. Microwave for 5 to 6 minutes until boiling. Soften corn starch in a small amount of water and add to strawberry mixture. Microwave 2 to 3 minutes or until mixture thickens, stirring once. Stir in butter and cool. Spread softened cream cheese on bottom of pastry shell and fill with remaining berries. Pour cooled glaze over the top and garnish with whipped cream.

Note: A microwave version of an "old friend."

Super Quickie Fudge

18 pieces

- 1 **pound powdered sugar**
- ½ **cup cocoa**
- ¼ **cup milk**
- ¼ **pound butter or margarine**
- 1 **tablespoon vanilla extract**
- ½ **cup chopped nuts (optional)**

Blend powdered sugar and cocoa in an 8 × 8 × 2 inch dish. Pour in milk and place butter on top. Cook in oven 2 minutes. Remove from oven and stir just to mix ingredients. Add vanilla and nuts if desired. Stir until blended. Place in freezer for 20 minutes or refrigerator for 1 hour. Cut and serve.

Jamaican Lime Pie

Crust:

½ cup coconut, toasted under broiler
1½ cups macaroon crumbs, crushed
¼ cup margarine

8 servings

Combine ingredients and press into a 9 inch glass pie plate. Cook 2 minutes in microwave. Cool. (A graham cracker crust could be substituted.)

Filling:

1 envelope unflavored gelatin
⅔ cup sugar
⅛ teaspoon salt
¾ cup water
2 drops green food coloring
1 6-ounce can frozen limeade
1 cup ice cold evaporated milk, or 2 cups prepared dairy topping

Mix gelatin, salt and sugar together. Add water and food coloring. Heat for 3 minutes, stirring 2 to 3 times scraping down sides. Gelatin should be dissolved. Add undiluted limeade and refrigerate until it mounds when dropped from a spoon, about 1 hour. Whip evaporated milk and fold into thickened mixture. Turn into pie crust and chill to set, about 2 hours. You may substitute frozen lemonade and yellow food coloring or frozen orange juice and orange food coloring for the limeade and green coloring.

Cheesecake Tarts

6 servings

3 tablespoons butter or margarine
½ cup graham cracker crumbs
1½ teaspoons sugar
1 8-ounce package cream cheese, softened
¼ cup sugar
1 egg
1 teaspoon vanilla extract
6 tablespoons berry or fruit jam

In a glass mixing bowl, melt butter for 1 minute in microwave oven. Blend in crumbs and 1½ teaspoons sugar. Line 6 glass custard cups with paper baking cups and spoon crumbs equally into each cup. With a spoon, press crumbs firmly over bottom and up the sides of the cups. Beat together cream cheese and the ¼ cup sugar until smooth. Add egg and vanilla and mix well. Spoon mixture equally into crumb-lined cups. Cook uncovered 1½ to 2 minutes, shifting inside cups to outside after 1 minute. Chill uncovered 1 hour. Cover when cold if stored longer. When ready to serve, spoon 1 tablespoon berry or fruit jam into each tart.

Cheesecake

16 servings

2	cups graham cracker crumbs
½	cup sugar
½	cup butter
½	teaspoon ground cinnamon
3	8-ounce packages cream cheese
5	eggs
1	cup sugar
½	teaspoon vanilla extract
2½	cups sour cream
1½	teaspoons vanilla extract
⅓	cup sugar

Combine crumbs, ½ cup sugar, butter and cinnamon in 9x13 inch pan and press firmly on bottom of dish. Cook in microwave for 2 minutes. Beat cream cheese until smooth and stir in eggs, one at a time. Mix in sugar and vanilla. Pour into crust and bake on low for 12 to 15 minutes, turning every 4 minutes. Combine sour cream, ⅓ cup sugar and vanilla. Blend well and pour mixture over cheesecake. Return to oven for 1 minute and 15 seconds. Chill. You may spread any fruit pie mix over the top. Cherry is our favorite.

Frozen Grasshopper Torte

9 servings

¼	cup margarine
30	chocolate wafer cookies, crushed
3	cups miniature marshmallows
¾	cup milk
¼	cup green creme de menthe
2	tablespoons white creme de cacao
1	cup whipping cream, whipped

Place margarine in a glass bowl and microwave for 45 seconds. Stir in wafer crumbs. Pat half of this mixture into an 8 × 8 inch glass dish. Chill. Place marshmallows and milk in a large bowl. Microwave for 1½ to 2 minutes, just until marshmallows are melted. Stir in liqueurs. Cool. Fold in whipped cream. Pour into crumb-lined dish. Top with remaining crumbs. Freeze until firm. Cut into squares and serve.

Raspberry Melba Sauce for Ice Cream

1½ cups

1	10-ounce package frozen raspberries
¼	cup sugar
½	cup currant jelly
2	tablespoons cornstarch
1	tablespoon cold water

Defrost raspberries in 1 quart casserole 1 minute or until thawed. Add sugar and jelly. Blend cornstarch and water and stir into mixture. Cook 5 minutes until sauce is thick and clear. Stir every 30 seconds. Cool.

Peanut Brittle

4 cups

2 **cups sugar**
1 **cup light corn syrup**
1 **cup water**
2 **cups raw peanuts**
¼ **teaspoon salt**
1 **teaspoon butter**
1 **teaspoon baking soda**

Combine sugar, corn syrup and water in a large glass mixing bowl. Cook in microwave 20 to 22 minutes or until mixture reaches 240 degrees on a candy thermometer. Stir in the peanuts and salt and cook 9 to 11 minutes more, until it reaches 290 degrees on the candy thermometer. Immediately stir in butter and soda and mix well. Spread the mixture evenly and thinly on a large buttered cookie sheet. Cool, lifting occasionally with a spatula to prevent sticking.

Note: If your peanut brittle sticks to your teeth, it has not been cooked long enough.

Baked Apples

4 servings

4 **medium cooking apples,**
    washed and cored
    raisins
¼ **cup brown sugar, packed**
4 **teaspoons butter or margarine**
    ground cinnamon
    whipped cream or sour cream

Place apples in a 2 quart baking dish. Put a few raisins in each cavity. Add 1 teaspoon brown sugar and 1 teaspoon butter to each. Sprinkle generously with cinnamon. Microwave for 8 to 9 minutes or until the apples are tender. Serve warm with sweet or sour cream. If apples are room temperature, cooking time will be slightly shorter.

Chocolate Surprise Squares

24 squares

1 **12-ounce package**
    chocolate chips
1 **12-ounce package**
    butterscotch chips
4 **ounces Spanish peanuts**
1 **3-ounce can chow mein**
    noodles

Place chips in a glass bowl and microwave for 4 minutes until melted, stirring until smooth. Stir in peanuts and noodles and pour into a buttered 8 x 8 inch glass dish. Cool until hardened and cut into squares.

STEAMBOAT SPRINGS

Hints from **Deer Trail**

The cook cooks! Others gather fire wood, clean, set up and strike camp.

Make a master check list. Before every outing, check the list to make sure you have every item. This includes planning menus and pre-preparing foods, wrapping them individually, and freezing and/or drying when possible.

Use Zip-Loc or Seal-a-Meal bags for heavy duty use.

A wire whisk is a must for mixing milk, dried foods, etc.

How did we camp before plastic bags, rubber gloves and asbestos gloves?

A nose dropper bottle filled with Clorox will substitute for a water purifier. Use 2 drops of Clorox to 8 ounces of water.

Packets of powdered Gatorade and ERG (found at Health Food stores) add variety to your drink choices and are great thirst-quenchers.

Keep butter or margarine for a long time by packing it in sterilized jars with tight fitting, screw-top lids.

Eggs dipped in boiling water for 10 seconds will keep longer in a camp ice chest.

Carry fresh eggs by breaking them into a tall, narrow olive-type jar, one at a time. They will pour out, one at a time.

To impart a barbecue flavor to broiled meats, sprinkle with instant coffee while cooking.

Baking soda has many uses in camp. It is an excellent fire extinguisher for flare-ups of the camp stove and soothing for the burn. It also doubles for toothpaste.

Food safety is important. Arrange to keep cold foods cold and hot foods hot, or omit them.

Take nothing—Leave nothing!

Deer Trail was once the center of a large sheep and cattle grazing area and a shipping point for livestock. Today it lies in a sparsely settled dry farming district just east of Denver. The land is covered with Russian Thistle, more commonly known as tumbleweed. Native to Russia, it was transported to this country by seeds mixed with imported grains.

Mother's Tea

1 gallon

1 quart boiling water
6 teabags
½ cup honey (or sugar)
2 lemons, juiced, reserve rind
6 sprigs fresh mint

Steep teabags in boiling water with mint, lemon rind and sugar. Cool. Dilute with 2 quarts cold water and add lemon juice. Remove rind and mint. Add ice to fill 1 gallon thermos. For variety, mix in any one or combination of juice mixes to suit your taste such as Tang, powdered lemonade, apple juice, pineapple juice or grape juice. Keep in refrigerator as a summer thirst quencher.

Mocha Mix

14 cups

1 8-quart box (10 cups) non-fat dry milk powder
1 16-ounce can (2 cups) pre-sweetened cocoa powder
1 6-ounce jar (1¾ cups) powdered non-dairy coffee creamer
1 2-ounce jar (¾ cup) instant coffee crystals (omit for plain hot chocolate)

Combine all ingredients thoroughly. Store in tightly covered container., Mix 4 heaping teaspoons in 1 cup hot water. Top with marshmallows.

Gorp

6 cups

1 cup quick-cooking rolled oats
1 cup shelled peanuts
¼ cup wheat germ
½ cup honey
½ cup pecans or walnuts
2 tablespoons vegetable oil
1 cup M&M candies
½ cup chopped, mixed dried fruit
½ cup raisins

In a bowl combine oats, peanuts, nuts and wheat germ. Combine honey and oil and stir into oat mixture. Spread out in a 9 × 9 × 2 inch baking pan. Bake at 300 degrees for 30 to 40 minutes or until light brown, stirring every 15 minutes. Remove from oven and transfer to another lightly greased pan to cool. Break up large pieces. Stir in candy, dried fruit and raisins. Store in a tightly covered container or plastic bag.

Note: Gorp is a high energy building snack that a cross country skier or backpacker should not be without!

Colorado Style Granola

½ **cup vegetable oil**
½ **cup honey**
3 **cups oats**
1 **cup wheat germ**
1 **cup sunflower seeds**
½ **cup sesame seeds**
1 **cup unsweetened coconut**

Add any or all of the following:
1 **cup miller's bran**
1 **cup roasted soy beans**
1 **cup wheat flakes**
1 **cup rye flakes**
1 **cup cashews**
1 **cup chopped almonds**
1 **cup flax seeds**

12 servings

Heat oil and honey and pour over mixture of dry ingredients. Mix well and spread in a 13 × 9 × 2 inch pan. Bake at 325 degrees for 15 minutes. Turn oven off and leave for 15 more minutes, stirring often. Cool and pack in a plastic container or bag.

Note: A great energy source while hiking or cross country skiing.

Fruit Leather

2 **cups fruit pulp (crabapple, apple, peach, pears, strawberries, apricots)**
½ **cup sugar**

2 cookie sheets

When using fresh fruit, cook and put through a food mill to remove stems and seeds. Or remove seeds and stems, chop and cook, then puree in a blender, one cup at a time.

Mix fruit and sugar. Spread on plastic wrap attached to a cookie sheet with scotch tape. Mixture should be very thin, perhaps only 1/8 to 1/16 inch thick. Bake in a slow oven (150 degrees) until it looks like leather (not sticky to touch) for as long as 2 hours. Leave door ajar slightly for moisture to escape. When done, roll up in a log. Can be cut shorter for individual packs.

Note: Kids love this and it is so much less expensive than the commercial kind.

Applesauce Leather

1 large or 3 small rolls

1   **16-ounce can applesauce**
¼   **teaspoon ground cinnamon**
½   **teaspoon fresh lemon juice**

Combine applesauce, cinnamon and lemon juice in blender. Puree until smooth. Spread mixture ¼ inch thick on plastic wrap or on a greased 15½ × 10½ inch cookie sheet. Dry in oven at 150 degrees until leather feels dry but tacky, about 6-8 hours. Leave door ajar during drying process. Remove from plastic wrap and roll. Cut into smaller rolls if desired. Store in covered jar or plastic in refrigerator.

Basic Beef Jerky

2   **pounds lean meat (flank steak, brisket, elk steaks)**
½   **bottle liquid smoke**
1½   **teaspoons meat tenderizer**
1½   **teaspoons seasoned salt**
1½   **teaspoons onion salt**
½   **teaspoon pepper**
½   **teaspoon garlic powder**
¼   **cup soy sauce**
½   **cup Worcestershire sauce**

Slice partially frozen meat as thinly as possible (with the grain for chewiness or against the grain for tenderness). Sprinkle the meat with any or all of the ingredients depending on how spicy you like it or whether you plan to use it just as a snack or in a backpacking meal with other ingredients. Marinate for a minimum of 24 hours in the refrigerator.

Drain and dry meat. Arrange on oven rack in a single layer. Place foil on bottom of oven to catch drippings.

Leaving door ajar, bake at 150 degrees for about 7 hours or until chewy and brittle. Blot drops of oil with a paper towel. Store in airtight container in the refrigerator.

Note: This supposedly keeps safely for 6 months, but no one has been able to keep it that long.

Foil Cooking

Foil is a blessing for every camp cook. Its indestructibility is the one objection, but if weight is a problem it can be carried to the nearest trash barrel after using. Few realize it, but hot coals alone are too hot. They must be mixed with ashes to temper the heat. The most popular use for foil is for baking potatoes or corn. Here are several other recipes that are fun and unusual. *Always use heavy duty foil.*

Mushrooms and Scallops in Foil

1 serving

¼ **pound fresh scallops**
¼ **pound fresh mushrooms,
      sliced**
2 **tablespoons butter**
1 **tablespoon minced parsley**
1 **12-inch square heavy duty foil**

Place ingredients on foil. Double fold foil and seal ends. Bake on a grill or in the coals for about 12 minutes.

Meat Loaf in the Coals

Make your favorite meat loaf recipe. Pour 2 tablespoons catsup or barbecue sauce into foil. Divide meat mixture into individual servings (about ¼ pound per serving). Wrap in foil and bake in coals about 30 minutes, turning every 10 minutes.

Note: This is guaranteed to stick so serve in the foil.

COLORADO CACHE COLORADO CACHE COLORADO CACHE COLORADO CACHE COLORADO CACHE COLORADO CACHE COLORADO CACHE COLORADO CACHE COLORADO

Campfire Foiled Chicken Dinner

6 servings

6	chicken breasts, precooked at home
6	carrots, sliced lengthwise, parboiled
6	small potatoes, sliced lengthwise, parboiled
1	onion, sliced into 6 slices
1	can cream of celery soup
1	can cream of chicken soup
4	tablespoons butter

Boil chicken breasts for 20 minutes at home. Place breast, carrots, potatoes, 1 onion slice, soups and pat of butter on 6 squares of heavy duty aluminum foil, dull side out. Seal tightly and freeze until needed.

At campsite, bury packets in hot coals. Cook 30 minutes, turning once or twice, until potato is tender.

Stuffed Zucchini in Foil

4 servings

4 - 6	small zucchini
1	pound ground beef
1	onion, chopped
1	egg
	salt and pepper to taste
½	cup seasoned bread crumbs
½	cup milk
1	cup grated Cheddar cheese

Mix together all ingredients except zucchini and ½ cup cheese. Scrape out center of zucchini, leaving ends. Fill cavity with hamburger mixture. Sprinkle grated cheese over top. Wrap heavy duty aluminum foil around squash individually. Place in coals and cook about 35 minutes.

Red Rocks Ham Rolls

10-12 sandwiches

2	cups cubed ham
¾	pound grated Cheddar cheese
1	large onion, chopped
1	4½-ounce can chopped, ripe olives
1	4-ounce can chopped, green chiles
1	8-ounce can tomato juice
2	tablespoons fresh lemon juice
10 - 12	hard rolls

Mix all ingredients except the rolls. Set aside. Slice the tops off the hard rolls, scoop out inside (save for bread crumbs) and fill with the ham-cheese mixture. Replace tops on rolls and wrap individually in foil. Bake in a very slow oven (275 degrees) for 1 hour. Wrap in newspaper or heavy towel and take to picnic site.

Ore-Bucket Cake

**cake batter, or
muffin batter
oranges, hollowed out**

Pour cake or muffin batter into a hollowed out orange until it is about half full. Replace the lid of the orange, wrap it in foil and bake over coals for about 10 minutes or until done.

Fruit Cobbler in Foil

**biscuit mix
fruit pie filling**

Prepare your favorite biscuit mix. Pat into oblong shape on 2 thicknesses of aluminum foil. Spread with ½ can of fruit pie filling. Fold over, seal and prick dough. Wrap completely in foil and bake about 7 minutes on each side. Serve with cream or plain.

Creole Eggs Colorado River—A Floater's Special

8 servings

Prepare in advance:
- 1 **28-ounce can stewed tomatoes**
- 1 **cup chopped celery**
- ½ **cup chopped green pepper**
- ¼ **cup chopped green onion**
- 1 **bay leaf**
  salt and pepper to taste

Combine tomatoes, celery, green pepper, onion, bay leaf and salt and pepper. Simmer covered until vegetables are slightly tender. Cool. Pour into heavy plastic bag (Zip-loc or Seal-a-Meal), seal and chill.

At campsite:
- 1 **16-ounce can peas**
- 1 **tablespoon cornstarch**
- 1 **tablespoon water**
- 10 **eggs (or more)**
- ¾ **cup cornbread crumbs**
- 1½ **cups grated Cheddar cheese**

In a heavy skillet, combine tomato mixture and undrained peas. Bring to a boil. Blend cornstarch and water and stir into mixture. Heat until thick. Remove bay leaf. Break eggs into skillet, one at a time. Cover and simmer for 7 or 8 minutes or until eggs are poached as you like them. Sprinkle with crumbs and cheese. Cover for 1 minute to allow cheese to melt.

COLORADO CACHE COLORADO CACHE COLORADO CACHE COLORADO CACHE COLORADO CACHE COLORADO CACHE COLORADO CACHE COLORADO CACHE COLORADO

"Breakfast on the Run" Bacon and Egg Bars

4-6 servings

1	**pound bacon**
⅓	**cup brown sugar, packed**
⅓	**cup butter**
¾	**cup flour**
½	**teaspoon salt**
¾	**cup quick cooking rolled oats**
1	**3-ounce package cream cheese**
¼	**cup milk**
8	**eggs**

Preheat oven to 400 degrees. Cut bacon into ½ inch pieces and cook until crisp. Drain on paper. Pour all but 1 tablespoon of bacon grease from the skillet. Cream butter and brown sugar. Mix in flour, salt and oats. Press ½ of the mixture in a buttered 8 × 8 inch baking dish. Whip cream cheese with milk. Add eggs and blend with electric mixer. Pour eggs and cheese mixture into skillet with 1 tablespoon bacon grease and cook slowly over low heat, stirring until it has the consistency of pudding. Add bacon to mixture in skillet. Spoon mixture over bottom crust. Top with remaining crumb mixture. Cook 20 to 25 minutes in oven. Cool slightly and cut into 9 or 12 squares. You may store overnight in refrigerator and reheat for breakfast 15 to 18 minutes at 400 degrees. You may substitute "Maypo" for ½ of the oats to add a maple flavor. When cooking eggs and cream cheese in skillet, avoid over-cooking as eggs must cook another 20-25 minutes in the oven.

Note: Prepare ahead of time before a busy week-end. Reheat before serving.

Skillet Stew

4 servings

1	**pound ground beef**
1	**medium onion, chopped**
1	**10½-ounce can beef consomme**
1	**1-pound can cream-style corn**
1	**1-pound can lima beans**
3	**large potatoes, diced**
	salt and pepper to taste

In a large skillet, brown beef and onion, stirring to chop meat into small granules as it cooks. Add consomme, potatoes, salt and pepper. Mix well. Cover and cook over low heat for about 25 minutes or until potatoes are cooked. Add corn and lima beans; heat thoroughly. Stir frequently to keep potatoes from sticking.

Note: This is excellent served around the campfire with fruit.

Camp Spaghetti

6 servings

2 packages McCormick's or Lawry's spaghetti sauce mix
1 8-ounce package elbow macaroni
2 2-ounce Wilson's meat bars
3 packages Lipton's cream of tomato "Cup of Soup"
2 tablespoons margarine

Cook macaroni in a 3 quart saucepan or Dutch oven. Add margarine. When done, crumble in meat bar and make sauce with seasoning mix in the same pan. Add the "Cup of Soup" packages and heat thoroughly.

Ham Chowder

6 servings

1 ham hock
3 potatoes, diced
1 large onion, chopped and sauteed
   salt and pepper to taste
2 teaspoons instant chicken broth
1 teaspoon dried parsley flakes
1 8-ounce box Velveeta cheese, cubed
2 cups cooked, cubed ham
1 pint half and half
½ box frozen peas

Cook ham hock in water to cover. Add potatoes, onion and seasonings. Simmer for about 15 minutes, then puree. Return to pan and add cheese. Heat until it thickens soup by melting. Add ham, cream and peas. Simmer for about 15 more minutes.

Note: Outstanding flavor and consistency. Could be served cold.

Green Chile Potatoes

4 servings

4 large potatoes, thinly sliced
1 large red onion, thinly sliced
1 green pepper, diced
1 large green chile, chopped
¼ cup vegetable oil
   salt and pepper to taste

Heat oil over campfire in a large heavy skillet. Add potatoes and fry until slightly tender. Add onion and green pepper. Cook a few more minutes, just to heat the onion and pepper, leaving them slightly crunchy. Add the green chile just before serving. Salt and pepper to taste.

Note: This was tested in Wyoming after an all day float trip. It put back everything the river had removed.

Ham, Taters and Peas

6 servings

1½ **boxes French's au gratin
     potatoes**
2   **packages Wilson's
     freeze-dried ham bits**
1   **package Mountain House
     freeze-dried peas**
½ - 1 **cup powdered milk**
¼   **pound butter or margarine
     salt and pepper to taste**

In a large saucepan or Dutch oven, cook potatoes according to directions with a little extra water until almost done. Add margarine. Add peas, ham bits and cheese sauce and stir until done. Should be thick and cheesy.

Gourmet Hamburgers

6 servings

2   **pounds ground beef**
1   **onion, chopped**
1   **tablespoon A-1 sauce**
¼   **pound bleu cheese**

Variations for filling:
     sliced onion
     pickle relish
1   **pat of butter with a few chips
     ice**
     **sliced mushrooms sprinkled
     with instant bouillon**

Salt and pepper meat to taste and mix with chopped onion and A-1 sauce. Make 12 thin patties. Crumble bleu cheese over 6 of these. Top with the other six patties. Press edges together. To freeze, place on cookie sheet until frozen and seal in plastic bags individually to take camping.

Hiker's Hot Dogs

6 servings

1   **tablespoon minced onion**
1   **12-ounce can beer**
1   **tablespoon Worcestershire
     sauce**
¼   **cup chili sauce**
12   **all beef hot dogs, quartered**
6   **French rolls, split**

Mix onion, beer, Worcestershire sauce, chili sauce and hot dogs together. Simmer for 30 minutes. Pour into a wide-necked thermos bottle. Serve on split rolls.

Note: This is especially good for an autumn dinner, skiing or skating supper or high-country camp-out. Can be frozen, sealed in a plastic bag and reheated at campsite.

Mountain Bread

16 squares

4	**cups whole wheat flour**
1	**cup water**
¾	**cup brown sugar, packed**
½	**cup honey**
⅓	**cup wheat germ**
⅓	**cup vegetable oil**
¼	**cup sesame seeds**
¼	**cup molasses**
3	**tablespoons non-fat, powdered milk**
1½	**teaspoons baking powder**
1½	**teaspoons salt**

Mix all ingredients until smooth. Pour into a well greased 8 × 8 × 2 inch baking pan and bake in preheated 300 degree oven for 1 hour, or until bread starts to pull away from sides of pan. Cut in squares and let stand uncovered overnight to dry a little. Seal in plastic bag or wrap.

Note: It will keep for weeks without getting moldy or stale and doesn't need refrigeration.

Pre-Fab Biscuits

12 cups

8	**cups flour**
2	**teaspoons salt**
¼	**cup plus 4 teaspoons baking powder**
2	**teaspoons cream of tartar**
2	**teaspoons sugar**
2	**cups shortening**
1½	**cups non-fat powdered milk**

Sift dry ingredients. Cut in shortening until mixture resembles coarse crumbs. Pack in coffee can, canister or plastic bag. At campsite, add ½ to ¾ cup water to 2 cups mix. Mix thoroughly and drop, one at a time, onto a lightly greased iron skillet. Bake covered until done; or wrap around a stick and toast over coals. Dip in honey.

Hot Banana Split

1 serving

1	**banana per person**
	chocolate bits or milk chocolate
	miniature marshmallows
	peanut butter

Peel back one section of a banana. Spread with peanut butter. Add chocolate and marshmallows. Replace the skin and wrap the banana in foil. Place the packages on the grill over the glowing embers. Cook for 10 minutes, turning frequently.

Chocolate Fondue

1½ cups

    3 **tablespoons margarine**
2 or 3 **tablespoons milk or water**
    2 **cups dry chocolate frosting
       mix**
    1 **teaspoon instant coffee (or
       ¼ teaspoon each ground
       cloves and ground
       cinnamon)**

Melt the margarine in a small saucepan over the campfire. Add milk or water and frosting mix. Mix the sauce thoroughly with a wire whisk or wooden spoon and heat until hot, but not boiling. Let everyone use his own fork for spearing fruit, cake, marshmallows or cookies. Provide plenty of napkins!

Dunkables:
       **angel food or day old pound
          cake**
       orange slices
       apples
       bananas
       strawberries
       peaches
       pineapple chunks
       sliced kiwi fruit

Apple in Hand

apple
**peanut butter
   (smooth or crunchy)**
raisins

Core whole apple. Mix peanut butter with raisins. Stuff mixture into hole in the apple. May be eaten whole or sliced.

Jello in the High Country

**Jello, or
pudding**

Make pudding or jello according to directions. Place in the stream, well anchored, in the morning and it will be ready in the afternoon.

Snow Ideas

Snow Ice Cream:

1	**egg**
¾	**cup sugar**
1	**cup milk**
1½	**tablespoons vanilla extract**
	dash of salt
	snow

Mix egg and add sugar, milk, vanilla and salt. Beat well. Add snow until thick and creamy.

Snow Cones, #1:

fruit juice concentrate
snow

Spoon snow into cups and pour undiluted juice over. Use straws or spoons.

Snow Cones, #2:

fruit-flavored gelatin mix
snow

Sprinkle powdered gelatin over snow and eat with a spoon.

Old Fashioned Lemon-Orange Ice Cream

2 quarts

	ice cream freezer
	ice cubes, to pack
	ice cream salt
	juice of 3 oranges
	juice of 3 lemons
1	**cup sugar**
1	**quart half and half**
1	**pint milk**

Fill inside container of freezer with orange juice, lemon juice, sugar and milks. Insert paddle and pack ice around container with salt. Freeze according to instructions. When thick and creamy, remove paddle and pack more ice around to ripen. If desired, freeze before serving.

Cover Mountain Carrot Cake

12-20 servings

1½　cups vegetable oil
1½　cups sugar
4　eggs, well beaten
3　cups grated carrots
2　cups unbleached flour
½　teaspoon salt
2　teaspoons soda
2　teaspoons ground cinnamon
2　teaspoons ground allspice
1　cup chopped pecans
1　cup raisins
1　teaspoon vanilla extract

Cream oil and sugar. Add eggs and carrots, and mix well. Mix dry ingredients. Add flour mixture to carrot mixture, a small amount at a time, beating well. When blended, add pecans, raisins and vanilla. (This mixture will fit into Cuisinart processor.) Pour into a 10 × 14 inch greased and sugared pan and bake at 325 degrees for 1 hour. Cool slightly before frosting.

Frosting:

½　cup margarine
1　8-ounce package cream cheese, softened
2　cups sifted, powdered sugar
1　teaspoon vanilla extract

Combine margarine and cheese with sugar and beat well. Add vanilla, mix well and spread on cooled cake
Note: Travels well; gets eaten quickly!

Peanut Butter-Date Cookies

2 dozen

1　egg, lightly beaten
½　cup granulated sugar
½　cup brown sugar, packed
1　cup peanut butter
½　cup chopped, pitted dates

Blend egg and sugars. Add peanut butter, mixing thoroughly. Stir in the dates. Roll into 1 inch balls. Place 2 inches apart on an ungreased cookie sheet. Using a fork or a glass with a design on the bottom, press the ball down to about ½ inch thick. Bake at 350 degrees for 10 to 12 minutes or until brown. Let cool about 2 minutes before removing from cookie sheet.

Hot Fruit Soup

¼ **cup raisins**
½ **cup dried prunes**
½ **cup dried apples**
½ **cup mixed, dried fruits**
⅛ **teaspoon salt**
½ **cup Tang**
1 **3-ounce package raspberry gelatin**
1 **cinnamon stick**
½ **cup instant whole milk**
1 **cup hot water**
½ **cup shredded coconut, optional**

4 servings

Cover dried fruits with water in a heavy saucepan or Dutch oven. Stir in salt, Tang, gelatin and cinnamon stick. Bring to a boil, cover, reduce heat and simmer 20 minutes or until fruit is tender. Stir dry milk into cup of hot water until dissolved, then add to fruit and mix. Garnish with coconut.

Note: For breakfast or dessert.

Picnic in a Pocket

Pocket, pita or Syrian bread is a round hollow single loaf that can be slit open or cut in half to hold a choice of fillings snugly without leaking and is perfectly portable.

Following are some suggestions for perfect portable sandwiches.

Venetian Pepper Filling

3 **sweet Italian pork sausages, cut in ½ inch slices (about ¼ pound)**
3 **hot Italian pork sausages, cut in ½ inch slices (¼ pound)**
 water
2 **tablespoons vegetable oil**
1 **large red pepper, cut in ½ inch strips**
1 **large green pepper, cut in ½ inch strips**
½ **teaspoon oregano**
2 **tablespoons tomato paste**
 salt and pepper to taste
3 **pita breads, cut in half**

6 sandwiches

In a large skillet, place sausages and ½ cup water. Cover and cook 5 minutes. Uncover and cook 10 to 15 minutes more, shaking pan frequently until sausages brown on all sides. Remove sausages and drain. Wipe out skillet. Heat oil and add peppers and oregano. Saute 10 minutes, stirring frequently. Stir in tomato paste, ⅓ cup water, salt and pepper. Cook 5 minutes. Return sausages to skillet. Cover and cook 10 more minutes, stirring until heated through. Place about ½ cup sausage mixture in each pita half.

Denver Stuffing

4 sandwiches

2 tablespoons margarine
½ cup chopped onion
½ cup diced green pepper
½ cup diced ham
4 eggs, well beaten
   salt and pepper to taste
2 pita breads, cut in half
1 cup grated Monterey
   Jack cheese
   Picante sauce to serve
   on the side

In a medium skillet, melt margarine. Add onion and green pepper and saute until tender. Add ham and saute about 1 minute. Pour eggs, salt and pepper into skillet and cook until eggs are set but still moist. Spoon into pita halves. Top each with ¼ cup cheese. Serve hot.

Curry Meatball Pita

6 sandwiches

Relish:
1 large cucumber, peeled,
   seeded and diced
½ cup sweet onion, minced
2 tablespoons fresh lime juice
2 tablespoons chopped parsley
½ teaspoon salt
½ cup chutney, optional

In a medium bowl, combine all ingredients for relish except the chutney. Set aside.

Meatballs:
1 pound ground beef
2 4-ounce cans diced
   green chiles
1 small onion, minced
1 egg
½ cup mashed potatoes
1½ teaspoons salt
1 teaspoon curry powder
3 pita breads, cut in half

In a medium bowl, combine the ground beef, chiles, onion, egg, potatoes, salt and curry. Shape into 1 inch balls and flatten slightly. Place on a cookie sheet with sides (to catch the grease) and bake in a 350 degree oven for about 20 minutes or until brown. Stuff 3 to 4 meatballs into each pita half. Add relish and chutney.

Pita Sandwiches with Shanghai Filling

4 sandwiches

3	tablespoons Tamari (natural soy sauce)
½	teaspoon sugar
½	teaspoon salt
1	tablespoon cornstarch
½	cup water
1	tablespoon vegetable oil
½	pound lean pork shoulder, cut into thin strips
1½	cups thinly sliced celery
1	cup sliced green onions
1	cup sliced water chestnuts
2	pita breads, cut in half

In a small bowl, combine soy sauce, sugar and salt. Set aside. In another small bowl, stir cornstarch and water until smooth and set aside. In a large skillet, heat oil. Add pork and stir-fry over high heat for about 3 minutes. Add soy sauce mixture and stir well. Add celery, green onions and water chestnuts. Stir-fry over high heat another 3 minutes. Stir in cornstarch mixture and continue cooking until sauce has thickened and vegetables are well coated. Spoon into pita halves.

Roast Beef Salad Spread

4-6 salad servings
10 pita sandwiches

½	cup chopped onion
¼	cup chopped celery
½	cup sour cream
¼	cup mayonnaise
2	tablespoons lemon juice
1	tablespoon chopped parsley
1	tablespoon horseradish
1	teaspoon prepared mustard
1	teaspoon salt
1	teaspoon oregano
¼	teaspoon pepper
1	pound mushrooms, thinly sliced
1	pound cooked roast beef, cut into thin strips (or ground in food processor)
	bean sprouts or shredded lettuce

Mix together all ingredients except meat and mushrooms. Toss meat and mushrooms separately then serve on pita bread with the dressing and sprouts.

323

Picnics and Camping

COLORADO CACHE COLORADO CACHE COLORADO CACHE COLORADO CACHE COLORADO CACHE COLORADO CACHE COLORADO CACHE COLORADO CACHE COLORADO CACHE COLORADO

Cold Brisket of Beef Sandwiches

10 sandwiches

5   **pounds beef brisket**
1½   **teaspoons salt**
2   **tablespoons Worcestershire sauce**
2   **tablespoons Tamari (natural soy sauce)**
½   **cup dry red wine**
1   **tablespoon honey**
½   **cup water**
¼   **teaspoon ground cinnamon**
1   **bay leaf**
1   **large onion, peeled and cut**
10   **onion buns or hard rolls**

Trim excess fat and rub salt on meat. Place in heavy duty foil. Combine Worcestershire sauce, honey, cinnamon and Tamari. Brush over meat. Add bay leaf, onion, wine and water to meat. Wrap and seal in foil. Bake at 350 degrees for 3 to 4 hours. Cool.

Sour Cream Horseradish Sauce:

½   **cup sour cream**
2   **tablespoons horseradish**
1   **tablespoon chopped parsley**
1   **teaspoon grated onion**
½   **teaspoon lemon juice**
  salt to taste

Combine and spread on onion buns or hard rolls. Fill with cold brisket. Wrap and take to picnic site.

French Burgers

6 servings

3   **tablespoons butter**
2   **green onions, finely chopped**
¼   **pound mushrooms, sliced**
1   **pound ground chuck**
½   **teaspoon salt**
½   **teaspoon garlic salt**
1   **cup shredded Swiss and Cheddar cheese**
  chopped ripe olives to taste
4   **French rolls, split**

Melt butter, add onions and mushrooms and heat, stirring until coated. Mix ground beef with ingredients. Pat meat mixture on each split roll. Bake at 450 degrees for 20 minutes until well browned.

Note: These can be made several hours in advance and baked just before serving. A change from hamburger and a hit with all ages.

STORM OVER COLORADO'S NORTHEASTERN PLAINS

Hints from **Sugar City**

In general, there are no set rules in modifying sea level recipes for high altitude use. Our recipes have been tested and found effective at approximately 5,200 feet. The following list may help you as a guide to necessary adjustments for your altitude.

To convert recipes in this book for altitudes from 2,500 to 4,000 feet:
- Increase baking powder ¼ teaspoon for each teaspoon used.
- Decrease liquid 1 to 2 tablespoons for each cup used.
- No change in sugar amount.
- Decrease baking temperature 10 to 15 degrees.

To convert low level recipes for altitudes of 4,000 to 6,000:
- Use 2 level teaspoons additional flour.
- Decrease baking powder, soda, or cream of tartar ¼ to ½ teaspoon or ¼ given amount.
- Decrease sugar ½ teaspoon per cup for each 1,000 feet rise in elevation.
- Increase liquid 2 to 3 tablespoons per cup. (Try smaller amount when two measurements are given.)

For adjustments at altitudes over 6,000 feet:
- Decrease baking powder ¼ teaspoon for each teaspoon used.
- Increase liquid 2 to 4 tablespoons for each cup used.
- Decrease sugar ¼ cup for each cup used.
- Increase baking temperature 10 to 15 degrees.

If you are unsure about using these recipes at sea level, consult your local county agent.

For flakey, tender pie crust use ½ as much shortening as flour, ½ as much **ice** water as shortening and ½ teaspoon of salt for each cup of flour. (For a 2 crust 8″ pie use 2 cups flour, 1 cup shortening, ½ cup ice water, 1 teaspoon salt.)

Sweeten whipped cream with powdered sugar to retain volume, and use super-fine sugar for meringues.

The addition of freshly grated coconut to white cake batter makes a moist cake and keeps it fresh longer.

When cooking with fresh fruits a dash of salt and 2 to 3 teaspoons fresh lemon juice will enhance the flavor and preserve the fruit.

A cake will be less likely to stick to the pan if you put the pan on a wet towel to cool as soon as you remove it from the oven.

Whipped cream will keep for a day or two if while whipping you add 1 teaspoon light corn syrup for each ½ pint of cream.

Split cupcakes in half, use frosting as a filling, put halves together for no-mess lunches or picnics.

Frosted grapes make a lovely garnish. Dip grape or clusters into slightly beaten egg whites or fresh lemon juice, then in granulated sugar.

Sugar City is situated on semi-arid land, once the grazing area of the buffalo and hunting grounds of the Cheyenne, Arapaho, Kiowa and Comanche Indians. Longhorn cattle supplanted the buffalo, and sugar beets for which the city is named are grown on the grazing lands. Rocky Ford, famous for its cantaloupe is located in this part of the Arkansas Valley.

Meringue Mushrooms

½ cup egg whites (3 to 3½) at
   room temperature
   scant ¼ teaspoon salt
¼ teaspoon cream of tartar
1 cup sugar
1 teaspoon vanilla extract
   cocoa
   chocolate (summer coating
      chocolate is best as it
      keeps weeks without
      discoloring, and hardens
      quickly at room temperature.
      Available at a cake supply.)

**24 large or
36 medium**

Preheat oven to 225 degrees. Cover cookie sheets with aluminum foil. Beat egg whites until foamy. Add salt and cream of tartar, beating until stiff. Add sugar, a rounded teaspoon at a time. Add vanilla. Beat an additional 7 to 8 minutes after all sugar has been added. Total beating time is 15 to 18 minutes. Using a 15 to 16 inch pastry bag and a 5/8 inch tip, shape stems by holding bag at a right angle, making stems 1 to 1¾ inches high. Place ½ to 1 inch apart on prepared cookie sheet. Strain cocoa lightly over stems. Place in upper ⅓ of oven. For caps, make even rounds 1½ to 1¾ inches wide and ¾ inch high, with tops smooth. Strain cocoa lightly across top. Bake in lower ⅔ of oven. Bake 1 hour or until meringues can be lifted easily. Then turn heat off and prop door open until cooled. Melt chocolate in top of double boiler (1 ounce will do about 5 caps). With cap upside down, spread layer of chocolate just to the edge. Attach stem. When set, remove and store.

Note: Store in non-airtight container. Will keep weeks. Pretty served in napkin-lined basket.

Peppermint Candy Cookies

1 cup butter (½ pound)
½ cup powdered sugar
2½ cups flour
½ cup chopped nuts
1 teaspoon vanilla extract

Filling:
½ cup crushed peppermint
   candy
½ cup powdered sugar
2 tablespoons cream cheese
1 teaspoon milk
   red food coloring

3 dozen

Cream butter with ½ cup powdered sugar. Gradually add flour, nuts and vanilla. Mix well and chill. Remove dough from refrigerator, and shape into balls. Make a deep hole with your thumb in the center of each ball and fill with about ¼ teaspoon filling. Seal and place on ungreased cookie sheet. Bake at 350 degrees for 12 to 15 minutes, or until set but not brown.

To make filling, combine candy and sugar. Blend cream cheese, milk and food coloring and add to candy mixture.

Potato Chip Cookies

1 pound butter (or half butter and half margarine)
1 cup sugar
1 teaspoon vanilla extract
3½ cups flour
2 cups crushed potato chips (4.5 ounces or 1 twin bag)
½ cup chopped pecans

7-8 dozen

Cream butter and sugar, add vanilla and stir in flour. Add potato chips and nuts. Drop by teaspoon onto greased cookie sheet. May put fairly close together as they do not spread. Bake at 350 degrees for 15 minutes.

Note: Delicious and keep very well. Surprisingly like shortbread.

Lemonade Drops

1 cup shortening
1 cup sugar
2 eggs
3 cups flour
1 teaspoon baking soda
½ teaspoon salt
1 6-ounce can lemonade concentrate, thawed

2-3 dozen

Cream shortening and sugar. Thoroughly beat in eggs. Sift flour, soda and salt. Add alternately with ½ the lemonade. Drop by teaspoons on a greased cookie sheet. Bake at 375 degrees for 15 minutes. Before removing from the cookie sheet, brush tops with the reserved 3 ounces of lemonade. Sprinkle with sugar and remove to cool.

Note: Quick and easy. Good with ice cream.

Cornflake Crispies

1 egg
1 cup margarine
1 cup sugar
1 teaspoon baking soda
1 teaspoon cream of tartar
1½ cups flour
2 cups cornflakes
pinch of salt

5 dozen

Mix all ingredients in large bowl in order given. Mix well. Drop by teaspoon onto ungreased cookie sheet. Flatten with fork. Bake at 350 degrees for 10 to 15 minutes.

Oatmeal Cookies "the Best"

6 dozen

- 3 eggs, well beaten
- 1 cup raisins
- 1 teaspoon vanilla extract
- 1 cup butter
- 1 cup brown sugar
- 1 cup white sugar
- 2½ cups flour
- 1 teaspoon salt
- 1 teaspoon ground cinnamon
- 2 teaspoons baking soda
- 2 cups oatmeal (substitute ½ cup wheat germ for more healthful cookies)
- ¾ cup chopped pecans

Combine eggs, raisins and vanilla and let stand for one hour, covered with plastic wrap. Cream together butter and sugars. Add flour, salt, cinnamon and soda to sugar mixture. Mix well. Blend in egg-raisin mixture, oatmeal, wheat germ and chopped nuts. Dough will be stiff. Drop by heaping teaspoons onto ungreased cookie sheet or roll into small balls and flatten slightly on cookie sheet. Bake at 350 degrees for 10 to 12 minute or until lightly browned.

Note: Delicious. Secret is soaking of raisins.

Cocoa Drop Cookies

4-5 dozen

- ½ cup butter, softened (or part butter and shortening)
- 1 cup sugar
- 1 egg
- ¾ cup buttermilk (or 1 tablespoon vinegar and milk to make ¾ cup)
- 1 teaspoon vanilla extract
- ½ cup cocoa
- 1¾ cups flour
- ½ teaspoon baking soda
- ½ teaspoon salt
- 1 cup chopped nuts

Mix butter, sugar and egg. Add buttermilk and vanilla. Blend in cocoa, flour, soda and salt. Mix well. Stir in nuts. Drop by teaspoon onto greased cookie sheet. Bake at 400 degrees for 8 to 10 minutes, or until no imprint remains when touched lightly with finger. May serve plain or with Mocha Chocolate Frosting.

Mocha Chocolate Frosting:

- 3 tablesoons cocoa
- 3 tablespoons strong, hot coffee
- 3 tablespoons butter
- ½ teaspoon vanilla extract
- 1½ cups powdered sugar

Combine cocoa and coffee. Add butter and vanilla. Beat until smooth. Add sugar gradually until mixture is of spreading consistency. Frost while warm.

Note: Children love these soft cookies.

Brown Sugar Nut Bars

20-25 bars

½   **cup butter**
1½ **cups brown sugar, packed**
1   **cup flour**
2   **eggs**
1   **teaspoon vanilla extract**
½   **cup chopped nuts**
    powdered sugar

Cream butter and ½ cup of brown sugar. Mix in flour. Press in bottom of greased 8 × 8 inch pan. Bake at 350 degrees for 20 minutes. Cool. Beat eggs and remaining sugar until smooth. Add vanilla and nuts. Spread over crust. Bake for 20 minutes more. Sprinkle with powdered sugar. Cut into bars.

Chocolate Cream Cheese Brownies

15-20 bars

1   **4-ounce bar German chocolate (or 1 cup chocolate chips)**
3   **tablespoons butter**
2   **tablespoons butter, softened**
1   **3-ounce package cream cheese**
¼   **cup sugar**
1   **egg**
1   **tablespoon flour**
1   **teaspoon vanilla extract**
2   **eggs**
¾   **cup sugar**
½   **cup flour**
½   **teaspoon baking powder**
½   **teaspoon salt**
½   **cup chopped walnuts**
1   **teaspoon vanilla extract**
¼   **teaspoon almond extract**

Melt chocolate and 3 tablespoons butter in top of double boiler. Set aside to cool. In a medium sized bowl, cream 2 tablespoons butter and cream cheese until fluffy. Blend ¼ cup sugar, 1 egg, 1 tablespoon flour and 1 teaspoon vanilla into the creamed mixture and set aside. In another bowl, beat 2 eggs, add ¾ cup sugar and beat until blended. Sift flour, baking powder and salt into egg-sugar mixture. Stir melted chocolate mixture, walnuts, vanilla and almond extracts into sugar and egg mixture. Spread ½ chocolate mixture evenly in bottom of greased 9 × 9 inch pan. Spread cream cheese mixture over chocolate layer. Drop spoonfuls of all remaining chocolate over the cream cheese. Swirl with a fork for marbled effect. Bake at 350 degrees for 40 to 50 minutes or until toothpick comes out clean.

Chocolate Peppermint Bars

24-30 bars

Layer #1:
- 2 **ounces unsweetened chocolate**
- ½ **cup butter**
- 2 **eggs**
- 1 **cup sugar**
- ½ **cup sifted flour**
- ½ **cup chopped almonds (optional)**

Melt chocolate and butter. Cream eggs and sugar. Add flour and chocolate mixture. Mix well. Bake in 8 × 8 inch pan at 350 degrees for 20 minutes then turn oven off and bake 5 more minutes.

Layer #2:
- 1½ **cups powdered sugar**
- 3 **tablespoons butter or margarine**
- 2 - 3 **tablespoons cream**
- 1 **teaspoon peppermint extract**

Cream sugar and butter. Blend in cream and peppermint. Spread on cooled first layer. Refrigerate until chilled.

Layer #3:
- 3 **ounces unsweetened chocolate**
- 3 **tablespoons butter**

Melt chocolate and butter together and pour over peppermint layer. Chill. Cut into small squares.

Note: Mint cream can be tinted red or green for Christmas.

Cheesecake Bars

20-25 bars

- 5 **tablespoons butter**
- ⅓ **cup brown sugar**
- 1 **cup flour**
- ½ **cup chopped nuts**
- ½ **cup sugar**
- 1 **8-ounce package cream cheese**
- 1 **egg**
- 2 **tablespoons milk**
- 1 **tablespoon lemon juice**
- ¼ **teaspoon vanilla extract**

Cream butter and brown sugar, add flour and nuts and mix. Set aside 1 cup of the mixture for topping. Press remainder in bottom of 8 × 8 inch baking pan. Bake at 350 degrees for 12 to 15 minutes. Blend sugar and cream cheese until smooth, add egg, milk, lemon juice and vanilla. Beat well. Spread over bottom crust, sprinkle with reserved 1 cup topping. Return to oven and bake 25 minutes more. Cool, then chill and cut into triangles. May double recipe and bake in a 9 × 13 inch pan.

Pie Crust I

1 double crust

½ **cup shortening**
¼ **cup butter**
1½ **cups flour**
⅛ **teaspoon baking powder**
   dash of salt
¼ **cup ice water**

Place shortening, butter, flour, baking powder and salt in electric mixer. Blend until "cut-in" and the size of small peas. Add water and stir until mixture leaves sides of bowl and forms a ball. Chill 15 to 30 minutes before using.

Pie Crust II

1 double crust

2 **cups sifted flour**
½ **teaspoon salt**
¼ **teaspoon sugar**
3 - 3½ **tablespoons butter plus enough shortening to equal 1 scant cup**
3 - 4 **tablespoons ice water**

Blend together butter and shortening. Refrigerate 1 hour or more. Mix flour, salt and sugar. Cut in shortening mixture until it is the size of small peas. Add water and mix lightly with a fork until dough holds together. Roll out on a floured pastry board.

Peaches 'n Cream Pie

6-8 servings

¾ **cup sugar**
¼ **cup flour**
1 **cup heavy cream**
¼ **teaspoon salt**
8 **peaches, peeled and sliced dash of salt to taste lemon juice to taste**
1 **9-inch unbaked pastry shell butter (about 2 tablespoons) cinnamon (about 2 teaspoons)**

Mix together sugar, flour, cream and salt. Slice the peaches, sprinkle with a dash of salt and a little lemon juice and place in unbaked pie shell. Pour other ingredients over peaches, dot with butter and sprinkle with cinnamon. Bake at 425 degrees for 15 minutes, then lower oven to 300 degrees and bake 40 to 45 minutes longer.

Sensational Rum Pie

6-8 servings

1   **cup milk**
½   **teaspoon ground nutmeg**
3   **eggs, separated**
⅓   **cup sugar**
½   **teaspoon salt**
1   **teaspoon unflavored gelatin,**
    softened in ¼ cup
    cold water
2   **tablespoons rum**
1   **cup heavy cream, whipped**
½   **cup milk chocolate**
    (approximately a
    4-ounce bar)
2   **tablespoons water**
1   **teaspoon rum**
1   **9-inch baked pastry shell**

Scald milk with nutmeg in top of double boiler. Beat egg yolks with sugar and salt. Pour milk slowly over egg yolks, stirring constantly. Cook mixture over boiling water until thick and creamy. Remove from heat and add softened gelatin. Cool. Add 2 tablespoons rum. Fold in egg whites which have been beaten until stiff but not dry. Pour into baked pie shell. Chill. When set, spread with half of the unsweetened whipped cream. Melt the chocolate in the water. Cool. Mix remaining half of the whipped cream with the melted chocolate. Add 1 teaspoon rum. Spread on top of pie and chill at least 1 hour.

Date Pie

6-8 servings

3   **eggs, well beaten**
18 - 20   **finely crushed**
    saltine crackers
1   **cup sugar**
1   **teaspoon baking powder**
1   **cup diced dates, scalded**
1   **cup chopped pecans**
    whipped cream for garnish

Pour boiling water over dates and let stand 1 to 2 minutes. Drain. Mix all ingredients and pour into a well buttered 9 inch pie pan. Bake at 350 degrees for 20 to 30 minutes. Cut into small wedges and top with whipped cream.

Pear Crumble Pie

6-8 servings

5 - 6	**cups sliced pears (about 8)**
½	**cup sugar**
1	**teaspoon grated lemon peel**
3	**tablespoons lemon juice**
1	**9-inch unbaked pastry shell**

Topping:

½	**cup flour**
½	**cup sugar**
½	**teaspoon ground ginger**
½	**teaspoon ground cinnamon**
¼	**teaspoon ground mace**
⅓	**cup butter**
½	**cup heavy cream, whipped and flavored with powdered sugar, vanilla or almond extract (optional)**

Peel, core and slice pears. Toss with ½ cup sugar, lemon peel and lemon juice. Arrange in unbaked pastry shell. For the topping combine flour, sugar, ginger, cinnamon and mace. Cut in butter until crumbly. Sprinkle mixture over pears. Bake at 400 degrees for 45 minutes or until fruit is tender. Serve warm with flavored whipped cream, if desired.

Peach Pecan Pie

6-8 servings

4	**cups fresh peaches, peeled and sliced**
½	**cup sugar**
2	**tablespoons tapioca**
1	**teaspoon lemon juice**
⅛ - ¼	**teaspoon almond extract**
¼	**cup brown sugar**
¼	**cup flour**
½	**cup chopped pecans**
¼	**cup butter**
1	**9-inch unbaked pastry shell**

Combine first 5 ingredients and let stand for 15 minutes. Combine brown sugar, flour, nuts and butter. Place ½ of nut mixture over bottom of pie crust. Add peach mixture. Sprinkle remaining nut mixture over peaches. Bake at 425 degrees for 10 minutes, then lower heat to 325 degrees and bake 20 minutes more.

Liqueur Pie

6-8 servings

1½	cups crumbs (macaroon, graham cracker, chocolate wafer or gingersnap)
¼	cup butter, melted
½	cup cold water
1	envelope unflavored gelatin
⅓ - ⅔	cup sugar (depending on liqueur and individual preference)
⅛	teaspoon salt
3	eggs, separated
½	cup liqueur or ¼ cup of two kinds
⅓	cup sugar
1	cup heavy cream, whipped

Combine crumbs and butter. Press into a 10 inch pie pan and bake at 350 degrees for 8 to 10 minutes. Cool. Pour water into a saucepan and sprinkle gelatin over it. Add ⅓ cup sugar, salt and egg yolks. Stir to blend. Place over low heat and stir until gelatin dissolves and mixture thickens. Do not boil. Remove from heat. Stir in the liqueur and chill until mixture starts to mound slightly. Beat egg whites until stiff, then add remaining sugar and beat until peaks are firm. Fold meringue into thickened mixture. Whip cream and fold into mixture. Pour into prepared crust. Chill several hours or overnight. Garnish.

Variations:

Chocolate Mint Pie:

¼	cup white creme de menthe
¼	cup creme de cacao
	chocolate cookie crust
	chocolate curls for garnish

Grasshopper Pie:

¼	cup white creme de menthe
¼	cup green creme de menthe
	chocolate cookie crust
	chocolate curls for garnish

Golden Dream Pie:

¼	cup Galliano
¼	cup Cointreau
¾	cup orange juice in place of water
2	tablespoons grated orange rind
	graham cracker crust
	toasted coconut for garnish

Irish Coffee Pie:

½	cup Irish whiskey
	double strength coffee in place of water
	graham cracker crust

Brandy Alexander Pie:

¼	cup Cognac
¼	cup creme de cacao
	graham cracker crust with a little nutmeg and finely chopped nuts
	chocolate curls for garnish
	sprinkle of nutmeg

French Silk Pie

Graham Cracker Crust:
- 1 **cup graham cracker crumbs**
- ¼ **cup butter**
- ½ **cup chopped nuts**
- ¼ **cup sugar**

Filling:
- ½ **cup butter**
- ¾ **cup sugar**
- 4 **tablespoons cocoa**
- 3 **extra large eggs**
- **pinch of salt**

Garnish:
- **whipped cream**
- **chopped nuts**
- **chocolate curls**

6-8 servings

Prepare graham cracker crust by mixing ingredients. Pat into an 8 or 9 inch pie pan and bake at 375 degrees for 10 minutes. Remove from oven and cool. To prepare filling, cream butter, sugar and cocoa for a minimum of 5 minutes. Scrape bowl often. Add each egg separately and beat for a full 5 minutes after the addition of each egg. Scrape bowl often. Pour into cool pie crust and refrigerate. Pipe whipped cream around edge and sprinkle with chopped nuts or chocolate curls. May serve refrigerated or frozen.

Note: Eggs must be at room temperature before using.

Pecan Cookie "Pie"

Crust:
- 2 **cups sifted flour**
- 1 **teaspoon baking powder**
- **dash of salt**
- ⅔ **cup brown sugar, firmly packed**
- ½ **cup soft butter**

Filling:
- 4 **eggs**
- ½ **cup brown sugar, firmly packed**
- ⅓ **cup flour**
- 1 **teaspoon salt**
- 1½ **cups dark corn syrup**
  (may use ½ dark and ½ light)
- 2 **teaspoons vanilla extract**
- ¾ **cup coarsely chopped pecans**
  ice cream or whipped cream

30 servings

Sift flour, baking powder and salt. Stir in brown sugar. Cut in butter with a pastry blender until it is well mixed. It will seem dry. Pat evenly into bottom of a well greased 9 × 13 inch pan. Bake at 325 degrees for 12 minutes.

Beat eggs until well mixed but not too light. Add brown sugar, flour and salt. Add corn syrup and vanilla. Mix well. Pour over the partly baked crust and sprinkle with pecans. Return to the 325 degree oven and bake 40 to 45 minutes. Cut into squares while still warm.

Note: May be served as a dessert with ice cream or whipped cream. If this is done, bake in an 11 × 7 × 1½ inch pan.

Veronika's Kirsch Torte

12 servings

4	eggs, separated, plus 1 egg white from buttercream layer
4	tablespoons water
1¼	cups sugar
1	cup flour
2	tablespoons cocoa
1	teaspoon baking powder dash of salt
½	teaspoon water
6 - 10	tablespoons Kirsch or Kirschwasser

Buttercream Layer:

1	whole egg
1	egg yolk (use egg white in cake)
¼	cup sugar
½	cup unsalted margarine
1	teaspoon cocoa
5	ounces seedless black raspberry jam
1	16-ounce can pitted sour cherries
½	pint whipping cream
2 - 3	teaspoons powdered sugar
½	teaspoon vanilla extract

Garnish:
semi-sweet chocolate curls

Preheat oven to 350 degrees. Grease a 9 inch springform pan and line the bottom with a circle of waxed paper. Beat yolks with water until foamy. Add sugar and mix thoroughly. Sift flour, cocoa and baking powder into egg mixture and mix thoroughly. Beat egg whites with salt and ½ teaspoon water until light and fluffy. Mix egg whites, flour and egg mixture. Bake at 350 degrees for 30 minutes on center rack in oven. Cool and split in half. Using an amount of Kirsch to suit your taste, sprinkle each half of cake evenly.

To make buttercream filling, place egg, egg yolk and sugar in a double boiler over hot water and stir constantly until thick. Let cool. Soften margarine and add cocoa. Add egg mixture slowly to margarine mixture. On bottom layer of cake make a circle of jam in the center. Spread a solid line of buttercream around the circle, then spread another circle of jam around the buttercream. Spread a final circle of butttercream around jam. Drain canned cherries and reserve 13 for top of cake. Push rest of cherries evenly into the 2 buttercream circles. Place top layer over jam-buttercream filling. Whip cream with 2 to 3 teaspoons of powdered sugar and vanilla. Pipe decoratively onto top of cake. Put 12 cherries around outside edge and one in the middle. Decorate with semi-sweet chocolate curls.

Note: Make the cake the day before you plan to serve the torte. Assemble the day before. Decorate buttercream top with whipped cream and cherries before serving.

Poppy Seed Torte

10-12 servings

½   cup poppy seeds
⅔   cup milk
½   cup shortening
1   cup sugar
2   cups cake flour
2   teaspoons baking powder
¼   teaspoon salt
3   egg whites, stiffly beaten

Soak poppy seeds in milk for 2 hours. Cream shortening and sugar. Mix dry ingredients and add alternately with milk and poppy seeds. Fold in egg whites. Bake in 2 greased and floured 8 inch layer pans at 350 degrees for 20 minutes or until it tests done with a toothpick. (May bake in an 8 × 8 inch pan and split layers or omit filling.)

Filling:
1   cup sugar
1   cup sour cream
3   egg yolks
1   teaspoon vanilla extract
½   cup chopped black walnuts
½   cup chopped English walnuts

Cook sugar, sour cream and egg yolks in top of double boiler until thickened, about 15 mintes. Remove from heat, add vanilla and beat with a rotary beater until smooth. Cool. Add nuts and spread between layers of cake. Frost with Chocolate-Mocha frosting or Fluffy White frosting.

Chocolate-Mocha Frosting:
6   tablespoons butter
3   tablespoons cocoa
3   cups powdered sugar
    hot strong coffee

Mix butter, cocoa and powdered sugar. Beat, moistening with hot coffee until spreading consistency.

Fluffy White Frosting:
2   egg whites
1½ cups sugar
¼   cup water
3   tablespoons light corn syrup
⅛   teaspoon cream of tartar
    dash of salt
1   teaspoon vanilla extract

Combine ingredients except vanilla and beat about 1 minute with electric mixer. Place over boiling water and beat for approximately 7 minutes. Remove from heat and add vanilla. Beat about 1 more minute or until spreading consistency.

COLORADO CACHE COLORADO CACHE COLORADO CACHE COLORADO CACHE COLORADO CACHE COLORADO CACHE COLORADO CACHE COLORADO CACHE COLORADO

Sacher Torte

8-12 servings

- ¾ **cup butter, softened**
- ¾ **cup sugar**
- 7 **ounces semi-sweet chocolate, melted and cooled**
- ¼ **teaspoon salt**
- ½ **teaspoon vanilla extract**
- 2 **egg yolks**
- 1 **cup sifted flour**
- 10 **egg whites, stiffly beaten but not dry**
- 1 **cup apricot jam**

Glaze:

- 2 **tablespoons butter**
- 2 **ounces unsweetened chocolate**
- 2 **tablespoons powdered sugar**
- ⅛ **teaspoon salt**
- 1 **cup heavy cream, whipped**

Cream butter and sugar until light and fluffy. Blend in chocolate, salt and vanilla extract. Add egg yolks, one at a time. Beat well after each addition. Gradually add sifted flour to chocolate mixture. Gently fold stiffly beaten egg whites into batter. Spread evenly in generously greased and floured 8 inch springform pan. Bake at 325 degrees for 50 to 55 minutes. Cool for 15 minutes. Remove pan sides and bottom. Invert cake on wire rack. Let stand until completely cooled. In a saucepan heat apricot jam, stirring frequently until boiling. Remove from heat. Press through fine sieve or blender. With cake bottom side up on wire rack, brush top and sides with jam. Let stand an hour to allow jam to set.

For glaze, combine 2 tablespoons butter, unsweetened chocolate, powdered sugar and salt in top of double boiler. Blend. Cook over simmering water, stirring until smooth. While glaze is still warm, frost top and sides of cake. Refrigerate until frosting has hardened. Transfer to a serving plate. Top each serving with a generous dollop of whipped cream.

Blintz Torte

8-10 servings

½　cup butter, softened
½　cup sugar
4　egg yolks, beaten
1　cup sifted cake flour
　　pinch of salt
1　teaspoon baking powder
5　tablespoons milk
1　teaspoon vanilla extract
4　egg whites
1　cup sugar
　　cinnamon sugar
⅓　cup sliced almonds

Cream together butter and ½ cup sugar. Beat in egg yolks. Sift together flour, salt and baking powder. Add flour mixture to butter mixture alternately with milk. Add vanilla, mix thoroughly and pour into 2 well greased and floured 8 or 9 inch layer pans. Set aside. In another bowl, beat egg whites until stiff and continue beating while gradually adding 1 cup sugar. Spread this meringue over batter in pans. Sprinkle meringues lightly with cinnamon sugar and almonds. Bake at 350 degrees for 25 to 35 minutes or until golden brown. Cool.

Custard:

6　tablespoons sugar
1　tablespoon cornstarch
½　cup sour cream
3　egg yolks, lightly beaten
1　tablespoon butter
1　teaspoon vanilla extract
½　teaspoon almond extract

Combine sugar and cornstarch. Add sour cream. Stir into lightly beaten egg yolks and add butter. Cook this mixture in double boiler, stirring constantly until thickened. Remove from heat and cool. Add flavorings. Chill. Use as filling between the two torte layers. Assemble shortly before serving. Place one layer, meringue side down, on a cake plate and spread with custard. Place second layer on top of custard with meringue side up. If desired, top with whipped cream and sliced strawberries. Store in refrigerator.

Garnish:

½　pint whipping cream, whipped
　　sliced strawberries

Torte Variations:

Use recipe for Blintz Torte following directions for batter and meringue. Bake and assemble much the same way, omitting cinnamon sugar, almonds and custard.

Variation I:
- ¾ cup chopped nuts, spread on both meringue layers
- 1½ cups heavy cream, whipped
- 1 cup drained, crushed pineapple
- 1½ teaspoons powdered sugar
- ¼ teaspoon vanilla extract

Combine whipped cream, pineapple, sugar and vanilla for filling.

Variation II:
- 1 4-ounce can shredded coconut
- 1 cup pecan halves
- 1½ cups heavy cream, whipped
  powdered sugar to taste
  vanilla extract to taste

On one meringue layer, sprinkle coconut and on the other arrange nuts. Use the flavored whipped cream for the filling.

Variation III:
- blanched, sliced almonds
- 1½ cups heavy cream, whipped
- 2 teaspoons powdered sugar
- ¾ - 1 cup lightly toasted coconut
- 1 - 2 tablespoons rum

Stud the top meringue with the almonds, placing slices close together. Combine whipped cream, sugar, coconut and rum and use for filling.

Denver Chocolate Sheet Cake

12-16 servings

2⅓ cups flour
2 cups sugar
1 teaspoon baking soda
1 cup butter
1¼ cups water
4 tablespoons cocoa
½ cup buttermilk
2 eggs, beaten
1 teaspoon vanilla extract

Mix flour, sugar and soda in bowl. Bring butter, water and cocoa to a boil in saucepan. Pour over dry ingredients. Mix thoroughly. Add buttermilk, eggs and vanilla. Beat well. Pour into a greased 9 × 13 inch pan and bake at 350 degrees for 30 minutes or until it tests done.

Frosting:

½ cup butter
4 tablespoons cocoa
6 tablespoons buttermilk
1 teaspoon vanilla extract
1 pound powdered sugar
½ cup chopped walnuts
    or pecans

To make frosting, heat butter, cocoa and buttermilk to boiling. Remove from heat and mix in vanilla, sugar and nuts.

Note: A delicious, moist, chocolate cake. The frosting will be runny but it hardens as it cools. Cake freezes well. Good with peppermint ice cream. It is also good with a 7 minute frosting.

Lemon Coconut Cake

10-12 servings

1 cup shredded coconut
2 tablespoons milk
¾ cup butter or margarine
1¾ cups minus 1 tablespoon
    sugar
2¾ cups sifted flour
½ teaspoon salt
2½ teaspoons baking powder
1 cup plus 2 tablespoons water
1 teaspoon lemon extract
4 egg whites, stiffly beaten

Soak coconut in milk. Cream butter and sugar until light and fluffy. Mix and sift flour, salt and baking powder together. To creamed mixture add dry ingredients alternately with water, mixing thoroughly after each addition. Add lemon extract and coconut-milk mixture. Mix very well. With rubber spatula, gently fold beaten egg whites into batter. Pour into 2 greased and floured 9 inch layer pans. Bake at 375 degrees for 20 to 30 minutes or until done.

Easy Lemon Frosting:

4 tablespoons lemon juice
    grated rind of 1 lemon
2 egg yolks
½ cups powdered sugar

Combine lemon juice and rind with egg yolks. Gradually add powdered sugar. Beat until spreading consistency. Refrigerate.

Sour Cream Pound Cake

12-15 servings

    1 cup butter
 2¾ cups sugar
    6 eggs, separated
  ¼ teaspoon baking soda
  ½ teaspoon salt
    3 cups flour, sifted before
        measuring
    1 cup sour cream

Cream butter and sugar. Add egg yolks, one at a time. Add soda and salt to flour and sift 2 more times. Then add flour mixture and sour cream alternately to the butter and sugar mixture. Beat egg whites until stiff and fold into batter. Bake in a greased and floured tube or Bundt pan at 350 degrees for 1¼ to 1½ hours or until toothpick comes out clean. When cool sprinkle with powdered sugar, if desired.

For Flavor Variations Add:
    1 teaspoon vanilla extract and
        1 teaspoon mace, or
  ½ teaspoon lemon extract, or
  ½ teaspoon orange extract and
        ½ teaspoon vanilla extract,
        or
        almond extract

Skier's Delight Date Cake

6-8 servings

  ½ cup butter, creamed
    1 cup sugar
    1 egg
    1 cup cake flour
    1 teaspoon vanilla extract
    1 cup chopped dates
    1 cup boiling water
    1 teaspoon baking soda
  ½ cup chopped walnuts
        (optional)
        whipped cream (optional)

Cream together butter, sugar and egg. Beat in flour and vanilla. Set aside. In another bowl mix dates, boiling water and soda. Let stand 10 minutes. Add to first mixture. Stir in nuts, if desired. Pour into well greased 8 × 8 inch pan. Bake at 375 degrees for 30 minutes or until toothpick inserted in center comes out clean.

Note: Very good served warm with whipped cream. Recipe can easily be doubled.

Sad Cake

15-24 servings

1   pound light brown sugar
4   eggs, well beaten
½   cup vegetable oil
2   cups biscuit mix
1   teaspoon vanilla extract
1   cup chopped pecans
1   7-ounce package flaked
      coconut

Mix sugar with eggs. Stir in vegetable oil, then biscuit mix a little at a time, until all ingredients are well mixed. Add vanilla, pecans and coconut. Bake in ungreased 9 × 13 inch pan at 325 degrees for 45 minutes.

Note: Do not be alarmed if cake looks strange. It is called "Sad Cake" because it rises fairly high, then caves in in the middle! It's delicious. Can be served warm with whipped cream or ice cream.

Drunken Casserole Cake

8-10 servings

4   eggs, separated
½   cup sugar
1   cup flour
1   teaspoon baking powder
¼   teaspoon salt
⅓   cup butter, melted
1   teaspoon vanilla extract

Sauce:
2   cups sugar
2   cups water
½   cup rum, brandy or sherry
      toasted chopped almonds or
         toasted shredded coconut
         for topping

Beat egg whites until stiff and add 4 tablespoons sugar. Beat egg yolks with remaining sugar and add to egg whites. Fold in dry ingredients and add melted butter and vanilla. Pour into a 2 quart casserole. Bake at 375 degrees for 30 minutes. Remove from oven and make holes in the top with an ice pick. Pour sauce over warm cake.

Boil sugar and water until soft ball stage. Remove from heat and add rum. Pour sauce over cake and before all the liquid is absorbed, sprinkle with almond or coconut.

Note: Good served warm or at room temperature the second day.

Mother Ann's Birthday Cake

15 servings

3 cups sifted flour
½ cup cornstarch
1 tablespoon baking powder
1 teaspoon salt
1 cup butter
2 cups sugar
1 cup milk
2 teaspoons vanilla extract
12 egg whites, at room
        temperature
    peach jam (about 10 ounces)

Sift together flour, cornstarch, baking powder and salt. Set aside. Cream butter until soft, then add sugar, a little at a time and continue mixing until smooth as possible. Add flour mixture and milk alternately, beginning and ending with flour. Stir in vanilla, then fold in stiffly beaten egg whites very gently and thoroughly. Pour into 3 well greased and lightly floured 9 inch layer pans. Bake in a preheated 350 degree oven for 25 to 30 minutes or until cake pulls away from sides of pan. Let stand several minutes before turning out of pans onto cake racks. When cold, spread peach jam between layers and frost sides and top with butter cream frosting.

Butter Cream Frosting:

½ cup butter, softened
1½ cups powdered sugar
2 tablespoons milk
½ teaspoon vanilla extract

Combine all ingredients and beat with an electric mixer at high speed until smooth and thick. If the frosting is too thin, add more sugar.

Note: An old-fashioned, "hearty" cake. The Shakers served this cake each year on March 1 to commemorate the birthday of their founder, Ann Lee, who was born February 29, 1736.

Perfect White Cake

8-10 servings

½ cup butter
1⅔ cups sugar
2½ cups cake flour, sifted before
        measuring
¼ teaspoon salt
1¼ cups cold water
1 teaspoon vanilla extract
2 teaspoons baking powder
4 egg whites

Cream butter and sugar. Sift flour and salt together and add alternately with water. Always start and end with flour. Add vanilla. Beat egg whites until frothy then add baking powder, a teaspoon at a time and beat until stiff. Fold into batter. Pour into 2 greased and floured 8 inch layer pans. Bake at 350 degrees for 20 to 30 minutes. Test by tapping center lightly with finger. When it springs back it is done.

ADO CACHE COLORADO CACHE COLORADO CACHE COLORADO CACHE COLORADO CACHE COLORADO CACHE COLORADO CACHE COLORADO CACHE COLORADO CACHE

Italian Cream Cake

14-16 servings

½ **cup shortening**
½ **cup butter**
1⅔ **cups sugar**
6 **eggs, separated**
1 **cup buttermilk**
¾ **teaspoon baking soda**
½ **teaspoon salt**
2 **cups flour**
¾ **teaspoon vanilla extract**
2 **cups shredded coconut**
1 **cup chopped pecans**
½ **cup quartered maraschino cherries (approximately 15 cherries)**
¼ **teaspoon cream of tartar**

Cream shortening, butter and sugar until light and fluffy. Add egg yolks, one at a time, and beat well after each addition. Add buttermilk alternately with dry ingredients, ending with flour. Stir in vanilla, coconut, pecans and cherries. Beat egg whites with cream of tartar until stiff. Fold into cake mixture. Bake in 3 greased 9 inch layer pans at 350 degrees for 30 to 40 minutes or until done. Cool 10 minutes, remove from pan.

Frosting:

½ **cup butter at room temperature**
1 **8-ounce package cream cheese, softened**
4 **cups powdered sugar**
¾ **teaspoon vanilla extract**
1 **cup chopped pecans**

Cream butter and cream cheese. Gradually add sugar and vanilla. Beat until smooth and creamy. Add pecans or sprinkle on top of frosted cake.

Chocolate Fudge Cake

10-12 servings

3	**squares unsweetened chocolate**
2¼	**cups sifted cake flour**
2	**teaspoons baking soda**
½	**teaspoon salt**
½	**cup butter or margarine**
2¼	**cups brown sugar**
3	**eggs**
1½	**teaspoons vanilla extract**
1	**cup sour cream**
1	**cup boiling water**

Preheat oven to 375 degrees. Melt chocolate over hot water. Cool. Sift flour, baking soda and salt. Beat butter until soft. Add brown sugar and eggs and beat until fluffy. Beat in vanilla and add cooled chocolate. Stir in dry ingredients alternately with sour cream, beating well with a wooden spoon. Stir in boiling water. Pour into greased and floured 9 inch layer pans. Bake at 375 degrees for approximately 25 minutes or until it tests done. Cool in pans on wire rack 10 minutes.

Frosting:

4	**1-ounce squares unsweetened chocolate**
½	**cup butter**
1	**pound powdered sugar**
½	**cup milk**
2	**teaspoons vanilla extract**

Combine chocolate and butter in saucepan until melted. Combine sugar, milk and vanilla in medium sized bowl. Stir until smooth. Add chocolate mixture. Set bowl in pan of ice water and beat with a wooden spoon until frosting is thick enough to spread.

Chocolate Roll

6 servings

4	**eggs, separated and at room temperature**
1	**cup minus 1 tablespoon granulated sugar**
½	**teaspoon vanilla extract**
3	**tablespoons cocoa**
½	**pint heavy cream, or more**
¼	**cup powdered sugar**
½	**teaspoon vanilla extract**
	powdered sugar for garnish

Grease a 9 × 13 inch pan well and dust a large sheet of waxed paper well with powdered sugar. Beat egg whites until stiff adding sugar gradually. Beat yolks until thick and lemon colored. Fold into whites. Add vanilla. Sift cocoa and fold into egg mixture. Pour into pan and spread into corners. "Cake" will rise then fall. Bake at 350 degrees for 20 to 30 minutes or until toothpick tests clean. Let stand 5 minutes. Loosen from sides of pan and turn upside down on powdered sugared paper. When cool, whip cream, adding powdered sugar and vanilla. Spread on top of cake and roll jelly-roll fashion, lifting waxed paper as you go. Garnish with additional powdered sugar. Chill at least one hour before serving.

Note: Also delicious served with Hot Fudge S (see index).

Caramel-Glazed Pear Cake

15-24 servings

1	cup butter
1	cup sugar
1	cup brown sugar, packed
2	eggs, beaten
1	teaspoon vanilla extract
2½	cups flour
2	teaspoons baking powder
1	teaspoon baking soda
½	teaspoon salt
2	teaspoons ground cinnamon
½	cup reserved pear syrup
1	16-ounce can pears, diced
1	cup raisins
1	cup chopped walnuts

Cream together butter and sugars until light. Blend in eggs and vanilla. Sift together all dry ingredients and add to butter mixture alternately with pear syrup. Stir in pears, raisins and nuts and pour into a greased 9 × 13 inch pan. Bake at 400 degrees for 25 minutes or until done. While still warm spread with caramel glaze.

Caramel Glaze:

¼	cup brown sugar, packed
1	tablespoon butter
2	tablespoons reserved pear syrup
½	cup powdered sugar

Bring sugar, butter and syrup to boil. Stir in powdered sugar and spread on cake.

Old Fashioned Lemon Tarts

4 dozen

	grated rind of 2 lemons
½	cup fresh lemon juice
2	cups sugar
1	cup butter
4	eggs, well beaten
4	dozen miniature baked tart shells

Combine lemon rind, juice and sugar in top of double boiler. Add butter and heat over boiling water, stirring until butter is melted. Add eggs. Continue cooking and stirring until mixture is thick enough to pile slightly, about 15 minutes. Cool. Spoon into tart shells just before serving. This filling may be stored in a jar in the refrigerator for several days.

To make tart shells use your favorite pie crust recipe or see index for Dwarf Date Cups and use the pastry recipe.

German Chocolate Butterfly Cupcakes

3 dozen

1	**4-ounce package German chocolate**
½	**cup boiling water**
¾	**cup shortening**
1¾	**cups sugar**
4	**egg yolks**
	pinch of salt
1	**teaspoon vanilla extract**
1	**teaspoon soda**
1	**cup buttermilk**
2½	**cups sifted all-purpose flour**
4	**egg whites, stiffly beaten**

Melt chocolate in water. Cool. Cream shortening and sugar, add egg yolks, salt, vanilla and melted chocolate. Blend well. Dissolve soda in buttermilk. Add flour and buttermilk alternately. Beat after each addition until batter is smooth. Fold in egg whites. Spoon batter into cupcake tins, lined with paper liners. Fill ⅔ full. Bake at 350 degrees for approximately 20 minutes or until it tests done. Cool. With a sharp knife remove large cone shaped piece from the center of each cupcake. Spoon coffee topping into each cupcake hollow. Split cones in half, stand on top of filling and drizzle with chocolate. Refrigerate.

Coffee topping:

1	**cup cold milk**
1	**teaspoon vanilla extract**
2	**teaspoons instant coffee granules**
2	**envelopes whipped topping mix**

Combine all ingredients for coffee topping and blend. Whip until peaks form and until light and fluffy. Then whip about 2 minutes longer.

Chocolate drizzle:

1½	**packages (6 ounces) German chocolate**
5	**tablespoons water**

Combine the chocolate and water in a saucepan. Cook over low heat stirring until chocolate is melted and smooth.

Brownie Cup Cakes

20 servings

4	**ounces semi-sweet chocolate**
1	**cup butter (½ pound)**
1¾	**cups sugar**
1	**cup unsifted flour**
4	**large eggs, lightly beaten**
1	**teaspoon vanilla extract**
	dash of salt
1	**cup chopped nuts**

Melt chocolate and butter. Cool slightly. Combine sugar, flour eggs, vanilla and salt. Add nuts to chocolate mixture to coat nuts. Combine the 2 mixtures. Mix only until blended. Do not beat. Pour into paper lined cupcake pans. Bake at 325 degrees for 30 minutes. Do not frost.

Note: These will not resemble traditional cupcakes.

COLORADO CACHE COLORADO CACHE COLORADO CACHE COLORADO CACHE COLORADO CACHE COLORADO CACHE COLORADO CACHE COLORADO CACHE COLORADO CACHE COLORADO CACHE COLORADO CACHE COLORADO CACHE

Everyone Likes Fruitcake

Approximately 5 pounds

1¼ **pounds seeded currants**
1¼ **pounds seedless raisins**
½ **pound chopped figs**
½ **pound diced dates**
5 **cups flour**
½ **teaspoon baking soda**
1 **tablespoon ground cinnamon**
1 **teaspoon ground nutmeg**
1 **tablespoon ground cloves**
2 **cups butter**
2 **cups brown sugar, packed**
5 **eggs**
½ **teaspoon salt**
½ **cup molasses**
¼ **cup brandy**

Wash currants and raisins in hot water to plump them. Drain and dry thoroughly. Add figs and dates. Mix and sift together flour, soda, cinnamon, nutmeg and cloves and combine with mixed fruits. Cream butter and sugar, blending thoroughly. Beat eggs with salt and add them to the butter-sugar mixture. Add molasses and brandy, alternately with the floured fruit mixture; beat well after each addition. Bake in a well greased or teflon coated tube pan. Place the pan in another pan containing 1 inch of hot water and bake at 275 degrees for about 2½ hours. Remove the pan with the water and bake the cake for 30 minutes longer. Cool. Cover with a cheese cloth soaked in brandy, wrap in waxed paper, and store in a tightly closed container.

Note: Flavor improves with age. Prepare at least 1 month before use.

Dwarf Date Cups

Pastry:
3 **tablespoons powdered sugar**
½ **cup butter**
1 **cup flour**
¼ **teaspoon salt**

20-22 cups

Cream sugar and butter. Add flour and salt. Mix thoroughly, making a soft dough. Press dough into tiny muffin cups, 1¾ inches, using fingers. Spread thin. Bake at 350 degrees for 15 minutes.

Filling:
4 **ounces pitted dates**
¾ **cup water**
scant ½ **cup sugar**
whipped cream for garnish

Combine dates with water and sugar. Bring to a boil. Simmer until soft. Cool. Fill pastry cups. Serve with a dab of whipped cream.

Butter Pecan Miniatures

10-12 tarts

- 1 **cup butter**
- 1 **cup light brown sugar, packed**
- 1 **egg**
- 4 **tablespoons flour**
- 1 **teaspoon almond extract**
- 1½ **teaspoons vanilla extract**
  few grains of salt
- 1½ **cups chopped, toasted**
  pecans, cooled
  whipped cream

Cream butter and sugar. Add remaining ingredients, mixing thoroughly. Put mixture into paper-lined cupcake tins and freeze. Remove from freezer ½ hour before serving. Top with whipped cream. To toast pecans, place them in a 300 degree oven, stirring frequently. This brings out the flavor and makes nuts crisp.

Individual Chocolate Frangos

24 servings

- 1 **cup butter**
- 2 **cups sifted powdered sugar**
- 4 **squares unsweetened**
  chocolate, melted and
  cooled
- 4 **eggs**
- 1 **teaspoon peppermint extract**
- 1 **teaspoon vanilla extract**
  pinch of salt
- 1 **cup whipping cream, whipped**
- 2 **cups vanilla wafer crumbs**

Beat butter and sugar with electric mixer until light and fluffy. Add chocolate and mix well. Add eggs and beat 3 or 4 minutes after each addition. Add flavorings and salt, mixing well. Fold in whipped cream. Place about 1 teaspoon crumbs into bottom of 24 paper lined cupcake tins. The foil backed cupcake liners work especially well. Fill with the chocolate mixture and sprinkle with remainder of the crumbs.

Topping:

- ½ **cup butter or margarine**
- 1 **cup powdered sugar**
- 2 **eggs**
- 3 **squares unsweetened**
  chocolate, melted and
  cooled

Beat butter and add sugar, beating until light. Add eggs and chocolate. Mix well. With pastry tube, pipe dollop of chocolate onto each pie, pressing slightly into mixture so it sticks when frozen. Freeze. When hardened may be stored in plastic bags. Serve frozen.

Note: Easy for group entertaining!

Tassies

48 tassies

1 cup butter
1 8-ounce package cream cheese
2 cups flour
dash of salt

Blend with pastry blender. Chill. Make into small balls and shape into miniature pans to make small tart. The 1¾ inch muffin tins work beautifully.

Filling:

2 eggs, lightly beaten
2 teaspoons melted butter
1½ cups brown sugar, packed
1 cup chopped pecans or walnuts (may substitute coconut, mincemeat or chopped dates for nuts)

Mix eggs, butter and sugar. Add chopped nuts. Fill individual pastry tarts with filling, not too full. Bake at 375 degrees for 10 to 15 minutes. Let tarts cool in pans before removing. Pastry tarts may be baked without filling to have individual pastry shells. Be sure to prick each pastry shell all over before baking. Cool.

Note: May prepare an assortment of these tassies with filling variations and freeze. Delicious and attractive displayed on a tray.

Filling Variations:

Lemon Cheese Filling:

3 eggs
¾ cup sugar
1 8-ounce package cream cheese
½ cup lemon juice
2 teaspoons lemon rind

Beat eggs in cold double boiler until thickened and fluffy. Continue beating while adding sugar, lemon juice and rind. Cook over hot water until smooth and thick. Cool. Soften cream cheese at room temperature. Gradually blend custard into cheese. Fill shells and top with whipped cream.

Strawberry Filling:

2 cups fresh strawberries, crushed
4 cups sugar
1½ teaspoons lemon juice
1 1¾ ounce box Sure Jell
1 cup boiling water

Mix strawberries, sugar and lemon juice and let stand. Mix Sure Jell and water and boil 1 minute. Add strawberry mixture. Cool.

Blueberry Filling:

1 15-ounce can blueberries
⅔ cup sugar
scant ½ teaspoon salt
2 large tablespoons flour
¼ teaspoon ground nutmeg
1 tablespoon lemon juice
1 tablespoon butter

Drain just a little of the blueberry juice off and put remainder of the can in a saucepan. Mix dry ingredients together and add to fruit. Mix well, but gently. Add lemon juice and butter. Cook, stirring constantly until thickened. Cool. Spread cheese mixture in pastry shells, then fill with blueberry filling. Reserve enough cheese mixture to put a small dollop on top of each tart.

353
Desserts

COLORADO CACHE COLORADO CACHE COLORADO CACHE COLORADO CACHE COLORADO CACHE COLORADO CACHE COLORADO CACHE COLORADO CACHE COLORADO CACHE COLORADO

Cheese Mixture:

1 3-ounce package cream cheese	Mix together until creamy.
½ cup sugar	
¼ cup heavy cream, whipped	

Individual Meringues

20 meringues

1 pound powdered sugar
6 egg whites at room temperature
1 teaspoon cream of tartar
1 teaspoon vanilla extract
1 teaspoon vinegar

Combine sugar and egg whites. Beat with electric mixer for 10 minutes at high speed. Add cream of tartar, vanilla and vinegar. Beat an additional 10 minutes. Bake on greased cookie sheets at 250 degrees for 15 minutes then raise temperature to 300 degrees and bake for 10 to 15 minutes. Remove meringues immediately from cookie sheets and place in tightly closed tins between sheets of waxed paper.
Note: These will keep indefinitely.

Hot Bananas Jamaica

4-6 servings

⅓ cup brown sugar, firmly packed
¼ cup orange juice concentrate
2 tablespoons butter
1½ tablespoons lemon juice
2 large bananas
¼ cup rum, warmed
1 quart vanilla or coffee ice cream
toasted sliced almonds for garnish

Place in a large skillet the sugar, orange juice concentrate, butter and lemon juice. Heat until sauce bubbles and blends together. Peel bananas and slice diagonally. Add to the sauce. Ignite a spoonful of warm rum and spoon, flaming, over the bananas. Add remaining rum and relight, spoon liquid until flame has burned out. Spoon bananas and sauce over ball of ice cream in dessert dishes. Garnish with almonds.

L'Orange Francaise Supreme

oranges
powdered sugar
Grand Marnier

For each person, use one orange. Peel and partially undo each section so that the orange is open at the top but still attached at the bottom. Place on a bed of powdered sugar in a sherbet glass. Serve on a dessert plate with a liqueur glass of Grand Marnier beside it. Eat with the fingers, dipping each orange section first in the Grand Marnier and then in the sugar.

Note: Easy, fun, different and a great conversation encourager!

Katie Stapleton's Peaches and Champagne

6 servings

6 **ripe peaches**
1 **bottle of champagne**

When ready to serve dessert, peel the peaches individually. Serve each guest a whole peach on a cold plate. Provide each guest with a salad fork, small knife and a glass of champagne. Guests then slice off a peach segment and dunk it in their champagne.

Brandied Green Grapes

4-6 servings

1 **teaspoon lemon juice**
¼ **cup honey**
2 **tablespoons Cognac or Drambuie**
1 **pound green seedless grapes**
½ **cup sour cream**
brown sugar to taste

Mix lemon juice, honey and Cognac. Pour over grapes. Let stand overnight in refrigerator. Four hours before serving, pour the sour cream over the grape mixture and sprinkle with brown sugar. Return to refrigerator until ready to serve. Serve in champagne glasses.

Fresh Pears with Ginger Sauce

6 servings

6   ripe pears
    fresh lemon juice
1½ cups sour cream
1   tablespoon honey
2   tablespoons Triple Sec
    crystallized ginger

Peel, core and cube pears and sprinkle with lemon juice. Mix with sour cream, honey, liqueur and ginger. Serve chilled. Do not prepare more than an hour or two in advance as the pears will get soft.

Strawberries Cardinal

8 servings

1½ quarts fresh strawberries
⅓   cup sugar
1   10-ounce package frozen
    raspberries, thawed
2   tablespoons sugar
1   tablespoon orange liqueur
1   teaspoon fresh lemon juice

Wash and drain strawberries. Slice if you wish and sprinkle them with the sugar. Toss, cover and chill. In blender, blend raspberries, 2 tablespoons sugar, orange liqueur and lemon juice. Cover and chill. Just before serving ladle sauce over strawberries.

Note: May use as a sauce over pound cake or ice cream.

Pike's Peak Spiked Apple Crisp

8 servings

5   cups peeled and sliced apples
    (Pippin, Jonathan or
    Winesap)
½   teaspoon cinnamon sugar
1   teaspoon grated lemon rind
1   teaspoon grated orange rind
1   jigger Grand Marnier
1   jigger Amaretto di Saronno
¾   cup granulated sugar
¼   cup light brown sugar, packed
¾   cup sifted flour
¼   teaspoon salt
½   cup butter or margarine
    cream, whipped cream or ice
    cream for topping

Arrange apple slices in greased 2 quart round casserole. Sprinkle cinnamon, lemon and orange rinds and both liqueurs on top of apples. In a separate bowl, mix sugars, flour, salt and butter with a pastry blender until crumbly. Spread mixture over top of apples. Bake uncovered at 350 degrees until apples are tender and top is lightly browned, approximately 1 hour. Serve warm with cream, whipped cream or with vanilla or cinnamon ice cream.

Rhubarb Cobbler

9 squares

1 **cup flour**
¾ **cup oatmeal**
1 **teaspoon ground cinnamon**
1 **cup brown sugar**
½ **cup butter, melted**
1 **cup sugar**
1 **cup water**
3 **tablespoons corn starch**
1 **teaspoon vanilla extract**
4 **cups sliced rhubarb**
   ice cream (optional)

Combine flour, oatmeal, cinnamon, brown sugar and butter. Press half of the mixture into an 8 × 8 inch pan. Cook 1 cup sugar, water, corn starch and vanilla until very thick. Add rhubarb and mix thoroughly. Spread into cake pan and top with remaining oatmeal mixture. Bake at 350 degrees for 1 hour. Serve warm or cold. Delicious topped with vanilla ice cream.

Lemon Float Pudding

4 servings

1 **cup sugar**
3 **tablespoons flour**
1 **tablespoon butter**
2 **egg yolks, beaten**
1 **cup milk**
   juice and rind of 1 lemon
2 **egg whites, beaten**
   whipped cream

Cream sugar, flour and butter. Add egg yolks, milk and lemon. Fold in beaten egg whites. Bake at 350 degrees for 40 minutes in a small casserole which is set in a pan of water. May need slightly longer baking time at high altitude. Garnish with whipped cream.

Amaretto Cheese Ball

6-8 servings

8 **ounces cream cheese**
¼ **cup Amaretto liqueur**
1 **3-ounce package toasted,**
   slivered almonds

Soften cheese and beat well with Amaretto. Form into a ball and stud with almonds in porcupine fashion. Chill.
   Note: Excellent for dessert with grapes, apples and pear wedges.

Old Fashioned Custard Cake

8-10 servings

- 1 tablespoon gelatin
- ¾ cup orange juice
- ¼ cup flour
- 1 cup sugar
- ¼ teaspoon salt
- 2 cups milk
- 3 egg yolks
- 1 tablespoon grated orange rind
- 3 egg whites
- 3 tablespoons sugar
  angel or sponge cake
- ½ pint heavy cream, whipped
  berries or mandarin oranges
    for garnish

Dissolve gelatin and orange juice. Cook flour, sugar, salt and milk in double boiler, stirring until thickened. While hot, add gelatin mixture, egg yolks and orange rind. Cool. Beat egg whites until stiff. Add 3 tablespoons sugar. Fold into custard. Break cake into bite size pieces. Layer with custard in greased mold or angel food pan. Refrigerate at least 12 hours. Unmold. Ice with unsweetened whipped cream. Garnish with berries or mandarin oranges.

Note: Very light.

Brandy Alexander Souffle

8 servings

- 2 envelopes unflavored gelatin
- 2 cups cold water
- 1 cup sugar
- 4 eggs, separated
- 1 8-ounce package cream
    cheese
- 3 tablespoons creme de cocoa
- 3 tablespoons brandy
- 1 cup whipping cream, whipped
    chocolate shavings, cherries,
      etc. for garnish

Soften gelatin in 1 cup water. Stir over low heat until dissolved. Add remaining water. Remove from heat and blend in ¾ cup sugar and beaten egg yolks. Return to heat and cook 2 to 3 minutes or until slightly thickened. Gradually add to softened cream cheese, mixing until blended. Stir in creme de cocoa and brandy. Chill until slightly thickened. Beat egg whites until soft peaks form. Gradually add remaining sugar, beating to stiff peaks. Fold egg whites and whipped cream into cream cheese mixture. Wrap a 3 inch collar of aluminum foil around the top of a 1½ quart souffle dish. Secure with tape. Pour mixture into dish. Chill until firm. Serve with a garnish.

Cold Lemon Souffle with Raspberry Sauce

10 servings

1	**tablespoon unflavored gelatin**
¼	**cup cold water**
5	**eggs, separated**
¾	**cup fresh lemon juice**
2	**teaspoons freshly grated lemon rind**
1½	**cups sugar**
1	**cup whipping cream**

Sprinkle gelatin over cold water to soften. Mix egg yolks with lemon juice and rind and ¾ cup sugar. Place in top of double boiler and cook, stirring constantly until lemon mixture is slightly thickened, about 8 minutes. Remove from heat and stir in gelatin until dissolved. Chill 30 to 40 minutes. Beat egg whites until stiff, gradually adding the remaining ¾ cup sugar. Whip cream until stiff. Fold egg whites and whipped cream into the yolk mixture until no white streaks remain. Pour into a 2 quart souffle dish and chill at least 4 hours. Serve with raspberry sauce or wine sauce.

Raspberry Sauce:
2	**packages frozen raspberries**
2	**tablespoons Cointreau**

Defrost raspberries and puree in blender until smooth. Strain through a sieve and add Cointreau. Chill.

Wine Sauce:
½	**cup sugar**
3	**teaspoons cornstarch**
½	**cup water**
1	**tablespoon fresh lemon juice**
1	**teaspoon freshly grated lemon rind**
2	**tablespoons butter**
½	**cup dry white wine**

In a small saucepan mix the sugar and cornstarch. Stir in water, lemon juice and lemon rind until smooth. Add butter. Bring to a boil, lower heat and cook until thickened. Remove from heat. Add wine and chill, stirring occasionally.

Fresh Apple Mousse

6-8 servings

4	**Jonathan or Winesap apples**
½	**cup sugar**
½	**cup water**
½	**teaspoon vanilla extract**
½	**pint whipping cream**
1	**tablespoon sugar**
1	**teaspoon vanilla extract**
1	**cup crushed peanut brittle**

Pare and core apples. Cut into ¼ inch slices. Combine sugar, water and ½ teaspoon vanilla in pan. Bring to a slow boil. Add apple slices and simmer 5 minutes. Remove from syrup. Cool. Whip cream, add sugar and 1 teaspoon vanilla. Fold apple slices into whipped cream carefully. In a glass serving bowl, place half the apple and cream mixture and sprinkle generously with crushed peanut brittle. Repeat the layers. Chill several hours before serving.

Brandied Orange Ice

4-6 servings

1   2-inch square orange peel
4   cups freshly squeezed
        orange juice
1   cup sugar
2   tablespoons apricot brandy
        or Grand Marnier
    juice of 1 lemon

With the metal blade of food processor in place, put orange peel, 1 cup orange juice, sugar, apricot brandy and lemon juice into feed tube. Process until mixed, about 15 seconds. Add processed ingredients to remaining 3 cups orange juice and mix well. Pour into 2 ice cube trays and freeze. Just before serving, with the metal blade in place, add frozen cubes, 1 tray at a time, to feed tube of food processor. Process, turning on and off rapidly, until a fine ice, free of all lumps, forms—about 2 to 3 minutes. Serve immediately.

Lemon Ice Cream

6-8 servings

¾   cup sugar
1   cup milk
¼   cup fresh lemon juice
1   cup whipping cream, whipped
        grated lemon rind, chocolate
        curls or frosted mint leaf
        for garnish

Dissolve sugar in milk and add lemon juice. Freeze for 1 hour, or until thick. Fold in whipped cream and freeze in 2 ice trays. Remove from freezer 15 minutes before serving. Garnish.
    Note: Sweet and light!

Orange Cream Sherbet

4 servings

1   cup heavy cream
2   slices orange rind, ½ × 3
        inches, white part removed
⅓   cup fresh orange juice
½   cup sugar
¼   teaspoon salt

Put all ingredients in blender and process until thick. Pour into freezer container and freeze until firm.

Strawberry Mousse Parfaits

8-10 servings

Mousse:

4	**cups ripe strawberries**
1	**cup sugar**
¼	**cup water**
	pinch of cream of tartar
6	**egg yolks**
¼	**cup Kirsch**
1	**cup whipping cream**

Sauce:

1	**cup strawberries**
1	**cup raspberries**
½	**cup sugar**
1	**cup strawberries sliced**
2 - 4	**tablespoons Kirsch**

Puree strawberries through a sieve and set aside. In a heavy saucepan combine sugar, water and cream of tartar. Cover, bring to a boil and cook until sugar is dissolved. Add strawberry puree and cook to 218 to 220 degrees. In a bowl, beat egg yolks well, then gradually pour in strawberry syrup and beat the mixture until it is cool. Add Kirsch. In another bowl whip cream to hold soft peaks and fold gently into the strawberry mixture and chill, covered.

Put strawberries, raspberries and sugar into blender and blend for 25 seconds. Transfer the puree to a saucepan, add strawberry slices, bring to a boil and simmer 6 minutes. With a slotted spoon, transfer strawberry slices to a bowl. Continue to cook puree until thickened. Cool slightly, then add Kirsch. Pour mixture over berries in bowl, cover and chill.

To assemble, spoon a layer of strawberry-raspberry sauce into each of 8 to 10 large parfait glasses. Fill ⅓ full with strawberry mousse. Add more sauce, then a scoop of vanilla ice cream. Continue to layer in this manner, ending with ice cream. Freeze for at least 4 hours before serving.

Note: Frozen berries can be used when fresh are not available.

Anytime of Year "Watermelon"

½	**gallon green ice cream**
½	**gallon red or pink ice cream**
6	**ounces chocolate chips**

Line a bowl with softened green ice cream (about 1 inch thick). Soften pink or red ice cream and fold in chocolate chips. Pour into the bowl and freeze. To serve, unmold and slice.

Note: Lime ice and raspberry ice or pistachio and peppermint ice creams are just 2 ideas!

COLORADO CACHE COLORADO CACHE COLORADO CACHE COLORADO CACHE COLORADO CACHE COLORADO CACHE COLORADO CACHE COLORADO CACHE COLORADO

Scrumptious Mocha Ice Cream Dessert

25 servings

24	Oreo or Hydrox chocolate cream sandwich cookies, crushed
⅓	cup butter, melted
½	gallon coffee ice cream
3	ounces unsweetened chocolate
2	tablespoons butter or margarine
1	cup sugar
	dash of salt
2	5½ to 6 ounce cans evaporated milk
½	teaspoon vanilla extract
1½	cups heavy cream, whipped
1½	ounce Kahlua liqueur
	powdered sugar to taste
½ - ¾	cup chopped nuts

Combine cookie crumbs and butter and press into the bottom of a buttered 9 × 13 inch pan. Refrigerate. When chilled, spoon on softened ice cream and freeze. Melt chocolate and butter. Add sugar, salt and milk. Bring to a boil stirring until thickened. Remove from heat and add vanilla. Chill and spread on top of ice cream. Freeze. Whip cream. Add Kahlua and powdered sugar to taste. Spread over chocolate layer and sprinkle top with chopped nuts. Freeze.

Variation: Excellent with peppermint stick ice cream, garnished with cookie crumbs or shavings of semi-sweet chocolate.

Ice Cream Pie with Raisin Sauce

6-8 servings

Crust:

1	egg white
¼	teaspoon salt
¼	cup sugar
1	cup chopped nuts

Filling:

1	pint coffee ice cream
1	pint vanilla ice cream

Sauce:

3	tablespoons butter
1	cup brown sugar, packed
½	cup half and half
½	cup golden raisins
1	teaspoon vanilla extract

Beat egg white and salt until frothy. Add sugar slowly, beating until stiff. Fold in nuts. Spread on bottom and sides of greased 9 inch pie pan and prick with fork. Bake at 400 degrees for 10 to 12 minutes.

Spread softened coffee ice cream over cooled crust for first layer and softened vanilla ice cream for second layer. Freeze after each layer.

Heat butter and sugar until sugar is dissolved. Slowly stir in cream. Heat for several minutes, then add raisins and vanilla. Sauce may be prepared ahead and refrigerated, covered. Warm to room temperature and serve over pie.

Note: Sauce may be heated slightly, if desired.

Raspberry Boccone Dolce

8-10 servings

3	**cups whipping cream**
⅓	**cup powdered sugar**

The night before serving, whip cream until stiff. Gradually add ⅓ cup sugar and beat until quite stiff. Line a strainer or collander with a double layer of damp cheesecloth. Pour whipped cream into strainer which has been placed in a bowl. Cover and refrigerate overnight. This drains liquid which usually accumulates when whipped cream stands, thus making a more stable dessert.

Meringues:

4	**egg whites at room temperature**
	pinch of salt
¼	**teaspoon cream of tartar**
1	**cup sugar**

Beat egg whites until frothy. Add salt and cream of tartar, beating until stiff. Gradually add sugar continuing to beat until the meringue is stiff and glossy. Line cookie sheets with brown paper and trace 3 circles, each 8 or 9 inches in diameter. Spread the meringue evenly over the circles and bake at 250 degrees for 35 to 50 minutes, or until the meringues are pale gold and still pliable. Remove from the oven and carefully peel the paper from the bottom. Place on cake racks to dry. The meringues may be made the night before.

6	**ounces semi-sweet chocolate chips**
3	**tablespoons water**
2	**10-ounce packages frozen raspberries, thawed and well drained (also may use 1 quart fresh straw-berries, sliced, reserving some whole ones for garnish)**

Melt the chocolate bits with water over hot water. To assemble, place a meringue layer on serving plate and spread with a thin coating of melted chocolate. Then spread a layer about ¾ inch thick of the whipped cream and top this with a layer of berries. Put a second layer of meringue on top, spread with chocolate, whipped cream and berries; then top with third layer of meringue. Frost sides and top smoothly with remaining whipped cream. Decorate top with melted chocolate, whole berries or piped whipped cream. Refrigerate 2 hours before serving.

Note: If whipped cream and meringues are prepared the night before, assemble the day of use. However, the dessert may all be made the same day it will be used (omitting the straining of the whipped cream).

Chocolate Cinnamon Cloud

8-10 servings

2 **egg whites at room temperature**
¼ **teaspoon salt**
½ **teaspoon white vinegar**
½ **cup sugar**
¼ **teaspoon ground cinnamon**
1 **6-ounce package chocolate chips**
2 **egg yolks, beaten**
¼ **cup water**
1 **cup whipping cream, whipped**
¼ **cup sugar**
¼ **teaspoon ground cinnamon**

Cover a cookie sheet with heavy brown paper. Draw an 8 inch circle on the paper. Beat egg whites, salt and vinegar together until soft peaks are formed. Gradually add ½ cup sugar and ¼ teaspoon cinnamon. Beat until very stiff. Spread mixture on paper, covering the circle. The meringue should be ½ inch high in the center and 1¾ inches high on sides. Bake in a preheated oven at 275 degrees for 1 hour. Turn off heat and leave meringue in oven for 2 hours longer. Peel off paper and place on a serving plate. Melt chocolate chips over water. Cool slightly and spread 2 tablespoons chocolate over the meringue. Chill. Add egg yolks and water to remaining chocolate. Mix well. Refrigerate until thickened. Whip cream until soft peaks form. Gradually add the remaining ¼ cup of sugar and ¼ teaspoon cinnamon. Whip cream until stiff. Spread ½ of whipped cream over chocolate on meringue. Fold remaining whipped cream into thickened chocolate mixture. Spoon this mixture on top of the whipped cream layer. Refrigerate several hours. Cut in pie-shaped servings.

Lemon Angel Pie

6-8 servings

Meringue Shell:
4 **egg whites**
1 **teaspoon cream of tartar**
  pinch of salt
1 **cup sugar**

Filling:
4 **egg yolks**
½ **cup sugar**
  juice of 1½ lemons
1 **tablespoon grated lemon rind**
2 **cups whipping cream**
½ **cup powdered sugar**
½ **cup toasted coconut**

Beat egg whites until foamy, add cream of tartar and beat until very stiff. Add salt, then fold in sugar slowly and carefully. Line a buttered 9 inch pan with meringue, building the sides a little thicker than the bottom. Bake in a slow oven, 275 to 300 degrees, for about 1 hour. Cool.

To make filling, beat egg yolks until light, add sugar, lemon juice and rind. Cook in double boiler until very thick. Cool. Whip cream until stiff and sweeten with powdered sugar. Put a light layer of whipped cream over meringue shell. Then spread on the cooled lemon filling. Follow with remaining whipped cream. Sprinkle with coconut. Refrigerate at least 3 hours or overnight.
  Note: Freezes well for later use. Thaw in refrigerator.

Luscious Lemon Meringue Torte

Meringues:
- 4 **egg whites at room temperature**
- 1 **cup sugar**
- ½ **teaspoon vanilla extract**

Filling:
- 4 **egg yolks**
- ½ **cup sugar**
- 3 **tablespoons fresh lemon juice**
- 2 **teaspoons grated lemon rind**
- ½ **pint whipping cream**
- ¼ **cup sugar**
- 2 **teaspoons vanilla extract whipped cream, strawberries or cherries for garnish (optional)**

8-12 servings

Cover cookie sheets with brown paper and draw 3 8-inch circles. Beat egg whites until stiff, adding sugar very slowly while beating constantly. Whip until stiff and sugar is dissolved. Fold in vanilla. Spoon onto circles and level out to edges with knife. Bake at 250 degrees approximately 60 minutes. Remove from paper before completely cool. Meringues may be baked the day ahead.

Beat egg yolks with ½ cup sugar until smooth. Add lemon juice and rind. Cook over gently boiling water, stirring constantly until smooth and thick as mayonnaise. Cool. Whip cream until it holds stiff peaks. Gradually add ¼ cup sugar and vanilla. Fold into lemon mixture. Spread between meringue layers and refrigerate several hours. Garnish with whipped cream and strawberries or cherries.

Note: May assemble and freeze. Keeps frozen for several weeks. Thaw before serving.

Cheesecake Supreme

Crust:
- 1¼ **cups graham cracker crumbs**
- ⅓ **cup brown sugar**
- ¼ **cup butter, melted**

Filling:
- 1 **pound cream cheese**
- ¾ **cup sugar**
- 5 **eggs**
- 1 **teaspoon vanilla extract**
- ¼ **teaspoon almond extract**

10-12 servings

Mix together the crust ingredients and press into a 9 inch springform pan. Bake at 350 degrees for 12 minutes.

Cream the cheese well, gradually beating in sugar. Add eggs one at a time, beating well after each addition. Add vanilla and almond extracts. Pour into crust and bake 35 minutes. Remove from oven.

Topping:

- 1½ cups sour cream
- ½ cup sugar
- 1 teaspoon vanilla extract

Mix topping and spread on "cake." Bake 5 minutes longer. Cool and chill.

Lemon Cheesecake

Crust:

- 2¼ cups graham cracker crumbs (about 25 single crackers, crushed)
- ¼ cup sugar
- 6 tablespoons melted butter or margarine

12-16 servings

Combine cracker crumbs, sugar and butter. Press into sides of an 11 to 12 inch springform pan. Bake at 350 degrees for 5 minutes. Cool before adding filling.

Filling:

- 3 8-ounce packages cream cheese, softened for 8 hours
- 3 eggs
- 1⅓ cups sugar
- 3 tablespoons lemon juice
- 2 teaspoons vanilla extract
- 1 teaspoon grated lemon rind
- 1 pint sour cream
- 3 tablespoons sugar

Glaze:

- ½ cup sugar
- 1 tablespoon plus 1 teaspoon cornstarch
- ½ cup water
- 2 tablespoons lemon juice

Beat cream cheese with electric mixer at high speed until completely smooth. Add eggs, one at a time, beating until smooth after each addition. Continue to beat, gradually adding 1⅓ cups sugar, then lemon juice and 1 teaspoon vanilla. Stir in lemon rind. Pour into cooled crust and bake at 350 degrees for 35 minutes. Blend sour cream with remaining 1 teaspoon vanilla and 3 tablespoons sugar. Set in warm place. Remove cake from oven. Gently spread sour cream over top of cake. Return to oven and bake about 12 minutes. Cool on rack for 30 minutes. Refrigerate until topping is cool but not completely chilled. Make glaze by combining sugar and cornstarch, blending in water and lemon juice until smooth. Bring to a boil, stirring constantly, until thickened. Cook 3 minutes. Chill until cool but not set. Spread top of cheesecake with lemon glaze. Chill several hours or overnight. Can also be frozen.

Petite Cheesecakes

18-22 servings

3 8-ounce packages cream
   cheese
1 cup sugar
5 eggs
1 teaspoon vanilla extract
2 cups sour cream
⅓ cup sugar
½ teaspoon vanilla extract
   any fresh fruit, such as
     strawberries or raspberries
     for topping

Cream until fluffy the cream cheese and 1 cup sugar. Add eggs and 1 teaspoon vanilla. Bake at 300 degrees for 40 minutes in paper lined muffin tins (⅔ full). Remove from oven and allow to "sink in". Frost with sour cream mixed with ⅓ cup sugar and vanilla. Return to oven for 5 minutes. Cool and freeze, muffin tin and all. When ready to serve, thaw at room temperature for about 30 minutes. Top with fruit.

Dessert Crepe Batter

**30 5-inch or
25 6-inch crepes**

4 eggs
1 cup light cream
1 cup club soda
3 tablespoons melted butter
¼ teaspoon salt
1 tablespoon sugar
1 cup unsifted all-purpose flour
½ teaspoon vanilla extract or
   citrus rind
   clarified butter for cooking
     crepes (see Index)

In a blender, combine eggs and cream and mix for a few seconds. Add soda, butter, salt, sugar and flour. Blend until very smooth. Scrape down sides of blender. Mix again for a few seconds until smooth. Let stand 1 hour, covered. Add flavorings just before cooking and stir well. Brush crepe pan with a little clarified butter and heat. To test for proper temperature, drop a bit of batter into the pan. If it browns quickly the pan is hot enough. Pour 2 to 3 tablespoons batter into pan and tilt so that the batter covers the bottom evenly. This should be just a thin film. Pour off excess. Brown lightly on one side, turn with a spatula and brown on the other side. If you plan to refrigerate or freeze crepes, place waxed paper between crepes, then wrap in foil. Can refrigerate for 4 to 5 days or freeze. To defrost, place the crepes, still wrapped in foil, in a 250 degree oven for 25 to 35 minutes. Separate carefully. Use immediately.

Lemon Crepes

8 servings

16 crepes (see index)
½ cup superfine granulated sugar
2 teaspoons grated lemon peel
¾ cup butter
¼ cup Cognac
¼ cup Cointreau or other orange flavored liqueur
2 tablespoons lemon juice
1½ ounces blanched, sliced almonds

Fold the crepes in half and arrange them in 1 layer, overlapping slightly, in a buttered shallow flameproof baking dish. Sprinkle crepes with sugar and grated lemon peel, mixed, and dot them with 2 tablespoons of the butter. Broil the crepes about 5 inches from heat until the sugar is melted and bubbling. In a saucepan melt the remaining butter, add the Cognac, Cointreau and lemon juice and heat, stirring until blended. Sprinkle the almonds over crepes and serve with the sauce.

Crepes Kahlua

**16 crepes or
8 servings**

¾ cup butter
¼ cup sugar
¾ cup almond macaroon crumbs or commercial coconut macaroons
½ cup Kahlua or other coffee liqueur
16 crepes
¼ cup butter
1 pint whipping cream, whipped
2 tablespoons Kahlua

Make filling by creaming first 4 ingredients. Spead thin layer of mixture over entire crepe and roll. Repeat until all crepes are used. At serving time, heat crepes in ¼ cup butter in a skillet. Serve with whipped cream flavored with 2 tablespoons Kahlua.

Crepes Fraises

Crepes:
- 2 **cups flour**
- 2 **tablespoons powdered sugar**
  dash of salt
- 5 **eggs**
- 2 **cups milk**
- 2 **tablespoons brandy**
  butter

Filling:
- 12 **ounces cream cheese,**
  softened
- ¼ **cup sugar**
- 3 **tablespoons fresh lemon juice**

Sauce:
- 2 **cups strawberries (frozen or**
  fresh sliced and sugared)
- 1 **tablespoon lemon juice**
- ¼ **cup slivered almonds**

8 servings

Sift flour, measure and then sift again with sugar and salt. Beat eggs and add dry ingredients and stir until smooth. Gradually add milk and brandy. Beat until smooth. Heat and butter pan for crepes. Pour in 2 tablespoons batter and tilt pan to spread evenly. Brown quckly on each side. Lay crepes on waxed paper to cool.

Beat cream cheese, sugar and 3 tablespoons lemon juice until fluffy. Put 2 tablespoons of this mixture on each crepe and roll. Place in a shallow baking pan and chill until serving time, then heat in a hot oven (400 degrees) just until crepes are heated through. Combine strawberries, 1 tablespoon lemon juice and almonds. Spoon over hot crepes and serve at once.

Note: This dish seems to be best if crepes are hot and strawberry topping is refrigerated.

Apricot Nut Frosting

- 12 **ounces cream cheese,**
  softened
- ¼ **cup honey**
- ½ **cup chopped dried apricots**
- ¼ **cup chopped walnuts**

Frosting for a single
9 × 13 inch cake

Cream the cream cheese until fluffy. Blend in honey, apricots and walnuts.

Note: Particularly good on carrot cake and spice cake.

Hot Fudge Sauce

1 pint

½   **cup cocoa**
1   **cup sour cream**
1½   **cups sugar**
½   **teaspoon vanilla extract**

Combine all ingredients in a double boiler and cook over boiling water for about an hour, stirring occasionally. This sauce will be thick and will keep for several weeks in refrigerator.

Fabulous Chocolate Frosting

Frosting for 2-layer cake

4   **ounces unsweetened chocolate**
2   **egg whites**
1½   **cups powdered sugar**
1   **cup butter**

Melt chocolate in double boiler. Set aside. Beat egg whites until stiff, then slowly add powdered sugar while beating. Mixture will be thin. In another bowl beat butter until soft, then slowly add egg white mixture, beating constantly. Add chocolate and beat thoroughly.

Note: Perfect for refrigerated or frozen cakes, but let sit a few minutes before serving.

Holiday Rum and Raisin Sauce

6-8 servings

½   **cup rum**
½   **cup seedless raisins**
½   **cup sugar**
¼   **cup water**
1   **stick cinnamon**
¼   **teaspoon vanilla extract**
1   **tablespoon freshly grated lemon peel**
1   **tablespoon freshly grated orange peel**
½   **cup pecan pieces**

Pour rum over raisins and let stand until raisins are puffed (several hours). Mix sugar, water, cinnamon and boil 2 minutes. Discard cinnamon, add raisins and rum. Cook 5 minutes. Add vanilla. Remove from heat and add lemon and orange peels and nuts. Serve warm over ice cream or pound cake.

Strawberry Cordials (Chocolate Covered Strawberries)

1½ pints covered berries

12 ounces semi-sweet
     chocolate chips
 1 ounce paraffin
 2 tablespoons butter
½ cup butter
 3 cups powdered sugar
 1 tablespoon milk
1½ pints fresh strawberries

Melt the chocolate chips, paraffin, and 2 tablespoons butter in the top of a double boiler while preparing the following. Cream ½ cup butter and slowly add powdered sugar. Add milk and continue to mix until smooth. "Dough" will be stiff. Roll out to about 1/8 inch thickness. Cut into squares the size necessary to cover berries. Place berry in center and gently bring dough around the berry to cover it completely. Dip the dough-covered strawberry into the melted chocolate mixture with a toothpick. Cover the candy completely with chocolate and place on a foil-lined cookie sheet. Remove the toothpick, dip it into the chocolate, and add a drop of chocolate where the toothpick left a hole. Chill. Remove from foil and store covered in the refrigerator. The strawberries will keep for 1 to 2 days.

Peanut Butter Candy Cups

About 4 dozen

⅓ pound graham cracker crumbs
     (11 double graham crackers,
     crushed)
½ cup butter, melted
½ cup margarine, melted
 1 cup peanut butter
 1 pound powdered sugar
     (4 cups)
 1 12-ounce package chocolate
     chips, melted over hot water

Combine first 5 ingredients until smooth. Press into a buttered 9 × 13 inch pan. Spread melted chocolate chips over mixture. Refrigerate until firm. Warm slightly at room temperature and cut into squares. (Chocolate will not crack when slightly warm.)

Note: You may make half a recipe using a 9 × 9 inch pan.

Peanut Butter Fudge

About 50 pieces

2	**cups sugar**
¼	**cup margarine**
½	**cup milk**
2½	**tablespoons marshmallow creme**
1	**cup peanut butter**
¾	**teaspoon vanilla extract**

Mix sugar, margarine and milk. Bring to a boil and cook for 3 minutes. Remove from stove and stir in marshmallow creme, peanut butter and vanilla. Pour into buttered 8 × 8 inch pan and cool.

English Toffee

About 60 pieces

1	**cup butter (do not substitute)**
1	**cup sugar**
3	**tablespoons water**
1	**teaspoon vanilla extract**
⅔	**cup ground or finely chopped almonds or pecans**
4	**1.05-ounce Hershey bars**

Cook butter, sugar, water and vanilla over medium heat stirring constantly until golden brown. It may smoke, but don't worry. Put ⅓ cup pecans or almonds in bottom of 9 × 9 inch pan. Pour "batter" on top of nuts. Place Hershey bars on top. Spread evenly when chocolate softens. Sprinkle top with remaining ⅓ cup almonds or pecans. When completely cool, break into pieces.

Fresh Pineapple with Grand Marnier

4 servings

1	**ripe, fresh pineapple**
½	**cup Grand Marnier**

Cut the pineapple lengthwise into quarters, leaving leaves attached. Cut fruit from skin into bite-sized sections, but leave it in the shells to serve. With a pastry brush, coat fruit sections with Grand Marnier. Chill before serving.

DENVER SKYLINE

Homemade Mustards

Basic Mustard:
- ¼ cup dry mustard
- ¼ cup white wine vinegar
- ⅓ cup dry white wine
- 1 tablespoon sugar
- ½ teaspoon salt
- 3 egg yolks

1 cup

Blend all ingredients except egg yolks and let stand 2 hours. Beat egg yolks into mixture. Cook, stirring constantly, over hot (not boiling) water until slightly thickened, about 5 minutes. Cover and store in refrigerator for up to a month.

Lime Mustard:
- ¾ teaspoon grated lime peel
- 1½ teaspoons lime juice

When adding egg yolks, also add lime peel and juice and follow basic mustard recipe. Serve with lamb, chicken or fish.

Tarragon Mustard:
- ½ teaspoon crushed tarragon

When adding egg yolks, also add tarragon and follow basic mustard recipe. Serve with lamb, chicken, shrimp or steaks.

Spicy Mustard:
- ¼ teaspoon ground turmeric
- ¼ teaspoon ground cloves

When adding egg yolks, also add turmeric and cloves and follow basic mustard recipe. Serve with ham, hamburgers or hot dogs.

Tomato Mustard:
- 1 teaspoon paprika
- 1 tablespoon chopped pimento
- ½ cup tomato paste

When adding egg yolks, also add paprika, pimento and tomato paste and follow basic mustard recipe. Serve with seafood, hamburgers, hot dogs or ham.

Dijon Mustard:
- 2 cups dry white wine
- 1 cup chopped onion
- 2 cloves garlic, minced
- 4 ounces dry mustard
- 2 tablespoons honey
- 1 tablespoon vegetable oil
- 2 teaspoons salt
- few drops of Tabasco sauce

2 cups

Combine wine, onion and garlic. Heat to boiling. Lower heat and simmer 5 minutes. Pour mixture into bowl and cool. Strain wine mixture into dry mustard in a small saucepan, beating until very smooth. Add remaining ingredients. Heat slowly, stirring constantly until mixture thickens. Cool. Pour into a non-metal container and cover. Chill at least 2 days to blend flavors.

Apple-Sage Jelly

4 cups

2½ **cups apple juice**
3½ **cups sugar**
6 **tablespoons liquid fruit pectin**
1½ **teaspoons powdered sage (or small sprigs of fresh sage)**

In a large saucepan bring apple juice and sugar to a boil. Stir constantly until sugar is dissolved. Add pectin and boil one more minute, stirring constantly. Remove from heat and skim off any foam. Stir in sage and pour into hot, sterilized jelly jars and seal with paraffin.

Note: If using fresh sage, place a sprig in each jar before adding jelly. Serve with pork or ham.

Brandied Apricot Jelly

4 cups

1½ **cups apricot nectar**
3½ **cups sugar**
¾ **cup brandy**
2 **tablespoons fresh lemon juice**
6 **tablespoons liquid fruit pectin**

Combine apricot nectar, sugar, brandy and lemon juice in a saucepan. Bring to a boil and cook for 2 minutes, stirring constantly. Remove from heat and stir in pectin. Mix well, and skim off any foam. Pour jelly into sterilized jars and seal with paraffin.

Note: Good served with fried or roast chicken.

Pepper Jelly

6 cups

1½ **cups cider vinegar**
5 **cups sugar**
1½ **cups chopped bell peppers, red or green**
1½ **tablespoons dried, crushed red pepper**
1 **6-ounce bottle liquid fruit pectin**
  a few drops green or red food coloring

In a saucepan boil vinegar and sugar. Add peppers. Boil again, stirring constantly. Remove from heat and stir in fruit pectin and food coloring. Pour into hot sterilized jars and seal with paraffin.

Pineapple-Orange Wine Jelly

4 cups

3¼ cups sugar
1¼ cups white wine
6 tablespoons liquid fruit pectin
1 6-ounce can frozen pineapple-orange juice concentrate, thawed

Combine sugar and wine in a saucepan. Bring to a boil and cook for 1 minute, stirring constantly. Remove from heat and stir in pectin and juice. Mix well. Pour jelly into hot sterilized jars and seal with paraffin.

Port Wine Jelly

4 cups

2 cups Port
3 cups sugar
½ teaspoon rosemary
6 tablespoons liquid fruit pectin

Bring wine, sugar and rosemary to a boil in a saucepan. Stir constantly until sugar is dissolved. Strain through cheesecloth. Add pectin and boil 1 more minute, stirring constantly. Remove from heat and skim off any foam. Pour jelly into hot sterilized jars and seal with paraffin.
Note: Great served with duck and game!

Sangre de Cristo Jelly

4 cups

2 cups Burgundy
3 cups sugar
6 tablespoons liquid fruit pectin

In a saucepan bring wine and sugar to a boil. Stir constantly until sugar is dissolved. Add pectin and boil for 1 more minute, stirring constantly. Remove from heat and skim off any foam. Pour jelly into sterilized jars and seal with paraffin.

Champagne Jelly

4 cups

2 cups pink champagne
3 cups sugar
6 tablespoons liquid fruit pectin

Bring champagne and sugar to a boil in a saucepan. Stir constantly until the sugar is dissolved. Add pectin and boil for 1 more minute, stirring constantly. Remove from heat and skim off any foam. Pour jelly into sterilized jars and seal with paraffin.

Creme de Menthe Jelly

4 cups

2½ cups sugar
1 cup green creme de menthe
1 cup water
6 tablespoons liquid fruit pectin
mint sprigs

Bring sugar, creme de menthe and water to a boil in a saucepan. Stir constantly until sugar is dissolved. Add pectin and boil 1 more minute, stirring constantly. Remove from heat and skim off any foam. Plunge sprigs of mint into boiling water for 1 minute and place a sprig in each sterilized jelly jar. Pour jelly into jars. Seal with paraffin.

Note: Good served with lamb or as an ice cream topping.

Tabasco Jelly

4 cups

1 cup water
⅓ cup lemon juice
2 teaspoons Tabasco sauce
3 cups sugar
6 tablespoons liquid fruit pectin
red or green food coloring

In a saucepan combine water, lemon juice, Tabasco and sugar. Bring to a boil, stirring constantly. Add fruit pectin and food coloring. Stir until mixture comes to a full, rolling boil. Boil 30 seconds more. Skim off foam. Pour into hot, sterilized jars. Seal with paraffin.

Note: Good with turkey, roast beef or game.

Western Slope Spiced Peach Jam

3 pints

4 cups peeled and finely chopped peaches
2 tablespoons fresh lemon juice
½ teaspoon ground cloves
½ teaspoon ground allspice
½ teaspoon ground cinnamon
5½ cups sugar
6 tablespoons liquid fruit pectin

In a large pot mix peaches with spices and bring to a boil. Add sugar and boil hard for 1 minute. Remove from heat and add pectin. Stir well and skim off foam. Pour into hot sterilized jars and seal with paraffin.

Note: For a wonderful ice cream topping, mix 1 tablespoon rum with each ½ cup jam.

Spiced Cranberries

4 cups

1 pound cranberries
2 cups sugar
2 tablespoons white vinegar
1 tablespoon ground cinnamon

Wash cranberries, do not dry! Cook cranberries and sugar over low heat in a saucepan until sugar dissolves. Add vinegar and cinnamon.

Fried Apples

6 servings

10 - 12 small apples, peeled, cored
 and sliced
 ¾ cup white sugar
 ½ cup brown sugar, packed
 ½ teaspoon salt
 1 rounded teaspoon ground
 cinnamon
 ½ cup butter

Mix white and brown sugars, salt and cinnamon and pour over apples. Stir so that apples are well covered. Melt butter in electric fry pan and add apples. Cover and cook at 300 degrees for about 5 minutes. Reduce heat to 280 degrees and cook for about 15 minutes more. Turn apples occasionally. Remove cover the last 5 to 10 minutes. Can be wrapped in heavy duty foil and taken to campsite.

Note: Great with pork or ham.

Baked Applesauce

5 cups

 5 pounds tart apples, peeled,
 cored and sliced
 1 10-ounce jar currant jelly
 ⅓ cup sugar
 ⅔ cup water
 ⅓ cup lemon juice
 dash of ground nutmeg

Place apples in casserole. Combine jelly, sugar and water. Heat until jelly is partially melted. Remove from heat. Stir in lemon juice and nutmeg. Pour over apples. Cover and bake at 350 degrees for 1¼ hours, or until apples are soft.

Cranberry-Orange Chutney

6 cups

 4 medium oranges
 ½ cup orange juice
 1 pound fresh cranberries
 2 cups sugar
 ¼ cup crystallized ginger, diced
 ½ teaspoon Tabasco sauce
 1 whole cinnamon stick
 1 medium clove garlic, peeled
 ¾ teaspoon curry powder
 ¾ cup raisins

Remove outer rind from oranges to make ¼ cup thin slivers. Remove all of membrane and remaining rind from oranges; discard. Cut oranges cross-wise in slices about ¼ inch thick. Cut slices in quarters. Combine orange rind, juice, cranberries, sugar, diced ginger, Tabasco, cinnamon, garlic, curry and raisins. In a saucepan, cook over moderate heat, stirring until sugar dissolves and cranberries pop open. Remove from heat. Discard cinnamon and garlic. Add oranges and mix lightly. Serve hot or cold. Store in refrigerator for up to 6 weeks or seal in sterilized jars.

Note: Serve with chicken, game or pork.

COLORADO CACHE COLORADO CACHE COLORADO CACHE COLORADO CACHE COLORADO CACHE COLORADO CACHE COLORADO CACHE COLORADO

Pear Chutney

3 quarts

Combine all ingredients in a large pot. Simmer 2½ hours. Spoon into hot sterilized jars and seal immediately.

5	cups peeled, cored and chopped hard pears
2	ripe tomatoes, peeled and chopped
3	apples, peeled, cored and chopped
3	peaches, peeled, pitted and chopped
2	lemons, seeded and chopped
1	lime, seeded and chopped
1½	cups raisins
3 - 4	teaspoons crushed, dried red pepper
1	large garlic clove, minced
2	cups cider vinegar
3	cups brown sugar, firmly packed
½	cup crystallized ginger
1	teaspoon ground cinnamon
1	teaspoon ground cloves
¼	teaspoon ground nutmeg
¼	teaspoon ground allspice
1	tablespoon salt

Pepper Hash

6 quarts

Coarsely grind the vegetables together and cover with boiling water. Let stand for 30 minutes. Drain off the liquid and add vinegar, sugar and spices. Bring to a boil and cook until sugar dissolves. Ladle into hot sterilized jars and seal immediately.

12	green bell peppers
12	red bell peppers
14	large, white onions (or 9 yellow onions)
3	small, hot red peppers, minus seeds
3	pints cider vinegar
6	cups sugar
2	tablespoons uniodized salt (pickling or plain)
2	tablespoons mustard seed
1	tablespoon celery seed

Tomato Apple Chutney

12 pints

¼ cup whole, mixed pickling spices
6 pounds tomatoes, peeled and chopped
5 pounds apples, peeled, cored and chopped
3 cups seedless raisins
2 cups chopped onions
1 cup chopped green pepper
4 cups brown sugar, firmly packed
4 cups cider vinegar
4 teaspoons salt
2 teaspoons ground ginger

Place pickling spices in a cheesecloth bag. Combine with the other ingredients in a saucepan and bring to a boil. Simmer until thickened. Remove bag and pour into hot, sterilized jars and seal immediately.

Jezebel

5 cups

1 18-ounce jar apple jelly
1 18-ounce jar pineapple jelly (or peach-pineapple or apricot-pineapple)
2½ ounces horseradish
1 ounce dry mustard
1 tablespoon ground white pepper

Mix thoroughly and keep covered in the refrigerator.
    Note: Serve with ham or, for an appetizer, spoon over a cube of cream cheese and serve with crackers.

Pickled Green Chili

3 cups

3 7-ounce cans whole green chiles
½ cup sugar
½ cup cider vinegar
1 teaspoon dill seed
1 teaspoon salt
½ teaspoon mustard seed
1 clove garlic

Remove seeds from chiles and slice into 1½ inch long strips. Boil the remaining ingredients until the sugar is dissolved. Add chiles. Refrigerate for several hours. Drain and serve with crackers.

Zucchini Relish

4 quarts

12	cups coarsely ground zucchini, unpeeled
5	medium onions
1	green bell pepper
1	red bell pepper
5	tablespoons salt
3	cups sugar
2½	cups cider vinegar
2	tablespoons cornstarch
1	teaspoon mustard seed
1	teaspoon turmeric
2	tablespoons celery seed

Coarsely grind onions and peppers and mix with zucchini and salt. Let stand for 3 hours. Drain and rinse well. Make syrup of remaining ingredients, boiling until sugar dissolves and mixture thickens. Add to vegetables and cook 20 minutes. Ladle into hot sterilized jars and seal immediately.

Dilled Green Beans

7 pints

4	pounds young, whole green beans
5	cups white vinegar
5	cups water
½	cup salt

Add to each pint jar:

¼	teaspoon crushed, hot pepper
½	teaspoon mustard seed
1	garlic clove
½	teaspoon dill seed

Wash beans and pack vertically into hot sterilized jars. Add spices to each. Combine vinegar, water and salt. Heat to boiling and pour over beans. Seal immediately.

Note: Great in martinis or in a tossed salad.

Banana Jam

4 quarts

3	quarts sliced, medium-ripe bananas (12 to 14)
6	cups sugar
1½	cups orange juice
¾	cup lemon juice

Cook all ingredients in a saucepan over moderate heat until sugar is dissolved. Simmer until thick, about 15 minutes. Pour into hot, sterilized jars and seal with paraffin.

Green Tomato Sweet Pickles

8 pints

16 **cups sliced, green tomatoes**
¼ **cup pickling salt**
9 **cups water**
1½ **teaspoons powdered alum**
1 **tablespoon whole, mixed pickling spices**
½ **teaspoon ground cinnamon**
1 **tablespoon celery seed**
3 **cups cider vinegar**
4 **cups sugar**

Sprinkle tomatoes with salt and let stand overnight. Drain and pour 8 cups of boiling water mixed with alum over tomatoes. Let stand 20 minutes. Drain and cover with cold water. Drain again. Combine spices and tie in a cheese-cloth bag. Place in a saucepan and add vinegar, 1 cup water and sugar. Bring to a boil and pour over tomatoes. Let stand 24 hours. The second day, drain off syrup and bring it to a boil. Pour over tomatoes and let stand 24 hours. On the third day, bring tomatoes and syrup to a boil. Pack into hot steril-ized jars and seal immediately.

Zucchini-Cauliflower Pickles

7 pints

10 **cups thinly sliced, unpeeled zucchini**
2 **heads cauliflower, broken into buds**
2 **large onions, thinly sliced**
2½ **cups cider vinegar**
1½ **cups sugar**
1 **tablespoon salt**
2 **teaspoons dry mustard**
2 **teaspoons turmeric**
½ **teaspoon celery seed**
1/8 **teaspoon powdered alum**

Combine all ingredients. Bring to a boil and simmer 15 to 20 minutes, until the squash becomes semi-transparent. Pour into sterilized jars and seal.

Port Cranberry Sauce

4-6 servings

2 - 3 **cups fresh cranberries**
⅔ **cup water**
½ **cup sugar**
1 - 2 **tablespoons butter**
4 **tablespoons Port**

In a saucepan, simmer cranberries in water and sugar until they pop. Add butter and Port and chill well before serving.
Note: A mellow change from the familiar.

Dilled Zucchini Pickles

8 cups

- 6 **pounds unpeeled zucchini, thinly sliced**
- 2 **cups thinly sliced celery**
- 2 **cups chopped onions**
- ⅓ **cup salt**
  ice cubes
- 2 **cups sugar**
- 2 **tablespoons dill seed**
- 2 **cups white vinegar**
- 6 **halved garlic cloves**

Mix zucchini, celery, onions and salt. Place a layer of ice on top. Cover and let stand 3 hours. Drain well. Combine sugar, dill seed and vinegar and heat to boiling, stirring constantly. Stir in vegetables and heat to a rolling boil, stirring several times. Ladle into hot sterilized jars. Put 1 or 2 pieces of garlic in each jar and seal.

Curry Powder

⅓ cup

- 1 **tablespoon commercial curry powder**
- 1 **tablespoon ground turmeric**
- 2 **teaspoons ground cumin**
- 2 **teaspoons ground ginger**
- 2 **teaspoons ground coriander**
- 2 **teaspoon fennel seed, ground**

Mix all ingredients and store in an air-tight container.
Note: Fresh curry powder enhances any recipe calling for curry.

Chinese Five-Spice Powder

⅓ cup

- 2 **tablespoons whole, black peppercorns**
- 36 **whole cloves**
- 12 **inches of stick cinnamon**
- 2 **tablespoons fennel seed**
- 12 **whole star anise**

Put spices together into a blender and pulverize into a powder. Store in a cool place in an air-tight container.

Poultry Seasoning

¾ cup

rind of 2 lemons, thinly
    shredded
½ cup parsley flakes
1 tablespoon salt
1 tablespoon thyme
1 tablespoon marjoram
1 teaspoon freshly ground
    pepper

Spread rind between 2 sheets of paper towel and let dry. Combine with remaining ingredients and store in an air-tight container. Sprinkle on chicken or pork, or use in stuffing or in a basting sauce.

Salad Seasoning

1 cup

¾ cup grated Parmesan cheese
¼ cup parsley flakes
1 teaspoon garlic powder
½ teaspoon freshly ground
    pepper
1 teaspoon chopped chives
1 teaspoon bell pepper flakes
1 teaspoon basil
½ teaspoon salt

Combine ingredients and store in an air-tight container. Sprinkle on tossed green salad, sliced zucchini or cucumber-tomato salad.

Herbed Crouton Snacks

2 cups

⅓ cup butter or margarine
½ teaspoon rosemary, crushed
¼ teaspoon garlic salt
¼ teaspoon thyme
¼ teaspoon mace
2 cups spoon-size shredded
    wheat biscuits

Melt butter in a pan in a 400 degree oven. Add seasonings. Stir in shredded wheat. Toss until evenly coated. Toast in oven 15 minutes, stirring every 5 minutes.

COLORADO CACHE COLORADO CACHE COLORADO CACHE COLORADO CACHE COLORADO CACHE COLORADO CACHE COLORADO CACHE COLORADO CACHE COLORADO CACHE COLORADO

Sweetened Condensed Milk

3 cups

4   cups instant powdered milk
1   cup hot water
2   cups sugar
4   tablespoons margarine or
      butter, melted

Mix in blender and store in refrigerator.
    Note: Costs approximately ½ that of a commercial brand.

White Sauce Mix

5 cups

2⅔   cups powdered milk
1   cup butter or margarine
1½   cups flour
3   teaspoons salt

Blend ingredients with a pastry blender until they become the consistency of sand. Keep in a jar in the refrigerator. To make 1 cup of white sauce, add ½ cup mix to 1 cup water.

Raspberry or Strawberry Butter

4 cups

1   10-ounce package frozen
      raspberries, or strawberries
1   cup butter
2   cups powdered sugar

The fruit and butter should be at room temperature. Cream butter and sugar and add berries. Keep refrigerated.
    Note: A treat on pancakes, waffles, French toast or muffins.

Teriyaki Almonds

2 cups

2   cups blanched almonds
¼   cup butter or margarine
2   tablespoons soy sauce
2   tablespoons dry sherry
¼ - ½ teaspoon ground ginger
        garlic salt to taste

Spread almonds on an ungreased cookie sheet. Toast for 20 minutes at 300 degrees. Melt butter and add soy sauce, sherry and ginger. Pour over almonds. Toast, stirring occasionally to coat evenly for 10 to 20 minutes more. Sprinkle with garlic salt to taste. Spread out on brown paper to dry. Refrigerate or freeze.

Peppy Cocktail Nuts

4½ cups

- 4 **tablespoons butter or margarine**
- 1 **tablespoon Worcestershire sauce**
- 2 **teaspoons Tabasco sauce**
- 1 **tablespoon salad seasoning (it has cheese, paprika, sesame seeds and poppy seeds in it)**
- 1 **teaspoon salt**
- ½ **teaspoon garlic salt**
- ¼ **teaspoon pepper**
- 1 **pound walnut or pecan halves**

In a large pan melt butter and add remaining ingredients except nuts. Stir until blended. Add nuts and toss to coat. Cook covered over low heat for 20 minutes. Stir occasionally. Drain on brown paper. Store in an air-tight container.

Curried Peanuts

1 cup

- 1 **cup roasted, salted, blanched peanuts**
- 1 **teaspoon curry powder**
- ½ **teaspoon seasoned salt**
- 1/8 **teaspoon garlic powder**

Combine spices and mix with peanuts. Spread on cookie sheet and roast at 350 degrees for 5 minutes.

Candied Pecans

2 cups

- 1 **teaspoon cold water**
- 1 **egg white**
- 1 **pound large pecan halves**
- 1 **cup sugar**
- 1 **teaspoon ground cinnamon**
- 1 **teaspoon salt**

Beat water and egg white until frothy. Mix well with pecans. Combine sugar, cinnamon and salt. Mix well with pecans. Spread on a cookie sheet. Bake at 225 degrees for 1 hour. Stir occasionally.

Spiced Nuts

1½ cups

- ½ cup sunflower nuts
- ½ cup Spanish peanuts
- ½ cup toasted corn nuts
- 1 teaspoon chili powder
- ¼ teaspoon cumin
- 1/8 teaspoon garlic powder
- 1/8 teaspoon cayenne pepper

Heat all ingredients in a skillet for about 5 minutes. Stir frequently.

Parmesan Walnuts

1 cup

- 1 cup walnut halves
  water
- 1 tablespoon vegetable oil
- 2 tablespoons Parmesan cheese
- ½ teaspoon garlic salt

Boil nuts in water for 5 minutes. Drain on paper towel. Spread nuts on a cookie sheet and roast at 350 degrees until crisp. Mix oil with nuts. Combine Parmesan cheese and garlic salt. Mix well with nuts. Roast for 5 minutes more.

Curried Popcorn

6 quarts

- 6 quarts popped corn
- ¼ cup butter or margarine
- 2 teaspoons curry powder
- 1 teaspoon salt

Melt butter and add curry powder and salt. Drizzle over popcorn and toss until well coated.

Sugar 'n Spice Popcorn

4 quarts

- 4 quarts popped corn
- 2 or 3 tablespoons sugar
- ¼ teaspoon ground cinnamon
- ¼ teaspoon ground nutmeg
- ⅓ cup butter or margarine

Melt butter and add sugar, cinnamon and nutmeg. Stir until sugar is dissolved. Drizzle over popcorn and toss until well coated.

Almond Tea

7 cups

3 **tea bags**
6 **cups water**
1 **cup sugar**
⅔ **cup fresh lemon juice**
2 **teaspoons almond extract**
1 **teaspoon vanilla extract**

Steep tea bags in 2 cups boiling water for 10 minutes. Boil sugar in 4 cups water for 5 minutes and then add lemon juice and flavorings. Combine the liquids and heat. Serve hot or cold.

Note: Will keep in refrigerator for 2 weeks.

Spiced Cider

3 quarts

3 **quarts apple cider**
10 **whole allspice**
10 **cinnamon sticks**
12 **whole cloves**
3 **small pieces fresh ginger, or**
  1 **tablespoon candied ginger**
¾ **cup brown sugar, packed**

Bring all ingredients except sugar to a boil. Stir in sugar and simmer 15 minutes. Strain and serve hot.

Hot Buttered Cranberry Punch

50 ounces

1 **16-ounce can jellied cranberry**
  sauce
⅓ **cup light brown sugar, firmly**
  packed
¼ **teaspoon ground cinnamon**
¼ **teaspoon ground allspice**
⅛ **teaspoon ground cloves**
⅛ **teaspoon ground nutmeg**
⅛ **teaspoon salt**
2 **cups water**
2 **cups unsweetened pineapple**
  juice
  butter pats

Crush cranberry sauce with a fork. Mix with sugar, cinnamon, allspice, cloves, nutmeg and salt. Add water and pineapple juice. Cover and simmer 2 hours. Ladle into mugs and float a pat of butter on each serving.

Spiced Peach Punch

- 1 **46-ounce can peach nectar**
- 20 **ounces orange juice**
- ½ **cup brown sugar, firmly packed**
- 3 **sticks cinnamon broken into 3-inch pieces**
- ½ **teaspoon whole cloves**
- 2 **tablespoons lime juice**

70 ounces

Combine peach nectar, orange juice and brown sugar in a large saucepan. Tie cinnamon and cloves in a small cheesecloth bag. Drop into saucepan. Heat slowly, stirring constantly, until sugar dissolves. Simmer 10 minutes. Stir in lime juice. Serve hot in mugs.

Hot Chocolate Mix

- 3 **cups powdered milk**
- ¾ **cup sugar**
- ½ **cup cocoa**
  dash of salt
  boiling water

4 cups

Sift together milk, sugar, cocoa and salt. For each serving, mix 8 ounces of boiling water with 4 tablespoons of mix.

Note: For an after dinner drink, make hot chocolate and add 1 ounce of Peppermint Schnapps. Top with whipped cream.

Apple Knockers

- 3 **cinnamon sticks**
- 2 **teaspoons whole cloves**
- ½ **teaspoon ground nutmeg**
- ½ **gallon apple cider**
- 1 **cup sugar**
- 2 **cups orange juice**
- ½ **cup lemon juice**
- 1 **cup brandy (any fruit flavor)**

3 quarts

Tie cinnamon, cloves and nutmeg in cheesecloth. Simmer cider and sugar with spices for about 15 minutes. Remove bag of seasonings. Add orange juice, lemon juice and brandy. Heat to bubbling and serve.

Note: Great apres ski!

Hot Buttered Rum Mix

6 cups

1 **pound butter**
2 **pounds brown sugar**
1½ **tablespoons ground cinnamon**
½ **teaspoon ground nutmeg**
1 **teaspoon vanilla extract**
 rum
 boiling water

Soften butter and mix with brown sugar, cinnamon, nutmeg and vanilla. Refrigerate or freeze. For each serving, use 1 tablespoon of the mix, ½ ounce to 1½ ounces rum and 6 ounces boiling water.

Note: This is much less expensive than a commercial brand.

Divine Rum

8 cups

1 **quart vanilla ice cream,**
   softened
1 **pound butter, softened**
1 **pound brown sugar**
1 **pound powdered sugar**
2 **teaspoons ground nutmeg**
2 **teaspoons ground cinnamon**
 rum
 boiling water

Cream all of the ingredients except the rum and water and freeze. To serve, put 1 ounce of rum and 3 tablespoons of the frozen mixture in a mug and fill up with boiling water.

Note: Good apres ski!

Banana Punch

5 quarts

7 **cups water**
3½ **cups sugar**
5 **bananas, mashed in a blender**
1 **6-ounce can frozen**
   orange juice concentrate
1 **6-ounce can frozen**
   lemonade concentrate
1 **46-ounce can pineapple juice**
1 **quart ginger ale**

Boil water and sugar for 5 minutes. Cool and add the remaining ingredients except ginger ale. Freeze. Remove from freezer 2 to 3 hours before serving. Mix with ginger ale.

May float assorted fruit in punch bowl. Vodka could also be added.

"Julius"

2 servings

3 ounces frozen orange juice concentrate, or
1 banana, or
6 ounces frozen strawberries, thawed, or
6 ounces frozen peaches, thawed
½ cup milk
½ cup water
¼ cup sugar
1 tablespoon vanilla instant breakfast
5 or 6 ice cubes

Mix all ingredients together in a blender until well mixed.

Tomato Juice Cocktail

48 ounces

1 46-ounce can tomato juice
4 tablespoons sugar
3 tablespoons vinegar
½ teaspoon onion salt
½ teaspoon salt
dash of pepper
½ teaspoon celery salt
1 teaspoon Worcestershire sauce

Mix all ingredients together and chill.

Limey-Piney

6 servings

1 6-ounce can frozen pineapple juice concentrate
1 6-ounce can frozen limeade concentrate
6 ounces soda water
6 ounces vodka, bourbon or rum
2 bananas (optional)

Place all ingredients in a blender. Fill with ice and blend.

Hummers

2 servings

Let ice cream soften a little. Put all ingredients in blender and blend. One sip and you hum!

Mocha:
- 1 ounce Kahlua
- 1 ounce creme de cacao
- 2 scoops vanilla ice cream

Golden Cadillac:
- 1 ounce Galliano
- 1 ounce white creme de cacao
- 2 scoops vanilla ice cream

Pink Squirrel:
- 1 ounce white creme de cacao
- 1 ounce creme de almond
- 2 scoops vanilla ice cream

Brown Velvet:
- 1 ounce Triple Sec
- 1 ounce brown creme de cacao
- 2 scoops vanilla ice cream

Mint Patty:
- 1 ounce green creme de menthe
- 1 ounce white creme de cacao
- 2 scoops vanilla ice cream

Spanish:
- 1 ounce Kahlua
- 1 ounce white rum
- 2 scoops vanilla ice cream

Brandy Pillow:
- 2 ounces brandy
- 1 scoop lemon ice cream
- 1 scoop orange sherbet

Angel Wings:
- 1 ounce creme de menthe
- 1 ounce brandy
- 2 scoops vanilla ice cream

Rocky Mountain:
- 1 ounce brandy
- ½ ounce white creme de cacao
- ½ ounce creme de menthe
- 2 scoops chocolate chip ice cream

Brandy Alexander:
- 1 ounce brown creme de cacao
- 1 ounce brandy
- 2 scoops vanilla ice cream
- dash of nutmeg

Coffees

1 serving

Add liqueurs and sugar to coffee. Top with a dollop of whipped cream or ice cream. Garnish appropriately.

Grasshopper:
- 6 ounces coffee
- 1 ounce creme de menthe
- 1 ounce white creme de cacao
- 1 teaspoon brown sugar
- 1 scoop chocolate ice cream

Spanish:
- 6 ounces coffee
- 1 ounce Kahlua
- 1 ounce light rum
- 1 teaspoon brown sugar
  whipped cream
  slice of lime or pinch of
  nutmeg

Velvet:
- 6 ounces coffee
- 1 ounce creme de cacao
- 1 ounce Triple Sec
- 1 teaspoon brown sugar
  whipped cream
  slice of orange or pinch of
  nutmeg

Alexander:
- 6 ounces coffee
- 1 ounce creme de cacao
- 1 ounce brandy
- 1 teaspoon brown sugar
  whipped cream
  pinch of nutmeg

Galliano

- 2 cups distilled water
- 1 cup white corn syrup
- ½ cup sugar
- 2 or 3 drops yellow food coloring
- 1¼ cups grain alcohol (188 proof)
- 6 drops anise extract
- 2 teaspoons vanilla extract

4½ cups

Boil water, corn syrup and sugar for 5 minutes. Add the remaining ingredients and stir. Cover and let stand 1 month.

Daiquiri Liqueur

- 4 limes
- 3 cups light rum
- 1½ cups superfine granulated
  sugar

1 quart

Pare very thinly the bright-colored rind from the limes (no white). Blot the peel on paper towels to remove any excess oil. Put peel in a 4 cup screw-top jar. Add 2 cups of the rum. Close the jar. Store in a cool, dark place for 2 days or until the rum has absorbed the flavor. Remove the peel and add the sugar. Shake vigorously until the sugar dissolves and add remaining cup of rum. Close jar and store in a cool, dark place at least 1 month to age.

Creme de Menthe

½ gallon

8　cups sugar
6　cups water
1　pint grain alcohol (188 proof)
1　ounce pure peppermint
　　extract
1　tablespoon green food
　　coloring

Bring sugar and water to a boil and simmer for 10 minutes. Cool. Add the remaining ingredients and stir. Cover and let ripen for 1 month.

Vanilla-Coffee Liqueur

5 cups

1½　cups brown sugar, packed
1　cup granulated sugar
2　cups water
½　cup instant coffee powder
3　cups vodka
½　vanilla bean, split (or 2
　　tablespoons vanilla extract)

Combine sugars and water. Boil for 5 minutes. Gradually stir in coffee. Cool. Add vodka and vanilla and mix thoroughly. Cover and let ripen for 1 month. Remove vanilla bean.

Caribbean Orange Liqueur

1 quart

3　large oranges
3　cups vodka
1½　cups superfine granulated
　　sugar

Pare very thinly the bright-colored rind from the oranges (no white). Blot the peel on paper towels to remove any excess oil. Put peel in a 4 cup screw-top jar. Add 2 cups of the vodka. Close jar. Store in a cool, dark place for 2 days or until the vodka has absorbed the flavor. Remove the peel and add sugar. Shake vigorously until the sugar is dissolved and add remaining cup of vodka. Close the jar and store in a cool, dark place at least 1 month to age.

Boerenjongens Cordial

4 pints

2	**cups raisins (can use ½ light and ½ dark)**
3½	**cups water**
2	**cups sugar**
2	**cups bourbon**
	lemon slices for garnish

Bring raisins and water to a boil. Simmer for 20 minutes. Add sugar and stir until dissolved. Remove from heat and stir in bourbon. Cover and let stand for 1 month. Serve in cordial glasses. Garnish with lemon slices, if desired.

Christmas Potpourri

5 cups

1	**quart fir needles**
1	**cup dried, mixed fruit (without membranes), thinly shredded**
1	**cup rosemary**
½	**cup basil**
2 - 4	**bay leaves, coarsely crumbled**
2	**cups coarse salt (not iodized)**

Mix and pour into little calico bags.

Hand Lotion

1 cup

⅔	**cup Bay Rum**
⅓	**cup glycerin**

Mix.

Note: This is great for cracked and dry hands and is very refreshing!

Play Clay

1½ cups

1	**cup flour**
1½	**teaspoons alum**
½	**cup salt**
1 - 2	**tablespoons solid shortening**
½	**cup water**
	a few drops of food coloring

Mix all of the ingredients and store in a plastic bag in refrigerator.

COLORADO ASPEN IN THE CHANGING SEASONS

A person wishing to dine out in Colorado can choose from hundreds of eating establishments throughout the state. Regional and ethnic cooking is well represented as is the more traditional classic continental cuisine. For Colorado Cache, we have selected 10 of our favorite restaurants. This is not meant to be a definitive listing of the best in the state, but rather a sampling of some of those restaurants our members consistently enjoy. Each restaurant has provided a recipe for one of its best liked offerings. They and we wish you Bon Appetit.

The Sunbonnet, Castle Rock

Specializing in distinctive luncheons with an art gallery and a gift boutique for browsing or shopping after lunch.

The Sunbonnet House Dressing

½ **cup**

¾ **teaspoon salt**
2 **tablespoons sugar**
1 **tablespoon minced parsley**
½ **medium yellow onion, minced**
¼ **cup olive oil**
¼ **cup red wine vinegar**

Mix all ingredients together and refrigerate for at least 2 hours. Toss with a combination of washed, dried and chilled salad greens. Tomato slices and chopped green pepper may be arranged on top.

The Normandy, Denver

Reminiscent of a French country inn. Wine cellar is one of the most complete in the region.

Escalopes de Veau Marie Antoinette

4 servings

3 **cups Brown Basic Sauce**
4 **cups Bechamel Sauce (see index)**
1 **cube chicken stock base**
3 **pounds veal**
2 **cups cooked mushrooms, pieces and stems**
4 **ounces grated Parmesan cheese**

This dish must be prepared in several stages. Make a rich brown sauce, or Sauce Espagnole. Make a thick Bechamel Sauce. To the finished sauce add a cube of chicken stock base and stir in until dissolved.

For each person, use two pieces of veal weighing approximately three ounces each. The meat should be from the veal round or rump. Pound the veal into thin escalopes no more than ¼ inch thick. Season lightly with salt and pepper, dip in flour and eggs and saute in margarine until brown on both sides.

Into individual casseroles, place enough brown sauce to cover the bottom generously, then add some sliced cooked mushrooms.

Place the two cooked escalopes on top of the brown sauce and cover the meat with thick Bechamel Sauce. Sprinkle grated Parmesan cheese on top of the white sauce so the surface is evenly covered.

Place the casseroles in a hot oven until the sauces begin to bubble, then quickly place under the broiler to brown the Parmesan cheese. Serve immediately, very hot.

The Quorum, Denver

Venerable meeting place of state officials and politicians, serving continental cuisine with a view of the State Capitol.

Filet de Boeuf en Croute (Beef Wellington)

8 servings

3 **tablespoons butter**
1 **4-pound piece of beef tenderloin (cut from thickest end)**
   flour
2 **cups chopped mushrooms**
2 **teaspoons chopped chives**
   dash of Cognac
¼ **tin pate de foie gras (goose liver pate)**
   freshly ground pepper to taste
½ **pound puff dough (available at your bakery or frozen food section)**
2 **egg yolks, beaten**

Melt the butter in a large, heavy skillet. Dust the meat with the flour and brown quickly on all sides. Remove meat and reserve in a warm place. Saute the mushrooms in the same butter in which the beef was browned, adding more butter, if necessary. Add the chives and Cognac. Remove from the fire and blend in the pate de foie gras. Cool slightly. Split the meat lengthwise through the center, making a pocket for the filling. Spread the mushroom and pate de foie gras mixture in the center of the fillet. Sprinkle with pepper to taste. On floured board, roll the pastry into a thin rectangle shape large enough to enclose the meat. Place the meat in the center of the pastry and wrap around the meat, placing the overlapping dough on the underside of the roll. Secure the ends by tucking them under the roll. Place on a buttered cookie sheet or shallow pan. Brush the pastry with the beaten egg yolks. Bake for 30 to 40 minutes in oven preheated to 350 degrees. Remove from the oven and let stand for 15 minutes before placing on serving platter. When moving the beef to the platter, be careful not to break the fragile crust. The beef can be sliced easily with a good bread knife or a sharp French knife. A Cognac or brandy sauce may be served with the beef.

COLORADO CACHE COLORADO CACHE COLORADO CACHE COLORADO CACHE COLORADO CACHE COLORADO CACHE COLORADO CACHE COLORADO CACHE COLORADO

Mon Petit, Wheat Ridge

A Victorian house renovated into intimate dining areas. French menu served with traditional elegance.

Duck a la Bigarade

4 servings

1 **4- to 5-pound duck**
   seasoned salt
2 **cups duck, chicken or veal**
   stock
   Bechamel Sauce (see index)
   fresh orange and lemon juice
   rosemary
   nutmeg
   ground cloves
¾ **cup Burgundy**
2 **tablespoons sugar**
   orange liqueur
1 **cup fresh mushrooms, sliced**
   dash of Cognac

Sprinkle the duck with the seasoned salt. Cover with foil and bake at 350 degrees for about 2 to 2½ hours. Let cool to room temperature. Meanwhile, thicken stock with Bechamel sauce. Add some orange and lemon juice. Add a few sprigs of rosemary, a touch of nutmeg and powdered cloves to stock mixture. Cook on low heat with Burgundy about 45 minutes to 1 hour. Caramelize sugar on low heat and slowly add it to the sauce and simmer another 20 to 30 minutes on low heat. Stir frequently. Add a few drops of orange liqueur. Cut duck in portions. Put in baking crock with 2 cups of the sauce and 1 handful of fresh sliced mushrooms and sprinkle with Cognac. Cover and bake at 350 degrees for 20 minutes. Serve over rice.

La Bola, Denver

Flautas and other Mexican specialties and giant margaritas are offered in three locations, each with a different south of the border atmosphere.

Chili Verde (Green Chile)

3 quarts

2½	**pounds pork roast (fresh shoulder preferred)**
1	**pound pork soup bones**
44	**ounces canned tomatoes (28-ounce and 16-ounce cans)**
23	**ounces tomato sauce (15-ounce and 8-ounce cans)**
1	**tablespoon garlic powder**
28	**ounces hot water (3½ cups)**
21	**ounces diced green chili strips (Ortega brand preferred, 3 7-ounce cans)**
¾ - 1	**ounce diced hot peppers (Ortega brand preferred, ¼ of a 3½-ounce can)**
1	**tablespoon sugar**
1½	**tablespoons salt**

Cut pork into ½ inch squares and with the pork bones fry over low heat until brown and the meat is slightly dry. If pork is very fat, pour off all but 4 or 5 tablespoons of the grease.

Using a colander, strain tomatoes into an 8 quart saucepan and coarsely chop tomatoes. Combine tomatoes, tomato sauce, garlic, hot water and cooked pork and bones in the same saucepan. Bring to rapid boil and continue boiling for 20 minutes. Add spices, chopped hot peppers and chopped chili strips. Continue boiling another 20 minutes.

Finish by cooking on medium heat until desired thickness, usually about another 20 minutes. Remove bones and green chili is ready to serve.

Note: May be kept refrigerated for a week or frozen for 3 months. La Bola uses green chili to cover burritos, chili rellenos and most of their specialties. Melt an equal amount of grated sharp Cheddar cheese and green chili for a chili con queso dip.

The Brown Palace, Denver

A Denver landmark since 1892, it fulfills the highest traditions of hostelry with the elegance and charm of the gold rush era. A variety of gracious dining rooms.

Roast Crown of Lamb Bouquetiere

8 servings

2	**racks of lamb**
1	**carrot**
1	**small onion**
1	**stalk of celery**
1	**pound lamb bones**
1	**quart stock**
1	**bay leaf**

Trim the two racks of lamb of excess fat. Tie racks to form a crown. Season lamb with salt, pepper and a little garlic salt. Place in a 12 inch braising pan. Place bones around crown of lamb. Cut 1 carrot, 1 onion, 1 stalk of celery into one inch pieces, wash and place around crown of lamb with bay leaf. Roast at 400 degrees for 1 hour or until medium. Remove from pan and keep in a warm place. Add 1 quart of stock to pan and reduce to 1 pint. Strain. This is lamb au jus for crown of lamb.

Bouquetiere:

2	**1-pound heads fresh cauliflower**
6	**large carrots**
2	**pounds peas**
6	**large mushrooms**
2	**pounds asparagus spears**
6	**large potatoes**
1	**pound butter**
½	**lemon**
3	**eggs**
	salt
	pepper

Clean cauliflower and peel carrots. Cut with parisienne spoon. Wash mushrooms and peel potatoes. Cook in individual pots. Cook all vegetables except mushrooms in salted water until tender. Drain. Add 1 tablespoon butter and season to taste with salt and pepper.

Simmer mushrooms in butter until half done. Add juice of ½ lemon and cook until tender.

Duchess potatoes: Mash cooked potatoes. Add 3 raw eggs, 3 tablespoons butter, salt and pepper to taste. Use pastry bag to force potatoes through on an 18 inch platter. Brown until golden brown.

To serve, place crown of lamb in center of the platter. Place vegetables and mushrooms around crown. Serve with au jus and mint sauce.

Red Lion Inn, Boulder Canyon, Boulder

The air of an authentic Bavarian inn serving a variety of dishes. Specialties are veal and game.

Rack of Venison

1 **rack of venison**
2 **quarts of buttermilk (approximately)**
5 **strips of bacon**
3 **tablespoons butter**
2 **carrots**
2 **stalks of celery**
1 **large onion**
5 **sprigs of parsley**
1 **pint sour cream**
2 **tablespoons Madeira**
¼ **teaspoon salt and pepper**
5 **juniper berries, crushed**

1 rack of venison

Place rack of venison in buttermilk for 2 days. After 2 days remove skin. Then salt and pepper the rack. Wrap bacon around rack and place in Dutch oven with butter. Brown on all sides. Add cut vegetables with the rest of the ingredients except sour cream and Madeira. Add enough water so meat and vegetables do not burn. Cook at 350 degrees for about 1¼ to 1½ hour. When done, strain sauce and add sour cream and Madeira to the remaining gravy. Thicken with flour and water or cornstarch to degree of personal preference. Serve with red cabbage.

The Broadmoor West, Charles Court, Colorado Springs

An aristocratic hotel offering continental cuisine served in classic surroundings of objets d'art. A view of the original hotel is mirrored in the lake.

Beer Batter for Fruit

4-6 servings

2   **cups flour**
    touch of salt
    touch of sugar
1   **bottle of beer**
5   **egg whites**
    small amount of vegetable oil
    cinnamon sugar
    vanilla sauce
    fresh fruit

This beer batter can be used for any kind of fresh fruit, strawberries, raspberries, etc. Combine the dry ingredients into a mixing bowl. Using a wire whip, add the beer slowly until it is a creamy consistency. Beat egg whites until they form stiff peaks and then fold them into the batter. If the batter is going to be sitting for awhile before using it, sprinkle the top with a very small amount of vegetable oil to keep a skin from forming on the top. More beer can be added if needed.

Dry each piece of fruit completely on absorbant cloth to make sure it is without moisture. Dip each piece of fruit in the beer batter and deep fry until golden brown. Take the fruit out of the hot oil and drain on absorbent toweling. Roll the fruit in cinnamon sugar until evenly coated. Serve on a bed of Vanilla Sauce.

Vanilla Sauce:

2   **pints of half and half**
    half a vanilla bean
    sugar according to taste
5   **egg yolks**

Bring first 3 ingredients to a boil in a double boiler. Place 5 eggs yolks in a mixing bowl and beat thoroughly with a wire whip. Add boiling cream mixture to the egg yolks stirring constantly. The best way to do this is by placing the mixing bowl in a hot water bath.

Laurita's, Georgetown

An alpine setting where seafood and Italian specialties are served in a family atmosphere.

Shrimp Rosemary

3-4 servings

olive oil
2 **tablespoons clarified butter (see index)**
⅓ **cup minced onion**
2 **garlic cloves, minced**
½ **teaspoon dried basil**
½ **teaspoon coarsely ground black pepper**
20 **large shrimp, shelled, deveined and butterflied**
½ **cup cream sherry**
½ **cup minced fresh tomatoes**
2 **tablespoons minced parsley**
garlic salt

Into a 12 inch skillet, pour olive oil to a depth of approximately 1/8 inch. Add butter and melt over medium heat. Add onion and garlic and saute until transparent. Add basil, black pepper and shrimp. Increase heat to high and saute 1 minute. Add cream sherry, tomatoes, parsley and garlic salt to taste. Swirl skillet until shrimp curl.

The Left Bank, Vail

Continental fare offered in a casually elegant atmosphere. Located in the heart of the ski area.

Cote de Boeuf Bordelaise

7 servings

7	**prime rib steaks**
	salt
	white pepper
8	**shallots**
2	**cups red wine**
1	**bay leaf**
2	**anchovy fillets**
2	**ounces butter**
½	**ounce flour**
	beef extract
	fresh lemon juice
7	**marrow bones**
	chopped parsley

Take a small (12 pound) western cut prime rib, with 2 to 3 weeks aging, and slice it into 7 steaks so that each one will have a bone. Trim excess fat and sprinkle meat with salt and pepper. Broil over a very hot fire. It takes 5 to 7 minutes broiling on each side over a hot flame to have the meat medium rare. When broiling meat rare, the broiler should be at the highest temperature.

In a heavy saute pan, place 8 finely chopped shallots, red wine (Bordeaux wine), bay leaf, chopped anchovy fillets and cook to reduce to half the quantity. Add butter which has been mixed with flour, a little beef base, salt, pepper and a few drops of lemon juice. This sauce should be strained and smooth.

Poach 7 marrow bones, then take out the marrow and put it on top of the steak and pour over the very hot sauce. Add a little chopped parsley.

Serve the following vegetables: fresh spinach, string beans and sauteed potatoes.

The Junior League of Denver would like to thank its members and their friends
who contributed so much to this book.

Edith Peters Acsell
Karen Keck Albin
Jane Alexander
Sally Stewart Alexander
Lucille Loeffler Allen
Jeaneene Fischer Anderson
Desse Pinckard Anthony
Nancy Apthorp
Diane Armstrong
Eirene Shields Arnot
Susan Suhm Ash
Susan Wild Baak
Catherine Ince Bader
Sue Dawson Baker
Sharon Thompson Bailey
Mimi Andrews Bain
Lindsay G. Ball
Pam Groteluschen Bansbach
Chris Baehren Barabasz
Barbara Holm Barendsen
Judith Heeren Baskette
Janice Heard Baucum
Lucy Rusnock Beale
Susan Smith Beasley
Jill Johnson Behr
Lindsay Bacon Bell
Mariette Howe Bell
Nancy Roberts Berge
Betsy Gregg Berry
Sharon Hager Beyer
Betsy Gensemer Blair
Marguerite Stone Bliss
Sandy Keller Blue
Jaydee Peterson Boat
Peggy Lynch Boerstler
Marianne Roberts Bolt
Karin Chapman Bond
Anne Lennox Borkovic
Joanne Renier Borg
Susan Taipale Bottoms
Betty Ann Mollin Bower
Barbara McCarthy Bowes
Shirley Sidles Bowman
Betty Pringle Boyd
Gay Baldwin Boyd
Martha Wheelock Brainard
Laurene Berger Brooks
Sylvia Knoblach Brown

Wilhelmina Shearer Bruhn
Penny Oliver Buckingham
Sheila Sherman Bugdanowitz
Karen Nelson Bush
Cynthia Strickland Butterfield
Janie Johnson Butterly
Nancy Peery Byrd
Sally Mahrt Cadol
Mame Blyth Cairns
Kathleen Koch Callendar
Catherine Cooper Campbell
JoAnn Conrad Cannon
Barbara Hardman Card
Ann Steinbruner Carey
Joan Summerton Carey
Jean Carlson
Trish Bowen Casson
Claudia Carbone Chambers
Kaye Chambers
Nancy Hall Chase
Susan Birchmier Cheley
Barbara Law Childs
Helen Hirst Christy
Sandy Adamson Clanahan
Jeannie Pinkerton Clancy
Betty Ward Clark
Chris Bower Clark
Phoebe Capron Clark
Lucia Thompson Clarke
Brooke Hurley Cogswell
Debbie Conant
Julie Harkness Condon
Betty Lou Reeves Conrad
Marilyn Gross Coors
Rosemary O'Donnell Corcoran
Linda Lees Crosby
Lynne Thurman Cundy
Jerry Huhn Cunningham
Liz Bauerfeind Cunningham
Hope Griswold Curfman
Anne Witte Curran
Marie Volkel Curran
Cathy Donohue Danielson
Barbara Considine Dangleis
Judy Snodgrass Davidson
Sally Hendricks Davidson
Debbie Enoch Davis
Lois O'Donnell Dean

Dorothy Rech Deane
Judith Steele DeBord
Margaret Archibald Decker
Kate Johnson Denious
Judy Fenton Dietz
Debbie Wing Dikeou
Joan Glover Disborough
Sally Campen Doty
Ann W. Douden
Medora Wilson Douden
Bonnie Page Downing
Lucia Pearson Doyle
Fay Pearson Dreher
Pat Hadley Duensing
Donna Archibald Duft
Marilyn Leclaire Dyer
Julie Eager
Mary Harding Eiseman
Janet Reidy Ellis
Garey Smith Erickson
Martha McElveen Ezzard
Elizabeth Cox Estey
Carol Turner Faber
Susan Rickett Farago
Barbara Olson Ferguson
Leslie Writer Ferguson
Sharon Stetzer Ferlic
Barbara Winter Fillmore
Bradone Bradley Fisher
Billie Jean Andrews Fitzgerald
Debbie Hand Flynn
Ann Gibson Forsey
Marie Lindquist Fredrickson
Kitsie Waltman Freund
Mary Grace Freyschlag
Jane Stuart Righter Froelicher
Sally Sloan Fullerton
Carolyn Drescher Gamba
Margaret Smith Garbe
Cecily Coors Garnsey
June Swaner Gates
Nancy Burgee Gerhardy
Nancy Winkler Giacomini
Alice Beardslee Gilchrist
Jane Bohan Glazier
Suzanne Seeley Golden

Marilyn Taylor Gordon
Marilyn Axel Gottesfeld
Connie Fox Graham
Carla Yancy Grant
Judy Lamme Green
Patty Pires Greene
Georgia Hendrix Grey
Vicki Taylor Griffith
Heidi Ager Grimditch
Dianne Price Groff
Norma Jean Carpenter Grow
Mary Williams Grow
Anne Kuzell Hackstock
Joey Dings Haeckel
Suzanne Cooper Hagan
Kay Wilson Hall
Barbie Gregg Halsell
Susan Nye Handwerk
Beverly White Hanselman
Jane Allison Harper
Lucy Dick Harper
Janie Thomason Harrington
Beverly Barrett Harris
Lois Kelly Harrison
Pat Anderson Harwood
Victor Hauser
Carole Cooper Hayward
Charlotte Standley Head
Cathy Fisher Heller
Helen Blandford Hempel
Clelia Windrum Hendee
Cynthia Madden Henry
Kitty Hancock Henry
Nancy Manning Hill
Arlene Friedman Hirschfeld
Sarah Hoper Hite
Jean Creamer Hodges
Joan Alexander Hollenbeck
Marilyn Adams Holmes
Nancy Gardiner Holmquist
Janice Cruzen Houston
Jane Snodgrass Houston
Linda Jorgensen Houston
Susan Oakes Houston
Donna de la Ossa Hultin
Karen Wolgast Howsam
Betty Lynn Dupy Jackson
Margaret Detweiler Jacobson

Sue Ann Brownlee James
Cindy Pate Jessop
Fleta Cooke Johnsen
Kay Durey Johnson
Lucia Moore Johnson
Winnie Unger Johnson
Jean Evans Jones
Karen Hillyard Jones
Cynthia Gaebe Kahle
Mikee Peoples Kapelke
Marlene Chandler Kearney
Jane Schack Kehl
Suzanne Woodward Kelly
Ann Sullivan Kennedy
Melly McGreery Kinnard
Sue Peabody Kinney
Sue Kullgren Kintzele
Shannon Burnham Kirby
Barbara Eckhart Knight
Helen Warner Koernig
Sarah Jones Koether
Jane Jubela Koontz
Bonni Radtke Kortz
Carol Watson Koser
Elaine Moore Krause
Gwen Williams Krueger
Karen Ellingson Kruse
Kathy Peavy Kugeler
Sue Hough Kuhn
Lucy Smyth Landes
Gail Lachmund Larson
Kay Whiteley Larson
Kelly Quinn Lasky
Edrea Matelich Learned
Mary Ann Mitchell Lee
Kaye Barnette Lemon
Mary Olson Lester
Merrilyn Maurer Leuthold
Meredith Miller Lewis
Blair Jolley Lindberg
Suzanne M. Little
Diane Gorsuch Long
Coleen Ness Love
Suzy Blommer Love
Mary Thorson Lucken
Betsy Boschen Lutz
Gay Elliot McPhail McClymont
Carole Lee Hand McCotter

Jan Coakley McCulloch
Marilane Schmierer McDermott
Carrie Kellog McDonald
Linda Landauer McDonald
Pat Bryan McElhinney
Georgene Wollgast McGonagle
Ann Cusack McMahon
Sandy Brown McMartin
Shirley Jackson McMillan
Sue Mellencamp McNamara
Christina McPhee
Marilyn Wells McWilliams
Billee Leonard Madsen
Susan Brinkerhoff Mammel
Carol Orem Mancini
Betty Scanlan Mangan
Anne Pierson Marquis
Susan Thorn Marr
Chartan Larned Martin
Susan Jarman Martin
Kathie Edmiston Massey
Joan Latcham Masten
Elizabeth Myer Matteson
Jan Perry Mayer
Eugene Megyesy
Mary McConnell Meinig
Carole Ruff Merkel
Janet Cooper Metzger
Donna Evans Miedema
Tim Miles
Janet Westbrook Miller
Shelly Suggs Miller
Donna Mendenhall Moore
Susan Hill Moore
Nancy Morgan
Beverly Byrne Morrato
Debbie Writer Mott
Rosemarie Palmerone Murane
Virginia Nielsen Muse
Cynthia Fels Nagel
Mimi Wilkinson Nelson
Nancy Mayer Nelson
Betsy Glaser Nevin
Muriel Staniford Newell
Judith Yrisarri Nichols
Barbara Stewart Norgren
Ann Barlow O'Donnell
Marvis Shearron Ogura

Catherine Hoover Olson
Sandy Sparks Olson
Virginia Cox Olson
Alfreda Mendenhall Orr
Stanya Burlew Owen
Barbara Beckley Page
Pat Patterson Panter
Virginia Lawhon Park
Debbie Duke Parsons
Sharon Kelly Pate
Joyce Tatum Payne
Carol Joplin Peck
Merlaine Meyers Peede
Jean Ostrander Peltier
Day Smith Peters
Carol Strandt Peterson
Liz Cowles Peyton
Nellie Chambers Philpott
Carol Ransom Pierce
Bonnie Halliday Pintaric
Ann McKenzie Polumbus
Gill Hansen Pool
Suzanne Hunter Presley
Susan Lowe Pryor
Jean Van Curan Pugh
Geisla Mussgnug Pytte
Carol Schildhammer Rand
Janice Latcham Rebstock
Karen Griffith Reder
Betsy Evans Reniers
Pat Wierman Rheem
Karen Parsons Rhodes
Nancy Blue Riley
Sally Winters Rippey
Linda Zimmerman Roberts
Patricia Hayes Roberts
Cille Burnside Robinson
Jill Newton Robinson
Kelly Donohue Robson
Ann Roning Roemer
Linda Miller Rogoff
Barbara Moore Rumsey
Mary Samford
Daphne Baine Sankey
Joan Martin Sare
Peggy Dolan Sawyer
Carolyn Sack Schaefer
Cheryl Eckel Schmitt

Sarah Wright Schmidt
Ellin Oberlin Schroeder
Marcia Peterson Seawell
Prim Hook Sebastian
Diane Rheem Seccombe
Julia Hutson Secor
Margaret Wagner Seep
Martha Carey Segelke
Susan Settlemyer
Rebecca Greer Sexson
Elinor Fiddler Siecke
Nathalie Osgood Simsak
Connie Hall Simpson
Carol Blackwell Siple
Dottie T. Sloan
Kathy Bowers Smith
Martha Mayne Smith
Sharon Larson Smith
Sheila Sullivan Smith
Virginia Moore Smith
Joan Stevenson Snyder
Kit Farrar Spahn
Betts Brennecke Stailey
Katie Hall Stapleton
Martha Smith Starick
Marne Tutt Steinegger
Louise Nichols Steinhauer
Deanie Ketchum Stenseth
Diane Hunt Stockmar
Joyce Naranche Straus
Caroline Landler Strickland
Diane Schwob Strong
Betty O'Donnel Stuckey
Georgia Mattern Sweeney
Meg Larkins Sweeting
Sarah Davie Swett
Marta Phipps Talman
Donna Ruth McIntosh Teel
Nancy Lawson Theis
Mildred Cobb Tierney
Lee Reuter Thrailkill
Joy Dunklee Tolin
Barbara Hudson Toltz
Betsy Bourne Tracy
Libby Cascio Trevor
Wendy Hall Trigg
Christie Kirkpatrick Truitt
Judith Weston Trumbull

Ann Hinds Tull
Suzanne Jay Unger
Roberta Rickard Urban
Adelaide Donnan Valentine
Nancy Crain Van Gilder
Jeri Comley Vanatta
Roxanne Shumaker Vierra
Beth Emery Vinton
Bernie Kirby Wagner
Betsy Ross Wahlberg
Pamela Parker Wall
Mary Dorsey Bass Wanless
Gay Schneider Warren
Paula Youngclaus Warren
Howell H. Watson
Ellen Kelly Waterman
Molly Mitchell Waters
Julie Chick Wattenbarger
Paula Wilson Weidner
Polly Edgar Weil
Linda Bailey Weiner
Julia Belden Weller
Ricky Hendricks Whitelaw
Susan Park Whitsit
Bonnie Jones Wicks
Laura Dumm Wierman
Mary Lou McCreless Wiggins
Jo Anne Richardson Wilbur
Jeanne Wilkins Wilde
Sharon Kullgren Wilkinson
Susan Pryor Willson
Glenda Carter Winker
Betty Andrews Winslow
Sandra Pflager Wischmeyer
Suzanne Iliff Witzler
Marcie Nelson Wolff
Frances Cotton Wollenweber
Sara Thomsen Woodard
Barbara Stearns Wootten
Esther Jane Center Worrell
Beth Hobbs Wright
Caroline Ennis Writer
Dee Davies Writer
Susan Beard Writer
Jane Ponting Yale
Karen Fleischman Yanish
Mildred Peterson Yrisarri

COLORADO CACHE COLORADO CACHE COLORADO CACHE COLORADO CACHE COLORADO CACHE COLORADO CACHE COLORADO CACHE COLORADO CACHE COLORADO

424 Index

C & C
Publications, Inc.
Colorado Cache • Crème de Colorado

The Junior League of Denver, Inc.
6300 East Yale Avenue
Denver, Colorado 80222
(303) 782-9244

Name _____

Address _____

City/State/Zip _____

Telephone _____

Please send me the best-selling classic cookbooks indicated below:

Title	Quantity	Price	Tax (Colorado residents only)	TOTAL
COLORADO CACHE	_____	$15.95	$.48 per book	$ ____ . ____
CRÈME DE COLORADO	_____	$19.95	.60 per book	$ ____ . ____
Total number of books ordered _____		plus $3.00 each for shipping and handling		$ ____ . ____
		(Canadian orders: $5.25 each for shipping and handling)		
			TOTAL ENCLOSED	$ ____ . ____

Please charge to my   VISA _____ or MasterCard _____

Expiration date _____

Please make checks payable to:
JUNIOR LEAGUE OF DENVER, INC.
Please do not send cash. Sorry, no C.O.D.'s

Card number _____
Cardholder's
signature _____

Send to: C & C Publications
The Junior League of Denver, Inc.
6300 East Yale Avenue, Suite 110
Denver, Colorado 80222 • (303) 782-9244

Profits from the sale of these cookbooks are used to support the purpose and programs of The Junior League of Denver, Inc.
Prices subject to change without notice.

The Junior League of Denver, Inc.
6300 East Yale Avenue
Denver, Colorado 80222
(303) 782-9244

TO: _____

C & C
Publications, Inc.
Colorado Cache • Crème de Colorado

The Junior League of Denver, Inc.
6300 East Yale Avenue
Denver, Colorado 80222
(303) 782-9244

Name _____

Address _____

City/State/Zip _____

Telephone _____

Please send me the best-selling classic cookbooks indicated below:

Title	Quantity	Price	Tax (Colorado residents only)	TOTAL
COLORADO CACHE	_____	$15.95	$.48 per book	$ ____ . ____
CRÈME DE COLORADO	_____	$19.95	.60 per book	$ ____ . ____
Total number of books ordered _____		plus $3.00 each for shipping and handling		$ ____ . ____
		(Canadian orders: $5.25 each for shipping and handling)		
			TOTAL ENCLOSED	$ ____ . ____

Please charge to my   VISA _____ or MasterCard _____

Expiration date _____

Please make checks payable to:
JUNIOR LEAGUE OF DENVER, INC.
Please do not send cash. Sorry, no C.O.D.'s

Card number _____
Cardholder's
signature _____

Send to: C & C Publications
The Junior League of Denver, Inc.
6300 East Yale Avenue, Suite 110
Denver, Colorado 80222 • (303) 782-9244

Profits from the sale of these cookbooks are used to support the purpose and programs of The Junior League of Denver, Inc.
Prices subject to change without notice.

Mailing Label – Please Print

The Junior League of Denver, Inc.
6300 East Yale Avenue
Denver, Colorado 80222
(303) 782-9244

TO: _____